Joseph Addison

Joseph Addison

AN INTELLECTUAL BIOGRAPHY

Dan Poston

UNIVERSITY OF VIRGINIA PRESS
Charlottesville and London

University of Virginia Press
© 2023 by the Rector and Visitors of the University of Virginia
All rights reserved
Printed in the United States of America on acid-free paper

First published 2023

1 3 5 7 9 8 6 4 2

Library of Congress Cataloging-in-Publication Data

Names: Poston, Dan, author.
Title: Joseph Addison : an intellectual biography / Dan Poston.
Description: Charlottesville : University of Virginia Press, 2023. | Includes bibliographical references and index.
Identifiers: LCCN 2023028639 (print) | LCCN 2023028640 (ebook) | ISBN 9780813950396 (hardcover) | ISBN 9780813950402 (paperback) | ISBN 9780813950419 (ebook)
Subjects: LCSH: Addison, Joseph, 1672–1719. | Addison, Joseph, 1672–1719—Criticism and interpretation. | Authors, English—18th century—Biography. | English literature—18th century—History and criticism. | Enlightenment—England.
Classification: LCC PR3306 .P67 2023 (print) | LCC PR3306 (ebook) | DDC 820.9/005—dc23/eng/20230727
LC record available at https://lccn.loc.gov/2023028639
LC ebook record available at https://lccn.loc.gov/2023028640

Cover art: Portrait of Joseph Addison by Godfrey Kneller, circa 1712. (Photo National Portrait Gallery, London)

To my parents, who taught me how to travel

Contents

Acknowledgments ix

Chronology of Addison's Life in Historical Context xi

Introduction 1

1. Addison the Ancient Author 37

2. Everyday Prose after Newton 80

3. Slavery in Addison's Discourse 116

4. Addison's Theory of the Imagination 149

5. Staging a Shadow King: Addison's Theatrical Politics 188

6. Addison's Cato 213

7. *Cato*'s Coda: Death after Tragic Fame 259

Notes 283

Bibliography 319

Index 337

Acknowledgments

This book began in Argentina, where I was grateful for the conversations with Jorian Schutz, along with Bridget Gleeson, Katherine Glover, Tony Maridakis, Ray McKay, Enrique Mitjans, Horacio Mohando, Paul Ryder, and Marcela Temes.

I am immensely thankful to Marvin Carlson and Jean Graham-Jones for their years of support, intellectual guidance, and reading at the CUNY Graduate Center. In the theater program there, I would also like to especially thank David Savran for his crucial advice and insights as I worked on this project. Among the too-many-people-to-name who filled the time at the Grad Center and Baruch College with wonderful seminars, friendly chats, lunches, and outings of all kinds: Joseph Alpar, Shane Breaux, Jordan Cohen, Annie Dell'Aria, Ryan Donavan, Peter Eckersall, Elisabeth Gareis, Ben Gillespie, Anna Harb, Jana O'Keefe Bazzoni, Nigel Philip, Seth Powers, Bess Rowen, Stephanie Vella, and Jim Wilson. I am also grateful in memory to Daniel Gerould and Lynette Gibson.

Working with Angie Hogan and the University of Virginia Press has been a wonderful experience, and I feel very lucky to have the opportunity to bring out this book with them. My thanks to the entire team there and especially to Wren Myers and Emily Jane Shelton for their support and acumen during the editing process. I am also very grateful to the thoughtful group of interdisciplinary reviewers whose feedback was immensely helpful in improving the book.

My warmest gratitude goes also to the many people at Harvard, NYU, and Bard who provided wisdom, guidance, and inspiration, particularly Michael Vannoy Adams, Sandra Bowie, Joseph Brown, Una Chaudhuri, Arthur Gibbons, Carmelo LaRose, Michelle Layser, Lindsay O'Connor, Elaine Scarry, Anna Deavere Smith, Richard Schechner, Karen Shimakawa, and Nikki Usher.

I am fortunate as well to have a great group of loyal colleagues in Tübingen, Berlin, and elsewhere in Europe: Matthias Bauer, Claudia Blümle,

Anne Enderwitz, Birgit Feller, Achim Geisenhanslüke, Çağlanur Gencer, Bernhard Greiner, Eva Haag, Anya Heise-von der Lippe, Hans-Christian von Herrmann, Jonathan Kassner, Julia Kerscher, Robert Kirstein, Andrea Krauss, Kim Luther, Katerina Magdou, Irmgard Männlein-Robert, Christoph Reinfandt, Max Roehl, Monique Scheer, Jörn Steigerwald, Elisabeth Strowick, Leonie Süwolto, Elisabeth Weber, Angelika Zirker. I attended two conferences that were exceptionally helpful for the preparation of this book: my thanks go to the colleagues and organizers for those fantastic days, especially to Claire Boulard-Jouslin and Klaus-Dieter Ertler for the Addison conference in Paris and to Francesca Saggini and Peter Sabor for the ISECS workshop in Viterbo.

For friendship, patience, conversations, housing et al. through the years in NYC, DC, Berlin, and beyond: Tonya Adair, Yasmine Alwan, Maya Anand, Ei Arakawa, Knud Breyer, Warren Clement, Scott Clift, Daniel Cohen, Karin DeGravelles, Mara Delius, Katie Deutsch, Bonnie-Kathleen Discepelo, Anne Dollason, Ulrike Eisenberg, the EoM Theatre Group, Joy Fairfield, Clint Froehlich, Libby Garland, Gregor Gumpert, Alisha Kerlin, Richard Koche, Elizabeth Long, Kelly Ma, Lesley Ma, Constanze Mackowiak, Jasmine Mahmoud, Christopher Moffo, Michael Moss, Julia Po, Braxton Poulos, Anna Raupp, Graham Sack, Peyton Sherwood, Melanie Sichler, Zhuo-Ning Siu, Martin Steffen, Jonathan Taylor, Martha Todd, Ewald Tucai, and Mike and Veronica Von Wiebner.

I never thought I would spend so many years learning and writing about Joseph Addison, and so I am immensely grateful, in impossible-to-write fashion, for another human being who shared that unexpected experience: so an important thanks to my husband, Eckart Goebel, for doubling the world, love, everyday, and a decade of listening to anecdotes about *Cato*.

Chronology of Addison's Life in Historical Context

	JOSEPH ADDISON	CONTEXTS
1660	Joseph's father, Lancelot Addison (b. 1632), made chaplain of the British garrison at Dunkirk	Charles II's restoration; royal patent theater duopoly established under Killigrew and Davenant
1662	Lancelot becomes chaplain of the British garrison at Tangiers	
1665		Five Mile Act expels Non-Conformist ministers; Great Plague: Newton works at home in Woolsthorpe; Second Dutch War
1666		Great Fire of London
1667		Dryden's *Annus Mirabilis;* Milton's *Paradise Lost;* Second Dutch War ends
1670	Lancelot returns to England, weds Jane Gulston (b. 1635), Joseph's mother; Lancelot appointed rector of Milston	

	JOSEPH ADDISON	CONTEXTS
1671	Lancelot's *West Barbary*	Milton's *Samson Agonistes*
1672	Joseph born (1 May) in Wiltshire, Lancelot and Jane's first surviving child	Third Anglo-Dutch War; Richard Steele born (12 March) in Dublin
1673	Brother, Gulston, born	
1674	Sister, Dorothy, born; uncle, John Addison, emigrates to Maryland	Milton dies; Third Anglo-Dutch War ends
1675	Lancelot's *The Present State of the Jews*	
1676	Sister, Anne, born	
1677		Behn's *The Rover*
1678		Bunyan's *Pilgrim's Progress*; Popish Plot
1679		Hobbes dies; Exclusion Crisis, birth of the Whigs under the 1st Earl of Shaftesbury
1680	Anne dies; brother, Lancelot, born	
1683	Father becomes dean of Lichfield	
1684	Father becomes archdeacon of Coventry; mother dies	Charles Montagu and Newton form a philosophical society at Cambridge
1685		Charles II dies; James II's accession
1686	Attends Charterhouse (under Thomas Burnet), where he meets Steele	

	JOSEPH ADDISON	CONTEXTS
1687	Enters Queen's College, Oxford	Newton's *Principia Mathematica*
1688		James II escapes to France; Glorious Revolution; Alexander Pope born; Nine Years' War
1689	Elected a demy of Magdalen College	Accession of William III and Mary II; Bill of Rights
1690		Locke's *Treatises of Government* and *Essay Concerning Human Understanding*; William III defeats James II at the Boyne
1691	Graduates and becomes a tutor at Oxford; publishes first volume of *Musæ Anglicanæ*	
1694	Verse publications in Tonson's *Miscellany*	Mary II dies; Montagu founds Bank of England, plans recoinage
1695		Stationers' Company monopoly lapses
1696		Via Montagu, Newton warden of the mint
1697	Dedicates his *Pax Gulielmi auspiciis Europeae reddita* to Charles Montagu	Treaty of Ryswick ends Nine Years' War; Dryden's *Works of Virgil*
1698	Becomes a fellow of Magdalen	Collier's *Short View of the Immorality and Profaneness of the English Stage*
1699	Royal grant, travels to France	
1700	Resides in Blois and Paris, meets Malebranche and Boileau	Congreve's *The Way of the World*; Dryden dies

	JOSEPH ADDISON	CONTEXTS
1701	In Venice, sees Pollarolo's opera *Catone Uticenze;* first drafts of "Letter from Italy"	War of the Spanish Succession begins; Act of Settlement establishes the Hanoverian Succession; Steele's *The Christian Hero*
1702	In Switzerland and Vienna	William III death; Anne's succession
1703	In Dresden, Hanover, Hamburg, Holland; father's death	
1704	In England, elected to the Kit-Cat Club; follows Locke as commissioner of appeals; *The Campaign*	Marlborough's victory at Blenheim; Swift's *A Tale of a Tub;* Newton's *Opticks;* Locke dies
1705	*Remarks on Italy;* long courtship with Charlotte (Myddelton) Rich has begun; mission to Hanover with Montagu	Steele's *The Tender Husband;* Steele marries Margaret Stretch
1706	Undersecretary of state	Steele appointed gentleman-waiter to Prince George; Steele's first wife dies
1707	*Rosamond* performed	Act of Union with Scotland; Steele appointed gazetteer, marries second wife
1708	Secretary of the Irish government under Lord Wharton; failing eyesight under the strain of work for two years	
1709	Brother, Gulston, dies in Madras; contributions to *The Tatler* begin	Steele begins *The Tatler;* Centlivre's *The Busie Body*
1710	Elected MP for Malmesbury; end of Irish Secretaryship; brother, Lancelot, dies in Madras	Sacheverell trial; Betterton dies; visit of the Four Iroquois "Kings"; Whigs fall, Tories ascend; Harley and Bolingbroke in power

	JOSEPH ADDISON	CONTEXTS
1711	*The Tatler* ends; *The Spectator* begins	Handel's *Rinaldo*; Pope's *Essay on Criticism*
1712	*The Spectator* concludes	Marlborough dismissed; Pope's *The Rape of the Lock*
1713	*Cato* premieres; buys estate in Warwickshire; *The Guardian*	Treaty of Utrecht ends British involvement in the War of the Spanish Succession and grants Britain the asiento trade monopoly
1714	*The Spectator* revival; regency secretary; secretary of the Irish government	Steele expelled as MP, manages Drury Lane theater; Harley and Bolingbroke fall; Anne dies; George I's accession
1715	Trade commissioner; begins *Freeholder*	Jacobite Rebellion; Montagu and Louis XIV die
1716	*The Drummer;* marries Charlotte Myddelton, Countess of Warwick	
1717	Secretary of state	
1718	Resigns due to illness	Quadruple Alliance; Steele's second wife dies
1719	Daughter Charlotte born (30 January); defends the Peerage Bill against Steele in *The Old Whig;* dies (17 June)	Spanish-backed Jacobites defeated at Battle of Glen Shiel; Steeles's *Plebian;* Defoe's *Robinson Crusoe*
1720		South Sea Company Bubble; Walpole PM; Steele's *The Theatre;* Trenchard and Gordon begin *Cato's Letters*
1721	Tickell's edition of Addison's *Works;* stepson, Edward Rich, dies	Cragg (heir to Addison's works) dies

	JOSEPH ADDISON	CONTEXTS
1722		Steele's *The Conscious Lovers*
1726		Swift's *Gulliver's Travels*
1727		Newton and George I die; George II's accession
1728		Gay's *The Beggar's Opera*
1729		Steele dies
1731	Charlotte Myddelton dies; *Rosamond* successfully restaged with Thomas Arne's music	Lillo's *The London Merchant*
1733		Voltaire's *Letters Concerning the English Nation*; Pope's *Essay on Man*
1737		Theatre Licensing Act
1739	Publication of *Discourse on Ancient and Modern Learning*	
1740		Tickell dies
1742		Walpole resigns
1744		Pope dies; Haywood's *Female Spectator*
1745		Swift dies
1755		Johnson's *Dictionary*
1759	Story of his death told in Edward Young's *Conjectures on Original Composition*	Voltaire's *Socrates*
1760		George II dies; George III's accession

Joseph Addison

Introduction

> The whole of the spiritual is between divine and mortal.
> —Diotima

Within the most central confines of London's Westminster Abbey, an observant visitor might notice the curiosity of one figure very unusually repeating in two distinct places and forms—once as a body buried beneath a loving gravestone in the chapel of Mary Tudor and her half-sister Elizabeth, the first modern English queens regnant; and once again as a free-standing statue in Poet's Corner: Joseph Addison.

If one took his two separate abbey monuments as end points of a short line, one would find the approximate midpoint in the chapel of St. Edward the Confessor—the rarefied posthumous neighborhood of England's most sacred kings. Given how relatively unknown Joseph Addison has become, it might come as a surprise for our observant abbey visitor to learn that the Addison statue now in Poet's Corner was nearly placed square amid that somber, exclusive royal slumber party, to stand upright above the grave of Thomas of Woodstock. If those nineteenth-century plans had come to fruition, the slightly higher than eye-level gaze of Addison's statue would have been a first uncanny encounter for newly anointed British monarchs at the end of their coronation ceremony, when they briefly retreat from public view into the heart of the abbey. There, flanked by their most legendary supine forebears, Addison would have paid a marked fixed witness to their taking off the heavy ancient sacred crown of Edward to first replace it with the lighter modern sign of ultimate sovereignty, the Imperial State Crown.

As this book will set out, the symbolism of the never-realized scene imagined above remains precisely in its lack of fruition an appropriate memorial to the Addisonian legacy. Disappearing as a middling authority among the persistent remains of sacred monarchs, the Addison effigy was an attempt to immortalize the gaze of a public worker who had successfully styled himself as a modern Censor and inviter-of-monarchs into their new ambivalent role as imperial servants of the people. The text accompanying Addison's white marble statue in Poet's Corner (designed by Sir Richard Westmacott and first erected in 1809) seeks to admonish a likely forgetful future about who an Addison at the center of culture had been. Inscribed in high-church Latin nearly a century after his death, it reads in translation:

> Whoever thou art who lookest upon this marble respect the memory of Joseph Addison; whom Christian piety, whom virtue and politeness, have ever found their indefatigable patron. His genius in poetry as well as in every other kind of exquisite writing, by which he has bequeathed to posterity the finest example of a pure style of composition, and learnedly developed the discipline of an upright life—stands sacred, and sacred must remain. In argument he happily blended gravity with mildness and in judgment, tempered its severity with urbanity: he upheld the good, and roused the imprudent, and, by a peculiar charm, turned even the guilty round to virtue. He was born in the year of Our Lord 1672, and augmenting his fortune by moderate degrees, at length arrived at the highest honours of the State. He died, in the 48th year of his age, the charm and ornament of Britain.[1]

Some hundred meters away, Addison's gravestone is more modestly set into the floor of the Albemarle Vault, proximately underneath the elaborate wall memorial of his patron and political mentor, the Earl of Halifax, Charles Montagu, an inventor of modern finance and a close prefiguration of the "prime minister."[2] As if in death reperforming an ambivalently modern/feudal subjecthood, Addison's poetical dignity is there politically relegated to subservience. A loyal foot soldier, his grave at the chamber's entrance symbolically guards the long British peace represented by the vault's funeral reunion of the two half-sister queens, Mary I and Elizabeth I, who in life had inherited bitter divided responsibility for the bloody Protestant-Catholic rift that had shaped the tragic destinies of their mothers, wives of Henry VIII.

Addison's gravestone was not inscribed until 1849, at which point a new, nonfeudal, industrial class configuration had firmly taken root. The middle and working classes were growing in conflict with each other and with the ruling bourgeoise, who were everywhere pushing the aristocracy to the sidelines. Robust democratic capitalism had already begun to make Addison's legacy as a driving cultural paragon pale—he who had so significantly helped cheer and shepherd society onto the track toward this energetic reorganization. The inscription on his abbey grave perhaps unwittingly marked this second, symbolic death in its mournful tone of final benediction: "Ne'er to these chambers where the mighty rest since their foundation, came a nobler guest, nor e'er was to the bowers of bliss conveyed a fairer spirit, or more welcome shade. Oh, gone for ever! take this long adieu, and sleep in peace next thy Lord Montague."[3]

Adapted by Francis Egerton, the powerful and wealthy first Earl of Ellesmere, from Thomas Tickell's 1721 eulogistic verses addressed in the first edition of Addison's collected works to his surviving stepson, the lines are not without irony. In their original context, they contributed the pathos of a personal friend's shocked grief to canonizing Addison—not only as an admired author but also as a sociable apparition interceding still in the world to spiritually call Tickell back to virtuous contemplation:

> If business calls, or crowded courts invite,
> Th' unblemished statesman seems to strike my sight;
> If in the stage I seek to soothe my care,
> I meet his soul, which breathes in *Cato* there;
> If pensive to the rural shades I rove,
> His shape o'ertakes me in the lonely grove.[4]

Tickell's original insistence that no guest among the abbey's memorialized host of mostly high-aristocratic and royal ghosts was more "noble" or "welcome" than Addison played on his time's wide celebration of a largely self-made man of the lower gentry, who indeed had advocated for a reformed, "fairer" society. Egerton's Victorian-era inscription reverses Tickell's sequence, reemphasizing Addison's permanent departure and his resting place adjacent to Montagu: the final words of the inscription change Tickell's sequentially earlier benediction of a rest side-by-side "thy loved Montagu" to a closing position next to "thy Lord Montagu."[5] Egerton's own Montagu-like ambitions as a writer, patron, and privy councilor might have resonated with the inscription's revision of Addison's claim to nobility as having less to do with the claim of affection and honorable work and more to do with the liberal permissiveness and protection of a higher, feudal order in which the once-blazing star of Addison now obligingly vanished into the pale welcome of a historically charted power constellation.

Addison, though, had created his own legacy in culture, politics, and literature. A few decades before Egerton's inscription, his second, statued "body politic" had prompted outraged royalist accusations of "leveling" when it almost elbowed its way as a just usurper into the sacred chapel of kings. When the controversy subsided, his statue found its permanent home mere yards away in the south transept of the abbey. It stands there still on its own feet in a location that he had been among the first to claim as the "poetical quarter" in a famous essay pondering the promiscuous mixing of bones of different social levels beneath the abbey's floor.[6] There, in the spiritual space of national authorship, the marble Addison remains elevated but, like his Mr. Spectator, sociable (albeit unknown) with crowds of international tourists and the effigies of other famous writers. His open, gazing eyes, grasped rolled-up scroll, and (fantastical) neoclassical garb suggest a countermodel of power: the future will be shaped by the active debates and discernment of freely associating people of letters, philosopher-citizens.

Discussing the 1808 debate about Addison's Westminster memorialization, Lawrence E. Klein writes that "modern moralism in its Addisonian form rattled the bones of the royal estate" by making the urbane gentleman an authority in himself.[7] Denizens of the nineteenth century celebrated Addison's cultural and political legacy as a long-lasting bulwark against "the twin corrosives of puritan hypocrisy and court corruption."[8] In his two memorialized forms, exposing an absence at the center of power, Addison today still silently rattles the polarized interpretation of middle-class existence as either proud self-standing liberation or faceless obsequious service to a higher power. His memorials in their displacement resonate with the dual figure of Edward the Confessor, lying at the heart of the abbey's equivocal project as either an archeological reconstruction of the decayed medieval nation or a projected blueprint for the future of a modern state and assembly. Edward was the first and only English monarch to be canonized but also effectively the last Anglo-Saxon ruler: the year of his death (1066) saw the quick defeat of his successor at the hands of invading Normans. He was and remains a model of English kingship because he represents an autochthonous, national sovereignty that was never to be, one in which worldly power could supposedly be wielded by sanctified, otherworldly heroes.

Addison's cultural figuration performed him as likewise uniquely able to straddle the world of power and spirituality in a manner foundational for a renewed national and international people. 1719, the year of his death, had marked another dual conversion of Britain as a modern, imperial nation: it was the year that British readers began to identify more with Robinson Crusoe than with Addison's walking Mr. Spectator or his antiquely Stoical Cato. Daniel Defoe's protagonist begins his ill-starred journey by rejecting his father's advice to ignore the seduction of sea-faring adventure for the best-possible, epicurean life of cultivating a modest garden at home—"the middle State . . . the most suited to human Happiness."[9] The language and arguments of the father's warning "Discourse" could have been taken directly from the periodical essays of Addison, the dying literary patriarch of the day; the anti-paternal rebellion of Defoe's hero resonates metaliterarily with the departure of a new literary age. In their reading, the British moved from the paradigm of the theater, where neoclassical culture had located the highest test of formal literary art, to the island paradigm of the novel, which would privately shape the roving imaginations of middle-class people for centuries to come.

Reading so, they mirrored the change in their politics, venturing like Crusoe away from the energetic domestic and European balancing act of cosmopolitan Addisonianism and toward a more unleashed, industrial-scale exploitation of offshored slavery and violent colonialism. Defoe's adventuring protagonist became the identificatory self-made man for the British body politic's anxious entrance into imperial dominance and capitalistic individualism. Half-German, Crusoe mirrored the Hanoverian Georges, those imported figureheads who were tasked with guiding their adopted nation and serving as exemplary characters for its consuming public. As the high medieval state would look back to St. Edward for the guiding fantasy of an autonomous, sacred-kingly nation that was not to be, modern readers in the eighteenth and nineteenth centuries would look nostalgically back to Addison for a "respected normative guide . . . a model social being" whose "style was taken as the mirror of his person."[10] Fixed in his gone-too-soon neoclassical effigy, Addison reliably provided for the backward-gazing subjects of later history a model of peaceable, urbane, middling sovereignty: a balanced modern sociability that had not (yet) fully usurped the mountain-like fortresses of feudal organization nor given itself fully over to the swallowing recklessness of adventurism.

Yet who was this Joseph Addison whom previous centuries admonish us to remember? His name was once synonymous with good English prose. Writers from Voltaire and Benjamin Franklin to John Steinbeck took him as a master to study and emulate.[11] At the tercentenary of his death, his fame as an exemplary theatrical and literary tastemaker has faded and receded into the annals of literary history, but his unparalleled success as a writer in his time lives on in the sound and style of everyday English. The Addisonian spirit, which ushered in an unprecedented era of domestic peace in Britain while eventually helping to inspire the French and American Revolutions, stirred the long breath of the Enlightenment period and coded many of the constitutional political and social agreements under which we live today.[12] A path-breaking journalist, poet, playwright, statesman, traveler, diplomat, philosopher, and businessman, Addison's understatedly colorful career championed moderation, middle-class existence, and the rights of all individuals to education, free debate, and political choice.

This book considers his highly influential contribution to British and transnational culture and politics through a comprehensive exploration of his performative writings, high-level political work, networked social life, and theatrical stagings. It is as an intellectual and artistic biography that functions in part as a broad critical exploration of the roots, intentions, directions, and receptions of Addison's work. In this regard, his overall progressive Whiggism is analyzed in the complex rendering of new light on how a cult of expanding liberty partially masked a simultaneous expansion of chattel slavery and the perpetuation of gender and class oppression. As an influential advocate for universal rights and education and increased equality, Addison's failures to draw critical attention to the abomination of the slave trade and to avoid passing on harmful racial and gender stereotypes in his own writing are particularly tragic and jarring given the clarity and forthrightness of his prose and its effects on his society. His memorialization as a moral authority is haunted by the much-less-memorialized suffering of masses for whom the rising British empire was not the liberating force lionized by Whig rhetoric. This book attempts to make his "silence" in these regards hearable by foregrounding the larger context in which he worked.

Navigating a period of world-shaking new scientific insights, a falling political order based on divine monarchs, and constant threat from foreign wars and violent civil factionalism, Addison shaped and directed new performances that set the scene for the emergence of modern nations—in the private imagination, in literature, in the playhouse, in royal courts, and in the halls of commerce and government administration. His theatrical transformation of quotidian private society was doubled by his creation of a new model for sovereign individuality taken up by monarchs and revolutionary leaders alike. A prototypical artist and public person of what Habermas called the "bourgeois public sphere" (*bürgerliche Öffentlichkeit*), much of Addison's work as a synthesizing cultural unifier has become invisible within our later spheres of specialized knowledges and research fields.[13] A study of Addison's life—one of the crucial founding performances of the modern public sphere—reopens the broad perspective that Habermas identified as "formerly reflected in the perspective of the traditional science of 'politics.'"[14] This book attempts a comprehensive reading of Addison's work and social persona along such contemporary "interdisciplinary" lines.

As an inventor of modern everydayness, Addison was naturally an early practitioner of the journalistic list, a form enjoying new ubiquity in our time of scrolling, strolling smartphone spectators. The two times' convergence in this respect beg the following:

WHAT TO KNOW ABOUT JOSEPH ADDISON

— He was the author of one of the eighteenth century's most popular and produced plays. His 1713 *Cato* was the first moral tragedy "to strike the imagination of the whole British people" and proved an extraordinarily influential drama throughout Europe and its colonies.[15]
— He was a foundational journalist and one of history's most impactful newspaper editorialists. His essays in *The Tatler* and *The Spectator* as well as in assorted other newspapers and pamphlets shaped discourse in London to an unparalleled degree between 1709 and 1719. *The Spectator,* which he published along with his lifelong friend Richard Steele, was one of the first daily English newspapers, becoming a must-read in coffeehouses and private homes. What was an extremely high circulation for its age (three thousand to four thousand copies per day) was dwarfed by its subsequent reprints in volumes held throughout Europe and the Americas,[16] as well as its reincarnation in copycat periodical publications that changed the political and social reality of the European world.[17]
— His other literary achievements also enjoyed remarkable success, be they his public poetry (*The Campaign*), his highly esteemed Latin poetry, his libretto for one of the early eighteenth century's only English operas (*Rosamond*), his guidebook for generations of English "Grand Tourers" on the Continent (*Remarks on Several Parts of Italy, &c.*), or his treatise on numismatics (*Dialogues upon the Usefulness of Ancient Medals*).
— Rising from a clerical familial background, he reached the top of the rapidly expanding British administrative state: as a powerful secretary of state, he held particular authority over British foreign and colonial policy at a crucial historical juncture. He was a major agent

in effecting and stabilizing the (Protestant) Hanoverian Succession, which moved Britain and the European world firmly away from the model of (Catholic) divine right monarchy. Sixty years later, David Hume claimed that since that achievement "public liberty, with internal peace and order, has flourished almost without interruption: Trade and manufactures, and agriculture, have increased: the arts and sciences, and philosophy, have been cultivated. . . . So long and so glorious a period no nation almost can boast of: nor is there another instance in the whole history of mankind, that so many millions of people have, during such a space of time, been held together, in a manner so free, so rational, and so suitable to the dignity of human nature."[18] This book attempts to integrate Addison's commitment to high-level political and administrative work, which often occupied the vast majority of his time, into the more typically developed picture of his literary and cultural accomplishments.[19]

— As a prototypical popularizer of science and philosophy, he helped to forge the role of the public intellectual. Not just in his religiously themed "Saturday sermon" *Spectator* essays but throughout the week, he occupied a "curatorial" role in the public sphere, forming national—and subsequently international—consensus on important cultural issues. Indeed, his work helped to create a coherent broader culture, into which disparate institutions, places, and fields of discourse were interwoven. One of his Victorian biographers, William John Courthope, called him "the chief architect of Public Opinion in the eighteenth century."[20]

— His essays were foundational for modern aesthetics and theories of the imagination. When subsequent philosophers and intellectual historians have investigated concepts of taste, preference, and beauty, they have found Addison's writings as a unique and rather subtle source of many ideas that then took on wider currency and shaped our experience of the world.[21]

— As an unmarried, traveling man until his last few years, he led a quietly unconventional life, building a network of friends and associates across two continents.[22] He theorized and critiqued fashion, embraced and defended popular forms like the ballad and the ghost story, and enthusiastically broadened the ecosystem and catalog of "types," creating models and classifications for a more cosmopolitan lifeworld. As a font of middle-class culture, Addison's expansive urbanity was a historically important counterweight to a scene later dominated by the stodgy bourgeois paterfamilias.

— By being all of these things and through his texts, he was a fighter for a progressive, balanced mode of liberation; a champion of domestic peace, increased international understanding and cooperation, and the middle classes avant la lettre. The now invisible scaffolding of our everyday cultural and psychological worlds owes much to Addison's popular work and its cultivation of a sociable middle of society working consciously together toward a more democratic, prosperous, and egalitarian modernity.

PERFORMING INTELLECT, THEATRICAL BIOGRAPHY

This book aims to provide a comprehensive picture of the intellect that Addison performed in the world. It takes as its point of departure the idea of Addison as a theatrical thinker and impactful theater-maker. When literary historians discuss Addison today, they focus overwhelmingly on Addison's legacy as the leading coauthor of *The Spectator*, which they often consider "the determinant of his cultural memory."[23] There are very sound reasons for such a consideration, even accounting for the natural tendency of institutionally bonded literary scholars to emphasize text as the source of primary cultural signification. *The Spectator* was and remains an event and a font of print publications with enormous, widespread impact whose reception shaped the lenses through which Addison's other performances were judged and understood, during his life and over the last three centuries, in both earlier popular contexts and in our smaller contexts of historically interested specialists today. This study benefits extraordinarily from the insights of the general literary historical discourse on Addison.[24]

With its attempt at a theatrical reframing, my approach does not aim to disagree with the primacy of Addison-the-prose-artist but rather to acknowledge and explore a different side of Addison and his reception that takes theater and performance as—sometimes, and often for Addison himself—providing the inspirational, existential, and aesthetic paradigm for historiography and biography. Even *The Spectator* (in its role, for instance, of running publicity for Addison's wildly successful tragedy *Cato*) can be usefully reimagined as one of the print era's first demonstrations of the ability to provide not just a small group of actors but an entire city's worth of actors with artful, quickly updated scripts for their novel and coordinated, artificial entertainments.

History and biography look very different depending on which aesthetic object or arrangement one takes to be at a given culture's "center." As this book will explore, there are many reasons to view Addison as primarily a theatrical or performative thinker in spite of his greater output of prose than dramatic literature. In *Conjectures on Original Composition,* his "monument" to his departed mentor and friend, Edward Young claimed that Addison should be thought of as "a *Roscius* on the stage of life," referring to the paradigmatic Roman actor.[25] Likewise, there are many reasons to think of Addison's culture as putting theater and the tragedy (sometimes) at the center of their cultural life. Moreover, when we approach what is now largely the obscure textual memory of a quintessential tastemaker, our necessary and wise interpretative remove is already theatrical: we witness former cultures through several historical layers still spectating the enormous glow and afterglow of Addison admiration, much of that witnessing—as will be explored below—under the influence of surviving printed tomes and memories of those family heirlooms in the hands of parents, grandparents, and others who had been, in their day, still genuinely and bodily moved by whatever cultural event or original fire it was that the name Addison once signified.

Theater historian Joseph Roach has argued that "the deep eighteenth century . . . isn't over yet. It stays alive among us as a repertoire of long-running performances."[26] Like Addison's, most of the eighteenth century's popular theatrical and literary performances do not survive today in our ordinary entertainment repertoire. The kind of performances that *do* survive, as Roach implies, are the constitutive ones: the rituals, habits, and traditions of our national and international governments and lives, significantly coded as they were by Enlightenment ideas and standards. Yet, without an understanding of the cultural background of the Enlightenment, the living structures that we have inherited from the people of that time lose something of their urgency and three-dimensionality. That loss of emotional and motivational connection to the still-performing institutional architecture of the Enlightenment is a pivotal historical development in our own era of contested, high-tech globalization and debates over postuniversalist futures. In the eighteenth century, emotional connection to the ideas and debates of the Enlightenment were forged not only in print but also in one of its dominant modes of entertainment: the theater. It was a golden age of acting, and theatrical audiences were large, diversifying, and growing.[27] During the Addison era, as Bridget Orr has recently argued, "the theatre was the site in which English (and British) audiences learned to feel together as Britons but also to feel for various people outside their own community."[28] Addison and Steele's periodicals and dramatic works both played expertly with the heightened theatricality of their culture and time; exactly through such performative, ludic virtuosity, their works became crucial media sources for the Enlightenment in Britain.

If one looked at the English and European world from the perspective of a child like Addison in the 1660s, the achievement of a social world remade by technology, enshrined rights to free expression, and institutionalized mass democracy would have seemed very far off. The politics of the day were deadly serious and dominated by war-making imperial ambitions and the restoration of monarchy, which it was hoped marked a decisive end to the preceding era of bloody civil wars and revolution. In such an environment, the profound energy of brilliant middling people wanting to liberate themselves and their society from dogma was turned away from the centers of acknowledged authority. Isaac Newton, for instance, turned instead privately to ordinary objects and charged them with a drive of curiosity and interrogation that established the universal laws of an intellectual regime change. Addison moved vocationally away from the hotbed of controversy and fighting in the church, where his family had for generations been employed, to develop the less contested liturgy of common conversation and quotidian ritual. The deceptively light touch with which he pursued his wide societal reforms—as with the bare explanatory mode of Newton's expostulations—belied the committed passion of a mind absorbed not in directly reshaping the official national religion but in reforging the broader cultural habitus, the neglected but de facto civic religion. Where Anthony Ashley Cooper, the 3rd Earl of Shaftesbury "advocated sociability and politeness in order to attack what he saw as the older intellectual order of the Church and the Court," aiming his partisan discourses "at the social and intellectual elite," Addison and Steele challenged the supremacy of old-style aristocrats on their own open turf by bringing broad public focus to politeness and its rules.[29] Constructing new ideals of polite social performance, they "sought not to discard ideals of refinement associated with the aristocratic elite but to reorient them toward what we would call aesthetic standards unmoored from any specific status milieu."[30]

The schisms multiplying in the society's religious life left a need for a common platform of moral instruction that periodicals had new power to meet; Addison and Steele's efforts publicly envisioned unprecedented socialization across a social body previously ridden with violent divisions.[31] The liberal politeness that Addison came to exemplify created a new ethic for public discourse, which facilitated for general social understanding the kind of "long conversation" that mathematics and science had enjoyed through millennia: "One had to talk in such a way as to allow the process of talking to continue, even if no agreement was ever reached."[32] Through its establishment of a norm of consideration for all points of view, the polite community of talk that Addison cultivated provided, as Christine Dunn Henderson argues, "a model of a tolerant civil society in which disagreement could be productive rather than destructive."[33]

THE DISAPPEARANCE OF THE SERVANT

Addison's tragic hero, Cato, was an elite, patrician Roman. But in Addison's retelling of classical history, he became also a private man who blessed in his dying moments a future interracial family in which strong women played leading parts and in which Cato himself fell as an absolute patriarchal authority. Addisonianism envisioned progress through the Catonic paradox: the reality of time's effects meant that even the true, just, and beautiful representative must accept its own destruction, like Cato, to further its ends. Ironically, the progress of the same Addisonian engine—its continuing success in our same time—creates the difficulty of recognizing Addison's sociability with us, less as a representative than as an equal collaborator, caught in and reforming particular historical circumstances.

Addison's politics and aesthetics were shaped by his attachment to the middling, commercial classes, not to the Shaftesburian or classical ideal of the elite philosopher's aristocratic withdrawal from the masses.[34] Some scholars of the period stress that the project that Addison and his contemporary Whigs pursued in forging a new public ethic of polite discourse encouraged tightly (self-)controlled groups of elite gentlemen to distance themselves from plebeian culture. But, even in its most elitist formulations, the Whig gospel of politeness and its sometimes restrictive or narrow-minded prescriptions also sought to authorize conversational topics and the participation of people previously excluded by older institutions and norms. Expanding norms and critique ambivalently go hand in hand with expanding representation, and Addison took the marked role of celebratory satirist and cheerleader for the early eighteenth-century culture of public politeness, through which "the forms of public life were expanded and elaborated."[35] Moreover, most Addison readers (and most of his historical reception) note his particularly energetic efforts to strike a steady progressive tone and involve a more inclusive set of actors in the societal picture and conversation. Klein, a leading Shaftesbury expert, has pointed out that even in contrast to his fellow Whigs, Addison's version of politeness pitched itself at a more expansive milieu. Unlike Shaftesbury's more patrician vision, "Addison associated the public, quite concretely, with the venues in metropolitan London, where men and women of the middling and upper sort could engage in discussion of matters of public concern."[36]

Addison, in other words, worked at more than a zero-sum game of empowering male bourgeois-aristocratic Whigs over male aristocratic Tories. As a leader, consolidator, and popularizer of the Enlightenment, his contribution toward middle-class and bourgeois identity was consistently a contribution toward a theatrically split, progressive subject of the kind that Jacques Rancière argues accompanies democracy: "The democratic distribution of the sensible makes the worker into a double being . . . giv[ing] him 'time' to occupy the space of public discussions and take on the identity of a deliberative citizen."[37] The early twilight of the Enlightenment, in which Addison lived and worked, was publicly still dominated by immensely powerful monarchs and aristocratic structures. Following in the heavy footsteps of public writers like Montaigne and Shakespeare, Addison was a key player in a long aesthetic movement that gave the mighty representative men who occupied those high feudal positions "time" to be depicted as more or less ordinary, disenchanted people engaged in trifling, domestic matters. The institution of broad polite culture, in turn, served as the field in which other less powerful and less public individuals could then also be afforded the time to mix as more or less equals in the pages of the same newspapers and literary works, the dividing lines of representational *Dignitas* increasingly blurred. The doubleness of reflective representation—politely extended beyond the elite aristocratic world—reached in Addison's vision even to those for whom the freedom of discourse and the imagination did not correspond with the freedom of social reality. Addison welcomed working people into the reflexive reading community of aesthetic subjects, as people he knew would have to make their own time and enjoyment. "I would have no Man discouraged," he wrote, "with that kind of Life or Series of Action, in which the Choice of others, or his own Necessities, may have engaged him. It may perhaps be very disagreeable to him at first; but Use and Application will certainly render it not only less painful, but pleasing and satisfactory."[38]

Making time in Rancière's sense meant also making time as such—history that progresses, allowing for meaningful change and perhaps a better future (personal and societal) to emerge out of an oppressive, delusive present. Epistemologically, the paradigm shifts and scientific leaps associated with Newtonianism had proven that true sight *depended* on progress that was not merely intellectual but technological as well: the refined mirrors and lenses and the rapid, comparatively cheap distribution of print that had made modern scientific discoveries possible, broadly repeatable, and widely known were part of a larger acceleration of European mercantilism. Due to a combination of historical circumstances, the England of Addison's lifetime was undergoing a uniquely rapid, continual increase in the number of people of many classes consuming a dizzyingly diversifying range of goods: a commercial revolution. The previously spare households of middling people were becoming cluttered with products that changed according to trends in fashion that were themselves being produced at an ever-accelerating rate. Goods (like a scientific education) that might previously have been bought once or simply inherited might now be bought several times in an individual's life. The activity of following the latest fashion and seeking actively to acquire novel consumer goods—long a habit normally confined to the aristocracy—became a normal, expected part of daily life for working nonaristocratic people. As the number of goods increased along with advertisement and demand, the commercial revolution would virtually remake society by the latter part of the eighteenth century, but it began much earlier.[39]

Already in the 1690s, when Addison was coming of age and entering into the commerce of intellectual life, a marked increase in consuming desire was being partially driven by the products of faraway imperial exploits and partially engineered by a wave of thinkers and writers who argued that consumer demand could drive a positive development of society and the economy. The effected democratization of consumption and rapid increase of commercialization was facilitated by the comparatively greater class mobility in England and the increased wage levels among the working classes. Population growth and the exceptional centralization of national culture in London were important factors in this development. Growing from about 200,000 to 900,000 inhabitants between 1600 and 1800, London was the largest city in Europe in 1700, and it drew a significantly higher proportion of its nation's citizens into its confines than other European capital cities. During Addison's period, probably about one in six English citizens lived in London at some point in their lives.[40]

The consumption of excised mass commodities increased in the period at more than twice the rate of the population, suggesting that other cultural factors were at work beyond simple, directly proportionate demographic change.[41] Addison and Steele's periodicals played a substantial role in producing and shaping this "excess" urban consumer desire. As mirrors, the journals guided their split, represented subjects through the labyrinth of newly marketed goods at the same time that they stoked their desire for the certain commodities that might materialize their more perfect, phantasmatic self- and group-actualization. There were now two Londons: the gothic, flesh-blood-and-stuff one that had existed even before William the Conqueror and the one more spectacularly performing itself for the expectant daily censorship of the ghostly modern national eidolon, Mr. Spectator. The periodicals were themselves perfectly elusive commodities in this respect, feeding previously unaddressed middle-class consumers' desire to read about themselves, become informed, feel perhaps a bit superior or smug, and belong to a group whose membership depended on a renewed daily purchase.[42] In their valence as active constructors of a middling society, Addison's periodical essays helped to found practices like consumer-choice identity differentiation and institutions like public fashion that, in turn, strengthened the reign of novelty—an engine of disenchantment with what had come before.[43] The consumer revolution and its implementation of a new regime of public, progressive time was part and parcel of the period's definitional shifts in the categorization of private and public whereby activities previously confined to "the household economy" became visible and publicly relevant, subject to important debate.[44] The pressure of this historical process of domestication worked in two directions: "downward" to "the common" from the heights of aristocratic and courtly self-fashioning and ecclesiastical and judicial governance; and "upward" to the coming regime of bourgeois citizenship in a generalizing movement that opened the private household to public display and importance.[45] The dual forces leave a strong artifact in the oversmooth flowing lines of Addison's middle style.

The unprecedented popular success of *The Tatler* and *The Spectator* heralded an era of politics and social life organized around the increasingly rapid and timely production of printed media. As Terence Bowers succinctly glosses, "Addison and Steele's journals . . . held up a 'mirror' to their readers, which enabled them to understand themselves as collectively constituting a new kind of community, one whose views ('public opinion') could claim to represent the interests of society in general because they seemed to transcend the narrow interests of any single group and were arrived at through reason, open communication, and critical discussion."[46] The quintessential model for this freer discursive community of modern public opinion was the textual community of classical authorities, who across millennia could be made to debate and articulate positions that had often been too dangerous for living authors to directly advocate. In his journal essays, Addison popularized the tales and reasoning of Homer, Socrates, and company by mixing them with news and tales from London and around the growing British empire. But the broad sociability of Addison's work heavily included recent and contemporarily active philosophers and scientists along with the ancients. The high accomplishments of the previous generations of French men of science and letters continued to inspire English intellectuals; Addison emulated their public work and disseminated their insights to a broad readership.[47] Shaping the domestic consensus, Addison's writing propagated in digestible form the modern world-shaping ideas of three key English thinkers: Milton, Locke, and Newton. Although we now take their towering influence on the general culture to be direct, their impact on early-eighteenth-century society at large owed much to Addison's writings in *The Spectator*.

Politically and aesthetically, all three of these men represented rather radical seventeenth-century departures from earlier conventions. Milton had advocated a head of state who served only at the will (and even the whim) of the governed; after the Restoration, he had made Satan—most beautiful of angels—the ambivalent tragic hero of his *Paradise Lost*. Locke had articulated a rational system of government premised on inalienable rights, the impossible coexistence of slavery and civil society, and a world populated mostly by good, reasonable people whose main political task was to prevent the harm that would be done by a few bad actors. Newton, however, was the figure whose remapping of the cosmos and the human experience most troubled and inspired Addison and many of his contemporaries. The historical disjuncture in sight, caused by the extension of that dominant human sense's range through prosthetic glasses and by Newton's demonstration of the radically contingent design of the eye, surfaces repeatedly as a driving thematic in Addison's work. His shaking insights shaped Addison's aesthetics. Moreover, the new power of Newtonian science on contemporary minds helps to explain the affective power Addison's work had for its original readers and audiences, if not for their twentieth-century successors. Addisonianism worked with the pathos of a culture newly theatricalized by the paradigm shift in human understanding effected by Newtonianism. One famous Addison admirer, Voltaire, was still struck by the different staging of the cosmos effected by Newtonian ideas two decades after the first run of *The Spectator*: "A Frenchman who arrives in *London*," he wrote in 1733, "will find Philosophy, like every Thing else, very much chang'd there. He had left the World a *plenum*, and he now finds it a *vacuum*." The abysses between Cartesianism (a fairly recent, modern cosmological system still prevailing in France) and the new English understanding of physics were immense: "A *Cartesian* declares that Light exists in the Air; but a *Newtonian* asserts that it comes from the Sun in six Minutes and a half. . . . The very Essence of Things is totally chang'd. You neither are agreed upon the Definition of the Soul, nor on that of matter."[48]

Newton's discoveries opened an immense vacuum out of which the ground of a truly modern world emerged. The visiting Frenchman pointed to the consequent rupture in human intellectual history: "The several Discoveries which Sir *Isaac Newton* has made on Light, are equal to the boldest Things which the Curiosity of Man could expect, after so many philosophical Novelties."[49] Decades before, Addison had argued similarly in essays Voltaire was likely to have read. The alienating light of Newtonian science exposed more starkly the human and its idiosyncratic, isolated position on a rock in space. The achievement and drive of modern subjectivity, I argue in the chapters that follow, was not *just* the result of ambition, socioeconomic changes, and the growth of populations and imperial schemes. Newtonianism was both a cause and effect of the bursting of the social bubble of the Roman church's parochial cosmos. With the advent of a Newtonian age, the denizen of the old central and closely managed terrestrial divine feudal system died to be reborn as a cosmopolitan creature, sociable with others as with distant physical phenomena, all subject to the same overriding laws. The now decentralized universe was one in which certainly no earthling (king, priest, or other) could reasonably claim a significantly special metaphysical position.[50]

In the context of sociable contingency, one of the larger, reflected gestures of Addison's work was the rejection of the notion that one can overcome human limits through the old means of traditional metaphysics or immersion into a supposedly transcendental social regime of arcane hierarchies. Newton's brilliant reasoning and optical discoveries had revealed each human to be forged and sustained by odd local forces; the earth itself was an accident of much more extensive mechanical laws. More than a philosophical quandary or intellectual adjustment, Newtonianism was for Addison and his audience a historical-material change in the felt experience of the human body and its environs: the "light" of the Enlightenment entered through eyes newly revealed to be little more than bizarre, highly subjective, and overwhelmingly flimsy lens-and-mirror contraptions. Addison understood this and committed, in turn, not a mere sociological or political act in dignifying the common human being, but an act of philosophy. It was rational in such a reality—bizarrely buoyed as we all are in a void at all sides—to take the human seriously as a scene of equal, interesting performative manifestations in need of a new, more plainly justifiable, and more egalitarian modern structure.

The poet and essayist Anna Laetitia Barbauld wrote that within Addison's texts one finds a uniquely affecting "alliance of the heart with the imagination."[51] Addison's writing urged and performed a steady moderate cheerfulness and optimism; the cold disorientation inherent in the opening, infinite

Newtonian cosmos played the silent background for his call to recommit to social, human values. Addisonian cheerfulness had to do much less with blitheness or kitsch than with health and duration on a planet now understood to be more like a small ship on uncertain seas than the fixed site of an eternal garden and its suburbs.

Overall, Addison developed a hermaphroditic discourse of life, balanced between the emotional, spiritual, and existential needs of the soul and the mind's drive toward the scientific sublime—Newtonian subjectivity's "original sin." In his critical essays, Addison laid the foundation for an understanding of "the egotistical sublime," the product of reflective negotiation between cold external perception and the vastness of inner psychological vision and experience; Milton was its poet laureate, and Addison gave him his public laurels.[52] After Addison, the sides of this hermaphroditic discourse—in which the vanguard of science still wore the full shimmering dress of "natural philosophy" and aesthetics emerged naked and nameless from culture's chilly, gripping bath in disenchanted physics—separated into different movements and institutions. To find a satisfying "holistic" discourse that attends both to health in all its aspects and to the frontiers of understanding in our hyperspecialized, postindustrial age is a desire likely to go unsatisfied. For a brief time and then for a longer time in the nostalgic gaze upon the past, Addison held together such a dream of comprehensive consensus for many in the English and European worlds. The *modern* subject became the *aesthetic subject of the imagination,* an Addisonian transformation explored in chapter 4.

As Richard Sennett argues, it is not only that our situation and our understanding of that situation that has changed: our structures of feeling have also moved on. After the breakdown of industrial paternalism, in which the bourgeois provider of employment was also supposed to cultivate his workers' well-being, the replacing idea of the worker's autonomy and freedom encourages a felt equivalence between disbelief and freedom. The flip side of this "liberation," however, is the ongoing power of the rich, now themselves liberated from the obligation to provide careful nurturance to peers outside their class level. The corresponding intellectual abandonment of regarding the whole person seriously and at length renders the historical Addisonian discourse and its contemporary analogues as alienated and cloyingly sentimental: their subtle turns and fine moderations become illegible in the sweep of a massive drive toward a freedom and autonomy that has abandoned to a large extent its reflected sociable aspect.[53] This historical development explains some of the difficulty we have in interpreting the eighteenth century, which we now for good reason tend to analyze as a temporal case study of lacking effective autonomy among the larger populace and the correspondingly unjust empowerment of a bourgeois paterfamilias. The riddling, positive aspect of the Addisonian Cato's sublimity—as a planned-obsolescent seizer and distributor of autonomy in an expanded cosmopolitan familial context—is lost in the rush to declare him merely a figure for masculinist, patriotic, British imperial ambitions. We condemn Enlightenment progressivism, in other words, at the risk of forgetting that even an eighteenth-century Cato stood against a real enemy in dire circumstances: a regressive regime centered solely around Caesar was waiting in the wings to destroy Cato's provisional senate-in-exile.

Since we are living through another historical moment when the turn of criticism is toward the inseparability of political struggles and aesthetics, the Addisonian legacy becomes newly legible again. The sublimity of prose and poetry in their separation from the body and context no longer, again, suffices in the cultural conversation. The Modernist dismissal of the "sentimental" Addison in favor of canonizing poets like Pope and Swift, who, in their own time, were criticized for meanness, melancholia, and elitism, presents itself with new, problematic valences. The "Newtonian" judgment and criticism of a writer like Edward Young becomes, again, differently accessible in a culture that no longer fully believes that the literary sublime or art for art's sake is a higher goal or achievement than the actions that real people take in the world. Demonstrating an Enlightenment consciousness of the inseparability of literary endeavor from politics, Young scientifically sorted the small, sociable circle of the three most preeminent British Augustan writers as such:

> To distinguish this triumvirate from each other, and, like *Newton,* to discover the different colours in these genuine and meridian rays of literary light, *Swift* is a singular wit, *Pope* a correct poet, *Addison* a great author. *Swift* looked on wit as the *jus divinum* to dominion and sway in the world; and considered as usurpation, all power that was lodged in persons of less sparkling understandings. This inclined him to tyranny in wit; Pope was somewhat of his opinion, but was for softening tyranny into lawful monarchy; yet there were some acts of severity in his reign. *Addison's* crown was elective, he reigned by the public voice.[54]

The broad appeal of Addison as writer and public person who could act as a moral authority had to do not only with his perceived virtue but also with the sense of his performativity itself. Bringing the word "egotism" into the English language, Addison marked a critical difference between his own public rhetorical display and that of Montaigne, who had avowed only his family and friends as audience and his plain "selfe" as groundwork for his seminal modern essays.[55] Beneath the everyday patina of Addison's more temperate middle style prose were darkly glistening pathos of a late Baroque sensibility, the irony of mise en abyme, the vaulting freedom of a theatrical generation who knew that any form of knowledge or lasting self they attained would be by default "mediated, approximated, provisional, and fictionalized."[56] Addison took as his classical master Virgil, who—he wrote—"loves to suggest a truth indirectly, and without giving us a full and open view of it, to let us see just so much as will naturally lead the imagination into all the parts that lie concealed."[57] He praised his modern master, Milton, similarly, for his "concealed beauties" and tendency to only subtly suggest meaning that must be meditated on and later interpreted.[58]

Addison, the poetic apprentice of Virgil and Milton's double optics, expressed his own genius in developing for his generation a prosaicness that resonated with the revealed abysses of Newtonian Enlightenment but performed a dignified tightrope walk over them. Readers responded affectively to the sense of textual theatricality, and Addison the literary critic authorized them to "know" how they should read Addison the literary writer. In his posthumously published *Discourse on Ancient and Modern Learning*, he stressed a context-dependent poetics of reading and writing, inviting by implication his contemporaries and we later readers to understand his works as buzzing with the specificity of the era and milieu in which they were written. The original readers of the classics, he argued, "being conversant with the Place, where the Poem was transacted, gave 'em a greater Relish than we can have at present of several Parts of it; as it affected their Imaginations more strongly, and diffus'd through the whole Narration a greater Air of Truth."[59] In the terms of contemporary art practice, Addison understood writing—and also reading—as an "installation," language set not just in its own discursive terms but in constellation with its time, culture, place, and social reality. As so much with Addison, it cut both ways, and he invited both: our distance from classical writers, he argued, also created new, real pleasures, often precisely *because* we might read them with a different sensitivity than their original readers, with productive ignorance or false impressions. A typical, uncanny Addisonian paradox ran lightly and poignantly through a piece rife with the suggestion of allegory that emerged as the last of his pieces to reach the public. The *Discourse* urges us to become better readers by consciously recognizing what we cannot recognize, the many inevitable rich slippages multiplying in the gaps between readers and dead author: "We can be sure, therefore, whatever imaginary Notions we may frame to ourselves, of the Harmony of an Author, they are very different from the Ideas which the Author himself had of his own Performance."[60]

In their overview of his multifaceted life and career, Edward and Lillian Bloom highlighted Addison's arduous, energetic efforts "to work out a comprehensive ethic for himself and his society."[61] He achieved this while blazing his own difficult middle path, striving toward and producing a more democratic and egalitarian order that would not more solidly exist until after his death. "A sociable animal," he looked at and led life holistically: "He did not merely observe the drama of his world; he participated in it," the Blooms wrote. He struggled, indeed, "for a stable world that lay just beyond his reach."[62] But he infused his classical, Virgilian ambition to be the georgic "tender husband" of a society in a rapid state of transition to empire with a modern perspective on the mechanical, programmable aspect of the odd, sociable human animal and its disenchanted post-Newtonian "sensoriolum."[63]

Writing at the beginning of the nineteenth century, Barbauld celebrated Addison's writings as "founding documents of the culture," which addressed a frightening lack of integration in society.[64] As a shaping force in Barbauld's own education, Addison had already become much more a stony monument than elegant-animal tightrope walker. But, in the context of her advocacy of dissent, gender equality, the French Revolution, and abolition, Barbauld's eulogy also speaks to Addison's inspiring position in a genealogy of progressivism that eventually set itself up more fully against racialized patriarchal bourgeois complacency. Thomas Macaulay would later give him credit for a "revolution" in the culture—"the greatest and most salutary ever effected by any satirist." Addison, he wrote, had turned the tables around so that vice could be mocked and virtue, which had previously been the object of scorn and ridicule, could be openly lived, praised, and valued. "Since his time," Macaulay argued, "the open violation of decency has always been considered among us the mark of a fool."[65] Addison's twentieth-century biographer, Peter Smithers, followed Macaulay's arguments to trace the link between Addison's salutary societal impact and our forgetting of him and his legacy: "It is this revolution in its completeness which has caused Addison's writings to pass from the list of favourite reading in the present century. So fully did mankind endorse his teaching that many of his precepts came to be thought trite, axiomatic, or even presumptuous, and to him was attributed an undisciplined romanticism which had no part in his make-up." When one looks at the historical record carefully, however, Smithers argued, "no other Englishman has influenced the social development of his country more powerfully."[66]

One of Addison's first biographers, Samuel Johnson, lends credence to Smithers and Macaulay's claims from a closer, eighteenth-century perspective, which was (in keeping with Dr. Johnson's character) less hagiographic than astutely critical. In our twenty-first-century age characterized by global performance imperatives, Johnson's precise identification of Addison's unique and unprecedented contributions gains new pertinence. "What he attempted," Johnson wrote, "he performed." The performance, then, because of its success, disappeared: "Addison is now despised by some who perhaps would never have seen his defects, but by the lights which he afforded them."[67] Already half a century after his death, Johnson testified at length to the peculiarly admirable "agedness" of Addison's site-specific work and the challenge it posed to the classical notion that great writing must be sublime writing whose affective power survives equally across eras:

> That he always wrote as he would think it necessary to write now, cannot be affirmed; his instructions were such as the character of his readers made proper. That general knowledge which now circulates in common talk, was in his time rarely to be found. Men not professing learning were not ashamed of ignorance; and in the female world, any acquaintance with books was distinguished only to be censured. His purpose was to infuse literary curiosity, by gentle and unsuspected conveyance, into the gay, the idle, and the wealthy; he therefore presented knowledge in the most alluring form, not lofty and austere, but accessible and familiar. When he shewed them their defects, he shewed them likewise that they might be easily supplied. His attempt succeeded; enquiry was awakened, and comprehension expanded. An emulation of intellectual elegance was excited, and from his time to our own, life has been gradually exalted, and conversation purified and enlarged.[68]

Addison's rapport with our modernity, in contrast with that of the eighteenth and nineteenth centuries, fits with what Pope described as his general pattern of sociability: "Addison's conversation had something in it more charming than I have found in any other man. But this was only when familiar: before strangers or perhaps a single stranger, he preserved his dignity by a stiff silence."[69] After Macaulay, Courthope picked up the theme of Addison's disappearance into the very structures he built, calling him "the chief architect of Public Opinion in the eighteenth century." The invisible Addisonian consensus, "in spite of its durable solidity, seems, like the great Gothic cathedrals, to absorb into itself the individuality of the architect. A vigorous effort of thought is required to perceive how strong this individuality must have been."[70]

Johnson had closed his well-known *Life of Addison* with the admonition that "whoever wishes to attain an English style, familiar but not coarse, and elegant but not ostentatious, must give his days and nights to the volumes of Addison."[71] Here was one of Addison's art's famous disappearing acts: into the "ease" of the "middle style" of writing. Later readers, familiar less with Addison than with essays by writers from Ben Franklin to Virginia Woolf who for two centuries took Johnson's once well-known advice seriously, take for granted a middle-brow essayistic tone that, hackneyed, seems to write itself on blogs, in magazines, and throughout literary criticism.[72] An overbusy tourist in Europe can feel the same when they visit yet another monumental stone cathedral in some capital city. Between Victorian grandiosity (with its ideal of sentimental service to God and country) and Johnson's invention of British Enlightenment sobriety, Addison's performance of disappearance had already proven uniquely pliable to the different ambitions and wishes of his interpreters and emulators. Hitting one of his trademark themes—time's "rust" collecting on even the most classic of texts—Addison implicitly demonstrated an awareness that any marks of his individual genius or hard-won originality would be invisible for the future readers of his polite, polished prosaic surfaces.[73] Antiquity, he argued, draws "a Kind of Veil over any Expression that is strain'd above Nature, and recedes too much from the familiar Forms of Speech." In contrast to an ancient text's original readers, we "take it for granted, that the Stile is beautiful and elegant, where they find it hard and unnatural. Thus has Time mellowed the Works of Antiquity, by qualifying, if I may so say, the Strength and Rawness of their Colours, and casting into Shades the Light that was at first too violent and glaring for the Eye to behold with Pleasure."[74] What disappears, finally, in Addison reception is the excitement and awe readers felt about a rather miraculous creation of prosaic, shared everydayness and a peaceful, accretionary discourse incorporating the blinding insights of modern science and philosophy into an expanding societal conversation.[75] With Addisonianism's success, the alien new light and voids of Newtonianism were woven, as if for us automatically, into the same humane, ordinary even kitschy domestic fabric that pleasingly covered, beautified, and incorporated the ongoing societal schisms threatening any individual and collective destiny.

Taking the flexible form of intellectual biography—rather than a strictly chronological telling of a life or a drier philological exploration of the influences and cognitive breakthroughs of an author—this book posits an Addison whose mind saw performance as its highest test: how to create good, useful work that would not, on the other hand become in time a poison for its readers, a theme Addison meditated on as the author's "purgatory" in *Spectator* 166.[76] The modesty of publishing in the vulgar, throwaway form of penny papers was one manner in which Addison marked his essays as "current coin," imbued with complexity and value but stamped definitively—even when printed in collected tomes for perpetuity—with a specific date.[77] This was in contrast to the published form of his one tragedy, *Cato,* which (although it also performed complexly with its specific time) the numismatist-author playfully had printed with images of antique Roman medals on its title page, signifying its author's ambition for his dramatic work to occupy a more noumenal position in the long game of culture. There is no final, conclusive portrait to be made of such a ludic and serious author and human actor, and this book attempts to follow Addison's moderating, slightly teasing spirit in flexibly comparing "the Poet and the Statuary together," allowing an Addison who thought like an interdisciplinary artist and cultural worker, both avant la lettre and in the sense of the Renaissance and its classical ideals of public citizenship.[78] A quintessential, warm humanist, Addison rather cheerfully sought to dissolve his author(ized)-function into the cold, progressive acid of unmarked subjectivity: this book seeks the Addison taking a mild garden-walk through the vacuum of the cosmos among the projected monuments of his own reception and the intense gravitational wells of his particular historical context—the same Addison who modestly and realistically sought to make a positive difference in the very real shared stage set of our consequential terrestrial life together here.

In his own lifetime, his political, literary, and theatrical work helped to effect a profound change in a feudal nation torn by civil war. As Smithers puts it, when Addison came of age and left his family home in the midst of the tensions that would lead to the unexpectedly "Glorious" Revolution, "no young man tasting the realities of the world for the first time could have predicted that from the violent happenings of those years there would spring two centuries of orderly constitutional development."[79] No one could have predicted such an outcome in part because it took Addison's contributions to help lay and stabilize the groundwork. "It was the task of Addison to carry on the reconciling traditions of our literature," Courthope wrote:

> It is his praise to have accomplished his task under conditions far more difficult than any that his predecessors had experienced. What they had done was to give instinctive and characteristic expression to the floating ideas of the society about them; what Addison and his contemporaries did was to found a public opinion by a conscious effort of reason and persuasion. Before the Civil Wars there had been at least no visible breach in the principle of Authority in Church and State. At the beginning of the eighteenth century constituted authority had been recently overthrown; one king had been beheaded, another had been expelled; the Episcopalian form of Church Government had been violently displaced in favour of the Presbyterian, and had been with almost equal violence restored. Whole classes of the population had been drawn into opposing camps during the Civil War, and still stood confronting each other with all the harsh antagonism of sentiment inherited from that conflict. Such a bare summary alone is sufficient to indicate the nature of the difficulties Addison had to encounter in his efforts to harmonise public opinion.[80]

From the relatively small corner of literary history, it would be enough to assert Addison's importance for our cultural self-understanding to repeat Smither's claim that "the influence of his prose style in modern literary history can hardly be overestimated."[81] Yet Addison's more comprehensive legacy was arguably in the performative act of dignifying and bringing public visibility and language to middling people, helping to forge, greet, and welcome an expanding citizenry of semisovereign participant-observers into the world of shared contemplation and cosmopolitan debate. This foundational act of emancipatory community creation lent his texts their oddly sacred aura so that Chalmers could claim in 1817 that *The Spectator* had "subsisted in the plenitude of its original popularity for nearly a century, and no composition merely human, has been so frequently printed and read."[82] The marks, inscriptions, and butter stains on surviving bound volumes of the original daily half-folio "penny paper" sheets suggest that *The Spectator* indeed had a wide readership beyond the cultural and political elite.[83]

Inside the roughly three thousand early eighteenth-century London coffeehouses where Habermas saw the origins of a bourgeois public sphere, the periodicals of Addison and Steele functioned as original, constitutional liturgical texts for a public imbibing the sacred drink of self-awakening. Through the pages of *The Tatler* and *The Spectator,* Habermas wrote, the new modern public was guided by Addison toward tolerance, civic morality, and practical wisdom. This new public "did not yet come to a self-understanding through the detour of a reflection on works of philosophy and literature, art and science, but through entering itself into 'literature' as an object."[84] Addison's performances of literary reform stand at the beginning of the "middling" classes' formal self-understanding, well before the term "middle class" or the modern theory of classes had taken root. He did not use the term "middling" that many of his contemporaries used to refer to the loose categorization of people who had to work for their living and who had some substantial economic agency, neither rich nor very poor. Nevertheless, he advocated for "the middle Condition" in life between riches and poverty and wrote affirmatively of the "middle Sort of People, who keep their Wishes within their Fortunes."[85] As Stephen Miller has argued, "Addison was not writing *for* a middle class. Instead he was writing in the hope of *creating* a larger middle class."[86]

In this book, I have chosen to use the tellingly uncomfortable word "middling" as a general signifier for the kind of people who would later be dignified with a socioeconomic concept—the middle classes—but who in Addison's time were newly and ambiguously forming as a public: people "of moderate means" but also "moderating," "negotiating," or even "interfering," meddling and needling in. Perhaps the awkward characterization remains true of middle-class existence, a station from which Mary Wollstonecraft would later in the century choose her intended female audience, since they were in "the most natural state," where virtue can be obtained.[87] It is, as Wollstonecraft's exceptional vindication proves the rule, a type of existence more often and easily criticized than celebrated, prone to a disavowal of sublimes yet an embrace of ambition, a condition routinely tied to complacency and ignorance yet commonly having more to do with striving, moral wrestling, active compromising, learning, adaptation, and educational attainment. As a writer, Addison was unusually socially evenhanded and aimed sharp, entertaining sentences also at the foibles, weaknesses, and failures of working people. But, instead of merely exploiting them for the sake of comedy (a vice of many writers of his time and of many literary ages), he consistently sought to recognize, bolster, and make representational space for them. He was, after all, defining and performing his own uncertain position in society. Although born into the privilege of a well-connected family as a son of an established dean of the Church and esteemed historian, the fact that he had to work hard for a position and livelihood with little guarantee marked him, like most of us, as middling.[88]

In the political, academic, and coffeehouse milieu of his London life, the former Oxford fellow Addison certainly enjoyed a built-in, inherited elite status in comparison with the vast majority of his contemporaries. Yet he and his Whiggish peers were helping to establish a new vector of history away from the authoritarian (aristocratic and/or ecclesiastical) and toward greater public inclusivity and the authority of the better argument.[89] Their liberal gospel of taste instituted a praxis of "standing back from ourselves and our private preferences," methodologically checking private inclinations and established dogma to produce a manifest sense of universality.[90] The act of debating and thinking with a degree of sociable disinterest required not only time but also new spaces, away from both the charged environment of immediate power and overdetermining rituals of allegiance (the court, parliament, and church) as well the less controlled traditional sites of more massive public assembly (the tavern, market, and fair). Coffeehouses provided ideal grounds for the reformist Whig project and its "urbanized" philosophy.[91] But one of the ways in which recent scholars lay bare some of the troubling contradictions and deep ambiguities of Whiggish progressivism is by drawing attention to the revisionist, nostalgic aspect of the Habermasian gaze on the "rational" coffeehouse, a gaze reinforced by Addison and Steele's glowing pictures of ideal coffeehouse culture. Rather than merely depicting a peaceable reality or wish, such depictions seem to express a censorious desire to legitimize and reform places that other archival sources reveal as sites of often "vulgar, popular, subversive, grotesque and sexual" sociability.[92] The mix of actual and representational exclusions in the coffeehouses celebrated by Addison and Steele create a deep ambiguity or even revulsion for contemporary readers contemplating the limits and self-serving, (self-)policing aspects of the era's Whiggish progressivism—a topic that subsequent chapters will explore more fully.[93]

In reality, the expanse of coffeehouse culture included houses with different mixes of classes and ethnicities—including houses serving a poorer and laboring clientele. Colonially produced caffeine was not the only stimulant driving many Londoners to visit different houses multiple times in a day: the success of the new cultural model was further fed by the excitement of debate between formerly segregated classes and groups, which included the "busy" elements in society, working people who also embraced the new Whiggish participatory ethic of politeness.[94] However, in one of the more significant "invisible" scenic exclusions of the forming liberal public, this excitement did not include the chance for people of different genders to publicly debate—women were largely absent from coffeehouses as clientele at the time.[95] Addison and Steele's popular periodicals pitched themselves, however, to women and filled up their pages with perspectives on and from "the female world." Designed to be read aloud in public places and in the private home, the essays we now read silently had a crucial performative role as props for ordinary people acting out the role of public rhetoricians for the first time.[96] Through the printed observations of Mr. Spectator and his circle, English men and women thus practiced at large scale taking on the perspectives of women and speaking about them as agents and co-observers in polite interaction. The significant contribution of two women to *The Spectator*'s printing and distribution throw into complex relief Addison and Steele's ostensible efforts to build women's presence into the reformed and expansive cosmopolitan community they advocated. Abigail Baldwin, the "A. Baldwin" on each number's imprint, was the venture's chief initial salesperson and sponsor. Sharing the imprint was the name of the printer, Samuel Buckley, whose capacity to turn out a mass daily paper resulted from his having bought the first long-running daily foreign news digest, the *Daily Courant,* from its founder, Elizabeth Mallet, who had originally published using a male pronoun.[97]

As will be discussed, Addison's actual representations of women were often highly problematic. In the long history of their popular reception, the many "readers who internalized their pronouncements and illustrations" were repeatedly fed the enclosing new bourgeois cliché equating women's nature with domesticity.[98] Paradoxically, for many appropriately critical gazes, the overdetermination of this restrictive leitmotif was part of the double-edged and often plainly contradictory effort on the part of Addison and Steele to strengthen the figure of a less assailable, publicly domestic woman: the consistent effort to address a female readership and to include some aspect of their concerns and lives in daily discourses provided a large new stage for women's broader civic assertion.[99]

The rate of literacy in England, which had fallen during the Restoration from the heights it had reached in the pamphlet-strewn Civil War period, began to climb again with the era of Queen Anne and Addison and Steele.[100] The popularity of the journals and the rise in literacy were mutually reinforcing: the sense was emerging again that the cultural signs being produced were meaningful and important for the larger population to decode. Addison marked his philosophically pedagogical interventions as modern mimeses of Plato's dialogues, which had also functioned as scripts for local performance and guides for how to have ideal conversations: the British coffeehouse reader acted in much the same way as Plato's original pupils, taking on the guise of a character in order to instigate reflective exchange through a somewhat lengthy speech or exposition.[101] Plato did not set his dialogues in a school setting but among people at leisure in diverse mostly noninstitutional settings. Addison and Steele's aim to renew philosophy in the coffeehouses can be seen in this light as a complex reenactment of the original philosophical movement, sidestepping the long-entrenched performative dispositions associated with Aristotle and his school-men, who had for centuries continued Plato's work in a dogmatic and less self-consciously performative manner. The lightness of Addison's texts has a coy aspect, but as a philosophical opus, they provided British readers with a solid entrance into "the dialectic" from a man who took on the role of a modern national "Censor," in the mold of Cato the Elder, himself already a latter figuration of Socrates. George Berkeley privately wrote to a friend that Addison was "a great philosopher, having applied himself to speculative studies more than any of the wits that I know."[102] Johnson, in his biography of Addison, painted a picture of a renowned public person who, by greatly expanding the practice and enthusiasm for philosophical reasoning into a common national discourse, attained in his time something like the esteem Socrates had once enjoyed in his own circle: "Of his virtue it is a sufficient testimony, that the resentment of party has transmitted no charge of any crime. He was not one of those who are praised only after death; for his merit was so generally acknowledged, that Swift, having observed that his election passed without a contest, adds, that if he had proposed himself for king, he would hardly have been refused."[103]

Because of particular historical situations at the end of the seventeenth century, like the breakdown of the Stationer's Company monopoly on printing and the resulting end of strong state control over newspapers and other literary material, England became in many respects the first leading example of a modern nation transformed by broad, democratizing public discourse. Profit-driven publishers like Jacob Tonson began to replace the feudal patron as the curator and source of livelihood for writers; it was the trader and the businessman who increasingly had the facility, resources, and networks to grant writers like Addison access to the larger developing markets of anonymously circulating goods, which would supply the eventual mass, middle-class society.[104] The model that England offered—coercively and more freely—to the rest of the world means that Addison's pivotal role during the period has meaning beyond its obvious importance for anyone who wants to understand what Britain was and has become: he was also a leader in the global, imperial, and cosmopolitan development of democratic nation-building more generally.

In many places of the world, readers of *The Spectator* and *Cato* reacted similarly: "The private people, come together to form a public, readied themselves to compel public authority to legitimate itself before public opinion."[105] By monumentalizing Addison—his texts and exemplary life—disparate communities of readers held up a mirror to magistrates in which was reflected an eloquent and plainly elegant spokesperson for their coming collectivity, an artist forging the self as a philosopher-citizen.

OUTLINE OF THE BOOK

The book proceeds in a roughly biographical fashion, moving from Addison's early life, formative cultural context, and "internal" intellectual and poetic life out to the public performances of his later theatrical, journalistic, and political career. As a bridge to a new acquaintance with Addison, the first four chapters thematize the disjuncture in his reception between the twentieth century and the two centuries prior to reveal, on the other hand, a new affinity between our own recent performative times and the British Augustan Age. Within the subtle interior turns of his writing, the Addison who would become the quintessential poet-statesman of his age began to shape a popular, modern style of individual sovereignty out of a philosophical confrontation with technological change and abyss-opening epistemological paradigm shifts. Drawing together influences ranging from the classical to the modern, this book participates in the project of intellectual history-writing for which Addison's own work was popularly foundational.

Why is Addison, one of the most successful, critically influential, and popular writers in literary history, so little known and read today? Chapter 1 attempts to answer that question by outlining his complex historical reception and looking at the powerful reevaluations of his work given by two giants of twentieth-century Modernist literature—T. S. Eliot and Virginia Woolf—and one of Modernism's most influential contemporary discontents, C. S. Lewis. After becoming a historicized, ambivalent, but still mighty figure for Victorian readers, the attacks on Addison's legacy by preeminent critics in the 1920s and 1930s (particularly Eliot and Bonamy Dobrée, whose biography named Addison as *The First Victorian*) caused Addison's reputation to rapidly and lastingly plummet.[106] A century after the Modernists' dismissal of Addison, the "performative turn" in literary studies and philosophy opens a path to productively discover his appeal to earlier audiences: working against the fragmentation of professional and social life and committed to a Whig poetics of literature's social utility, Addison's writing envisioned a different future of general, progressive sociability. A reformist "in the spirit of liberal guidance rather than puritanical castigation," Addison's sentimentality was misunderstood by twentieth-century intellectuals focusing on the importance of critical debate for constructing the "bourgeois public sphere."[107] Those later cultural workers' efforts to analyze and complicate an overgrown cultural blandness took for granted the kind of general "contact at a distance" and bonhomie that Addison's work seeded: a feeling of social cohesion through "sentimental connections as insurance against social disruption."[108] Picking up where less frequent periodicals like Ned Ward's monthly the *London Spy* left off, *The Tatler* and *The Spectator* performed daily for and with their broad readership what Manushag Powell calls "the subtle but marked shift from spy to spectator," whereby "the increasing acceptability, even desirability, of looking *openly* around oneself" became instilled "in English (or at least London) culture." The Addisonian Gestus of emancipation moved readers from the position of sidelined arrivistes in national public life to central sovereign subjects, granting them a stable citizen-community of their own.[109] Woolf's ironically ambivalent label of Addison as "pure silver" points the way to understanding the poetics of a self-consciously quotidian author who aspired above all to be useful in his own time. It also provides a strong and appropriately satirical critique of Addison's imbalanced and often condescending representation of women, which lapsed at times into misogynistic tropes and participated in propagating new and old gender stereotypes at the same as "gallantly" opening a door to women's participation in the coming public order.[110] As such, Woolf's essay provides a model for meditating on writing from monumentalized progressives of the past, whose prejudices and failures are all the more exposed for not being cloaked in an apolitical, ahistorical sublime.

Chapter 2 reads Addison's contributions to *The Spectator* as informed by an everyday, existential sense of incongruence between simple perception and recently acquired scientific knowledge about the scale and nature of the universe and the human body. Blind like moles, Addison suggested, humans after Newtonian science face the alienating incongruence of living necessarily procedural lives while experiencing the frightening and alienating grandeur of newly revealed infinite scales and material contingency. Addison's new cosmographic account of life helped to spawn both the Romantic sublime and an expanding sense of middle-class, practical realism, which would significantly separate and then re-merge two centuries later in Modernism. Echoing M. H. Abrams's *The Mirror and the Lamp*, this chapter complicates Abrams's theory of the origins of Romanticism: Addison's texts show how Newton's new, empirically proven conception of the eye as essentially "creative" pushed literature toward a self-conscious aesthetics of prosaic artificiality. At the same time, the chapter highlights Addison's efforts to integrate this awareness of terrestrial artificiality into a coherent and devoted religious faith, a project central to the oeuvre of an author who often professed a strong feeling for divine omnipresence.[111]

Addison's devotion and ethical commitments take on an aspect of distasteful, sentimental paint for contemporary readers partially because of what chapter 3 analyzes as the historically specific partialities, distortions, and incompleteness of his popular moral sermons. "Sentiment," Julie Ellison argues, "arises from a world of racial difference."[112] The bubble of domestic peace, liberty, and prosperity in England that Addison's work helped to grow had a profound shadow in Britain's increasing imperialism and exploitation of African slave labor. Britain's involvement in colonial slavery grew throughout Addison's lifetime and career as a largely "offstage" phenomenon in Queen Anne's London that deeply inflected the period's cultural output and inflects our reception of its cultural figures. I follow Ellison's lead in weaving this context of Addison's work into the complex historical emergence of a performative culture of sympathetic "sensibility." Many contemporary historians and cultural critics argue that the philosophical and political discourse of British liberty, in which Addison was a leading voice, was fueled by imperial ambitions and enabled the growth of chattel slavery and the exploitation of racial difference. Early eighteenth-century Whigs' compromised language attempted to pragmatically and conveniently ignore the specifics of racialized slavery while generally attacking the slavery of feudalism and absolute monarchy, part of a larger strategy to challenge Europe's authoritarian Old Regime of Catholic monarchs on all fronts—cultural, political, and economic. This chapter locates Addison's disappointingly brief discussions of racial politics and his relative silence on the slave trade (in spite of his leading position within British foreign affairs) historically between Cromwell's "Western strategy" and mid-eighteenth-century Whig abolitionism. The growth of massive outsourced cruelty contradicted a long tradition of Britain associating itself with exceptional freedom from a global norm of slavery, a patriotic tradition that in the seventeenth century mixed with neoclassical Roman arguments for liberty in a successful bid to legally corner feudal and monarchical oppression. Addison's quiet progressivism, impactful as it was, is situated in an uncomfortable historical balance between too-quiet perpetuation of a system of mass exploitation and realpolitik alliance-making between liberal-minded, self-advancing men and their powerful patrons.

Published in the midst of his vita activa wrestling with official duties and political controversies, Addison's defense of moderate, individual escapism, *On the Pleasures of the Imagination,* inaugurated a new discourse of aesthetic subjectivity. The groundbreaking 1712 essay originally appeared as eleven sequential daily issues of *The Spectator* and became in its many reprintings "familiar to every man of letters" in his century.[113] "One of the most important and seminal texts of Enlightenment modernity, the series," as Frédéric Ogée has recently described it, "is also one of the founding texts of British aesthetic discourse."[114] Chapter 4 develops a new reading of Addison's ironically most "weighty" essay as a landscape of the imagination for which the Latin and Greek epigraphs above each installment provide a telling, contrapuntal map. That map for the "knowing" reader points to Ovid's myth of Hermaphroditus and Addison's underlying proposal of the imagination's essential role in moderating between epistemological optimism and the nihilism of stringent materialism. The essay self-consciously echoes Platonism and the classical tradition while incorporating a Newtonian worldview that, somewhat conversely, motivates his calls for a more equal footing between the fanciful and the understood. Addison had arrived already, via Stoicism and scientific contemplation, at the Modernist paradox: the high achievements of human reason—the arts, architecture, abstruse insight, and technology in general—could remake the sensual world to such an extent that reason could not claim to build a stable map over the top of sensual experience. The artifacts and residues of human reason overwhelmed the human, but the imagination persisted as a restoring reservoir. Reason and beauty, in Addison's philosophical intervention, are acknowledged as providing the healthful balance that sustains the individual body.

Though the structure of the book, which climaxes in a reading of his tragedy, suggests the emphasis given to the importance of theater and tragedy in particular in Addison's thinking, the extended analysis of his imagination essay occupies the book's center because of the importance of unpacking a piece whose intellectual-historical impact is belied—in precise Addisonian style—by its relatively simple, light surface. The main gesture of Addison's essay is to propose and synthesize the important role of the imagination as an educative and yet satisfyingly relaxing modality of cognition in a refined person's life. The move of validating imaginative exercise as a useful and good pastime, a positive means of establishing individual sovereignty, had far-reaching effects—making middling appreciation of art and landscape fashionable. Addison's essay "made pleasure not only safe for Anglo-American culture but essential to it."[115] Providing one of the first critical treatments "of the conditions of perception and reception," his intervention placed new emphasis on the reader and viewer's experience and their self-conscious *creation* or *allowance* of that experience.[116] Addisonian aesthetic experience thus philosophically bolstered the sociable home of middling subjectivity, simultaneously an "upward 'refinement' of the crude senses and an imaginative, downward 'domestication' of the rarefied understanding."[117] Although the practice of individual sovereignty he theorized held only a "virtual" territory in the fancy, it was a starting place from which to build, in Hannah Arendt's sense: "Freedom as an inner movement of man is identical with the capacity to begin."[118] Its validation of aesthetic citizenship in the world for proto-middle-class subjects—in Laura Baudot's terms, the essay's establishment of "an immaterial property . . . and a reified interiority to store that property"—laid crucial groundwork for the separate-yet-collective imaginative communities of large stable modern nations and international orders.[119] Imagination, "the essential idea" of the Enlightenment, drew the expanding different branches of art and thought into one discursive body—a "university" or unified field whose orientation around health and pleasure remains vital.[120] In this respect, to use Walker's words, "Addison is beyond enlightenments, old and new."[121] The essay in this chapter's reading functions as a keystone for the rest of his performed life, especially in the valence of his ambitions as a playwright-philosopher in the long tradition of Plato.

The second part of this book turns to the active world of eighteenth-century British politics to show how the poetic and philosophical ground that Addison established in his writing was enacted and reproduced through concrete real-world administration, diplomacy, and theatrical stagings. Addison rose to high ranks in Whig circles at the turn of the century due to the strength of his poetry and the careful cultivation of well-placed patrons. Chapter 5 examines his subsequent rise in government administration vis-á-vis his canonical poem *The Campaign,* his opera libretto *Rosamond,* and his well-known numismatic interest in coins and medals as political propaganda. Addison, "a central figure in the forging of a modern Whiggism," and his Tory rivals wrestled for symbolic control of the state apparatus through attempts to stage convincing images of the absent (and future) king, a figure that disquieted Queen Anne's reign in various guises just as it had Elizabeth I's reign.[122] The doctrine of "the king's two bodies"—legally enunciated by leaders of the Catholic opposition to Elizabeth and developed popularly on the Elizabethan stage—haunted the British Augustan Age and charged the event of Addison's *Cato* with a political, historical, and religious energy that transformed subsequent representational politics.

Chapter 6 takes up that revisionist historical tragedy, an international success and one of the most popular plays of the eighteenth century. *Cato*'s triumph helped to jettison Addison into the upper echelons of the British government, where he was charged with responsibility for Queen Anne's funeral, George I's arrival, colonial affairs, and the response to Jacobite plots and invasions through military, diplomatic, and propagandistic means. English theater already had a long propensity for an allegorical aesthetic of the "simultaneous expression of myth and event."[123] Within the eighteenth century, theater in the Anglo-American world continued this tradition, shaping the political communities, compromises, and living performances that would transform the paradigm of English divine right kingship under the conditions of republican democracy. Addison chose the muse of history (Clio) to shape his play, but his revisions of Cato's classical tale therein yielded a tragedy that metatheatrically performs art's modernizing, Dantean role as a purgatory through which an old world can be mourned and a new tragicomic one can emerge. Examined not only as a dramatic text but also as public ritual of restored national unity, Addison's *Cato* functioned as a prototypical theatrical restoration of the body politic of the king in a revised, nostalgic Roman republican form. Following Ernst H. Kantorowicz's historical insights in *The King's Two Bodies*, chapter 6 reads *Cato* as a founding middle-class tragedy and as a discordantly Protestant high mass that claimed one aspect of the sacred body of the king for a new Whig regime of cosmopolitan, representational democracy.

Addison's early death at the age of forty-seven marked the brief tenure of the neoclassical poet-politician as a dominant model for the British statesman. As the era of the novel and the professional politician dawned, Addison's bubble of balanced statesmanship and philosophy gave way to the accelerating machinery of far-flung imperialism. His final split with his lifelong friend, Steele, prefigured the epochal division in British history and Whiggism as the prototypical modern island nation threw itself into the unbridled greed of worldwide empire during the Walpole age. Classical tragedy was relegated to an ennobled past and sidelined in the aristocratic spectacle of opera, but Addison and his *Cato* were remembered nostalgically for their moral and—in some contexts—revolutionary example. In the final chapter, a brief overview of Addison's death and authorial afterlife show how his disappearance as a household name and leading cultural figure over the last two centuries paradoxically continues the success of his work in comprehensively bending the shape of our cosmopolitan everyday lives toward rational procedure, optimistic debate, and egalitarian inquiry.

1
Addison the Ancient Author

Virtue confess'd in human Shape he draws,
What Plato thought, and God-like Cato was.
—Alexander Pope, prologue to *Cato*

His beauties sparkle, but do not warm; they sparkle as stars in a frosty night.
—Edward Young on *Cato*, *Conjectures on Original Composition*

EVERYDAY OZYMANDIAS

Addison's popularity and influence established him in his own lifetime as "the natural monarch of a literary kingdom," whose stature as "the dominating figure of the English literary world . . . had in no way lessened but had increased after the Battle of Waterloo a century later."[1] Yet, as is well-known among literary historians, reading of Addison's fame today has an effect akin to what Percy Shelley described upon hearing about the astonishing faraway feats of the forgotten ancient king Ozymandias (Ramses II): if one feels compelled to obey history's half-buried admonishment to attend to his once mighty works, one has to (imaginatively) clear away a lot of desert to discover anything that looks like grandeur. The archeologically uncovered bubble of Addisonian literary triumph presents itself as another grand confirmation of mortal humility, a "colossal Wreck," inviting the warm-blooded reader into a reading experience "boundless and bare" in which "the lone and level sands stretch far away."² Addison's glory was the middle tissue of the Enlightenment. The words remain, but after the Napoleonic Wars and the rise of Romanticism, the spirit if not yet the stature was gone.

Those remaining texts seem often preserved for a dusty corner of an undervisited museum: stiff, constrained, trite, and overly moralistic. It is hard to understand the enthusiastic reception of his work at the time when, Colley Cibber tells us, *Cato* infused "the noble Spirit of Patriotism into the Breasts of a free People, that crowded to it" and through its "affecting Force" raised "in every sensible Hearer such conscious Admiration . . . as even *demanded* two almost irreconcileable Parties to embrace, and join in their equal Applauses of it."³ *Cato,* indeed, now haunts theater history as a quintessential example of a play that once tremendously moved audiences almost universally but that leaves modern readers cold, a symbol of untranslatable historical paradigms of experience and left-behind structures of feeling.

Addison himself suggested explanations for this conundrum. His essay on reading ancient poetry, for instance, takes up the problem of modern readers who, unlike their ancient counterparts, no longer feel engaged by much of a classic text because they do not know "the secret History of a Composure: What was the Occasion of such a Discourse or Poem, whom such a Sentence aim'd at, what Person lay disguis'd in such a Character." Published in 1739, twenty years after his death, the essay contrasts poignantly with Pope's *Dunciad,* whose transparently veiled satirical attacks on the time's literary milieu had been published in 1728. While Pope draws readers into the thickness of decoding the intrigues, judgments, and back-biting relations of his literary age, Addison lets the reader go and forget. Pope's acerbic Juvenalian spirit would monumentalize his more mediocre writing colleagues by nailing them down to the details of their inanity; Addison's essay, which does not need at all to be read as an allusion to his own work and its future reception, weightlessly—and, only if you will, ironically—contemplates how writing like ancient sculpture loses color over time and thereby lives a kind of second life, as purer form. Whereas the Ancients "cou'd see their Author in a Variety of Lights, and receive several different Entertainments from the same Passage," modern readers "can only please ourselves with the Wit or good Sense of a Writer, as it stands stripp'd of all those accidental Circumstances that at first help'd to set it off: We have him but in a single View, and only discover such essential standing Beauties as no Time or Years can possibly deface."⁴ Here, in its purest distilled form, is the seeming paradox that frustrates and enlivens the latter-day reception of Addison's practiced poetics. In one sense, it is simply a difficult-to-swallow simplicity arrived at through elaborate erudition and arcane reflection: the temperate resignation of a moderate human being. Literary ambition and achievement might typically be abetted by a commitment either to the dense, competitive effervescence of a particular present literary scene or to the ideal of literary immortality. Addison practiced, observed, and admired both commitments, but he chose for himself and his labor a middle way, a commitment to positive realist thinking and positive real effects that celebrated a historical theatricalization of literature and authorship—the latter most enjoyably seen "in a variety of Lights."

Looking back at what he called his "Performances" in the newspapers *The Tatler* and *The Spectator*, he took as his chief concern the social and political effects those writings had had on the public. His aim, he wrote, had been to create a healthier literary culture that would redirect overly strong satirical energies against real vice rather than against "Persons and Things of a sacred and serious Nature." His motto in the endeavor was a religious one: "*Inservi Deo et Laetare, Serve God and be cheerful.*"[5] Opposing the inertia of an established literary scene, Addison believed his own cultivated popularity and literary endeavors had their test not in enduring as left-behind eternal masterpieces for subsequent generations to reverentially admire but in effectively constructing a broad and sustainable new civil politics.

Writing in a perhaps milder moment, Pope eulogized his one-time friend in multiply resonating terms that pick up on the uncanny disappearance of Addison's authorship, his virtuous aim to restore a certain innocence of human health and sentiment, and his texts' classical fading into truth, form, or the emptiness of old paper:

> No whiter page than Addison remains.
> He, from the taste obscene reclaims our youth,
> And sets the passions on the side of truth,
> Forms the soft bosom with the gentlest art,
> And pours each human virtue in the heart.[6]

Pope's verses tellingly mimic the Addisonian style of smoothness, a seemingly effortless stream of prose that hides its own seams and subtle constructions, allowing an in fact highly particular craftsman to pour carefully distilled formulae directly into an equally carefully formed vessel—a reader's bosom (a fantasy that can be flipped around to suggest Addison and his soft textual prothesis breastfeeding the reader).

Other writers might have hoped or labored to produce such a medicine and audience that would continue to produce magical effects until the end of time. Whether primarily out of skepticism about its general possibility, modesty, a critical awareness of lacking skill, or a sacrificial choice to be a physician of his own time and milieu, Addison did not believe his own works were headed toward literary immortality. If his works reached the success he hoped for them in his own time, they would largely suffer the fate of many classical passages of text: "Those very Phrases, that are in themselves highly proper and significant, and were at first perhaps study'd and elaborate Expressions, make but a poor Figure in Writing, after they are once adopted into common Discourse, and found over familiar to an Ear that is every where accustomed to them. They are too much dishonour'd by common Use, and contract a Meanness."[7] The diminishment of a work's effect and reputation as a result of the familiarity coming through its success proved to be a common and distinctively overdetermined trope of Addison reception from its earliest days on. Addison not only discussed the trope of successful reception's soft tragedy repeatedly but also seems to have designed his work to hide ostentatious flare-ups of genius, sacrificing high, lasting literary reputation for broad recognition and digestibility. Critics from Johnson onward have admired and puzzled over the concealment of originality and craft in Addison's work. Leslie Stephen, for instance, "depicted Addison as a man who was influential enough to make his opinions seem conventional when in fact they were largely of very recent manufacture. Addison was an artificer of the first order, and Stephen was fascinated by his skill."[8]

In broad terms, this aspect of Addison's writing marks one influential origin of a middle-class style of modest procedural, periodical writing, a practice of public assertion balanced by the imperative to reach success through "blending in." Smithers argued that Addison's literary work was an important part of a longer, central historical process, stirring and calling to virtue again "the middle-class element in the British character," which "had been dominant at the Commonwealth period, and subdued but never destroyed during the Restoration."[9] His stated Socratic intention to bring philosophy down from the clouds and into the coffeehouses—in short, his invention of the "middle style" in English prose—spurred on the long glorious revolution of middle-class people and institutions gradually taking more administrative control of the English state and European states more generally. This, at least, was a central plank of the teleological Whig interpretation of history, an interpretation double-cast as performative assertion. But it was not just because Addison was an influential, partisan Whig reformer and minister that he professed the Whiggish idea that literature's value was crucially tied to its reformist social effect. His cultural milieu uniquely celebrated and understood itself via the paradigm of theatricality, in which language and text always necessarily serve another higher, wider, and more impactful art.

The time was a heyday of theater, when houses were expanding, the admiration of actors was on a steep ascendance, and the medium had unprecedented breadth and influence. After Addison's death, the growth of private reading in multiplying comfortable private houses made theater less essential as a mode of entertainment in a way that prefigured (still from a great distance) the advent of radio, television, and the personal computer. Theater would adjust, creating, for example, bigger stars (e.g., David Garrick, Sarah Bernhardt), the lavish nineteenth-century melodrama and twentieth-century megamusical, and more fantastic illusions and sharper aesthetic experiences in the age of realism and the director. But Addison's lifespan was the peak of a certain theatrical culture in which the magic still happened inside the present and relatively approachable actor's body. Only today do we again have access to an analogous moment of theatricality, with the ubiquity of personal screens and the new ease of video production making the site of compelling magic inside the performing body unsettling in both its closeness—just another twitching consumer performing for the screen—and ubiquity. The analogy with today's performative video culture has many important disparities, yet it gives us experiential access again to the sense of a culture permeated and created from the inside out by theatricality: not just by long hours witnessing fictional drama but by the sense that the real of identity itself is produced simply by the decision to start performing. In our time, that decision is signified by pressing record and sharing; in Addison's London, it was regularly witnessed up close when someone like Betterton and his many colleagues (whom you might see very easily elsewhere in London) transformed themselves live into different people every night, just a few feet from where you were sitting. These were not, as in later popular theater cultures, actors who performed only one role over a long run of single shows and then hid themselves away in the shadow of megacelebrity. Rather, these were people who were convincingly very different people each night in different plays, who mingled often promiscuously with their audiences, like TikTok or YouTube celebrities in an unmoderated live chat. The "mirror" they provided as staged human beings was uncannily, excitingly close; it posed every question imaginable about why you thought you had to return at the end of the nightly show to the same stage set, drama, and repeated character.

Within this theatrical era and its afterglow, Addison's claim to a peculiarly intense and long-lasting reputation turned on the subtle complexity with which he gently exposed the absurd pathos of a world of actors. His was a world into which, in fact, no one fit naturally, despite their efforts to appear to do so and despite any belief that others might actually do so. Bringing the more unspoken and less official norms and rules of such a provisional world to consciousness to make them topics of conversation and debate, he supported his reflective readers in their shared deeper background feeling that the progress of the world demanded that they become different, make *themselves* new. Addison thematized this modern difference in life-feeling metatheatrically. In his prologue to Steele's 1705 *The Tender Husband,* Addison (to whom the play was dedicated) contrasted "the first rise and infancy of Farce," which was "rich in originals" because "plays were scarce" with the current age of stock comic characters and an abundance of plays wherein "punks of different characters we meet, / As frequent on the stage as in the pit."[10] The stage and the audience were equally dramatized in his age, and the mimetic effects were not just evidenced in playwrights' iterative re-creation of known characters but also in people in their real lives "punking" or prostituting themselves as characters from the stage. The effects of this dramatization of society (to cite Raymond Williams's argument, avant la lettre) were intense enough that originality was hard to find, presumably also in the search for an authentic self; "modern wits are forced to pick and cull" and search long into character's lives to find novelty and inspiration.[11]

Addison named the mass of existential flaneurs for whom he wrote "the Fraternity of Spectators who live in the World without having any thing to do in it. . . . In short, every one that considers the World as Theatre, and desires to form a right Judgment of those who are the Actors on it." Mr. Spectator's famous ambition was to be a middling British Socrates: "It was said of Socrates," he wrote, "that he brought Philosophy down from Heaven, to inhabit among Men; and I shall be ambitious to have it said of me, that I have brought philosophy out of Closets and Libraries, Schools and Colleges, to dwell in the Clubs and Assemblies, at Tea-Tables and in Coffee-Houses."[12] *The Spectator* was at the beginning of middle-class social industrialization on a large scale, and Addison as writer was at one with his medium as message; he recommended reading the paper to all "well-regulated Families, that set apart an Hour in every Morning for Tea and Bread and Butter." His literary career was a conscious effort at subjective coding: *The Spectator* "lay a Claim to . . . the Blanks of Society," who, he wrote, "lie at the Mercy of the first Man they meet, and are grave or impertinent all the Day long, according to the Notions which they have imbibed in the Morning."[13]

He gave a script for a host of new actors, middle-class people reading for the first time something that pertained to them, pages filled with the promise that the future was drawing them in. The emphasis can be debated: Did Addison and Steele's periodicals *construct* a new public middle class, or did they merely find and successfully exploit an already existing but still untapped middle-class consumer desire to read about themselves, become informed, and perhaps feel a bit superior or smug?[14] Addison would have side-stepped the question. Even his playfully high and low Socratic ambition performs the typical warm (self-)irony of the coauthor of *The Tatler*'s Sir Roger de Coverley, a founding "great example in English of the [Quixotic] figure of sympathetic naivety."[15] Cicero had more seriously appraised Socrates's role in philosophical history as "the first to call philosophy down from the heavens and set her in the cities of men and bring her also into their homes and compel her to ask questions about life and morality and things good and evil."[16] Addison lightly adds the tinkling of fastidiously selected china and silver tea spoons to his own time and discourse's translation of metaphysics into worldly ethics. Theatricality surged with the existence of a new kind of consciousness vying for cosmopolitan participation in an increasingly imperial, market-oriented society. *The Tatler* and *The Spectator*, Mackie argues, "were crucial agents in the definition of the cultural ideals of [the middle] class"; in their valence as wildly successful "lifestyle magazines," they sold "new and improved ways of living" and sought "to refashion the textures of daily life."[17] With their roving, gathering Horatian gaze, they also sought to refashion classicism, to make the world safe for modern-day Ciceros and Socrateses, who might find a new longer life less as individual martyrs and more as members of a large and potentially powerful expanded public seeing itself "live" in real time for the first time. If they were blankly shopping rather than exceptionally dying, they might still be shopping for a truer, more modern, practical, yet spiritually satisfying understanding of their human condition.

It could perhaps better be argued in reverse: for all its relatively new performance theory, our time is naive about theatricality in comparison to Addison's. Our time believes in some possibility for literature to function outside of immediate social, political performance. Our time believes in the possibility of some historical subject—some Addison, if you will—who was not primarily performing and then, necessarily, if being at all, reforming. Rather than standing sublimely alone, an Addisonian text functions within the larger public performance of an artist reaching various audiences through many different media, modes, and time-specific actions. The study of Addison's texts from the vantage of performance reveals another site from which we as readers might reclaim a participatory social ideal of art against the influential

Romantic and Modernist reformulation of taste around the lonely exquisite literary object.

ADDISON ACTS ACTEON

Like all authors whose works become important touchstones for a culture's self-definitional discussions, Addison's reception modulated significantly during the more than two hundred years of his playing a leading and ultimately tragic part in shifting Anglophone and European literary canons. His own predictions and hopes for his works cast their fate as akin to well-used coins, which eventually, through their very usefulness in changing hands, lose their shine and even their valuable substance.[18] In one of his earliest poems, the 1694 "An Account of the Greatest English Poets," he already displayed a tendency to think of great literature as modern utilitarian currency: Chaucer's verses were rusted over, and the best of English writing shone in the freshly minted poems of John Dryden, William Congreve, and Charles Montagu.[19] The committed classical scholar and passionate antiquarian numismatist returned often and faithfully to ancient authors, whom his last posthumously published essay called "the Poet's Countrymen."[20] But he argued for a certain modesty and openness in how we approach them, cautioning that none of us are "intimately enough acquainted with them, and never met with their Expressions but in Print, and that too on a serious Occasion."[21]

Though his works would be later published and referenced like bibles, his essays—in their original penny-paper form—did not shy away from what is half-celebrated today as trashiness. In contrast to the more "stable" and serious form suggested by subsequent "literary" collections and scholarly discussions, *The Spectator* playfully reveled in juxtaposing conversations of the utmost seriousness with commercialism and spoof, real and mock advertisements.[22] Unlike the Modernist wasteland—a planet filled with discarded and incessantly manufactured consumer goods and everywhere noisy with engines, roads, and factories—the world of Addison and his contemporaries was just undergoing a first, transformative explosion of imperial mercantilism. *The Spectator* did not stand aloof from the consumer revolution flooding London and other cities with novel goods and options for how to spend one's time and money. Rather, Addison and Steele stepped energetically into the role of authors immersed in the excitement and bewilderment of the new agency promised by the modern acceleration of consumer choice. As both comically sympathetic commiserators in the chaos and orienting normative guides to how to behave and what to buy in such a brave new whirl, the authors of *The Spectator* cultivated a timely, dynamic relationship with an audience shaped in and by the unprecedented amounts of differentiated, socially manufactured and mediated material surrounding them.[23]

A paradigmatically Horatian satirist whose favorite mode of analysis was comparatist, Addison's periodical texts (like those of Steele and his more occasional cowriters) were framed by an essential, ludic fictionality bespeaking their easy repartee with theatrical market culture.[24] Their first-person discourses were assigned to fictional characters, often writing in marked, specific fictional settings. Nicholas Ridout has recently suggested that we reread *The Spectator* essays as a continuation and heightening of experimental theater praxes from the seventeenth century, rather than as journalism or as the collected, confessional commonplace book many critics now take them to be.[25] Even the eventual avowal of authorship—via a key provided in Steele's final number of *The Spectator* revealing Addison as the writer of all the preceding essays signed with any of the letters that spell out "CLIO"—played with authorial and generic displacement: Had it really been Addison writing or four fragmented modes of Addison through which the muse of history simply, for a while, sang?[26] Any serious literary scholar must recognize that *The Spectator* delighted in posing such not very serious riddles for its contemporary and future audiences.

One of the traditional roles of theater—to display the stories, beauty, and wisdom of literature and the discourses of the learned to a large, general audience—was increasingly taken over by printed literature itself. Now more massively and directly available, literature in the forms of reactionary pamphlets, play editions printed immediately in the days after successful performances, along with Addison and Steele's daily papers, also began to rob theater of some of its claim to superior "liveness." The cathartic experience of an ideal Aristotelian tragedy was increasingly accessible in private, at home, away from social pressure and the gaze of others. Even or specifically at this peak age of theatrically, far before the age of the television set and the computer screen, the printed products of increasing mechanical reproduction provided new possibilities for entertainment in the home. Accordingly, theater's status had already begun to shift for middle-class people from a necessary social act (if entertainment was to be had) to a chosen, consciously social act.

This subtle but important shift in theater's ontological status as a social act was masked by the same mechanical and cultural processes expanding the ease of audiences gathering, theater construction, and production processes in general, along with the gradually increasing distribution of economic agency in England throughout the century. But the sense of relatively nascent competition between theater and literature for the souls of the masses resulted in Addison's age in a unique balance or exhilarating indistinctness between the two forms of mass media. To act was still to declaim a text on stage; to be in the audience (despite the popularity of scenic innovation) was still called "hearing" rather than "seeing"; and to read was often to read a play script, to become prompted into social action, to think carefully not merely about enjoyment but about the effects of a given text on one's standing, one's behavior, one's self-articulation in society. In their first reception milieu of coffeehouses and tea tables, Addison's essays were read aloud as timely theatrical positions, rehearsals for both identifying and disidentifying with particular kinds of public characters, voices, and opinions.

As a performing author, Addison functioned as a consolidator of culture, not only in his wide-ranging topical discourses but also in his display of movement between genres. His very public literary career demonstrated the individual mind performing itself in various literary and theatrical modes. In addition to his many polyvocal periodical essays and numerous early Latin poems and translations, Addison the author published more singular works of different high classical literary genres, most attaining a high degree of success: one poetic address to the king, one georgic poetic epistle, one short epic poem glorifying a returning warrior, one prose travelogue, one treatise-in-dialogue, one opera libretto, one war pamphlet, one tragedy, one timely satirical pamphlet of political allegory, one comedy, one poetic ekphrasis, one unfinished religious defense. In the archive as in his culture, Addison performed the literary journeyman, less a jack-of-all-trades or polymath than a Proteus expressing time and self through various genres and occupational roles. This kind of metaperformance marks the larger historical literary period with its efforts to institute an English literary canon and establish the role of the professional literary writer. The historical performative paradigm—the public author with a heightened theatrical relation to the self—can be seen in the conscious contrast Addison drew between Montaigne's foundational modern essayistic project and the inauguration of his own.

The very first *Spectator* essay begins, like the prefatory author's note of Montaigne's collection of essays, with a short meditation on the slippage and independence between book and self. A Latin epigraph from Horace signals that the author's intent is not to give "smoke after flame" but, rather, "after smoke the light," an intention in keeping with Addison's general poetics of valuing modern clarification (*Aufklärung*) over literary modes that created the illusion of depth and value by gripping readers through emotional turmoil and excitement. The vernacular opening then proceeds: "I have observed, that a Reader seldom peruses a Book with Pleasure 'till he knows whether the Writer of it be a black or a fair Man, of a mild or cholerick Disposition, Married or a Bachelor, with other Particulars of the like nature, that conduce very much to the right Understanding of an Author."[27] From the start calling attention to the superficial, mask-like categories of social judgment, the Spectator's self-consciousness ironically mirrors Montaigne's stated desire to portray himself through his essays as nakedly as possible, "without contention, art or study."[28] The writing Spectator is identified as a "Silent Man" with a small but ancient hereditary estate who does not care much for conversation. The plain self-exposition here, of course, is fictional. The "genuine, simple, and ordinarie" self that Montaigne sought to write down in early retirement from his former urban court life was as alien to the theatrical literary and social milieu of Queen Anne's London as Montaigne's own small "hereditary estate" in Dordogne had been to seventeenth-century Paris.

"I have acted," the Spectator continues, "in all the parts of my Life as a Looker-on, which is the Character I intend to preserve in this Paper." Again echoing Montaigne's ambitions, the Spectator declares: "I am resolved ... to Print my self out, if possible, before I Die."[29] The image of sociability that the Spectator gives is theatrical, paradoxically lonely and social. The most adept of social performers, perfectly entitled to his modest claim to English citizenship (since William the Conqueror's Norman invasion) and able without effort to participate in any social scene or profession, he is nonetheless perfectly solitary, without attachment or entangling emotional relationships. In the sense that modern journalism has one origin-point in Addison's Spectator, it begins with a somewhat strange yet compelling existentialist fantasy, not so distant from a Modernist figure slipping fluidly in and out of trains or roving through a city's rooms and half-deserted streets.[30]

The foregrounded split between silent looker-on and social man-about-town alienates the confessional act of Montaigne: it is the fictional eidolon rather than the flesh-and-bone author who professes the drive to print himself out publicly. Actually, the audience will learn nothing directly of the author; it is all a play, a bit of augmented reality. To nostalgically hear in Mr. Spectator a pure authorial voice or the journalist's serious will to objectivity would be a misreading. What Addison intended and what his contemporaries heard was an enigmatic shell, a character and roving subjectivity finding its partial way through the urban acceleration process that was just beginning. He was not Montaigne's naked self-portraitist but a masked practitioner of clubby yet distanced metropolitan politeness in the modern city and the hastening full morning of the print age.[31]

Frequently fantasizing about his legacy's eventual disappearance into utility, perhaps Addison, the ambitious classical scholar with a strong will to see the modern break through, identified with the similarly named Actaeon, an unfortunate hero of one of his earliest major translation projects, book 3 of Ovid's *Metamorphoses*.[32] The fate of Actaeon (the hunter transformed into a deer and killed by his own dogs after he accidentally intruded upon the goddess Diana bathing) echoed in Addison's anticipation of his own oeuvre falling victim to the tearing progress of time, whose spirit it sought to inspire and unleash. As the dogmas of literary culture shifted through the decades and centuries, the hunted-for, rather antidogmatic Addisonian *Geist* shifted in character, quarried often beyond recognition by fixated enemies and zealous followers. In the age of Modernism, finally, the bedraggled Addison effigy was left on the platform as the select train of canonicity took on new speed and mettle.

Paul Davis tells us that one important modulation in Addison's reception had taken place already in the 1740s, when "new imperatives of sensibility and primitivism began to take hold in British culture," causing poetry to become increasingly "equated with visionary excitement and sublime power—'original' or natural 'genius.'" Addison, who had started his career as a sophisticated neoclassical poet before taking his long performative ambulation through public everyday prose, consequently became just a few decades after his death "immovably associated in his guise as Mr. Spectator with the previously dominant values of polite urbanity."[33] His fame persisted, his reputation altered and diminished. By 1815, the Addisonian project had undergone, writes Gregory Dart, "a gradual transition from virtuous expansion to complacent decline." In that year, Leigh Hunt assessed the state of Addisonianism in the full sun of Romanticism, borrowing the numismatic language of Addison's own prophecies about his work's long-scale reception: "Character first gives way to polish . . . polish by little and little carries away solidity."[34] The city flaneur and rhapsode of the ballad and the free English landscape garden had become, by his very success, associated inevitably with the confined Romantic classroom rather than with its liberties and ranging rambles.[35] He was transformed, in essence, into one of the "Schoolmen" away from whom he himself had originally sought to steal the flame around which serious thought so long had circled, to bring it into the freer public street and rowdy coffeehouse.

When the dialectic of history shifted again, Addison's legacy—along with the rest of monolithically conceptualized eighteenth-century literature—became the necessary bogeyman and fatwood of Victorian projection, self-positioning, and cultural polarization. With alternating dispassion, hyperbolic ardor, and oversharp criticism, the collective figure of Addison and his colleagues was (inconsistently) defended or denigrated as "an aristocratic enemy who had been vanquished" or as loathsomely middle class: artificial, unpoetic, demonstrating little understanding of the classics at the same time as being pretentiously "Classic," rule-bound, utterly conventional.[36] Though overall his reputation and relevance seemed to be fading as the nineteenth century progressed, Addison remained a central subject of deliberations about the English literary heritage. The period produced several important and lengthy Addison biographies: Lucy Aikin's 1843 two-volume *Life of Addison*, Macaulay's essay on Addison published as a response the same year, and W. J. Courthope's biography of 1884. As an ambivalent icon around which Victorian identity stabilized itself, Addison was marked, especially for the generations to follow, as a "First Victorian," redrawn along the lines of public manliness that people like Macaulay, Leslie Stephen, and the Earl of Ellesmere imagined for their own performances.[37] The critical clang of Modernism, with its own generational drive to disrupt the stuffed complacency of Victorianism, found in the mythical spiritual hero of such performances a grave over which to ring a more heavily discordant death knell. Hunting for the underlying totems that upheld the previous regime, that next literary generation found a hot trail in such lionizing passages as Courthope asking and answering, "To whom do we owe the comparative harmony we enjoy? Undoubtedly to the authors of *The Spectator*, and first among these, by universal consent, to Addison."[38]

In turn, it is—as Paul Davis has recently put it—the after-effects of the "dogmatic certainty" of famous Modernist critics that "we are still trying to shake off" of Addison's transformed and mostly buried corpus.[39] If we want to hear across such distance from the singer himself, we need to consider picking Addison up from the station where the Modernists denied his boarding. This is, however, not an argument for Addison's reinclusion in a reimplemented canon but, rather, a suggestion for how to begin rethinking a once immensely popular oeuvre from a historical context uniquely generative of still-running engines of debate, democratization, and public institution-building. By looking carefully at the moment of Addison, the writing performer, being finally torn, after almost two centuries, from the literary canon, we have the opportunity to reflect about what a literary culture and history not oriented around the deathly "promise" of literary immortality could have or could again look like. Whether we want such a literary culture is perhaps of secondary importance to whether we have the capacity to understand, imagine, and—in Eliot's sense—*feel* the historical alterity and possibility such a literary culture.

The dismissal of Addison as an author worth reading played a surprisingly crucial role in several influential Modernist authors' public articulations of their aesthetic taste. In *Addison and Steele Are Dead: The English Department, Its Canon, and the Professionalization of Literary Criticism,* Brian McCrea argued that the Modernist condemnation of Addison was decisive for the disappearance of his texts from the standard education of the twentieth century. As one of the most influential critics of the century, T. S. Eliot's vehement rebukes were especially damning to Addison's later reputation.[40] In his 1933 *The Use of Poetry and the Use of Criticism,* he remarked that "Addison is a conspicuous example of . . . embarrassing mediocrity, and he is a symptom of the age which he announced." While granting Addison a large historical importance, Eliot treated the paragon of the literary Augustan Age to a barrage of insults, preceded by this confession: "It is perhaps as well to warn you that Addison is a writer towards whom I feel something very like antipathy." Characteristic of his writing, according to Eliot—the ex-pat London-banker son of an American industrial tycoon—is an exhibition of "smugness and priggishness."[41] Addison was symptomatic of the deterioration of society after Dryden; he had everything to do with the superficiality of the middle class, theology masking itself as poetry. Echoing Pope's attacks against "Atticus" in the former's "Epistle to Dr. Arbuthnot," Eliot declared him "a bourgeois literary dictator," nothing more than "a popular lecturer."[42]

We might, with Eliot's contemporary, Sigmund Freud, be slightly suspicious of such a heavily poisoned disavowal. Indeed, Addison provided the straw man for Eliot's own arguments for what the poet was and what the poet should be. In his influential essay "The Metaphysical Poets," Eliot identified the disease that broke out in English literature of which Addison would become the greatest symptom and for which Eliot himself would act the part of curing physician. "In the seventeenth century," Eliot wrote, "a dissociation of sensibility set in, from which we have never recovered. . . . while the language became more refined, the feeling became more crude." The idea of a historically widening abyss between feeling and poetry pointed toward a lost kind of true poetry that would have to be recovered or reinvented by the Modernists. For Eliot, this true kind of feeling poetry assumed the function of poetry to be a comprehensive translation in language of a poet's total experience. Modern poetry must be difficult because civilization had become immensely complex: "The poet must become more and more comprehensive, more allusive, more indirect, in order to force, to dislocate if necessary, language into his meaning."⁴³ The apparent directness, simplicity, morality, neoclassical order, and sentimentality of Addison were, to this project, anathema.

Naturally, Eliot's insistence on the function of poetry being the recovery of full experience is historically and culturally specific. An ideal of full translation of full subjectivity performs its contradiction. It passionately hides in plain sight the asocial ecstasy of its author and that ecstasy's shadow: the author's everyday body without the cutting rudder or sail of transcendent thought, a potential mimetic teacher of totalitarian passivity. Thought and ideology are to be less shaping forces than ingredients of a manufactured total articulation by an industrial subject resigned to the acceleration of technological complexity. What is performatively masked in Eliot's account of the poet is that the ideal inspired poet of modern complexity would not look like the full and roving, segmented subjectivity that the writing would mimic. The unseen poet would more likely look like an isolated, still, thinking, remembering banker busy at a desk, the writer and perhaps the reader. For Eliot, the idea of a passing Spectator looking in at his writing closet would have been understandably an unbearable distraction and painful awakening.

The recovery of full experience in language, in urging no action or overriding, conceptual thought, would translate into separated, sedentary people addicted to the transcendental theater of their minds, in which fullness and the totality of relative emotional states were not denigrated into the need for choice and public deeds. Such writers and readers would leave the actual theaters empty of broadly social bodies. Pathos would be preserved (*aufgehoben*) in a separate sphere of art; enabling day jobs and societal arrangements would transpire in another alienated sphere to be at best later aesthetically remembered. The imaginative space of literature in the Modernist ideal resonates fully in the individual's inspired mind; the practical art of the Enlightenment public sphere and its literary cheerleader, Addison, need to be squeezed out, left simply in the dark to die unmourned. So too the qualities that might have suggested Addison's writerly kinship with Eliot's Modernist ideal— its allusive, neoclassical dislocation of language, its performatively indirect comprehensiveness.

A fantasy of Addison's death—carrying the tone of ambivalent literary *Vatermord*—is pointedly conjured at another famous, seminal birth-site of the Modernist writer.⁴⁴ In James Joyce's *A Portrait of the Artist as a Young Man*, Stephen Daedalus's religious awakening and call to the life of a writer takes place as a priest concludes his sermon with the famous anecdote of Addison's death scene: "Was it not Addison, the great English writer, who, when on his deathbed, sent for the wicked young earl of Warwick to let him see how a christian can meet his end. He it is and he alone, the pious and believing christian, who can say in his heart: *O grave, where is thy victory?/O death, where is thy sting?*" Lost in the miasma of masturbatory fantasy, the teenage Daedalus identifies with both Addison as the great writer ("He it is and he alone") and the wicked young earl of Warwick. He seems to awake, as if called by Addison to realize that "every word of it was for him," that he is the surviving son, the next mystical incarnation of genius.[45]

The Modernist's valorization of the sensitive genius's total subjective experience as the proper mimetic object of art was indeed at significant odds with Addison's own poetics. In *Spectator* 225, Addison wrote: "I have often thought if the Minds of Men were laid open, we should see but little Difference between that of the Wise Man and that of the Fool. There are infinite *Reveries,* numberless Extravagancies, and a perpetual Train of Vanities which pass through both. The great Difference is, that the first knows how to pick and cull his Thoughts for Conversation, by suppressing some, and communicating others; whereas the other lets them all indifferently fly out in Words." An exposure of the total mind, a stream of consciousness, would have lacked for Addison the discretion necessary to transform experience into a sociable work of art. Differently put, Addison might have readily agreed with Eliot's dedication of *The Waste Land,* in which he called his editor, Ezra Pound, the better craftsman. (Of course—and to the point—he would have had issue with both men's politics and abstruse poetic styles.) "Accordingly," he continued, "if we look into particular Communities and Divisions of Men, we may observe that it is the Discreet Man, not the Witty, nor the Learned, nor the Brave who guides the Conversation, and gives Measures to the Society. A Man with great Talents, but void of Discretion, is like *Polyphemus* in the Fable, Strong and Blind, endued with an Irresistible Force which for want of Sight is of no use to him."[46]

Eliot's critique of Addison and Addison's own poetics intersect in the association of modernity with a certain necessary alienation from pure direct poetic singing. As Paul Davis has pointed out, the blinded (Samson-like) cyclops Polyphemus was a figure Addison personally associated with the shadow side of Milton, a towering poetic hero but also a threatening specter whose singular optics, radical politics, and vocation as bard Addison experienced as dangerous, better to be left in the past, disavowed.[47] Perhaps for Eliot there was something Prufrock-like about Addison's mid-career turn to being a poet of prose, the urban everyday, the modern flaneur or "traveler" rather than the classical heroic, conquering poet. Yet their poetics also intersected in the censure of small-mindedness. Where Eliot sees in Addison a petty sentimental artificiality and narrowing of experience, Addison—whose work accomplished an unprecedented historical expansion of literary conversation—believed that the crucial narrowing of experience came through the falsely clever myopia of self-absorbed thinking:

> At the same time I think Discretion the most useful Talent a Man can be Master of, I look upon Cunning to be the Accomplishment of little, mean, ungenerous Minds. Discretion points out the noblest Ends to us, and pursues the most proper and laudable Methods of attaining them: Cunning has only private selfish Aims, and sticks at nothing which may make them succeed. Discretion has large and extended Views, and, like a well-formed Eye, commands a whole Horizon: Cunning is a kind of Short-sightedness, that discovers the minutest Objects which are near at hand, but is not able to discern things at a distance.[48]

The long, transcendent view linked Addison's artistic work to social functionality, to politics, morality, history, and religion. Art was social performance with social ends. Fame and selfish success might be won by cunning, but what mattered was the accomplishment measured at the larger scale to which the discrete oriented their perspectives and actions. Sociable artistic production, like social performance in general, had strategic choice and not mimesis nor even formalism as its highest criterion. The discrete man must "consider what will be his Condition millions of Ages hence, as well as what it is at present. He knows that the Misery or Happiness which are reserved for him in another World, lose nothing of their Reality by being placed at so great a Distance from him. The Objects do not appear little to him because they are remote."[49]

Such passages, as many in Addison's essays, made explicit his religious convictions and the importance to him, not just of being seen by an All-knower but of living for redemption in another world to come after death. This was a crucial—and, today, often forgotten—disjuncture in sensibility between the assumptions of earlier Addison readers and those of the less religiously normative twentieth century.[50] With the backdrop of centuries of (forced) religious conformity, the preaching style that Eliot detested can be read (and was read by its original readers) as a light, playful, yet powerful appropriation of the mandatory Sunday discourse of the pulpit by a milder, reforming, urbane voice. In his moderate, progressive mode, Addison publicly practiced a conscious resyncretism of Christianity with Platonism and Stoicism. His "Saturday Sermon" *Spectator* essays moralized, but his theological assertions usually took a general, abstracting tone that opened them, perhaps subtly, to spiritual, philosophical, or practical dimensions beyond a particular dogma, an ecumenicism that not infrequently included the insights of other faiths entirely.

If one takes together his statements about virtuous living and the aims of artistic production, Addison advocates a poetics of pragmatic, performative choice. He urges that actions be founded on discrete judgment of their ensuing real effects on humanity, in the longest, human scale, against the pressure of conformity in more contingent contexts. "A wise Man," he wrote well before Kant, "will suspect those Actions to which he is directed by something besides Reason, and always apprehend some concealed Evil in every Resolution that is of a disputable Nature, when it is conformable to his particular Temper, his Age, or way of Life, or when it favours his Pleasure or his Profit."[51] The primacy of thought both in shaping literary and theatrical pursuits and their ideal reception was a standard tenet of Addison's neoclassical criticism. Rehearsing the famous French debate between the Moderns and the Ancients, Addison wrote in *Spectator* 39 that when it came to the exemplary Ancient tragedies, "tho' the Expressions are very great, it is the Thought that bears them up and swells them." The moral import of theater was more important for Addison than any other aesthetic value it had, and, when it came to morality, the modern theater (and perhaps its larger religious context) fell short: "The Modern Tragedy excels that of *Greece* or *Rome*, in the Intricacy and Disposition of the Fable; but, what a Christian Writer would be ashamed to own, falls infinitely short of it in the Moral Part of the Performance."[52]

With his twentieth-century bemoaning the loss of complex *feeling* in the poetry of Addison's age, Eliot might actually have found an ally in Addison himself, who as an advocate of the meditative use of the imagination criticized his fellow modern writers for doing nothing to elevate the "vicious Taste of their Readers, who are better Judges of the Language than of the Sentiments."[53] Sentiment, of course, is a tricky word in eighteenth-century texts, combining thought and feeling.[54] For Addison and the Platonists, the mixing of the two encouraged fuller and more complex thinking, which ultimately meant fuller and more complex existence and insight within a soul that was eternal or at least—all things going well—progressively climbing the scales of virtue. At issue between an Addisonian and a Modernist ideal of art was not the *mixing* per se of dried-up conceptual memory and desire. Instead, the antagonism between the two critical ideals has to do with a simple reversal of which—prescriptive thought or desire—was associated more with life and which more with death. Eliot's industrial world demanded a medicinal recovery of deep feeling. The ordered, massively slicing, procedural landscape of thought had to be challenged and made secondary. Addison's post–Civil War, opening Newtonian world, on the other hand, demanded that the whirlwind of feeling be captained by the decisive charting of thought.

A quintessential example of Addison's poetological priorities in this regard is his reworking of Aristotle's theory of catharsis. In *Spectator* 40, Addison concurs with Aristotle that "the principal Design of Tragedy is to raise Commiseration and Terror in the Minds of the Audience." But, already in this translation of the famous classical doctrine, Addison tweaks the purpose of tragedy in the direction of social empathy, using "commiseration" instead of the typical translation of *éleos* as "pity." A further Addisonian revision involved the jump from this long-established Aristotelian dogma to the neoclassical article of faith that theater must primarily transmit and inspire clear and noble thought. Addison accomplished this bit of argumentative quick-stepping by asserting that "Terror and Commiseration leave a pleasing Anguish in the Mind, and fix the Audience in such a serious Composure of Thought as is much more lasting and delightful than any little transient Starts of Joy and Satisfaction."[55] The linking of "a serious Composure of Thought" with delight was quintessentially Addison, but the actual link—a "pleasing" kind of psychological anguish—would likely have smacked for Eliot too much of Addison wanting to have his catharsis and his dry contemplative distance, too.

In difference to a traditional idea of catharsis (a large social outpouring or individual affective cleansing) as a sanitary end in itself, Addison espoused individual contemplation as the proper end of tragic entertainment. Yet even while the individual's reflective process was key to Addison's ideal, the social aspect of the audience's dramatic experience remained vital. The sublimity of witnessing a staged tragedy lay in the unique collective experience that followed pity and terror: the recognition that both the self and a large group of others, emotionally cleansed of illusion, were moved to a state of dispassionate, serious, existential contemplation. Such experiences convinced Addison and his age that refined feeling had a specifically sociable and theatrical essence. Shared clear thought and artificial, high sentiment balanced, supported, and produced each other's verticality; in the analogy and identity of individual and group experience, that verticality was multiplied; and the union of sentiment and thought operating in this repeating series of group epiphanies gave the direction of moral action.

From a later perspective, Addison the taste-making critic sought to "fortify a link between the aesthetic experience and the moral preservation of moral society."[56] The clarity of identifying that "link," however, is formally anachronistic, since a modern discourse of "the aesthetic" finds early groundwork in

Addison's writing, as will be explored more fully in chapter 4. What we call "the aesthetic" needed no link for Addison and his readers: they lived at the peak of theatricality, at the cusp of the coming processes by which theatricality and the aesthetic would be rigorously separated out from real, social, and moral life. They knew and felt as people who still—regularly, physically together—read Aristotle and attended large performative events that such a peak implied the probability of tragedy. Even those of us who eccentrically make ourselves latter-day experts of something like the old physical theater lack the theatrical attunement to tragedy as an organizing, cumulative social artwork and experience that we can presume the average regular theatergoer of those days had. Such a sensibility, which will be explored as formative for the metatragic event of Addison's triumph, *Cato*, in chapter 7, knew more than it could dryly articulate. It knew in its tragic praxis that the rupture of historical climax coming with the entering new order of the modern implied not just mourning but irrecoverable loss, horrible, out-of-control shredding loosed from sovereign, poetic control. A turned-around Addisonian gaze on Modernist critics would inquire about the dissociation of sensibility from consequence, the failure to *feel* any longer the moral *purpose* of literature in everyday life, with actual other people (and not just our ideas of them) present. Had Eliot been a more sympathetic reader of Addison, perhaps he would have shifted politics sooner in what became the entr'acte between the two world wars.

FAULT LINES OF FEELING

McCrea sees in Addison's work the relic of a preindustrial mixed life that had a different kind of fullness than Eliot sought to recover in his ideal kind of poetry. Addison and his contemporary poets, in McCrea's estimation, "all led much less fragmented lives than the modern author Eliot describes."[57] McCrea positively evaluates the mixed sentimentality of the Augustan Age's literature, in which "political, social, religious, philosophical, economic and, ultimately, emotional values are associated, not dissociated. For Addison and Steele, as for Swift and, perhaps, Pope, a purely literary act or work could not exist." Reviewing Addison's periodical essays, McCrea concludes that "we tend to live within categories that he did not see." Our sandboxed, postindustrial categories of life experiences destroy our taste for a heightened literature that was full of the mundane and the everyday and did not keep things like "business matters and emotional matters" (or politics, social arrangements, and the ideal of art) separate.[58]

Alongside this tragic temporal and historical disjunction between the Addisonian age and that of Modernism, however, was another transhistorical disjunction that persisted and modulated from Henry VIII's reign through Modernism and beyond. This other disjunction—articulated and fought with the means of historiography itself—was the partisan rift: in various guises and formulations between Protestants and Catholics, Parliamentarians and Royalists, Whigs and Tories. After Modernism and its accompanying world wars, such an old European partisan rift receded behind the bloody, nuclear urgencies of new, more pressing partisan rifts (e.g., intercontinental, postmodern, and secular or postsecular). But for the paradigmatic critic Eliot, "who styled himself a Royalist in politics, and who could use the term Whiggism as a term of abuse," the old partisan rift remained operative and even, arguably, determinative.[59] In terms of literary history and canon formation, it reached back across the historical disjuncture discussed above to foreground different heroes and genealogical points in the true and false flowering of history and aesthetic achievement. From their own period through Modernism and—less transparently—until today, Pope and Swift bolstered the Catholic, Royalist, Tory sense of what literature did best during the Augustan Age. Addison and Steele fell away during the complex mid-to-late twentieth century in which Protestantism and democratic debate were taken for granted as stabilizing institutions of establishing consensus. Protestantism's spirit of dissent became invisible as its hard fought-for ideals and reforms became the central, procedural DNA of the West.

Nevertheless, the knowing, intellectual persistence of the old partisan rift can be seen in the way Eliot's British contemporary, C. S. Lewis, pointed—more positively than Eliot—to Addison's crucial role in the pre-Modernist history of English literature and feeling. While Eliot's reading of Addison mourned the supposed loss of fine, deep feeling between Shakespeare, Donne, and the later Restoration period, Lewis's reading of Addison's oeuvre hinged on its progressive proximity to Romanticism and its status as an influential early herald of the Romantic age. Addison's close connection to what would become the Romantic movement had to do with the fact, in Lewis's words, that he "stands at the very turning-point in the history of a certain mode of feeling."[60] What persists in the different Addison receptions of the two influential twentieth-century critics is a divide between a backward-looking, Anglo-Catholic, Tory perspective (Eliot) and an incrementally progressive, classically liberal, Anglican perspective, which, by Lewis's time, had no neat moniker but, in Addison's time, was simply called Whiggism.

While Modernists like Eliot could complain of the loss of a heightened sensuous world inside British Augustan literature, no such postindustrial privilege could have been expected of Addison's actual readers, who were still uncomfortably close to the reality of nature as a likely swallowing quagmire. Lewis thus suggested that it was Addison who helped to originate a new, reflective, distanced aesthetic intimacy with the nonhuman world—a significant step toward modern subjectivity. Addison, in his analysis, was instrumental in transforming the structure of feeling through which society approached nature: "It is the change from an age when men frankly hated and feared all those things in Nature which are neither sensuously pleasing, useful, safe, symmetrical, or gaily coloured, to an age when men love and actually seek out mountains, waste places, dark forests, cataracts, and storm-beaten coasts. What was once the ugly has become a department (even the major department) of the beautiful."[61]

Addison's creation of the "natural" aesthetic ground for what would become Romanticism was, for Lewis, essential to understanding his historical potency as a writer. The usual paradox of the monstrous father destroyed by his monstrous progeny applied. Once Addison had helped to establish the proto-Romantic sublime—the sociability of the forlorn wilderness with the magnificent and the beautiful—the socially integrated, urban author would be pushed offstage by the scene change to literary country houses and hermit huts. One of the supporting, constitutive backdrops in front of which this new literary scene unfolded was a mild, cosmopolitan Addisonian fabric, connecting hectic London assemblies to lonely, exotic mountainscapes. But for those left cold by the long-running Protestant play of industrious reform and progress, Pope and Swift remained archetypal Augustan poets in part because they had so acerbically satirized their own age, city milieu, and Addison himself. Their reputation as writers increased, Lewis argued, because of what was, in their own age, their melancholic, distemperate characters.[62] The contrast with the social characters of Addison and Steele is evidenced in the Romantic critic William Hazlitt's comparison of his own periodical venture with that of its archetypal predecessors. The authors of *The Tatler* and *The Spectator*, he wrote, had benefited from their era's "honeymoon of authorship"; public favor had taken on a new "gloss" as Addison and Steele inaugurated a novel humble authorial performance as "companions," who in turn collared "wisdom" to submit to "social esteem." Their essays, Hazlitt wrote, "were among the first instances in this country of learning sacrificing to the graces, and of a mutual understanding and good-humoured equality between the writer and the reader." But this was before public favor "had become tarnished and common—before familiarity had bred contempt."[63] Addison remained subtly peculiar, conversationally sly, and historically undismissible, a conversation piece and a monumentalized civic institution. But for readers and writers drawn to the exclusive, privy depth of projects like Coleridge's *Friend* (a consciously post-Addison periodical attempt to reclaim philosophy for the coterie and the thinking classes), Addison might be admired for his middle style but he belonged fundamentally to the vulgar, not the Vulgate.[64]

Indeed, Addison had built his career by moving out of the exclusivity of (literal) Latin poetry into vernacular prose in a manner that consistently honored a broad socioeconomic cross-section of his society. His treatment of the folk ballad to the same weight of critical discussion as other more traditionally seriously treated literary genres and artifacts played an important role in generating the broader, respectable discussion of folk poetry that would seed Romantic sensibility.[65] As a crucial conduit through which the historically strong down-to-earth and democratic vein of British literary culture flowed, Addison's essays aimed to engage readers beyond the elite. His classical, poetic exemplars—the poetry of Virgil and the odes of Horace—taught him to aim in his prose for the middle between the extremes of vulgarity and pompous complexity: such an approach yielded "expressions very sublime, but at the same time very natural."[66] Crafted so, his essays' easy style and common themes often belie the elegance, originality, and intellectual grit of their thought, especially for later readers already familiar with ideas that actually first appeared in Addison's texts but were subsequently taken up by more abstruse, properly "philosophical" writers.[67] In hagiographic mode, Macaulay reminded Victorian readers that the discreet modesty of Addison's work had served to reach the readers of his present: critics, immersed a century later in the wide reading culture he had helped to establish, had lost their sensitivity for Addison's genius. Macaulay's historically insensitive colleagues might mistakenly judge his work as hackneyed or dryly old-fashioned, but in fact Addison "was not so far behind our generation as he was before his own."[68] Another century after Macaulay, Lewis found that Addison's work was essential for understanding not only Romanticism but also the intellectual background of the modern world in general. Addison, he wrote, "appears to be (as far as any individual can be) the source of a quite astonishing number of mental habits which were still prevalent when men now living were born."[69]

The installation of good habits in his society was central to Addison's ambitions as a writer, and his success in doing so had surely to do with the repeated validation his essays gave to the middling sort of people, even as he curried elite favor and position. In *Spectator* 464, characteristically he wrote: "The middle Condition seems to be the most advantageously situated for the gaining of Wisdom. Poverty turns our Thoughts too much upon the supplying of our Wants, and Riches upon enjoying our Superfluities; and, as *Cowley* has said in another Case, *It is hard for a Man to keep a steady Eye upon Truth, who is always in a Battel or a Triumph.*"[70] True sublimity, for Addison, lay not in the momentary psychophysical experience but in literature and art structured around the actual ongoing needs of the average person. The disavowal or deferral of ultimate, aristocratic fulfilment was not just preferable for practical reasons but was abidingly and universally correct as a chosen mode of responding to the contingency of life as it was given. "The middle Condition," he wrote in the same essay, "is most eligible to the Man who would improve himself in Virtue; . . . it is the most advantageous for the gaining of Knowledge."[71]

Lewis's broad historical gaze allowed him to link the political divide between the Tories Swift and Pope and the Whig Addison to their differing styles of social performance. These contrasting styles were ultimately suggestive of the origins of the Tory and Whig parties in the conflict between the flamboyant courts of Charles II and James II and the more Anglican and Puritan opposition of the late seventeenth century. In Lewis's perspective, one of Addison's most important accomplishments was his success in helping to abolish "the old flamboyancy" of previous English culture. Replacing Shakespearean extravagance and general courtly exaggeration, Addison focused the English-speaking world on middle ways of looking and expression: "That sober code of manners under which we still live today, in so far as we have any code at all, and which foreigners call hypocrisy, is in some important degree a legacy from the Tatler and the Spectator."[72] Addison preached modesty and an avoidance of ostentation as national virtues.[73] In doing so, he did not neglect—so Courthope had suggested—drawing his more courtly audience into a fuller social fabric that included puritan elements: "It was Addison's aim to prove to the contending parties what a large extent of ground they might occupy in common. He showed the courtiers, in a form of light literature which pleased their imagination, and with a grace and charm of manner that they were well qualified to appreciate, that true religion was not opposed to good breeding."[74]

In the *theatrum mundi* of the British early eighteenth century, Addison represented a successful, consistent, and inspiring example of the artist-citizen forging a new expanded order in the social sphere. Lewis's account did not leave Addison "smug" or "priggish," as Eliot would have had him. Because for Addison art was properly subordinated to social purpose, his texts advocated and strove to instill a moderate and enduring cheerfulness with which middling people could profitably and functionally labor, live, and reflect. His periodical essays can be interpreted in their historical context as serving aristocratic patrons—whose imperial ambitions required an increased pool of reliable administrators and an efficient general social machinery—but Addison's own expressed sentiments signaled that their achieved intent was rather to provide a means of transferring sovereignty to people of lesser socioeconomic status.

Of course, public art generally must hold the pressure of simultaneously functioning as a pleasing ornament for elite gatekeepers and as an effector of sublime or otherwise meaningful experience among a wider audience. But Addison's liminal work moved consistently in a progressive direction, shedding the skin of the transcendental ideal of literature that served conservative structures and more radically violent but ultimately cyclical (i.e., revolutionary) movements. The sublimity of Shakespeare, whose divine kings were ground into the dirt only to be replaced by higher renewed royal authority, gives way in Addison to the social goal of passing on the rational frame of mind and cheer necessary to continue with steady work. Biographically and in his poetical writings, Addison was forthright in setting out the social function of art as its highest purpose.

Lewis's milder, sympathetic evaluation of Addison picks up on this intent by stressing literature's place in the reflected working life. Eliot's Modernist poet sought existential integration through the sublime moment's unification of what was otherwise impossibly fragmented experience. The convivial Augustan poet par excellence sought, on the other hand, to husband the loneliness of sublime experience and reactive passion to the steadiness necessary for a consistent, unified, and sociable performance. Lewis wrote that "the Addisonian world is not one to live in at all times, but it is a good one to fall back into when the day's work is over and a man's feet on the fender and his pipe in his mouth."[75] The Addisonian world was a nostalgic one for Lewis, perhaps the fantasy of a pre-feminist and pre-Freudian world where a pipe could just be a pipe and a "hard-working man" would always be played by an actor of only one certain gender. Lewis and Eliot both pitch literature as a place of recovery and retreat, be that place one of ecstatic recuperation of feeling (in Eliot's ideal) or one of rest and delight (in Lewis's palliative vision). Lewis agreed that history had moved on from the Addisonian world but differed from Eliot in still feeling under the layers of history the cheer with which Addison attempts to greet his laboring compatriots.

The twentieth-century Modernist attack against Addison, voiced so strongly by Eliot, had its roots in disapproval of middle-class values and commerce's disruptive effects on traditional society.[76] As necessary and compelling as that critique is and was, the alternative that Addison was fighting against in his own time—the continuation of feudal structures without a strong, steady co-alitional counterbalance—might give us contemporaries historical pause. At the very least, the importance of Addison's writing in the moment in which it was engineering a turn of public feeling was not the "mere" soothing effect it would provide two centuries later to Lewis's settled patriarch drifting into a nostalgic evening nap. What Addison saw and addressed in his own time was the need for a great Horatian literature that was not literature for its own sake but a useful source and company for the balanced, performed life: a crucial, unprecedented, and uncertain kind of life whose value like all new currencies was contingent on the actions and sayings of a like-minded community.

THE WHIG PARADIGM OF THE PERFORMING AUTHOR

At a time without an established middle class in which literacy and literature were becoming more affordable as preindustrial mechanical reproduction in general began to gather speed, Addison represented a broadening of neoclassical culture and its attendant politics and public. In Klein's words, his was "a modern Whiggism that linked the establishment of liberty, the growth of commerce, and the refinement of manners in a comprehensive and progressive ideology of enlightenment."[77] Addison and his reformist Whig colleagues worked in and around long-established feudal structures, effectively outflanking their political adversaries where they could not achieve results via direct confrontation: "generic transgressiveness" was a key feature of Whiggism "in literature as well as politics."[78] With the speedy development of new forms in the period, many of these transgressions became invisible. Here again we encounter the trope of Addison's handiwork disappearing because of its success, this time in the larger context of the "Whig Interpretation of History": a teleology toward "a democratic, utilitarian, middle-class society."[79]

The strategically combined Whiggish ideal of history, politics, and literature shaped Addison's oeuvre, but, today, understanding its literary culture requires an act of recovery of the sort that David Womersley undertook in his late 1990s exploration of literary Whiggism.[80] Ancients, Addison wrote, lived in the scene of their poetry, and the scene "gave a thousand pleasing Hints to their Imaginations," building an ecosystem of signs, memories, works, authors, and events that enhanced their enjoyment and understanding of how a given work and author participated in their unfolding culture.[81] Womersley argued that we similarly fail to imagine the scene of Addison's writing because we imbibe our history of the literary period from the "opposition party" who were busily scribbling at the period's margins. "Today," Womersley wrote, "we still approach the literature of this period in accordance with the habits of reading, the principles of judgement, and the hierarchizing oppositions disseminated by Pope and his lieutenants." Through works like the *Dunciad,* the Scriblerians relegated Whig poets and critics to the status of "tradesmen in words rather than artists." What this only subsequently hegemonic "Tory version of the English literary past" suppressed in its seemingly "superb dismissal of a disreputable crew of literary chancers" was the period's disinterest in the (later, post-Kantian) disinterestedness of aesthetic taste. The Whigs' "self-consciously modern programme for English poetry," articulated in the 1690s and 1700s by writers like Addison, held popular and ascendent political sway. This "combatively Christian" program sought "to identify the literary forms and models appropriate to a nation which, with the Glorious Revolution of 1688, had grasped its political liberty and entered into possession of itself."[82] In the Addisonian period, Whig writers and critics validated a mode of writing in which the metaphors of the text slipped easily between personal, aesthetic, historical, and political registers, in which judgments of writers and texts were mixed with the contextual politics they performed.

Addison and the Whigs' modern aesthetic for poetry prized "negligence, grace, looseness and familiarity"—a prosaic poetics.[83] Ironically, of course, as Addison well noted, the difficulty of achieving familiarity with a historical period's literature tends to increase with the extent to which the salient works of that period achieved their effect by creatively participating in a mutual sense of familiarity spread over a broad contemporaneous cultural field, as today with the difficulty of projecting the influence of an important blog post into a distant historiographical future without elucidating its concatenation in a meaningful net of other social and traditional media outputs. But the hoped-for future of literary immortality was not the Whigs' aim. While "the received account of English literary history from the Restoration to the accession of George III," as Womersley argued, was in fact shaped exceptionally by those who failed to shape either the history or the larger political future—by Jacobite sympathizers, in fact—it was the Whigs who dominated the actual politics of the century and their writers who captured the popular imagination en masse.[84] To Addison the scholar, the truth of written history was often, and perhaps inherently, defective because writers naturally write in response and reaction to a larger "Tradition" they leave out in proportion to its obviousness to all who lived in the period: the contextualizing "Comment on the Story" is thus "now quite lost and the Writing only preserv'd for the

Information of Posterity."[85] The extent to which the sidelined Tory literary critics were successful in creating "a template for virtually all the subsequent literary history of that period" is an argument *for* the orienting of a writing life and culture around a pragmatic ideal of literary immortality.[86] For Addison and his Whig colleagues, however, aesthetic thinking was consistently and urgently shaped by a more present political realism.[87]

With industrialization's breakdown of traditional societies and acceleration of change, the link between inwardness and immortality was strengthened. The Modernist critique against politicized poetry resulted in a mid-twentieth-century consensus that, according to Adam Rounce, associated the poetic with "retreat, isolation, and interiority" in opposition to "history and politics."[88] Womersley bemoaned that "such unbalanced and injudicious critical investments have led to the scanning of the Whig poetic tradition."[89] Virginia Woolf's turn away from the positivistic public writing championed by Mr. (Arnold) Bennett and toward the mysterious anonymous psychological reality of Mrs. Brown had become paradigmatic. Addison could not be popular anymore because his essays, as Stephen Miller puts it, "are familiar but not personal."[90] But as postindustrialization's continued accelerations restage even the soul and other designated interiors of subjectivity as mechanically (re)produced construction sites, immortality and value move again in the direction of the external. Recent turns in literary conversation open new vantage points on Addison's praxes and theories, in which "the bond between taste, morality, and society" was "sophisticated, vigourous, and unrelenting."[91] Rereading dismissed "Whiggish poetry" and considering its culture in this time "challenges us," wrote Womersley, "to justify our habitual valuations and to defend our customary ways of reading."[92]

At the cusp of Romanticism, still writing in the tradition of public Enlightenment in which the sound of Addison's voice resonated strongly, Mary Wollstonecraft argued that popular opinion gives to a century a "family character," shaping the total education of individuals.[93] In spite of efforts at self-education, individuation, in Wollstonecraft's view, necessarily took place in the context of a somewhat temporally intimate social dynamic, which logically results in some of the important meanings of one age becoming lost to another age's "family." An influential celebrator of rapture, lonely visions on city and country walks, and popular folk ballads, Addison was also a founding architect of expansive modern public opinion, what became the active British and European national and international "discourse communities" or communication matrices. Naturally falling on the Protestant, Whig side of the spectrum, the arc of his performative, political, and literary efforts as a sermonizing "Censor" of everyday urban life aimed toward bridge-building, out from the middle. That he could often be an effective partisan fighter, helping to cement through his writings the long Whig dominance over the eighteenth century, does not belie the historical truth that Addison also had unique success in building a large-scale, peaceable national consensus and conversation across the divides of party, class, and taste.

But the theatrical impersonalness of his writings exhibits a certain formality, stiffness, and coolness that contrasts with the warmer style of his cowriter and almost lifelong friend, Steele. Where Steele exuded a literal wish to understand and transform the nation into a family, Addison's less personal *familiarity* drew a social world together in sympathy and debate that could yet maintain enough distance to stay open, to be not just broad but broadening.[94] Lewis and Eliot in their dichotomous Addison assessments both made the error of evaluating Addison as writer for the established middle-class nighttime parlor or the professional literary man's study sanctuary, each already a nostalgically Romantic setting. They ought instead to have taken their copy of Addison's performances along with them and their historical imagination to the more appropriate receptive settings of the rushed morning table, their day-job coffee breaks, and crowded, glancing commutes among fellow social-climbers. Lewis's sentimental return to Addison with its evocation of the thoughtful worker enjoying a reflective pipe at the end of a long day understood the progressive gesture of Addison's work: literature as a mode of support for the working life, not a mode of aristocratic remove or a decadent source of existential trauma for its own sake. At a great historical distance, however, even Lewis's ambivalently positive evaluation of Addison separated him from the further progress of Whiggism by tying him in the end to the comfortable domestic refuge of the middle-class paterfamilias. By becoming "literary" in the twentieth-century sense, Eliot and Lewis's Addison participated in the segregation of a domestic, personal world from a male business, scientific world. In that fantasy of an all-too-comfortable Whiggism, a historically odd Addison emerged: a male figure in a domestic literary world, who in his own time had in fact fictionally domesticated politics to encourage wider participation and discussion on the streets and in public commerce and institutions. By preserving him as a literary sermonizer or quaintly palliative patriarch instead of reenlivening his efforts at purposefully mild progressive provocation, Eliot and Lewis, on different sides of the partisan fence, created a new Addisonian reactionary bogeyman, whose roving, multifaceted Horatian irony was reduced to a soporific delight or dismissed as priggish or nonexistent.

Before putting his feet up on his fender and his pipe in his mouth, Lewis's relaxing Addison reader notes that "if it were at all times true that the Good is the enemy of the Best, it would be hard to defend Addison. His Rational Piety, his smiling indulgence to 'the fair sex,' his small idealisms about trade, certainly fall short of actual Christianity, and plain justice to women, and true political wisdom. They may even be obstacles to them; palliatives and anodynes that prolong the disease. In some moods I cannot help seeing Addison as one who, at every point, 'sings charms to ills that ask the knife.'"[95] The Whiggish mode of criticism would beg to understand Lewis's contemplation in the context of his writing at the close of World War II and its unfathomable revelations. In 1945, watching the opening twilight of nuclear warfare from a now safe distance, questions of previous appeasement and failed moderation seemed to have horribly clear, certain answers. The kinship of Lewis's prepalliative postwar judgment—which he ties to his generation's modern hatred of Victorianism—with Eliot's harsh interwar Addison criticism suggests a consensus that leaves both writers perhaps too comfortable. After all, as they and their partisanly split intellectual milieu debated a program for modern literary life, they failed to prevent the kind of utter catastrophe that Addison had feared if his own politics did not succeed in preventing the renewed outbreak of civil war. On their speeding straight course toward the modern sublime, they left a sacrificial bogeyman-effigy on the platform marked indeed as a too mild, politically unwise hindrance to the immortal, gallantly masculinist, Christian perfect.

That Lewis later may have revised his vision of Addison as unwise might be seen in late changes he made to a 1938 poem about a bird he hears singing on the beloved Oxford path outside of Magdalen College called Addison's Walk, named in the poem's opening line. His 1931 conversation with J. R. R. Tolkien and Hugo Dyson (covering very Addisonian topics) on that path precipitated his famous conversion to Christianity, referenced in his 1938 poem by the bird's cheerful hope that the coming summer might this time really bring salvation: "We shall escape the circle and undo the spell." As the formerly grand skies of Victoria's old empire closed more definitively a second time above him, the poet conditionally yet arrogantly and bitterly remarked that the sung prophecy "might prove truer than a bird can know; / And yet your singing will not make it so." Toward the end of his life, Lewis revised the poem, perhaps reversing the accusation of naivete by cutting his younger self's wise pronouncement, giving the urgently cheerful, Addisonian singer the last, admonishing couplet: "Often deceived, yet open once again your heart, / Quick, quick, quick, quick!—the gates are drawn apart."[96] By allowing the Addisonian voice to sing more fully through the poet, a reflective Lewis might signal a renewed validation and respect for a writer whose reworking the scene of mundane life had played a crucial role in one of the most profound turning points of his own brief chance on earth—a writer in whose dismissed effigy he had left an important "naive" part of himself.

What aided, in any case, the creation of Addison-as-bogeyman in both its "positive" and "negative" formations was, of course, the passage of time, the progress of history, and, crucially, Addison's own partially historical and partially personal insensitivity, ignorance, and failures on issues like race and gender. From its outset, *The Spectator* had sought to engage a female readership in a historically innovative way, and this was likely Addison's idea, following the success of the *Athenian Mercury* (1691–97) and the model of the *Female Tatler* (1709–10).[97] As chapter 3 will develop, Addison's thematization of race—let alone his outreach to nonwhite readers—was virtually absent when compared to his frequent appeals to women readers and discussion of topics drawn (at least in his fantasies) from their lives. But as will be explored, Addison's progressive "gallantry" had a "knowing, double-edged nature" specifically tied to the construction of the kind of segregated domesticity that Lewis's hard-working middle-class patriarch believed it should be his privilege to enjoy.[98] Addison in his periodical essays gave witness to a rise of women's participation in public politics and claimed to address them and their concerns directly but often mixed praise for their public patriotism with preaching the doctrine of separate spheres whereby "the Sex" should confine itself to peacemaking domesticity. Critics have noted that, in doing so, his essays often give "almost classic statements of eighteenth-century notions of gender difference, public/private distinctions, and mannered middle-class respectability."[99]

The complex work of recovering historical context and Whig poetics suggests that the story is not so simple: witness the monarchical Tory feminism of Aphra Behn and Mary Astell and the comparative twentieth- and twenty-first-century marginalization of Whig female writers from the period like Elizabeth Rowe.[100] Rarely lacking self-irony or practicing an ideologically rigid consistency, Addison's construction of "natural" feminized domesticity went hand in hand with what can be taken as his larger reformed Whig project of simultaneous naturalization and domestication: supporting natural, domestic fashions against those foreign and elaborate; the "polite and aestheticized imagination" against undisciplined fancy and enthusiasm; decent bourgeois taste against depraved aristocratic taste. One of the most problematic of his relatively common critical stances was his tendency to praise the domesticated woman while satirizing the sophisticated woman.[101] The idea of the natural, "domestic" woman of simplicity was anything but simple at the time, ruled over as it was by a childless female monarch whose politics and succession depended on elaborate foreign agreements yet who performed a kind of modest Protestant domesticity in contrast to seventeenth-century, French-leaning Stuart court extravagance. Rather than giving women a forum for self-representation as the *Athenian Mercury* had done, Addison and Steele's periodicals were prescriptive and paternalistic in their normatively defining women's nature, casting them as principally daughters and wives. As Kathryn Shevelow has argued, this constructed, desirable model of femininity—"'the angel in the house' devoted to husband and family—corresponded to a new ideology and domesticated model of both family and masculinity."[102] In one sense, Addison represented normative gender difference in the same manner that he represented partisan difference. Both women and Tories like Sir Roger de Coverley were "lovably" satirized and sentimentally tied to their domestic lives and spaces. Fictionalizing the representatives of the other sides of what were for him potentially dangerous and combustible "partisan" splits, Addison's mode of naturalizing and eternalizing sociably polarized character types aimed at achieving general collective peace or at least avoiding violently escalatory spirals of alienation. Using the same pattern they applied to representing stereotypical members of partisan clubs, "Addison and Steele established a social ideal predicated upon the harmonious interaction of gender oppositions."[103]

But just as, for Tories, Addison's performative nonpartisanship proved a frustratingly effective tool in its "fair" representation of fictional Tory characters and positions, so did his depiction of women prove less than equanimous and peaceable. Shevelow writes of the "reformed" manner of discursively confining women, to which Addison's works heavily contributed:

> As upper- and middle-class Englishwomen increasingly began to participate in the public realm of print culture, the representational practices of that culture were steadily enclosing them within the private sphere of the home. That is, at the same historical moment that women were, to a degree unprecedented in western Europe, becoming visible as readers and writers, the literary representation of women—whether as members of an intended audience, as writing subjects, or as textual objects—was producing an increasingly narrow and restrictive model of femininity.... Many of the very agents that were enabling, even actively promoting, women's participation in print culture were also those engaged in containing it.[104]

Shevelow goes on to analyze the historical turn in representation as such: "In *The Spectator*, as in *The Tatler* before it, the witty and willful young aristocratic woman of Restoration comedy gave way to a new idealized woman—the largely middle-class wife and mother."[105] E. J. Clery, however, stresses the "vital point" that in this context "it would be a mistake to see the legislation of female manners as an end in itself." Witnessing the bust of previous models of feminization that had allowed women to fall again into stigmatized sensuality, Addison and Steele, Clery argues, "attempted to define a new kind of woman, whose highly public brand of domestic virtue would be proof against every test."[106] This historiographical complication points again to the complexity of defining social progress and understanding Whig positions in the period when writers like Elizabeth Rowe contributed, along with Addison and Steele, to a "progressive" model of women's liberty that critics now often interpret as retrograde in comparison to the models provided by earlier, libertine Restoration writers.

One reason for this difficult interpretative ambiguity has to do with what Michael McKeon contends was Addison's notable and repeated "insistence on the face of sexual difference" as part of his participation in the larger, programmatic discursive separation of the middle-class, bourgeois family from the state. This multivalent historical process posited a modern normative "domestic" space (both private and national) that would enclose a new, potentially extendable public realm of politics.[107] Women became problematically central in such a publicly important yet adamantly private domestic sphere. Addison's role in figurally staging them there was contradictory and productive of a large swath of the overweening sentimentality that (productively) alienates contemporary readers from his work. The next section of this chapter analyzes the particularities of Addison's representation of women via a third influential Modernist return to his work found in Virginia Woolf's artfully ironic essay commemorating the bicentennial of his death.

TARNISHED SILVER

"But there are none to whom this Paper will be more useful than to the female World"? With a more assertive bit of punctuation, Addison signaled in *Spectator* 10 what was certainly a wise business decision, albeit one that risked stretching his authorial representative scope to the point of absurdity for twenty-first-century readers, and likely for a large number of his contemporary readers as well. The paper went on to claim, with the condescension of reforming intent, that for "ordinary" women—who previously lacked the edification of a publication like *The Spectator* to address them as "reasonable Creatures"—"the Toilet is their great Scene of Business, and the right adjusting of their Hair the principal Employment of their Lives."[108]

Many of Addison's sociological viewpoints, as captured in his sometimes contradictory writings, are jingoistic, racist, ethnocentric, sexist, and, yes, "priggish." Many of those adjectives, unfortunately, do not distinguish him from the average writer of his time and place, though there were certainly more truly discerning and equitable writers competing—less successfully in terms of numbers—for the same readership. However that may be, even in his own time, Addison's awkwardness with the female gender was fairly idiosyncratic. His relations with women reportedly evinced distance, distrust, and low opinion of their intellect and capacity for logic; he seemed to have no intimate friendships with women or insight into their deeper thoughts. Philologists can often identify the essays and essay sections of unknown authorship that are likely by Addison as opposed to Steele and other collaborators through the particularly condescending manner with which Addison's speakers tend to address female characters and readers.[109] In writing, according to Smithers, "when he wished to address himself specifically to women, Addison usually assumed the weapons of raillery and banter rather than the methods of logic."[110]

When he did address women with argument, the call was often to urge them to become something like inspiring neoclassical statues, to (as he urged women in *Spectator* 10) "join all the Beauties of the Mind to the Ornaments of Dress, and inspire a kind of Awe and Respect, as well as Love, into their Male-Beholders."[111] Togas and tunics—rather illogically for the learned classicist that he was—did not carry the duplicitous potential of modern fashion. Erin Mackie points out that the Addisonian maneuver of labeling fashion as feminine (and a bad kind of feminine at that) was another example of Addison's rhetoric having enough success that today we are tempted to take it for granted. In his own time, extravagant fashion actually had a strong masculinist association with the Restoration culture of aristocratic men, fops, beaus, and rakes competing to look like the freshest arrivé from Louis XIV's court. By stigmatizing fashion as the occupation of "ordinary," unelevated women, Addison participated in a larger societal trend of critiquing increased retail trade as deceptively theatrical and suspiciously sexualized and feminized. On the other "straight" side of Addison and Steele's transitional satire stood their effort, praised by Lewis, to codify a new sober public *masculinity* against aristocratic seventeenth-century norms.[112] The nascent, Addisonian middling everyman-ideal would be a "masculine character . . . a domesticated man who, nonetheless, is not a fop; an unequivocally masculine man who, nonetheless, is not a rake; a man with a certain degree of worldly savoir faire who is by no means a beau or a pretty fellow."[113] Using the figure of fashionable femininity as a scarecrow for both genders, *The Spectator*'s advocacy of "tasteful" simplicity in dress constructed attainable costumes for the new public actor and actress, plain styles that would not overtax middling people with the need to participate in the growing markets of goods at the impossible-to-sustain level of the aristocracy.

Even accounting for an anti-aristocratic bent, the fact that Addison and Steele left in place a misogynistic hierarchy and blamed women's influence for social instabilities of various sorts (e.g., the advent of wasteful consumer culture and fashion) cannot be so easily read over. Their ploy to simultaneously, often teasingly, condemn and pardon women ran afoul of some of their original readers—*Spectator* 34, for instance, reports that female readers have objected to raillery against "the Dress and Equipage of Persons of Quality."[114] Even Lucy Aikin's panegyric nineteenth-century biography singles out Addison's irritating proclivity toward "coarse reflections" on women and patronizing "banter" directed to them.[115] The attempted codification of a restricted domestic social role for women, after all, went beyond the sumptuary, even when he invoked the powerful neoclassical archetype of the Roman matron. *Spectator* 81 urged women to avoid partisan politics in favor of focusing on beauty and more peaceable virtues, uniting rather than dividing; like classical women, they should "distinguish themselves as tender Mothers and faithful Wives, rather than as furious Partizans. Female Virtues are of a Domestick turn. The Family is the proper Province for Private Women to Shine in."[116] Addison praised women's equality as a demonstration of exceptional British liberty, but linked their "sexual virtue" to their partisan political views, portraying female prostitutes negatively as supporters of Jacobitism.[117] He built up women's domestic role "to the female equivalent of a male profession" but warned against their more direct and active involvement in politics and chauvinistically accused them of being unanswerable to argument once they had taken up an error or prejudice as a group.[118] His ironic tone often turned or invited the reader to turn and extend the same criticism also to men, yet the brunt of the "cheerful" misogynistic satire remained where it first landed.

And yet *The Spectator* was one of the first mass periodicals to address female readers explicitly on a regular basis, to treat their presumed concerns, and to invite them and their representatives into the debate about politics and philosophy.[119] Addison and Steele's journal, following Habermas, is granted a crucially inspiring and shaping agency in the development of the bourgeois public sphere, and from the beginning, the public that it was imaginatively forming was a reading and speaking public of more than one gender. In this light, as Thomas Alan King argues, their "historical success" was to develop a public "heterosocial model of male subjectivity" in opposition to an older philosophical tradition—carried forth by Shaftesbury, for instance—of homosocial debate. They emphasized and naturalized male and female gender roles as innate but simultaneously contributed to the progress of gender equality by making the inclusion of both "complementary" genders necessary for correct, balanced thinking, conversation, and reflection—for the forming of a real public worthy of the name.[120]

The Restoration theater also had a large role in shaping the emerging, dual-gendered public sphere, and there again the structural sexism of condescension toward the female gender—in the era of Aphra Behn and then Susanna Centlivre—was complex. As in Addison's work, female characters, now usually played by actresses instead of boys, often performed a dangerous and bewildering, or amusing and potentially regressive emotionality. Spectators, as Felicity Nussbaum argues, came to the theater to see reliably the survival of "old," persistent ways of feeling in spite of a progressive, imperial modernity that demanded constant, rational openness to new, cosmos-changing data, perspectives, and theories. The theater of the time staged the split between a more archaic, bodily mode of feeling and an accompanying new artificial rational-sentimental discourse by emphatically displaying the passionately suffering female character. Embodied intensely by renowned actresses who had only legally been allowed to practice their trade since Charles II's return from France, this popular theatrical trope captivated audiences. They watched on stage what they felt in themselves: the conflict between fresh liberation and alienated suffering that went along with a world being remade as well as the paradigm shift in feeling that adaptation to such a world required.[121]

British Augustan periodical literature and theater, in this sense, served for its public an individually reintegrative function, partially by exploiting, staging, and perpetuating a strong regime of gender roles. Around 1910, when Virginia Woolf suggested that female literary figures stepped with Mrs. Brown as equal passengers into the same speeding train of time as male literary figures, Modernism undid the energies of this contradictory Enlightenment procedure of individual-integration-via-gender-segregation: women would no longer act as the clichéd reservoir of feeling, men no longer sit comfortably as the spectating scientific jury. Addison occupied a crucial position in Woolf's autobiography-laden, fictional depiction of the reflective female writer coming to modern assertion—in a manner that distinctly resonates with Joyce's invocation of Addison in his own *Portrait* of artistic coming of age and with Addison's ghostly, singing presence in Lewis's meditations on his coming to modern faith. Woolf's father, Leslie Stephen, had written extensively about Addison, who served as a foil for his own ambitions and with whose decision to reject a university clerical occupation in favor of a literary life in London he came to identify.[122] In *Orlando,* her 1928 fictional "biography" of Vita Sackville-West and her family, Addison haunts the eponymous hero/heroine as a model man and author through her epoch- and gender-shifting transformations. When the critically nostalgic, Elizabethan poet Greene reappears toward the novel's end as a plump, prosperous Victorian professor of literature with a depressing respectability in a gray suit, he mentions Addison as the last of the dead heroes of literature shortly before Orlando—disillusioned now with literature—accidentally lets fall out from her bosom what will be her first publication, "The Oak Tree." Greene promptly compares the poem with *Cato.* The poem (an allusion in the novel to Sackville-West's 1926 Georgic poem *The Land*) will then win a prize, "this culmination to which the whole book moved," shortly after which Orlando realizes she has been haunted and then becomes "a single self, a real self" who promptly gets the respectful, nodding approval of her old friends "Dryden, Pope, Swift, Addison."[123]

Before *Orlando* and her other major novels, Woolf had wrestled with the Addisonian ghost in a significant critical essay in 1919 commemorating the two-hundredth anniversary of his death. Woolf's essay stresses the surprise a modern reader might find in actually encountering an author whose reputation (in her time) very much preceded him: "Addison is very well worth reading. The temptation to read Pope on Addison, Macaulay on Addison, Thackeray on Addison, Johnson on Addison rather than Addison himself is to be resisted, for you will find, if you study *The Tatler* and *The Spectator,* glance at *Cato,* and run through the remainder of the six moderate-sized volumes, that Addison is neither Pope's Addison nor anybody else's Addison, but a separate, independent individual still capable of casting a clear-cut shape of himself upon the consciousness, turbulent and distracted as it is, of nineteen hundred and nineteen."[124]

But Woolf's take on Addison overall fell in line with that of Samuel Johnson, one of her role models. Indeed, the very first sentence of her somewhat Addisonian book of essays *The Common Reader,* in which her essay on Addison was reprinted, explains that she took the phrase "Common Reader" and the inspiration from Johnson, a man from Addison's hometown who became one of his first and most influential biographers.[125] Woolf's virtuoso analysis, full of fine allusion to Addison's work and commitment to antiquarian numismatics, playfully indicates a close familiarity with his oeuvre and bears on many of the concerns addressed above:

> It seems so often scarcely worth while to go through the cherishing and humanising process which is necessary to get into touch with a writer of the second class who may, after all, have little to give us. The earth is crusted over them; their features are obliterated, and perhaps it is not a head of the best period that we rub clean in the end, but only the chip of an old pot. The chief difficulty with the lesser writers, however, is not only the effort. It is that our standards have changed. The things that they like are not the things that we like; and as the charm of their writing depends much more upon taste than upon conviction, a change of manners is often quite enough to put us out of touch altogether. That is one of the most troublesome barriers between ourselves and Addison. He attached great importance to certain qualities. He had a very precise notion of what we are used to call "niceness" in man or woman. He was extremely fond of saying that men ought not to be atheists, and that women ought not to wear large petticoats. This directly inspires in us not so much a sense of distaste as a sense of difference.[126]

Woolf directly critiques the necessity of imagining the context of his work, arguing for greatness in the literary field being tied to a transhistorical universal appeal and against Addison's famous misogynistic fashion criticism: "Any historian will explain; but it is always a misfortune to have to call in the services of any historian. A writer should give us direct certainty; explanations are so much water poured into the wine. As it is, we can only feel that these counsels are addressed to ladies in hoops and gentlemen in wigs—a vanished audience which has learnt its lesson and gone its way and the preacher with it. We can only smile and marvel and perhaps admire the clothes."[127] The turn of Woolf's phrase is characteristically wicked in its inversion of Addison's argument. In the *Spectator* essay (435) she singles out to ridicule, Mr. Spectator was critiquing—as so often—the "Extravagancies" of women's fashion.[128] After he gave himself credit for "so effectually quashing those Irregularities" he had previously criticized, he mused that he was

> afraid Posterity will scarce have a sufficient Idea of them [i.e., the discarded items of fashion] to Relish those Discourses which were in no little Vogue at the time when they were written. They will be apt to think that the Fashions and Customs I attacked, were some Fantastick Conceits of my own, and that their Great-Grandmothers cou'd not be so whimsical

as I have represented them. For this Reason, when I think on the Figure my several Volumes of Speculations will make about a Hundred Years hence, I consider them as so many Pieces of old Plate, where the Weight will be regarded, but the Fashion lost.[129]

A self-effacing Addison, it seemed, anticipated C. S. Lewis's ambivalent praise in the twentieth century: he had abolished "the old flamboyancy" so effectively that subsequent generations did not understand the need for his works.

In an irony to which Woolf was likely sensitive, *Spectator* 435 bears traces of repressing a different kind of internal "flamboyancy" then projected censoriously onto female "fashion victims," in a maneuver that Tita Chico suggests was typical for certain male writers of the period gazing across gender lines into the mirror, as it were. "The dissembling woman, seated at her dressing table" became "a paradigmatic provocation" for self-fashioning, sociable middling men like Addison, who saw reflected in her an illegitimate, uncontrollable masculine will to power through deceit and performance, a desire to realize the public self as a work of art. In general, the reading, costuming woman became an ambivalent figuration of the "becoming" subject of the new public sphere.[130] The excitement and detailed critical passion with which Addison observed female costuming may have carried particular personal significance, of which his texts might show a conscious or at least sublimated awareness. The era was one, like many, in which sex between members of the same gender regularly resulted in violent and potentially lethal legal and extralegal sanctions; the Societies for the Reformation of Manners, for instance, actively persecuted "sodomites" and others in the period. Pope's published remark—after Addison's death—that Addison and Steele were "a couple of H—-s" (probably using the word "Hermaphrodites," a common epithet for men who had sex with men at a time before the invention of the term "homosexual") shows the dangerous, edgy context in which Addison wrote publicly about topics touching on gender, especially as he was aiming as a reformer for the Apollonian "moral middle" of the public discourse and not for the Dionysian space of carnivalesque art.[131] During a scene heavy with hints of homoeroticism in his 1714 comedy *The Drummer,* a comical slippage in dialogue offers a recognizable slang understanding of "your Hermaphrodites, as they call 'em": double men, married and not married.[132]

Reading a knowing, teasingly subversive, or simply fascinated "closet" sensibility in Addison's writings does not rid them of misogynistic and "naturalizing," binary pronouncements. But it does throw some of his more condescending and normative passages into the slight relief of heightened (self-)

irony, even into the suburbs of early modern camp and textual drag. Indeed, the figure of Hermaphrodite/Hermaphroditus emerges in a few key places in Addison's life and thinking (as subsequent chapters will also explore), suggesting his "middle style" might be understood in various registers as a "hermaphroditic" discourse. His translation of the myth of Hermaphroditus in book 4 of Ovid's *Metamorphoses* was one of his earliest publications, and *Spectator* 435 takes its Latin epigraph from the pivotal moment in that tale when a rejected lustful nymph has her prayers answered through an underwater merger of her body with the body of Hermaphroditus: "Nec duo sunt at forma duplex, nec fœmina dici / Nec puer ut possint, neutrumque & utrumque videntur." Addison's own earlier translation of the same passage reads: "Both bodies in a single body mix, / A single body with a double sex."[133] Mr. Spectator picks up on the hermaphroditic theme by revealing his proclivity to play gender police: "I think it however absolutely necessary," he declares, "to keep up the Partition between the two Sexes, and to take Notice of the smallest Encroachments which the one makes upon the other."[134] Disapproving of a new fashion of cross-dressing among Cavalier or equestrian English ladies, the Spectator relates a recent encounter with a character that could be out of Woolf's *Orlando*: a fashionable female Cavalier, a "Gentlewoman... in a Coat and Hat," a monstrous hermaphrodite in "Amphibious Dress" riding through a country field drew a crowd of country folk out of their houses to stare at the apparition.[135] From his beginning, Mr. Spectator's viewpoint was set off from the author's by an uncertain, playfully ironic distance and characterization. That aspect of light comedy is accentuated in an essay like *Spectator* 435 replete with the frivolity of the Spectator's visit to the estate of the ridiculous but lovable conservative country gentleman, Sir Roger de Coverley. The teasing, double-edged satire comes to a head when, in spite of the Spectator's self-righteous protestation of the benevolence of his service to the "She-Disciples who peruse these my daily Lectures," he reports recently running into some resistance against his efforts at enforcing a code of gender norms. Encountering one of his unhappy "Female Readers in Hide-Park," the Spectator relates how she "looked upon me with a masculine Assurance, and cocked her Hat full in my Face."[136] In *Orlando*'s queer sense of time, Addison and Woolf perform for each other across a two-way textual mirror.

Woolf's essay on Addison notes his habit to do "his best to count" the innumerable follies of "the fair sex" of his time "with a loving particularity"; he does so, however, Woolf says, "very charmingly."[137] The thematization of gender difference in his literary and theatrical output was, as discussed, peculiarly central to his poetics. The figure of the fashionable, equestrian hermaphrodite capped a sequence of essays (*Spectator* 433 and 434) in which he told the tale of a male commonwealth and a female commonwealth that joined into one state, with the "moral" that men make women more charming (hence, Woolf's subtly ironic use of the compliment above) and women refine men, as an alchemist might refine a metal.

Neither refining him nor shaping him into a more charming creature for the modern world, Woolf remains the clear Johnsonian critic, even as she allows a deeper current to move under her Addison evaluation. In difference to Eliot's dismissal and Lewis's nostalgic living-with, Woolf's giving Addison grief allows the pathos of grieving. The surfacing of this deeper current begins in her essay with the recitation of that trope in Addison reception that Addison himself began—namely, that Addison was so successful in the reform of the social world he took on that his works now read to us as empty cliché, that in his invention of everyday culture (even "office culture") the precious metal of his creativity, boldness, and ingenuity disappeared into an unthought-of medium of exchange. "Undoubtedly," the essayist Woolf wrote, "it is due to Addison that prose is now prosaic—the medium which makes it possible for people of ordinary intelligence to communicate their ideas to the world." She then turned to what was for her the medium in which Addison was still captivating, and the movement of grief in the essay begins, only to collect exquisitely with cutting Woolfian irony in the delayed final word of the essay—a tear that holds the cosmos, in which she herself as author indicated she might see herself, perhaps only momentarily, inside or merely reflected. The motif of mourning starts with the essayist's profession that "we have lost the art of writing essays. What with our views and our virtues, our passions and profundities, the shapely silver drop, that held the sky in it and so many bright little visions of human life, is now nothing but a hold-all knobbed with luggage packed in a hurry. Even so, the essayist will make an effort, perhaps without knowing it, to write like Addison."[138]

The "silver drop," the admired handiwork of the bard of Queen Anne's Silver Age of British literature, alchemically shifts back and forth from an inaccessible, kitschy cultural antique depicting an undesirable, long-passed social milieu to a nostalgic twentieth-century dream of perfect artistic capture, impossible now in a relativistic cosmos held together only in the individual mortal mind, "nothing but a hold-all knobbed with luggage packed in a hurry." What shone through was the seeing—empty or clear—of the numismatic tragedian. "In all these matters," Woolf asserted, "Addison was on the side of sense and taste and civilisation. Of that little fraternity, often so obscure and yet so indispensable, who in every age keep themselves alive to the importance of art and letters and music, watching, discriminating, denouncing and delighting, Addison was one—distinguished and strangely contemporary with ourselves."[139] She identified him with his own allegorical description of men who play the lute, a quiet and beautiful antique instrument often drowned out by more bombastic talents, discernible only by very cultivated ears. Here she quoted Addison: "The lutanists, therefore, are men of a fine genius, uncommon reflection, great affability, and esteemed chiefly by persons of a good taste, who are the only proper judges of so delightful and soft a melody."[140] And she marked her grief by rejecting Macaulay's argument that Addison's importance as an author is chiefly genealogical. The merit of his essays, she argued instead, "consists in the fact that they do not adumbrate, or initiate, or anticipate anything; they exist, perfect, complete, entire in themselves."[141]

Woolf's essay mimics movingly and delightfully a general pattern of Addison reception, strangely consistent and strangely known to be consistent. The typical reader wrestles simultaneously with the work's frigid, designed sentimentality; its overly mild, stock nature; and the reports of its profound sociological effects in fomenting publics, nations, catharsis of all kinds, even revolutions. They puzzle in particular, like Woolf, over the normally astute Dr. Johnson's belief that *Cato* was "unquestionably the noblest production of Addison's genius" when the tragedy reads today as dry, obsolete "collector's literature."[142] Here there is usually a disjuncture. On the one hand, critics like Lewis and Macaulay attempt to aesthetically revalidate and recover the work in light of its historically transformative effects. They take Addison's own invitation to take time: to use "polite Learning" to "consider what Pleasure the Contemporaries and Country-men of our old Writers found in their Works, which we at present are not capable of; and whether at the same Time the Moderns mayn't have some Advantages peculiar to themselves, and discover several Graces that arise merely from the Antiquity of an Author."[143] Woolf declared, however, that "that is not the way to read. To be thinking that dead people deserved these censures and admired this morality, judged the eloquence, which we find so frigid, sublime, the philosophy to us so superficial, profound, to take a collector's joy in such signs of antiquity, is to treat literature as if it were a broken jar of undeniable age but doubtful beauty, to be stood in a cabinet behind glass doors."[144] In this respect, she seemed to agree with critics like Eliot and Addison's contemporary John Dennis, who declared the Augustan emperor naked and his works impotent and derivative, a poor tobacco for anyone's evening pipe, aged or not.

In the end, however, Woolf took the more critically muscular approach of bending both streams together and acknowledging an uncanny affecting quality that still sublimates out of Addison's work. Her essay ends with a precise and implicit, diaphonic reflection on the concept of purity and secondary, middling status, even as it highlights and agrees with Addison's own prediction for his writing's reception: "Two hundred years have passed; the plate is worn smooth; the pattern almost rubbed out; but the metal is pure silver."[145] The "Sterling" remains a signifier of particular British value, just as silver remains the typical pride of the formal middle-class dining room, the treasure of accomplished domesticity. In Addison's day, silver was the standard—it would only be eclipsed as the fever of gold-extracting imperialism took firm hold in Britain in his final years and after. In his 1740 autobiography, Colley Cibber was giving no mere second medal to Addison's *Cato* when he testified to its popularity at Oxford in 1713: "Applause was not to be purchas'd there," he wrote, "but by the true Sterling, the *Sal Atticum* of a Genius."[146]

Woolf's brilliant distillation of the tragic Addisonian ghost is itself haunted by Newton, whose third career after alchemist and professor of universal physical laws was as master of the mint, from which post he engineered the de facto shift from a silver to a gold standard during the years of Addison's final highest political preeminence. The Modernist claim that great art must be immanent and held up to a transhistorical standard is intuitively appealing, itself the ecumenical union of Catholic wholeness and Protestant direct, individual revelation (no priestly historians allowed). But, as a claim, it of course paradoxically insists on the power of one present culture to determine what is and what is not transhistorically sublime. Addison as a performative artist insisted, on the other hand, on the value of art that would not necessarily last, on performances whose success would disappear with their success: on a literature of its time, self-reflexive, metatheatrical, posing a humanistic figure against the factions of discipline that would come to separate engineer, journalist, politician, poet, and impresario. The critic Addison advocated for an ideal of literature shaped by the constraint of artists' need or want to be useful in a paradigmatically shifting world. Like the transexual antique silver shilling who tells his life story in one of Addison's more famous *Tatler* essays (249), the Addison that managed to print himself out has many times changed hands around the world, been exhibited in the place of high honor and forgotten for decades in dark corners, been pulled out, recoined, and thrown away for all sorts of purposes, but has never been happier than as an active currency being put to good, sociable use.[147]

2

Everyday Prose after Newton

> Our own art is so much an art of emphasis, and even of over-emphasis, that it is difficult to consider the possibilities of an absolutely unemphasized art, an art where the author trusts so implicitly that his auditor will know what things are profound and important.
> —Ezra Pound, *Noh,* 1916

> For here the mind, which is always delighted with its own discoveries, only takes the hint from the poet, and seems to work out the rest by the strength of her own faculties.
> —Addison on Virgil's *Georgics,* 1697

EARLY SIGHTLINES: ADDISON'S FATHER FIGURES

Addison did not, of course, develop his aesthetics of the socially useful artist in isolation. His early influences reveal much about the milieu in which he was operating and the ghosts that haunt his performative work. He began life as the son of a provincial but fairly well-connected Anglican clergyman of moderate means. His father, Lancelot Addison, established a strong patriarchal role as a cosmopolitan polymath, successfully navigating the difficult career of a political churchman, author of theological treatises, and pathbreaking historian of North African Judaism and Islam.

Lancelot's brother, John, had escaped the difficult times for Royalists during the Commonwealth period by emigrating to Maryland, where he married and prospered. Lancelot, on the other hand, stayed in England until the Restoration, at which point he took up adventurous, loyal service to the king as a garrison chaplain at Dunkirk and then Tangiers. In 1670, he returned to England, where his father had also been a churchman, and married Jane Gulston, whose own relatives' connections in the church ensured their budding family a stable income and place. Joseph was born in 1672 as their first surviving child.

Lancelot published several influential books on the histories and religious traditions of the Barbary Coast, based partially upon his time of service in Tangiers. The first was his 1671 *West Barbary, or a Short Narrative of the Revolutions of the Kingdoms of Fez and Morocco*.[1] This was followed, in 1675, with what was for its time the fairly broad-minded *The Present State of the Jews*, which included an ethnographic account of the Barbary Coast Jewish communities along with a description of the Jewish religion as it was then practiced.[2] He subsequently published what Justin Champion has called "one of the first and most successful anti-Islamic histories" — *The First State of Mahumedism; or an Account of the Author and Doctrines of That Imposture*, in which he argued that Muhammad had cynically used a hodgepodge of religious traditions in order to achieve his primary goal of a political empire.[3] Although Lancelot's works are almost completely forgotten, they had a sizable impact on the British theological and intellectual cultures of his time. The reconstructed list of Isaac Newton's books, for instance, contains two works by Lancelot (*The Present State of the Jews* and a theological treatise on the catechism), in addition to many volumes of his more famous son's periodical essays.[4]

Lancelot's moderate royalist politics earned him gradual promotion, so that by the time Joseph came of age, his father was the dean of Lichfield and the archdeacon of Coventry. Joseph followed in paternal footsteps at Oxford, where he became a well-known poet and fellow. Connecting himself to the national poet laureate, Dryden, as well as the Whig publisher Jacob Tonson and several powerful Whig politicians, Addison earned high respect for his classical scholarship, translations of Ovid and Virgil, and original Latin poetry—with glaring disrespect to centuries of competitors, including Ovid et al., Edmund Smith later described Addison's 1697 paean to William III (*Pax Gulielmi Auspiciis Europae Reddita 1697*) as "the best Latin Poem since the *Aeneid*."[5] His education, one might argue, continued in differing form along the lines of his father's life pattern: leaving Oxford, he went on an adventurous grand tour of the European continent, sponsored by the Crown for the purpose of preparing him for its service. That tour, conducted at a height of military tensions when France had occupied Italy, integrated him into the

Whig diplomatic network and resulted in one of his most important poems, "A Letter from Italy" to Charles Montagu, and his *Remarks on Several Parts of Italy,* which became a popular guidebook for future travelers. Along the way, he had significant meetings and conversations with eminent figures like Boileau, Malebranche, Leibniz, and the Electress Sophia of Hanover.[6]

Returning from Amsterdam to England only after his prominent father's death in 1703, the trained classicist, traveler, and diplomat entered the folds of a powerful group of patrons: the rising Whig ministers who would form the core of the Kit-Kat Club and cement their societal influence through hard-fought political intrigue and the financial support of leading poets, journalists, and scientists. Addison's work would pave the way for a normatively bourgeois and middle-class period to follow, but his own time and century were still dominated by monarchical and aristocratic power structures, in which neoclassical taste was a necessary refinement for participation. The teleological historical energy may have been on the side of the bourgeoisie, but the ruling class for Addison's time remained aristocratic and the outcome of any ensuing class struggles were far from certain or inevitable, even though the strategic Whig historians and prophets of a triumphant modern world may have successfully wished and written so. Dominant networks of aristocratic and royal patronage largely determined what (and who) could be printed and reach a wide audience in a financially stable fashion.[7] Although no aristocrat, Addison had some initial access to these networks through his well-connected father, Lancelot, and other familial relations among the clergy. Performing neoclassical erudition and discipline as Addison did through his Oxford education and early Latin poetry publications had a value similar to the requisite elaborate dedications to aristocratic patrons prefacing most of the literary works of the period: it gave him a privileged status in the networks of the aristocratic and monarchical elite who could fund or ruin his enterprise to pass on the necessary shibboleths and wisdom of neoclassical culture to a broader public audience.[8]

Although British neoclassicism in the period had a long connection to the Stuart and French royal courts, its inflection had significantly altered after the Glorious Revolution of 1688. Solidifying their new power over the more constitutionally limited monarchs they had put on the throne, the aristocratic oligarchy of William and Mary's reign became the energetic champions of Greek and Roman cultural aesthetics. As self-styled virtuous guardians of liberty, this oligarchy sought to defend their preeminence by celebrating their own likeness to Roman republican patriots like Cato and Cicero. Their dignification via association with idealized classical images was no mere intellectual project. Pursued with its shadow of brutality, oligarchic neoclassicism changed the physical setting of England dramatically: "Tenants were turned out and villages demolished to create the English landscape garden. The only limits to self-indulgence were those imposed by a very expensive rule of taste" of the sort delightfully urged by their peer, the 3rd Earl of Shaftesbury.[9] Addison's work bears the marks of a landscape transformed by neoclassical, aristocratic-monarchical power struggles. The resulting distributed nodes of oligarchical authority, production, and censorship signaled the dawn of Foucault's administrative state with its more spread-out, abstract, and specialized social networks of control—an updated Hobbesian Artificial Man with more mechanical joints, just beginning to gather steam and costumed in a retro toga, as it were.[10]

Addison's performative employment and popular modification of neoclassicism reveals the ingenuity of middling people in contesting and carving out a greater public sphere between and for themselves within an old, ever-evolving authoritarian context now at least in words committed to "liberty." When we read Addison in order to understand Addison, rather than to experience his texts as a kind of direct natural impact upon ourselves, we have to understand his language as part of that complex ecosystem. He remains a paradoxical figure in literary and cultural history in part because his popularity signified a dual, tragic accomplishment: on the one hand, he climbed to the heights of a powerful aristocratic-monarchical system by celebrating a certain pitched peak of its imperial power via a robust pageant of neoclassicism; on the other hand, he heralded the end of that system by serving as the spokesperson for the classes and political alliances that would dominate the new more expansively imperial, bourgeois, and middle-class system. It is exactly the heavy neoclassicism of Addison's public works that points to the invisible performative energies undergirding his and his contemporaries' invention and embodiment of what we take for granted as quotidian, upwardly aspirational, middle-class interaction and societal administration. His success in founding and entrenching a new middle-class social system and public language cloaked the synthetic, produced, deliberate, and artistic nature of the endeavor, except in the now-telling garishness of its neoclassical garb. For Addison, however, such a pragmatic bending to elite taste was for artists at least as old classical culture itself: the very little that one could learn about Homer's life, he wrote, nevertheless demonstrated that the ur-bard of Western culture had "endeavoured to gain Favour and Patronage by his Verse; and 'tis very probable he thought on this Method of ingratiating himself with particular Persons."[11]

One of those very particular persons whom Addison signaled out as a potential patron was Charles Montagu, a lapsed poet and playwright and dominant political player of the era, who had a uniquely long and close relationship with Isaac Newton. Montagu had become intimately acquainted with Newton in 1678 upon the former's entrance to Trinity College Cambridge. Though nineteen years separated the elder Newton and the younger Montagu, they founded a (short-lived) Cambridge philosophical society together. In the latter part of the 1690s, around the same time that Montagu was helping Newton to obtain the well-paid post of warden of the mint and to secure housing near his own in London, Addison had begun to benefit from Montagu's patronage.[12] In those years, Montagu's literary successes were still fresh in the cultural consciousness—most notably his verses on the death of Charles II and his collaboration with Matthew Prior on *The City Mouse and the Country Mouse,* a burlesque of Dryden's *The Hind and the Panther.*

John Dennis reported that Montagu (later created Earl of Halifax) received more literary dedications than any other person of his time.[13] The Montagu model of turning an early reputation as a poet and playwright into a high-flying political career was one that many men of the period would attempt to emulate. In the protégé Addison's case, a far greater ultimate literary success would continually open the gates to ministerial posts, whereas Montagu's extraordinary achievements as an administrator and politician far outshone his reputation as a poet once he entered government work and largely left behind the professional literary field. As a role model and patron, Montagu performed a crucial role in helping the young Oxford poet to modulate the destiny handed down to him by his successful father. Some of Addison's closest literary colleagues would later privately judge that he had always been "a priest in his heart."[14] Indeed, the legacy of his family—consisting of multiple generations of churchmen on both sides—remained strong in his "clerical" mission to reform society and raise the general level of peaceful societal interaction. When formulating the larger plan for his paper, Addison had Mr. Spectator defer to the highest authority in his Club, a revered clergyman who urges him to avoid satirizing the weak and depressed and to use cheerfulness "to assault the Vice without hurting the Person," resulting in his vow to never "publish a single Paper, that is not written in the Spirit of Benevolence and with a Love to Mankind."[15] According to Smithers, much of Addison's writing in that paper treated "matters which had been declaimed from the pulpit to drowsy congregations for many years but which now received a new life and interest because presented as a part of daily conduct as lived by the 'polite.'"[16] Joseph's choice of an urban public life marks a contrast to Lancelot's ultimate path as a high provincial clergyman, but the contrast is not so stark if one considers the son's passionate service to the state and the broader Anglican "church" of British culture, in which *The Spectator* functioned as an unprecedented daily-updated written social liturgy and constitution.

According to Richard Steele, Montagu played gatekeeper at this juncture of fate, not only helping to arrange the financing for Addison's European tour but also using his political clout to free Lancelot's son from the clerical obligation under which almost all fellows of Oxford fell. Montagu's letter convinced the president of Magdalene College to grant Addison a rare dispensation from taking orders. This allowed Addison to remain a securely funded fellow but be absent from campus for extended periods of time. Urging his case, Montagu wrote, according to Steele's memory of the letter, "that however he [Montagu] might be represented as no Friend to the Church, he never would do it any other Injury than keeping Mr. Addison out of it."[17] One of history's greatest financial architects, Montagu effected the crucial transfer of Addison's talent from the Church to the secularizing state.

Much of Addison's literary and theatrical career, in keeping with the continuing strength of aristocratic patronage throughout the British eighteenth century, can be suggestively tacked to the influence and rise and fall of Montagu. A founder of the Bank of England and the system of public credit, Montagu served as president of the Royal Society from 1695 to 1698.[18] It was he who connected Newton, the warden of the mint, to the young traveling writer of *Dialogue on Medals;* who ushered the unemployed classical scholar into the halls of London power shortly after the death of his father (around the time Addison put the first four acts of *Cato* on a shelf for almost a decade); whose temporary fall from power created the window of unemployed time Addison used to write and publish *The Spectator;* and whose comeback paved the way for Addison's ultimate political rise as secretary of state. Montagu himself was crucial in creating the role of the modern British minister of state, a role that Addison would help to further transform and claim for the ambition and interests of middling people. The paternal role of Montagu in Addison's life speaks to the secularizing energies of Addison's projects and particularly—if one remembers Montagu and Newton's first collaboration on a philosophical club at Cambridge—to his immersion in that great alternative discourse of ultimate meaning that ran slightly in the shadow of Christianity: Platonism.

Addison's self-declared goal (cited in chapter 1) to bring the philosophy of Socrates down from the heavens and into the coffeehouse, to circulate among middle-class households, is a consistent key to his poetics and theatrical drive. Plato's movingly ironic, resistantly tragic dialogue *Phaedo* was an inspiration for the would-be playwright, who spoke of a desire to transform the death of Socrates into a tragedy for the English stage of the early eighteenth century.[19] Since the historical Cato famously took Socrates as a model for his life and his tragic end, Addison's *Cato* can be considered a dramatic surrogate for that unwritten Socratic drama, highlighting how Addison, like many learned individuals through the centuries, took the wily, unwriting Athenian as an admired master. When he looked, as Socrates urged his followers to do after his death, for the best living replacement—the new mapmaker of the cosmos—Addison and many other learned individuals found Isaac Newton to be the age's most awe-inspiring truth-teller.[20]

Although there seems to be no known correspondence between the two discourse-founders, Newton and Addison shared a tellingly close connection in Montagu.[21] Besides being the most important political patron for both men, Montagu was a close private friend of Newton, who left the latter's admired niece and ward, Catherine Barton, a somewhat scandalously large inheritance, in part for her "conversation"; Barton had served as something of a housekeeper for him after his wife's death. Newton was heavily involved in the negotiations that divided Montagu's estate between Barton and Montagu's principal heir after his death in 1715, the same year that Newton would purchase an essay on medals by Addison, the poet-statesman who would a few years later himself be buried in Westminster Abbey at the foot of Montagu's grave.[22] The connection speaks to the period's uniquely tight knot of Platonism, innovative forms of mathematics and experimental science, energetic associations between long-unmarried men and women, reinvented finance, Whiggism, the administrative transformation of the state, and the strong necessity of aristocratic patronage for middling people. The next section of the chapter turns to investigate the shaping juncture between Platonism, Newtonianism, and Addison's modern reception of both, resulting in a new sociable world of theatrical epistemology.

IN NEWTON'S EYES

By the time Addison was born in 1672, Newton had already accomplished some of his most stunning scientific work. Addison and his contemporaries would be deeply affected by Newton's many convincing and often unsettling new descriptions of light and the rest of the physical universe. Indeed, it seems difficult to overestimate Newton's impact on subsequent intellectual life. Inside of this novel scientific paradigm itself were the shaking effects of cultural, political, and theological change: the accomplishment and reception of Newton's work signified a historical opening for scholars of middling backgrounds to supplant elite, authoritarian paradigms of knowledge through writing, argument, and demonstration. Moreover, because much of Newton's redefinitional work was accomplished in relative isolation and away from great urban centers, he stood culturally as a modern archetype of the lonely, revolutionary genius building a picture of the world in the wild, from the ground up (as it were).

The son of a deceased father and stepson of a clergyman, Newton benefited from an excellent education at a local grammar school and at Trinity College Cambridge, where he later became a fellow. But a study of his biography and notebooks bears out that many of the startling insights he eventually passed on to his contemporaries were the result of a relatively radical process of experimentation and rethinking the nature of the world from scratch.[23] As such, Newton's accomplishments represent an increased validation of middle-class individual experience based upon rigorous, direct observation and long, careful investigation and thought. The archetype of the modern genius as prophet of a previously hidden order of things went hand in hand with Protestantism's validation of the individual reader's inspired, direct connection to God. Indeed, in Newton's notebooks, the mixed proximity of his notes and expositions relating to scientific and theological inquiries often suggest their simultaneity and imbrication in each other.[24]

Addison, a preacher of polite neoclassical taste, was one of the most important popularizers of science in the Enlightenment.[25] From one perspective, he was working on behalf of patrons to strengthen the aristocratic conception of England as a new Rome; from another perspective, the British-Roman stage set he designed was placed squarely on a strange, recently discovered Newtonian planet. Citizens must comport themselves as if they were ever in the service of new Rome's network of patrician family rulers, but the planet—the ground and its inviolable laws—more than ever belonged to the practical class and their mathematically sound divine hermeneuticist, Newton. Subsequently, as a London state official, that foremost patriarch of modern physicists would become a consumer of Addison's collected essays. Prior to those essays being written, however, Newton had given to English intellectuals what any would-be cultural engineer could only dream of if they were looking (as Addison was, to a degree) to reconstitute society on a firm and stable basis: a new Nature, both historically revolutionary and verifiable through common sense and common reason. The fatherless young man from Woolsthorpe turned Cambridge scientist so boldly validated his own middle-class epistemological worth that he dismissed experts throughout Britain and the continent in favor of his own experimental findings and calculations, eventually refusing even to present his work to the Royal Society unless he could do so without questions, dissent, or debate. Because his bold assessment of his own scientific intellect turned out to be accurate, he met with unparalleled success, not just in setting forth new universal physical laws but in radically changing how we understand a fundamental basis for the shared sense-world: our eyes.

This seismic shift in understanding had subtle yet monumental consequences through which Addison guided his readers. After Newton, the idea that plain light simply reveals the essential colors of objects became untenable. Rather, Newton revealed, plain light was itself a mixture of all colors, a mixture so ubiquitous in our experience that our eyes were formed to regard it as colorless. Our experience of color became, in this new paradigm, only the eye and the mind's reaction to objects' very small differential reflection of light. Color was a practical tool for navigating the surface of our particular planet, not itself anything essential. This simple and demonstrable seventeenth-century insight painted nature as such an alien landscape that language and thinking still strain themselves in trying to translate it into our backward quotidian experience.

At the same time, Newton's other physical discoveries participated in a redrawing of the map of the cosmos. That fundamental revision was already well underway, thanks to a resurgent Platonism in which both Newton and Addison were fluent. By the early eighteenth century, most educated people rejected a medieval geocentric picture of the universe, believing instead in the Copernican model of the earth revolving around the sun. Moreover, influenced by Cartesianism and the arguments and demonstrations of astronomers like Galileo and Giordano Bruno, the educated part of British society at the time tended increasingly to adopt a "modern conception of the scale of magnitude and the general arrangement of the physical world in space."[26] Cartesianism's modern cosmography painted a picture even more radical than a heliocentric universe: the courtly schema of the earth moving around the sun in a solar system surrounded by a fixed array of stars gave way instead to an acentric universe, a scattered aggregate of almost infinite potential worlds. This change, as Arthur O. Lovejoy has argued, was the decisive blow to the medieval imagination. It upset the spatial underpinning for the medieval theological assumption that Earth "alone contained a race of free creatures half-material and half-spiritual—the middle link in the Chain of Being—for whose allegiance the celestial and the infernal powers competed."[27]

Descartes's seventeenth-century, expanded acentric cosmography was in a certain respect only a neoclassical synthesis of elements "carried in solution in medieval thought": its acceptance as a new system had less to do with empirical evidence than with a shift in philosophical and theological authority. The Platonic doctrines of multiple times, multiple worlds, and divine plenitude had persisted for centuries in the esoteric confines of Scholastic debates about the finitude or infinitude of creation. Bruno's late sixteenth-century astronomical observations had given those Platonic doctrines fresh support, but their new widespread acceptance by the end of the seventeenth century was bolstered by theological arguments made prominently by Montaigne and then Descartes for the good of humility as a corrective against man's delusional capacity for egotism.[28] The popularity of man's egotism and theological certainty had taken significant hits due to the still threatening trauma of horrific religious civil wars, most recently the Thirty Years' War on the continent and the related English civil wars. The English Restoration of the monarchy and Newton's simultaneous lonely experimental and observational work were, in this regard, part of a new epistemological balance in society at the time between the traditional, orienting (Hobbesian) sovereignty of a collective spiritual body with a singular, martial head and an emerging modern sovereignty of equal individuals working separately and through correspondence toward consensus. The two sides of the epistemological balance roughly implied two different cosmographies and two different class systems: medieval and feudal on the one hand, modern and liberal-capitalistic on the other.

Lovejoy's famous Modernist intellectual history left Newton's decisive impact in effectuating the "Cartesian" cultural transition between the medieval and the modern imagination relatively suppressed. It can be indirectly inferred, however, through the connection Lovejoy drew between Descartes and another eminent culture-maker: Addison. As evidence for Descartes's central, synthesizing role in creating common acceptance of the modern cosmography, Lovejoy cited Addison's Latin oration at Oxford in 1693. In that oration, one of his first public successes, Addison declared that it was Descartes who "destroyed those orbs of glass which the whims of antiquity had fixed above," and who "scorned to be any longer bounded within the straits of crystalline walls of an Aristotelic world." A performative academic exercise advocating the Moderns over the Ancients, the oration was reprinted much later in 1728 and throughout the 1730s as an appendix to a translation of Fontenelle's *Entretiens sur la pluralité des mondes* titled "Mr. Addison's Defence of the Newtonian Philosophy." The editor of that edition, aside from pitching the speech as arguing for Newtonianism (rather than Cartesianism), claimed in a footnote that when Addison wrote "the *great Ornament* of the present Age," he meant "NEWTON."[29] This attribution of reference is almost certainly an error produced by an overly strong interpretation of the English translation of Addison's oration, but, as an error, it attests both to Newton's sway in changing the direction of "philosophy" and, correspondingly, to Addison's crucial cultural role as an enthusiast and popularizer of Newton. The editor of the Fontenelle edition likely recalled Addison's use of similar laudatory language in *Spectator* 543, where he wrote of "Sir Isaac Newton, who stands as the Miracle of the present Age."[30]

The younger Latin poet Addison of 1693 may have been in the thrall of an ornamental Descartes, but the older vernacular Addison would help to transform the intellectual climate in the direction of a practically miraculous Newton. His oration's argument, moreover, was that the names and labels do not matter so much as the recovery of an *ancient* philosophical tradition. That older philosophical tradition, he argued, was ironically more modern than the Scholasticism that then held sway because it—the so-called new philosophy—was based on common sense. The promising Latin scholar and poet queried, "Shall we stigmatize with the Name of Novelty that Philosophy, which, tho' but lately revived is more ancient than the *Peripatetic,* and as old as the Matter from whence it is derived?"[31] Addison's play on the greater authority of the simultaneously more ancient and more modern natural philosophy when compared to the Scholastics' Aristotelian peripatetic discourse hinted at the grounding of the new empiricism on the playwright Plato's staging of his teacher Socrates's antitextual discourse. Attacking Plato's student, Aristotle, and his centuries of followers, Addison gave intellectual marching orders to his generation: "We no longer pay a blind Veneration to that barbarous *Paripatetic*-Jingle, those Scholastic Terms of Art, once held as Oracles, but consult the Delicates of our own Senses, and by late invented Engines force Nature herself to discover plainly her most valued Secrets, her most hidden Recesses."[32] The bravado of Addison's assertion belied the paradox inherent in Newtonianism, which would return the older Addison again and again to the problematic epistemology of vision and blindness. Addison's later writings would moderate his exuberance about those "late invented Engines" or glass prosthetic eyes—the telescope, the prism, and the microscope—that had enabled the shattering of Aristotelian orbs. Seventeenth-century glassworks, in the same gesture of extending human vision, had helped to empirically disprove the objective reality of human vision.[33] The broken shards of the orbs symbolized the human world's unbalanced wedding to an acentric cosmos that could only be experienced indirectly by peering into finely wrought, manmade lenses and carefully observing the light that they scattered.

SELLING PROGRESSIVE VISIONS:
NEWTONIAN NEOCLASSICISM

A sensitivity for seeing ran through much of Addison's poetic and theatrical work and perhaps informed his famous sympathy for the writings of John Milton. Addison seems to have identified with the republican poet laureate of Hobbes's generation partially through a concrete fear of blindness: when Addison was at his busiest with administrative work, his eyesight often rather frighteningly failed him, forcing him to take days off to recover.[34] His special philosophical concern for sight was, in a longer mode of thinking, an inheritance from Socrates, whose description of the highest attainment of heaven in *Phaedrus* was linked to the sight of the beloved and ultimately to the gods circling frictionless around a vision of whole perfection. Seeing and being seen—the theater of existence—was not, for Addison, a mere sideshow but as close as one could come to the measure of true existential dignity. In *Spectator* 111, he took up the Socratic argument for the immortality of the soul and wrote that "Among . . . other excellent Arguments for the Immortality of the Soul, there is one drawn from the perpetual Progress of the Soul to its Perfection, without a Possibility of ever arriving at it." He called this "perpetual Progress" of the soul "towards the Perfection of its Nature" the most "pleasing and triumphant Consideration in Religion." The projected rhapsodic vision followed: "To look upon the Soul as going on from Strength to Strength, to consider that she is to shine for ever with new Accessions of Glory, and brighten to all Eternity: That she will be still adding Virtue to Virtue, and Knowledge to Knowledge, carries in it something wonderfully agreeable to that Ambition which is natural to the Mind of Man. Nay, it must be a Prospect pleasing to God himself, to see his Creation for ever beautifying in his Eyes, and drawing nearer to him, by greater degrees of Resemblance."[35] Rather than accepting the zero-sum game of a static "Creation" in which one person's ambition meant another's downfall, Addison and many of his contemporaries validated ambition as part of the divine plan of endless progress, a growing nearer and nearer to the image of a watching God, the universe as an evermore-blooming flower. Lovejoy called this development in the history of the ideas the "temporalizing of the Chain of Being": a new doctrine of spiritual and religious evolution of the whole cosmos.[36] The Chain of Being, a concept derived from Plato, Aristotle, and Plotinus, linked minerals, plants, animals, angels, God, and all forms of being imaginable in a scale of good or reason. The hierarchy itself demonstrated what the good was partially through what was lacking in the lower scales and through the evident greater scaled perfection as one ascended. It was thus an argument for why the existence of evil or imperfection in the world did not contradict the notion of an omnipotent, perfect, and benevolent creator—a solution to the old problem of theodicy.

The traditional schema of the Chain of Being—a central organizing metaphor in European philosophy and theology for centuries—was, according to Lovejoy, "rigid and static." It presented a universe created with perfect continuity and completeness. As a master theological schema, this traditional version of the Chain complemented feudal power structures and a unified church propped up by ancient dogma and tradition. By fully reworking the traditional schema to theologically validate progress and a spiritual ambition that was synergetic with the more terrestrial, individualistic ambitions validated by Protestant mercantilism, Addison was one of the first authors of the eighteenth century to significantly challenge the old fixed world-picture.[37]

Addison's temporalization of the Chain of Being balanced the old philosophical doctrine of optimism, which held that we live in the best of all possible worlds, with modern hope—the eighteenth-century conviction that a better world might be possible if enough people took the decision to challenge some of the supposedly permanent evils of the world, like horrific civil wars. The notion of progress was introduced into the traditional theological picture by way of a new picture showing that a perfect universe might not exhibit all kinds of perfection at every time. Forms and beings might pass away and come into existence in time as the universe perpetually, performatively neared the absolute perfection that, taken as an eternal whole in a kind of theological integrative calculus, it was.[38] As an infinitesimal part of this evolving universe, a human being, in Addison's modified Christian vision, was an "organism that never stops improving, a kalon zoon that becomes ever more beautiful in the afterlife and a zoon holon whose full perfection is only partially realized on earth."[39]

Addison's revised version of a progressive, historically and permanently shifting Chain fit with the new acentric, expansive, and evolving Newtonian cosmos for which he was also an influential spokesperson. Both reworked master schemas complemented the social age that was witnessing the formation and rise of the European middle class. The structural, synergetic homology of the new Addisonian master schemas with their shifting historical social matrices, however, speaks also to the strong, historically specific persistence of the older hierarchical, feudal arrangement. When one considers the ambiguous flexibility of Addison's Chain or a universe structured around Newtonian law against a more Romantic schema of boundless space and chaos or a Modernist Einsteinian world-picture of relativity, one sees the historical limits of Addison's progressivism vis-à-vis more thoroughgoing revolutionary ardor or sublime individualism. Addison's revision of the Chain of Being, exuberant as it was, celebrating eternal progress as it did, was not as bombastic as we might expect of a proper class warrior, in the later revolutionary Romantic tradition. Nor did it collapse the eternally judging Divine gaze into the encountering subjectivity of an autonomous woman on a speeding train. The links in the Chain became greater, the gaps between beings of different stations smaller, but the different spheres of different beings remained, in Addison's account, eternally separate in spite of universal progress—they became sociable but not entirely social. One hears, perhaps, a certain offer of (gender-coded) appeasement extended from the ambitious writer to his noble patrons in the way he approaches *Spectator* 111's conclusion:

> That Cherubim which now appears as a God to a human Soul, knows very well that the Period will come about in Eternity, when the Human Soul shall be as perfect as he himself now is. Nay, when she shall look down upon that degree of Perfection, as much as she now falls short of it. It is true, the higher Nature still advances, and by that means preserves his Distance and Superiority in the scale of Being; but he knows how high soever the Station is of which he stands possess'd at present, the inferior Nature will at length mount up to it, and shine forth in the same Degree of Glory.[40]

Contemplating progress within the Chain, Addison argued, would rid the rational being of envy since each being might perpetually and successfully strive for betterment. At the same time, a certain more fluid baroque hierarchical order of discreet, eternal souls would be maintained. The man or the journalist might move upward into an angel or a duke's palace, but the angel and the duke would meanwhile move into an unimaginably more luxurious dwelling. The new Chain resonated terrestrially with a Whig doctrine of wealth creation not as a zero-sum competition or revolution but as chance for all to better their conditions in a dynamically hierarchical society; the liberty of each industrious individual climbing the ladder would increase the heavenly harvest and create the conditions for all of society's flowering. The twinned promise of increased general wealth and imperial expansion was sold as a self-generating panacea, the product, enabler, and aristocratic anodyne of increased English liberty. The serf would gain access to a world of goods and free movement, but the Queen could be content: she would become empress.

In Addison's writing, positive, large-scale social and spiritual progress became possible—and even likely—through the developments of time and history. Time and its myriad changes were part of the larger, unfolding eternal perfection; they were no longer mere mortal trials and distractions from meditating on a mostly fixed and static cosmos presided over by a sometimes-interfering God. A positive conception of both individual and collective temporal change facilitated, to a critical degree, a heightened moral and spiritual interest in news, fashion, and consumer culture: How, after all, should human beings most ideally costume, feed, and surround their bodies and minds in order to achieve the best conditions for themselves and their societies? For Addison, as John Brewer has argued, "Man was a creature of his cultural and social environment, shaped by his changing circumstances and stimuli."[41] Because humans were among "the most changeable Beings in the Universe," guided strongly neither by instinct nor by intuition, the species was shaped by different moments of history in a similar way to how an individual's proceeding life stages "produce Changes and Revolutions in the Mind."[42] Lovejoy suggested that Addison and his contemporaries provided in this respect "the foreshadowings of the Faust-ideal," which celebrated diversity, novelty, and man's insatiable nature—"an interminable pursuit of an unattainable goal" rather than the medieval "final rest of the soul in contemplation of Perfection."[43]

The Faustian ideal Lovejoy had in mind was the Romantic Faust of Goethe, but it is useful to consider Addison as poised in the European theatrical tradition between Marlowe and Goethe. Marlowe's Faust was condemned by his lust after a diverting "Grand Tour" of demonic visions and superficial visits to European courts; a liminal Renaissance figure, his adventurous spirit is crushed anew within the strict confines of feudalism after a few enticing glimpses of a riskily emerging modern cosmopolitan liberty. Goethe's Faust, on the other hand, rejects the mass sociality of cosmopolitan rebirth (symbolized in the play's opening Easter scene outside the town walls) to embrace the Romantic *imbalance* between individual withdrawal and industrial-fueled, wide-flung adventuring, the unrestrained carnival of world travel and radical creative transformation. At times satiated by the totality of diverse imperial experience, the industrialist, Romantic Faust is even saved in the end by love and the Mater Gloriosa: matter itself yields and bends to human passion and ingenuity, altering even the basic terms of the supposedly eternal contract.

Addison's Spectator took his daily constitutionals at a mid-point historically and experientially between the two lonely yet übersocial Fausts. Free and content to stroll at whim through an active and diverse social milieu,

Mr. Spectator was called into a flowering cosmopolitan theater produced as if magically, naturally by each day itself. Steady, diurnal time was the benevolent daemon-impresario dutifully throwing visions before the anonymous Everyman-Emperor of his own domain. For the Fausts, a more devilish figure of temporality functioned as the theater-maker-within-the-play—the event-maker Mephisto with his various demonically distracting toys and illusions. In Marlowe's Elizabethan vision, time's tricks reduce to nothing but absorbing illusions masking an eternal contract. There is nothing really new under the sun; Faust can be saved or condemned in a forever of little historical change and none of real consequence.[44] In Goethe's two-part Romantic tour de force, on the other hand, industrial time's magic reshapes Faust's community, nation, and cosmos until even its dark aspect—the tyranny of time over a mortal frame, Mephisto himself—seems about to melt away: he is revealed as perhaps nothing but a disguised angelic jester whose chaotic bending of the world to man's desire was a form of comic grace, beguilingly guiding unwitting man toward his marriage and reunion with a maternal eternal. The ambiguity of Goethe's Romantic staging hits with the final theatrical moment and the realization that the captivating, overrhyming figure of time (Mephisto) might simply be an impresario so successful that we forget his old function as the con fooling us with gripping, pleasing illusions right up until the very lights go out.

Mr. Spectator's Faustian dilemma is exquisitely distilled in his brief Orientalized manifestation as Mirzah, the visionary wanderer of one of Addison's most famous and most mystically theological essays. The succinct allegory encapsules Mr. Spectator's historically specific existential position: an observer whose liberation to observe the capturing illusion of his society within a much vaster, infinite Newtonian frame does not (yet) grant the fundamental power to alter his basic, practical situation. Rather than being condemned to suffer in the no-time of a harsh, settled social order as Marlowe's Faustus, rather than being led as Goethe's Faust through an endless carnival of shocks and transformations to arrive at a solipsistic transcendence with no steady ground or certain source of light, Addison's Mirzah is returned at the midpoint of the early modern Faustian theater to the Earth, to the unchanged classical biblical ground of pastoral exile where transcendence collapses into the gravity of the long chronicle's merely daily progress. High above the hills of Baghdad, the reading Spectator meets not Mephisto but a mysterious Genius, a flute-playing shepherd—the fleeting revealer of the split experience of post-Newtonian temporality itself. The "Vision of Mirzah" in *Spectator* 159 evinces a historical conception of a man ambiguously condemned to play out the role of a terrestrial animal after the revelation of an infinite, differentiated cosmos, in which he is relegated to a very small and illusionary corner.

The first vision granted to Mirzah by the shepherd Genius is of a bridge to nowhere—riddled with small distractions, mundane forms of torture, and trapdoors—over a vast sea: the mortal scale of a busy society, structuring and absorbing human lives within its own close architecture of time. Everyone falls through the bridge at some point, and some are swept across a clouded expanse into an infinite ocean spotted with countless shining paradisiacal islands. The islands, the Genius explains, are "the Mansions of good Men after Death, who according to the Degree and Kinds of Virtue in which they excelled, are distributed among these several Islands. . . . Every Island is a Paradise accommodated to its respective Inhabitants." When Mirzah asks the Genius to show him the other half of the ocean, to which the less-good half of the human race is condemned, the Genius and his vision disappear: "instead of the rolling Tide, the arched Bridge, and the happy Islands, I saw nothing but the long hollow Valley of *Bagdat*, with Oxen, Sheep, and Camels, grazing upon the Sides of it."[45] Mirzah's moment of revelation, closing then like a theatrical illusion, implicates the world to which he returns (from which he never left) as a new kind of hell. Only remembered symbolic architecture—the bridge to nowhere—lifts human life to a level of meaningful striving, but even that transcendental architecture is largely an architecture of delusion. Everyone must walk forward on the London Bridge commute, but there is no sense to the required direction of the herd; what matters is only to be good in the midst of the torturing illusion.

In a way that corresponds with Addison's status as Whig writer and propagandist, the vision presents no real solution (hence its Orientalized displacement) but a new problematic, in which the grazing domestic animals become the embodiment and reminder of an eternally repetitive, parochial, nonprogressive life. Lacking technological, theatrical prostheses, the domestic animal does not trade in visions. It has only one: a singular terrestrial landscape, on the margins of which it consumes. The Whiggish ideal, in contrast, held forth a new imperial, cosmopolitan merger between trading ventures, liberation, and nation. In homology with an expanded, acentric, evolving cosmos interpellated into human experience by the abstract revelations of technology and middling experiments, Hobbes's sovereign Artificial Man was to be disrupted and remade by the business of shipping and integrated, exotic exchange. The vision of socially transformative transcendence and middle-class nationalism was still inchoate: it would bloom much later with the industrial Romanticism of the elder Goethe's Faust, who represented the liberated energy of free people constantly negotiating exchange and resynthesized world-pictures as they came and went from all directions over the globe, the shadow cleared from the final overbright stage lights.

The metatheatrical Faust myth reflected ambivalence about the growing theatricalization and marketization of society, two coemerging and intimately related historical processes in England. At first temporally and physically confined regions of suspicion where different social orders and relationships to truth were tolerated, markets and theaters—where a seductive stranger might sell glimpses of an eccentric world—became more and more constant, necessary presences in the world of the English subject. In the eighteenth century, Agnew argues, the market became virtually omnipresent, effectively theatricalizing society. The feudal subject, reimagined as a kind of domestic animal or slave (see chapter 3), was transformed via the promise of the market. That promise entered his or her daily life to an extent that was legally, physically, and practically proscribed before. The spreading technique of marketing—with its impossible guarantees, wild tales from faraway, and exaggerated claims about relatively tiny objects—theatricalized life, at first disruptively and then increasingly more ontologically.[46] The unsettling, daemonic stranger-salesman of Marlowe's marginalized traveling markets became Mirzah's entrancing Genius: a good merchant whose services must be attracted and valued highly if a society or an individual was to gain in knowledge, prestige, and spiritual truth.

By the early eighteenth century in Britain, the scene of the market was everywhere expanding and diffusing into the "eternal" picture of feudal and domestic life, accelerating modernity's theatrical constitution: the sense was growing that any place or time could be instantly revealed as a very different place or time altogether.[47] In contrast, the Oriental landscape of the Spectator-Mirzah's mystical tale sketched an old theological understanding of life on Earth as a staging ground for ultimate judgment, with hell and paradise discreet spaces generally outside our mortal purview. But in Addison's modern theological revision, hell was replaced by the unchanging terrestrial ground of the animal. Only the spell of a Genius could split that persistent mild purgatory of mortal life, the timeless pastoral scene of classical and biblical myth.[48] The merchants' product was no longer a delusive analgesic. It was becoming a necessary cure, a curtain pulled open on truth: to frame and undo the meager, contingent enchantment of society's theatrical life (a temporary show) and to reveal the eternal paradises of individual self-fulfillment.

In his more ordinary incarnation as the eidolon of the everyday, Mr. Spectator's marvelings were not on abstruse conversations with vanishing desert spirits but on the real new seeing of natural philosophers peering through the latest telescopes and microscopes, theatrically reconstituting modernity by revealing scales and vistas previously veiled from human consciousness. For Addison, the great herald, Genius, or hawker of modernity was Isaac Newton. As an adolescent boarder in the practically magical space of an apothecary shop, Newton had taken the Faustian path toward obsessive, secretive, and lonely study and alchemical investigations.[49] The pragmatism of his working, middling background shone through, however, in the tight solidity of his empirical and mathematical proofs. Those proofs greatly facilitated the era's decisive intellectual break with the Aristotelian-Ptolemaic system that had seemed certain for many centuries and whose gradual fading as a satisfying explanatory theory over the previous century had already troublingly undermined general confidence in reason's power. This historic "loss of intellectual security" was ameliorated by the innovatively convincing modern form of Newton's proofs and their positing of a new universal system of mathematical laws over the now cognitively enlarged vacuums of space.[50] Newton's calculations signaled verifiable confirmation of the Platonic-Cartesian cosmography and the inception of a new age of reason, a Restoration and Settlement of a century of discursive warfare, anxiety, and doubt.

Just as the forming Modernist literary canon elided Addison's contributions from view, the corresponding, contemporaneously forming "history of ideas" inaugurated by Lovejoy's work on the Great Chain of Being suppressed Newton's profound contribution to the modern cosmographic shift. In analogous fashion to Addison being relegated in the literary field to the status of a middling, lesser popularizer (in contrast to Shaftesbury, Pope, and Swift), Newton became in the history of philosophy a kind of tinkering, calculating workhorse enabling the smooth elite Cartesian transition from Aristotle to modern Platonism. Underthought in Modernist discourse was the radical performative element of both men's work. Their impactful cultural interventions were more than well-accomplished feats of public engineering, marketing a pre-agreed intellectual historical shift of influence. They represented more so the rising of a new kind of sovereignty, signified in effigy by the middling scientist and the popular political writer-for-the-masses arriving among the ghosts of Westminster Abbey. The foundational gesture of what would become Addison's ideal of sociability was arguably already encoded in the sentence that Newton inscribed above the first page of his early experimental notebook: *Amicus Plato amicus Aristoteles magis amica veritas*, "I am a friend to Plato and Aristotle, but my greatest friend is Truth."[51] Problematizing Lovejoy's narrative of a social and institutional shift between opposed neoclassicisms, Newton's declaration signaled a different paradigm. It was not one of elite people making points in a centuries' old debate, but one of an emerging, far-flung community of lonely devotees to individual reason, social enough to follow and discuss the old discourses but asocial enough to insist on the primacy of their singular, reasoned judgments.

The historiographically suppressed celebration of both men's work in their time is shadowed by the forgotten pathos that went along with their works' contemporaneous reception. The new surety provided by Newton's proofs in his *Principia,* which contained the universal law of gravitation, came with a different difficult-to-swallow epistemological pill on top of his optical work's overturning previous ideas about human vision. His elaboration of the Copernican system and demonstration of its convincing predictive capacities assumed the earth as a useful provincial laboratory from which to draw conclusions about the mechanically unfolding events of the larger universe. Crucial to this assumption was that the emergence of material systems, like the solar system, within absolute space was a relatively rare and sporadic event. In the new theory, the time of material existence—a totality that far exceeded human experience—was itself extremely odd and limited. The Newtonian system's restoration of human intellectual security came, paradoxically, at the price of positing the actual human position on the fringes of a vast, contingent universe.[52] Just under its surface, the early eighteenth-century celebration of renewed stability and confidence in mankind's ability to reason was bedeviled by the continued epistemological threat of endless disruptive successions as well as by the new existential reality of the solar system and all its wondrous times and sites (e.g., terrestrial life) being such a small and brief sideshow that a busy Deity might reasonably pay it little—if any—mind. If the Newtonian settlement was then taken as a model, what was exposed, transhistorically speaking, was the persistent underlying loss of legitimacy to *any* claim of sovereign knowledge in such a radically shifting universe.[53] As Addison's contemporary Shaftesbury put it, the earth that we experience is "a mere point still, a very nothing compared to what remains . . . only a separate by-world . . . in the wild waste." At some point, "Old Father Chaos" would "by a furious inroad recover his lost right," ending our accidentally ordered world.[54]

DIFFERENT COSMIC LENSES

A hint of this shadow to rational progress can be read in the work of Addison's close poetic colleague and sometimes friend Alexander Pope. Utilizing the

Great Chain of Being motif, the Tory-leaning Pope wrote in *An Essay on Man* that angelic superior beings,

> when of late they saw
> A mortal Man unfold all Nature's law,
> Admir'd such wisdom in an earthly shape,
> And shew'd a NEWTON as we shew an Ape.[55]

In the opening dedication of that work (to the former Tory leader and repentant Jacobite, Lord Bolingbroke), Pope wrote:

> The science of Human Nature is, like all other sciences, reduced to a *few clear points:* There are not *many certain truths* in this world. It is therefore in the anatomy of the Mind as in that of the Body; more good will accrue to mankind by attending to the large, open, and perceptible parts, than by studying too much such finer nerves and vessels, the conformations and uses of which will for ever escape our observation. The *disputes* are all upon these last, and I will venture to say, they have less sharpened the *wits* than the *hearts* of men against each other, and have diminished the practice more than advanced the theory of Morality. If I could flatter myself that this Essay has any merit, it is in steering betwixt the extremes of doctrines seemingly opposite; in passing over terms utterly unintelligible; and in forming a *temperate* yet not *inconsistent,* and a *short* yet not *imperfect* system of Ethics.[56]

As so often in early-eighteenth-century writing, the passage above alludes to the haunting specter of dispute turning "the hearts of men against each other" in order to justify the attempt, for which Addison was frequently given the highest credit, at striking a tone and goal of moderation that would avoid the conflagration of civil war and discord. Pope's epistemological conclusion was not unlike Addison's in its declaration of the harmful prodigality risked in studying matters either too small or too large. Although the latter wrote (in *Tatler* 216) that he "would not discourage any Searches that are made into the most minute and trivial Parts of the Creation," Addison warned often against "the Mind of Man, that is capable of so much higher Contemplations" becoming "fixed upon such mean and disproportioned Objects."[57] Scientific realism meant for both poets the need and wisdom for humans to remember their scale. Yet Pope's *Essay on Man* exhibits a conservatism (befitting the author's Catholic Tory politics) that would short-circuit the insights of present and future science to arrive back at a stable ethics and catechism of eternal truths, a certain demand that all times rhyme. For Pope, the mass-marketing of Newton's theater of glasses was a sociologically dangerous experiment.

Addison's imperial, Protestant Whig politics matched, on the other hand, his essays' more enthusiastic—though still ambivalent—exploration of scientific discovery and embrace of the plenitude of new worlds that science would continually reveal.[58] In prose, Addison was willing to revel in the extremes of technological sensory prosthesis and the conjectures to which it led him. Like a good Whig, however, all his far-out expeditions were bent in the end toward a stable, classical, epistemological home: progress was, as it had always been, an eternal feature of the world, not the old world's overturning. The difference between Pope and Addison in this regard can be plainly laid out with a brief comparison of their different employment of the Great Chain of Being.

The first epistle of Pope's *An Essay on Man* sermonizes against pride. Although his intent may have been to deliver a moderate response to the intellectual crises brewing around the new science and its opponents, Pope's version of moderation lands fairly far on the side of rejecting the notion of scientific progress and the permeability of spheres of experience. In so doing, the satirized "wiser thou" of his poem could be read as Addison himself, a man who before his death had become an embittering rival for Pope and the direct replacement in the high ranks of government for Pope's addressee, Bolingbroke. The *Essay* was published in 1733, fourteen years after Addison's death, but with Addison's reputation still high, Pope's poem performed as a political corrective to the dominant Protestant Whig ideology for which Addison had secured overweening influence.

Rather than Addison's urging toward cheerful action, a progressive modernity, and a new sovereignty constructed from trade and global exchange, Pope's poem urged submission to higher order, action only inside one's designated sphere, and a caution against overoptimism in trade and notions of improvement. Like the weather, Pope argued, so the mind of man: one cannot realistically expect the Addisonian citizen, "Men for ever temp'rate, calm, and wise."[59] His ambitious fellow citizens had forgotten the humility of their ever-returning nature:

> In Pride, in reas'ning Pride, our error lies;
> All quit their sphere, and rush into the skies.
> Pride still is aiming at the blest abodes
> Men would be Angels, Angels would be Gods.
> Aspiring to be Gods, if Angels fell,
> Aspiring to be Angels, Men rebel.[60]

The age of telescopes and microscopes that shattered the Aristotelian orbs in Addison's 1693 oration is for Pope no real progress but an age of delusion. The strolling Spectator found overwhelming positive sentiment in the noisy peace of markets: those interdependent shrines of cosmopolitan consumption summoned forth cheerful citizens of the world with an intelligent taste for products that eased the peculiar disadvantages of their particular climates. One's identity was to grow in richness and complexity with an ever-wider perception and experience of the faraway and the different. The speaker of Pope's essay, on the other hand, urged a turning away from the theatrical ambiguity of progressive hybridity and scientific extension. Instead, one should submit to one's fate in the fixed sphere—of species, world, scale, and country—to which a higher order assigned one.

> The bliss of Man (could Pride that blessing find)
> Is not to act or think beyond mankind;
> No pow'rs of body or of soul to share,
> But what his nature and his state can bear.
> Why has not Man a microscopic eye?
> For this plain reason, man is not a Fly.[61]

Each system, in Pope's view, must operate independently in its own sphere, or risk the destruction of the whole. It is "absurd for any part to claim / To be another, in this gen'ral frame."[62] Distinctions must be recognized and upheld, as in the Great Chain, so in the society and the mind:

> What thin partitions Sense from Thought divide?
> And Middle natures, how they long to join,
> Yet never pass th' insuperable line![63]

The referents of Pope's speaker slip somewhat ambiguously between the concrete and the allegorical, the psychological and the concrete, the theological, philosophical, political, and sociological. In the longing of "middle natures" who never finally cross the decisive line, one could read an indictment of the Addisonian sentimental mix of emotion and thought, never ultimately being either. As the following stanza makes clear, one must also read an advocacy of turning away from "pressing" or revolutionary energies toward the decision to suffer the unavoidable passions of acting one's natural, prescribed part in an established hierarchical chain—animal, human, angel; serf, vassal, lord.

In contrast, Addison's cosmography, distilled in *Spectator* 519, began with the subtle affirmation of a dualistic perspective. The material universe, "that System of Bodies into which Nature has so curiously wrought the Mass of dead Matter," could maintain a provisional independence from the spiritual.[64] Unburdened by prohibitive spheres or the psyche's provinciality, "dead Matter"—though "only the Shell of the Universe"—provided a shared commons, a kind of interstate highway on which many species and angelic forms could theoretically and relativistically share points of perspective. Pope also noted the diversity of traditionally known sensing beings and worlds of different scales, but in Addison words of commonality and abundance slipped in floods past the old Aristotelian censors, charged with the excitement of a just dawning scientific age: "Every part of Matter is peopled," Addison's Spectator declared. "There is scarce a single Humour in the Body of a Man, or of any other Animal, in which our Glasses do not discover Myriads of living Creatures." His sometimes ecstatic extrapolation of new telescopic and microscopic discoveries projected a relative universe of life-forms at every scale, on every surface, "Beings adapted to their respective Situations."[65]

Unlike Pope's later cautionary *Essay,* Addison's cosmological statement was a theological celebration of fluid multiplicity. "The exuberant and overflowing Goodness of the Supreme Being," was evidenced by "his having made so very little Matter, at least what falls within our Knowledge, that does not Swarm with Life: nor is his Goodness less seen in the Diversity, than in the Multitude of living Creatures." A particular existential fate was not a crystalline prison to which one must submit but a fine subjective glass through which to temporarily encounter a common universe: the good Supreme Being "*specified* in his Creation every degree of Life, every Capacity of Being. The whole Chasm in Nature, from a Plant to a Man, is filled up with diverse Kinds of Creatures, rising one over another, by such a gentle and easie Ascent, that the little Transitions and Deviations from one Species to another, are almost insensible. This intermediate Space is so well husbanded and managed, that there is scarce a degree of Perception which does not appear in some one part of the World of Life."[66]

Addison's gospel of progressive plenitude, like Pope's ode to resignation, attempted to make the gaps genitive of God. Though both men insisted on a hierarchical arrangement, the material construction of the "chain" for Pope was more like a strand of inviolable individual pearls, only God providing the fine string of connection. For Addison the "chain" was more like an enfolded fabric of microscopic gold links, God's handiwork visible as an intricate, minutely interlocking design: through the electric intertwining of different scales, a soul's progress might indeed range from the dregs of the material world to the more universe-spanning flights of angels. The whole itself was not fixed in one permanent state but might bloom and bloom again like an eternal coffee flower, beauty and perfection without limit. While not denying abysses and distances in the Great Chain, Addison's Whig cosmography followed Locke in positing that the gaps between man and angel or plant and animal and man were rather flexible and full of intermediates. Pope's "insuperable line," a gap of a different order, lay in Addison's revised cosmography only between "the highest created Being, and the Power which produced him."[67] The universe of social life, on the shell of dead matter, was an interconnected, open order, assured of a certain imperfect egalitarianism by the primary gap between that teeming plenitude and the lonely monarch-creator spectating from afar.

Pope and Addison's competing renderings of the Great Chain of Being are paradigmatic for reactionary-versus-progressive responses to novel epistemological challenge. The Newtonian revolution troubled people in the era with the cold awareness that even the most ingenious human architectures of knowledge would only ever give them "partial, provisional glimpses of larger truths."[68] This prompted from Pope a strain of submissive nihilism that propped itself up on a traditional hierarchy and a fixed, eternal frame for understanding a zero-sum world. The same intellectual revolution prompted Addison's textual performance of bullishly embracing slippery infinite scales and a temporally progressive, never statically perfect, potential bettering of the whole cosmos. This would happen, in his aesthetic vision, less through accepting the old limited spheres of action than through divinely interconnected individuals moving with some liberty across scales and places in pursuit of knowledge and virtue.

In keeping with this view, Addison was an epistemological optimist about scientific prosthesis, believing, at times, nature to be somewhat benevolently concealing herself behind veils. In *Tatler* 119, he wrote: "There is a great deal of Pleasure in prying into this World of Wonders, which Nature has laid out of Sight, and seems industrious to conceal from us. Philosophy had ranged over all the visible Creation, and began to want Objects for her Enquiries, when the present Age, by the Invention of Glasses, opened a new and inexhaustible Magazine of Rarities, more wonderful and amazing than any of those which astonished our Forefathers." At his most scientifically ecstatic he imaged the modern universe made visible by new optical instruments as "a Variety of Worlds and Suns placed one above another, and rising up to such an immense Distance, that no created Eye can see an End of them."[69] But these isolated moments of rhapsody could be misleading if not contextualized in the larger fabric of his work, which, like Pope's, was haunted also by the darker revelation of human reason's deceptive contingency.

For Addison, this grappling was more historically specific than a general intellectual reckoning with the immensity of the cosmos. In *Spectator* 565, he marked this difference by juxtaposing the biblical King David's humility before the Heavens—composed relatively neatly of the Moon and the Stars—with the Spectator's latter-day consideration of "that infinite Hoste of Stars, or, to speak more Philosophically, of Suns. . . . with those innumerable Sets of Planets or Worlds, which were moving round their respective Suns." Extending the modern cosmography hypothetically to "another Heaven of Suns and Worlds rising still above this which we discovered," he reasoned that if the Earth's Sun and all its planets were "utterly extinguished and annihilated, they would not be miss'd more than a grain of Sand upon the Sea-shore." The result was a "secret Horror" of his status as a being "afraid of being overlooked . . . and lost among that infinite Variety of Creatures, which in all Probability swarm through all these immeasurable Regions of Matter."[70] Where once a storied king had been sovereign over a world dwarfed by its attendant heavens was now a perhaps unwitnessed, middling creature, somewhere: the heavens themselves were likely mostly elsewhere, out of even telescopic sight. And sight itself, of course, had been revealed by Newton to be a way of knowing radically contingent to peculiar existence on a clumped happenstance of matter, the human mother planet. Another dramatic figure began to reemerge as the emblem of the modern sovereign: the blind, decrowned Oedipus, dying invisibly in an unknown location. Even the "good" afterlife revealed to Mirzah was an endless ocean landscape of separate islands, each shaped contingently to match its inhabitant's idea of the good: this was no vision of shared full communion but rather a horizontal paradise still eternally, epistemologically conscribed. If on earth we were no better than momentarily saved by Providence from drowning in an unpredictable, chaotic sea, in heaven our best reward would be a bespoke resort for self-optimization in a calmer section of the same separating water superintended by the same distant Supreme Being.[71]

AFFIRMING SENSORIOLA—THE SOCIABLE CONTRACT

In *Spectator* 121, Addison allegorized the human condition under the shadow of general epistemological relativity through his description of a mole's life. "Her Eye," Addison wrote of the excavating rodent, "is said to have but one Humour in it, which is supposed to give her the Idea of Light, but of nothing else, and is so formed that this Idea is probably painful to the Animal. Whenever she comes up into broad Day she might be in danger of being taken, unless she were thus affected by a Light striking upon her Eye and immediately warning her to bury her self in her proper Element. More Sight wou'd be useless to her, as none at all might be fatal."⁷²

Seeing Providence's work in even such "Blemishes" as the mole's blindness, Addison turned his readers' attention to gratitude for "the several Endowments which it has variously bestowed upon such Creatures as are more or less refined and compleated in their several Faculties, according to the Condition of Life in which they are posted."⁷³ Despite the positivistic redirection, the harsh allegorical light thrown upon the blind human sensory system could not, perhaps, be reburied. In a later *Spectator* issue (565), he equated the sensory experiences of humans and "brutes" in their diminutive scale below the "insuperable line," coining a new English word from Newton's original mint: "The noblest and most exalted way of considering [the new cosmography's] infinite Space is that of Sir *Isaac Newton,* who calls it the *Sensorium* of the Godhead. Brutes and Men have their *Sensoriola,* or little *Sensoriums,* by which they apprehend the Presence, and perceive the Actions of a few Objects contiguous to them. Their Knowledge and Observation turns within a very narrow Circle." Robbed of a premodern world-picture that at least had the condescending grace to shroud the universe's unfathomable scale from sight and understanding, Mr. Spectator ends his meditation on our species being lost in vast space by identifying with Job's despair and inability to find God in the physical world: he must rely on faith and reason to be assured of his omnipresence and omniscience.⁷⁴ Both modern and biblical heroism meet horrible loss and abandonment with a faithfully (Stoic) resolve to nevertheless rebuild something positive within the harshly limited human *Sensoriolum.*

One origin of what Eliot called the "priggishness" of Addison's essays was their attempt to construct a social consensus over a new and yawning epistemological abyss. The world of the eighteenth century was pre-Modern in its lacking the large industrial machinery driving the masses, a machinery that Eliot and his compatriots could hardly slow down, stop, or fail to rely upon. Where we turn on the television for Addison was just the air and Newtonian silence. Human effort—the decision—was still the motor that made society work or not, and a convincing code of behavior required a certain stridency and social consensus where no philosophical match could be found between the world of the relativized senses and the proven cosmos of infinite scales. Addison and Steele's discipline in steadily bringing forth Mr. Spectator to imaginatively walk the London streets six days a week performed a daily exercise of reliable self- and society-composition, starting a new discursive engine of orientation on our planet that began to teach us how to become, as if automatically, a modern diurnal collective.⁷⁵

In *Spectator* 465, Addison directly connected ideological decision and individual regulation of life with the abstruse, proven conclusions of Newton's new calculus:

> Nothing is more laudable than an Enquiry after Truth, so nothing is more irrational than to pass away our whole Lives, without determining our selves one way or other in those Points which are of the last Importance to us. There are indeed many things from which we may with-hold our Assent; but in Cases by which we are to regulate our Lives, it is the greatest Absurdity to be wavering and unsettled, without closing with that Side which appears the most safe and the most probable. . . . It is in this manner that the Mathematician proceeds upon Propositions which he has once demonstrated, and tho' the Demonstration may have slipt out of his Memory, he builds upon the Truth, because he knows it was demonstrated.[76]

The argument, with its citation of the general Socratic procedure, spoke to Addison and his compatriots' Job-like understanding of the frightening potential randomness of human knowledge and decision: the requirement of a resolute, theatrical artificiality in faithfully walking forward, exercising a somewhat arbitrary sovereignty over their own lives.

A mind trained to cling rationally to the esoteric truth of the new natural philosophy would struggle to find a corresponding coherence or symmetry in the bustling spaces of human civilization. One antidote was Addison's prescribed (proto-Romantic) practice of retiring from sociality to commune with unreformed nature.[77] "In Courts and Cities," he wrote in the same essay,

> we are entertained with the Works of Men, in the Country with those of God. One is the Province of Art, the other of Nature. Faith and Devotion naturally grow in the Mind of every reasonable Man, who sees the Impressions of Divine Power and Wisdom in every Object on which he casts his Eye. The Supream Being has made the best Arguments for his own Existence, in the Formation of the Heavens and the Earth, and these are Arguments which a Man of Sense cannot forbear attending to, who is out of the Noise and Hurry of Human Affairs.[78]

Had Addison given in to his "Romantic" side, the Enlightenment would have lost one of its strongest advocates, perhaps to obscurity. He felt, indeed, the temptation: "He who reads over the pleasures of a country life as they are described by Virgil," he wrote ironically in his 1697 preface to Dryden's translation of the *Georgics,* "can scarce be of Virgil's mind in preferring even the life of a philosopher to it."[79] But an opposed choice between artificial cultural production and natural divine wonder was too facile for the era of Newtonian neoclassicism. Addison performed rather the difficult, tenuous, two-way work of keeping "human constructions and institutions in touch with nature."[80] Art and philosophy were, after all, crucial guides and prods toward a life of liberty and truth. Likewise, the nature that one could see with one's unadorned eyes was, in a sense, nothing but the illusionary art of a particular, human sensoriolum.

Perhaps it was this turn in the dialectic of his thought that caused Addison to skip the famous opening line of Psalm 19 in his own poetic adaptation, with which he ended *Spectator* 465. Leaving out "The Heavens declare the Glory of God," Addison opened not with direct divine bombast but with the subtler, framed firmament showing the handiwork of God, as a remote copy:

> The Spacious Firmament on high,
> With all the blue Etherial Sky,
> And spangled Heav'ns, a Shining Frame,
> Their great Original proclaim:
> Th'unwearied Sun, from day to day,
> Does his Creator's Pow'r display,
> And publishes to every Land
> The Work of an Almighty Hand.[81]

The sky—like the paper on which the copy of *The Spectator* was printed and distributed in the arduous performance of regularity and dailiness—read as a proof of higher order. Yet Addison's psalm was not a mere poetic reinterpretation of the original, but an updating of its spirit in Newton's light. A secondary, framed proclamation rather than a primary declaration spoke to post-Newtonian humans, who existed now on the fringe of the universe and whose enlightenment depended on decoding distant, strange, and more general truth from within a limited, distorted sensoriolum. The second verse likewise avoided the certain direct divine connection of the standard Prayer Book psalm. Instead of one night certifying another, Addison merely staged the paradigmatically beautiful, reflective moon taking up the secondary tale, headlining the night show with "the Story of her Birth," while a chorus of stars and planets appeared illusorily around her to confirm the "Tidings"—the language playfully overemphasizing the planetary confines and plain geological processes of the spectator's position.

While the biblical psalmist had praised the vast but largely earthbound dominions of God, Addison's third verse performed a crucial zoom-out befitting eighteenth-century awareness of a larger acentric cosmos:

> What though, in solemn Silence, all
> Move round the dark terrestrial Ball?
> What tho' nor real Voice nor Sound
> Amid their radiant Orbs be found?[82]

Here Addison reworked as questions the Prayer Book psalm's proud paradoxical assertion that in spite of the heavens lacking language and speech, their sound and words reached "the Ends of the World." Contrastingly, his rhetorical inquiries emphasize the troubling disjunction between the human sensory system and the reality of the larger universe, which was not really revolving around the peculiar happenstance of terrestrial existence. Earth's new known isolation among space and silence (the negative to the exuberance of positivistic plenitude) problematized a celebration of theological certainty. What remained, as conclusion, was not an assumed universal experience of the heavens leading inevitably to a feeling of divine grandeur but, in its place, an affirmation of reason's triumph over the senses. The eternal crystalline orbs, transformed physically into mere provisional orbits of mute faraway masses, had a second life as patterns revealing abstract law and design to thought, if no longer directly to the physical bodies and senses of earthly creatures. No longer resounding obviously with clear declaration, "In Reason's Ear they all rejoice, / And utter forth a glorious Voice."[83] Abstract reason as a prosthetic, intermediate sense organ was to save the human world from becoming lost in vast, asocial contingency.

FINDING GEORGIC GROUND

One of the manifestations of Addison's extensive popularity in both the eighteenth and nineteenth centuries was the use of this concluding poem from *Spectator* 465 as the lyrics for a widely sung nineteenth-century hymn. The music for the hymn was taken from the oratorio, *The Creation*, by the Austrian composer Franz Joseph Haydn, who had followed in the tradition of Addison's contemporary theatrical competitor, Handel, by composing for English audiences. Haydn's music was full of passionate color and thundering, cascading mimeses of natural and theological themes; one can hear in it the attenuated Classical passage from the age of the Baroque to the Romantic. As something of an anti-Romantic gesture, the replacement of the original *Cre-*

ation lyrics with Addison's text in nineteenth-century hymn books showed the enduring affinity between Addison's worldview and that of religious readers and singers. The textual passage from Haydn's oratorio erased in the hymn books by Addison's poem concerned the end of the fourth day, in which God created the heavenly bodies. Concluding part 1 of the oratorio, a trio sang a paraphrase of Psalm 19, rendered "In all the land resounds the word, / never unperceived, / Ever understood," a phrasing that contextually carries a Christological implication, linking the Hebrew psalmist to the universal claims of the Christian gospel. Colin Jager analyzes the Haydn libretto (whose author remains unknown) as "an amalgam of *Paradise Lost* and the early chapters of Genesis," whose "basic energies are decidedly those of natural theology: inductive, reasonable, and confident."[84]

The relativistic questions of Addison's text, on the other hand, do not afford the same bombastic performance of confidence in answer but rather a more restrained assertion of the right or necessity to celebrate reason's more abstruse conclusions. Poised between two historical forms of denial reactions—on the one hand, the passionately regressive embrace and earthy reaffirmation of gothic sensuality (Romanticism) and, on the other, the conservative disavowal of the novelty and validity of scientific discovery—the Addisonian discourse risked the priggishness or timidity of sentimentality to chart a moderate course. Eliot's later attempt to bury the literary totem Addison (who had been a grandfather to Romanticism, as Haydn had been a father) by arguing for a return to the maze of (Catholic) Baroque feeling was anticipated in Freud's century-turning, neoclassical 1900 epigraph to *The Interpretation of Dreams*. There, Freud declared with Virgil's Juno: "If I cannot bend the Higher Powers, I will move the Infernal Regions."[85] Modernism, as announced by Freud, moled further into the psyche in an attempt to release the repressed libidinal energies that Romanticism's societal-level spasms had somehow failed to represent or satisfy. What remained haunting was the silent yet teeming Newtonian sky, the Father-God's higher heavenly array: an oppressive, detached, distant order, out of communion with human experience, an unbending impersonally physical architecture of power.

After Woolf's window on multiperspectival cosmopolitanism, Einstein's relativity, the later Freud's (Catonic) death drive, and the subsequently returning trauma of global war, we moderns, with Addison, are not so sure that our minds are the perfect fit with any objective cosmos. Addison's pre-Romantic, pre-Modernist emphasis on the societal recognition of space, nothingness, and the effort involved in designing a terrestrial architecture of behavior based not on affect but on reason may gain a quiet appeal, as it did for some denizens of the nineteenth century. Rather than being simply a rejected historical relic or counterexample for Modernism, Addison in fact prefigured the Modernist attempt to synthesize and moderate between gothic sensuality and reasonable perspectives on the alienated individual and society in an era of an acentric, technologized cosmos. Freud's epigraph, in this regard, is an invitation to connect Modernism's impulse to that of the neoclassical poet and journalist who was often hailed as a tender husbander of society, the British Virgil.[86] One of Addison's subtle yet consistent provocations was the emphasis he placed—against the dryer sublime of pure philosophical discourse—on the beauty and importance of directly accessible pleasures, the kind of pleasures that the living and working underdogs of society could find and cultivate in their own experience, quickly and for free.[87]

Of course, the reflective release of repressed libido—like the opportunity to spend hours on Freud's couch—arguably required a high degree of leisure, resources, and education. Addison's retirement plan, the purchase of an estate at Bilton two to three days travel from London, fulfilled his ambition to live in the model of "the Augustan statesman" who had a country seat to which a soft retreat from "Rome" was possible.[88] As a worker in an urban, elite, factional social world, he won the ability to afford limited escapes, and it is in his paeans to gardening that one finds him at his most personal, on his own, scaled paradisical island. The garden, whose philosophy he discussed in *Spectator* 477, was the site where an ideal balance between the wildness of nature and the elegancies of art could be practiced and worked out. Such a balanced garden-ideal was prefigured in *Tatler* 218, where Addison takes Isaac Bickerstaff, the journal's fictional author, on a stroll through the country to gain an outside perspective on the craze of trade, finance, politics, and scandal that so often dominated London professional life. Sheltering from a storm, Bickerstaff eavesdrops on a group of strangers in a house seeming to discuss nonsensical high-level secret intelligence or historical interpretations; it turns out they are actually opining about rare and expensive tulips carrying the famous names of past and present political leaders. Bickerstaff confesses that he remained immune to the strangers' "Tulippomania" and could not be brought to value a tulip according to its rarity or financial worth; instead he values the gaiety, color, and beauty of flowers that can be found just as easily or even more exquisitely in the common meadow, among daisies, violets, daffodils, and cowslips.[89]

As he would in his long meditations on medals and coins, so in his lonely musing on tulips Addison rejects the notion that the progress of science and engineering is more associated with increasing instrumentality and zero-sum games than it is with the increase of beauty and means toward sociable political goals. Through Bickerstaff, Addison reimagines the representative, elite primal scene of nascent capitalism—what is often taken to be the pivotal tableaux of his historical era—as a publicly accessible, outdoor Newtonian laboratory: "Sometimes I considered the whole Bed of Tulips, according to the Notion of the greatest Mathematician and Philosopher that ever lived, as a Multitude of Optick Instruments, designed for the separating Light into all those various Colours of which it is composed." The sublime of sophisticated art, like the highs and lows of financial charts or various royal courts, paled in a world redescribed analytically by Newton as a real theater of fantastic illusion. Validating again the quotidian, the earthy, and the freely abundant—so alien, artificial, and strange under the gaze of the new empirical science as any curated heightened reality—Bickerstaff focused his artificially tulip-sharpened vision on wildflowers. He "walked Home in this Temper of Mind through several Fields and Meadows with an unspeakable Pleasure, not without reflecting on the Bounty of Providence, which has made the most pleasing and most beautiful Objects the most ordinary and most common."[90]

Addison readers "learned to be both inside and outside at the same time," Ridout writes, adding: "They have learned to live and act as though they were invisible."[91] Eavesdropping and escaping into country fields with *The Tatler*'s Bickerstaff or walking anonymously through the man-made metropole with Mr. Spectator, readers were invited into a foundational fantasy of journalism, a new subjectivity mirrored in "the passive, anonymous, visually-oriented surrogate with no particular commitments," who, Anthony Pollock writes, "can appeal to a much wider demographic than more concretely embodied, discursive, and obviously opinionated personae."[92] Some recent critics like Ridout emphasize the particular privileged ("bourgeois") status of Mr. Spectator and his "Fraternity," whose way of life "leaves them at leisure to look at the world around them as a source of entertainment, rather than as a set of relationships in which they must participate in order to survive." Their "entertainment" aligned with their duty as neo-Platonic Guardians of the nation: living the freedom (*eleutheria*) from labor in order to study and determine the best politics of state.[93]

Yet imagining the Addison reader as a Guardian, who Socrates argued should be taught to perfect being *one* person from *one* particular place, highlights the other side of the reader's identification: not with an unmarked, ghostly bourgeois Spectator but with the everywhere spectated, with the living, bloom-like social body of changing individuals—artificially natural and naturally artificial—activated by Mr. Spectator's gaze and their daily habit of mass communal reading.[94] In this identification, readers also learned to disappear, but not as the featureless, walking, unitary sovereign eidolon. Instead, they disappeared back into the city as people who had been made visible as representatives of a particular mode of being in a set of historical circumstances. Rather than being absorbed only into the backstage stance of a universal, disinterested subject watching from a nontheatrical eternity, they had been finally seen as the hopelessly interested, hopelessly schematic and contingent actors they were. The change and progress of man-made, daily news-time made them part of this new kind of partial, programmed and reprogrammed universality. They were, as George Eliot would put it, a "mysterious mixture" behaving differently "under the varying experiments of Time."[95]

Bickerstaff taking in the garish Newtonian laboratory-garden and its incomprehensible political discourse, like the statue of the king overseeing the bustling international merchants at the Royal Exchange, was an emblem of the artificial human sovereign gazing upon the artificiality of its own most ideal or beautiful man-made construction.[96] The quintessence of science, for Addison and his first readers, revealed the empirical reality that human knowledge was mere art mirroring art and thus revealed again the necessity of faith exactly where one might have hoped to find godlike liberation.[97] This was and is not just a bourgeois position, since contemplation and the effort of constructing advanced world-pictures has never belonged only to the bourgeois. Instead, the subsequent victory of the bourgeois under the conditions of industrialization and the ability of those few humans directing massive projects of coordinated human activity organized around capital to effectively create an absorbing earthbound modern religion of materialism have fueled a critical drive to find the origins of such cynicism in a publication that first hooked readers on the sovereignty of manufactured time: *The Spectator*. But Addison was not such a cynic, flawed as he was (as we will see in the next chapter). Making astonishing tulips, seeing with eyes through elaborate glassworks, working out the strange, fixed destinies of gravitation—these were godly activities for Addison, but only in the sense of evincing a will to understand and grow closer to the "Supreme Being." If the activities of making and understanding were done wisely and reflectively, they showed with a plainness directly proportional to their genius their inadequacies, abysses, and paradoxes. They moved us forward and connected us to a larger, teeming, and fluid life-world and universe below the insuperable line, but they demonstrated in the self-aware fragility of their masterful constructions that, as he put it in *Spectator* 441, "we are under the Care of one who directs Contingencies."[98] The director was invisible but certainly no bourgeois.

Just as Addison imagined the statue-king's gaze over the Royal Exchange collecting the individually dispersed local values and knowledges of the world under a single, recombinatory point of oversight, so the work of Newton was gathering together an unprecedentedly far-reaching and powerful description of the cosmos—as demonstrably accurate as could be deduced within the human sensoriolum.[99] The historically and geographically local gravitational forces of these contexts—Newtonianism and British neoclassical imperialism—exerted strong pressures on Addison's work, as viewed from our later vantage point. They combined to form an influential yet alien aesthetic, a cold-reading Newtonian neoclassicism. The newness of Newtonianism for Addison and his contemporaries left important literary traces not often apparent to modern readers, who paradoxically experience a comforting intellectual home in dry Newtonian regularity after the unsettling twentieth-century revelations of relativity and quantum entanglement. In inverted historical fashion, modern readers generally find the nostalgic intellectual home of Addison and his contemporaries to be a major stumbling block in their appreciation of early eighteenth-century literary relics: sentimental neoclassicism and its accompanying stuffy ambience of judgmental, privileged decorum block the reading of texts that come off as stiff and pretentious exercises in form. Within our more high-tech, genetically engineered, historiographic lab distillations, the era of Newtonianism now appears like a nostalgic historic garden laboratory, full of gaudy, artificial flowers and incomprehensible concerns, but taking on the naturalized dross of wildflowers, formed in its own reality by the chaos of circumstance and the irrationality of conflicting human wills. In his staging of Bickerstaff's encomium to both the state-of-the-art analytical flowers and their divinely created, "simpler" and "extrahistorical" pastoral cousins, Addison offered another telescope in which to discover not a proto-master-of-the-universe but a noncontemporary contemporary.

In a Latin ode addressed to Thomas Burnet, a theologian whose famous work *A Sacred Theory of the Earth* was admired by Newton for its effort at syncretizing modern and classical natural philosophy and Christian doctrine, Addison asked, "Who is so steely in his stout heart that he does not walk in trembling with a timid foot, when you disclose the frail calamities of this treacherous world?"[100] Departing from his own syncretic theologian father's commitment to the Church, Addison performed his theatrical-political career in the self-expanding commons. A real-life eidolon of the commons, he roved like Bickerstaff and Mr. Spectator with understated boldness between administrativizing royal courts, publicizing private families, politicizing social and business clubs, and nationalizing wilderness gardens.

The gesture and persistence of Addison's ventures to open a middle space in culture, science, and government may read as charged with cloying normativity, moral self-righteousness, and simplifying sentimentality, per Eliot's general line of critique. But his efforts were received in his own time by others who knew that he walked, like them, newly empowered yet almost blind through an uncharted cosmography, only freshly, conceptually opened. The declamations of old Roman ghosts were conjured up in Addison's pages not out of bombast alone but out of a daily need for courage to tread a bit forward on a timid, poetic, creative foot, as imperial as that trek appears in certain crucially critical lenses, as ambiguously and incompletely emancipatory as was the poet and prosaist's quotidian work toward a middling peace.

3
Slavery in Addison's Discourse

> Imperial wonders raised on nations spoiled,
> Where mixed with slaves the groaning martyr toiled
> ... all her triumphs shrink into a coin.
> —Pope, "Epistle to Mr. Addison"

> In each how guilt and greatness equal ran,
> And all that raised the hero, sunk the man:
> Now Europe's laurels on their brows behold,
> But stained with blood, or ill exchanged for gold;
> Then see them broke with toils or sunk with ease,
> Or infamous for plundered provinces.
> —Pope, "Epistle IV," *Essay on Man*

LIBERTY'S SPLIT SCREEN

Addison's *Cato* provided a dramatic blueprint for the patriot-martyr of the eighteenth century, who would profess and sometimes demonstrate his or her willingness to die in the name of liberty. The expansion of liberty—one of the major projects of Enlightenment discourse—was a theme that Addison urged throughout his writing and worked for in his political life. In *Spectator* 287, he wrote: "Liberty should reach every Individual of a People, as they all share one common Nature; if it only spreads among particular Branches, there had better be none at all, since such Liberty only aggravates the Misfortune of those who are deprived of it, by setting before them a disagreeable subject of Comparison."¹ Striving for a sociable middle style, Addison often left certain key terms, like "a People," undefined or intentionally vague, allowing of a certain pragmatic flexibility. The conjunction of "a People" with "one common Nature" here, however, suggests that Addison had in mind a stable, hereditary, and probably geographically confined group as the social unit inside of which political liberty could and should be (universally) organized. This raises significant problems for contextually interpreting Addison's British Enlightenment concept of liberty into contemporary discourses of liberty, which assume multicultural nations, a globally mobile population, and well-established debates and principles concerning transnational human rights.

To make the quick-step of assuming Addison's vague notion of "a People" with "one common Nature" could be progressively mapped onto our modern notions of national citizenship or, even further, general human belonging would be too historically facile. Such an extension, however, would not run against the spirit of much of Addison's writing, which advocated consistently for cosmopolitan world-expansion, albeit—again problematically—a kind of expansion tinted strongly with British imperial colors. Addison viewed patriotism as a positive balancing passion between private/familial interest and an unrealistic universalism. In *Freeholder* 5, he advocated the feeling of kinship and desire to help the community into which one was born as natural and good, urging that people of all countries should practice patriotism as a means of making the human race happier overall: the reader should think of "what Opportunities he has of doing Good to his Native Country" rather "than to throw away his Time in deciding the Rights of Princes, or the like Speculations, which are so far beyond his Reach."²

Typical among many intellectuals of a time before industrial travel and telecommunications, at a crepuscular moment in the forming modern conceptions of race, Addison's discourses on national and ethnic differences assumed a "natural" working of climate, ecosystem, and tradition on the denizens of different countries and, implicitly then, a world of relatively stable local populations with relatively essential characteristics. Living in a different place and climate, he wrote, for instance, may cause "Alteration in the animal Spirits, and the Organs of Hearing.... The Sounds which the Ear has ever been most accustom'd to, insensibly conform the secret Texture of it to themselves, and wear in it such Passages as are best fitted for their own Reception." Of course, here again we find a typical Addisonian ambiguity. In stressing the biological developmental adaptability of the human organism and particularly the "secret Textures" of its sense organs to its environment, he also finds the origin of tragic inflexibilities of mind, culture, and taste, which then reinforce themselves even more detrimentally at the group level. "National Prejudice, and Narrowness of Mind, makes everything appear odd to us that is new and uncommon," leading to the common experience that "what is tuneful in one Country, is harsh and ungrateful in another."[3] Along the same ambiguous lines, he believed that the "tunefulness" of liberty was more likely to take hold in certain soils or bloods—the English type of both being the prime, most fertile example. Nonetheless, his cosmopolitan advocacy of liberty was flexible and optimistic; climate, culture, history, and blood were less important in producing liberty and enlightenment than a nondespotic government that took care of the needs and wants of its people.[4]

A related large problem for modern critics of Addison's discourse on liberty presents itself only invisibly: through the absence of essays from Addison addressing the epoch's growing British participation in African chattel slavery. His silence here is specifically noteworthy. Although his strongest loyalties may have lain with British men of different classes, he was not reticent about the need for liberation among other types of people. The emancipation of women and non-British Europeans were topics that Addison approached again and again, often with notable condescension but without significant reserve. Since a strengthened discourse of liberty was one of Addison's most important legacies—shaping the revolutionary births, negotiated constitutions, and performative legacies of not just particular nations but of the modern nation-state more generally—it is important to critically read the absence of his addressing racialized slavery. This chapter attempts to contextualize that speaking silence via its particular genealogy in British historiography and politics, shadowed as they were already at Addison's birth by the growth of the transatlantic slave trade.

A key component of Addison's ideal of sociability was his belief in the efficacy and importance of representation. After the previous century's revolution, civil wars, commonwealth, monarchical restoration, and parliamentary coup (the "Glorious Revolution"), Addison was convinced that the formality of political representation had good effects upon society, most basically in sublimating group conflicts away from outright violence. Expanded political representation was the best way to guarantee liberty for an entire body politic. In *Spectator* 287, he wrote: "The greatest Security a People can have for their Liberty, is when the Legislative Power is in the Hands of Persons so happily distinguished, that by providing for the particular Interest of their several Ranks, they are providing for the whole Body of the People; or in other Words, when there is no part of the People that has not a common Interest with at least one part of the Legislators."[5] The period in England and Europe was one in which absolute monarchy and the hierarchized, centralized religious vision of Catholicism were often synonymous and collaborative: Hobbes's *Leviathan* stood as the philosophical monument to that seventeenth-century synthetic political "reunion," a reaction to the gruesome violence of religious civil war and the rise of Protestant democratic regimes.[6] Hobbes argued that individual liberty would be best preserved from the threat of invasion and internecine conflict by a social contract granting an absolute monarch power over a unified body of subjects. Against this ideology, Addison's Whiggish vision posited the good of a pluralistic, representative legislature to match a "Body of the People" that was not whole unless it consciously incorporated many parts and ranks as substantial, free equals.[7] Where this was not the case—for instance, in parts of the European continent where people still lived under singular rulers with sole ultimate legislative power—Addison contended that citizens were reduced to slaves. Even if the ruler were benign, allowing his subjects a fair degree of latitude and high levels of education, the true condition of slavery would persist. Such had been the case, Addison argued in *Spectator* 287, in Rome under Augustus and his imperial successors: unless the people governed themselves through a representative legislature, they would enter a depraved state of servitude that would lead eventually and inevitably to societal degeneration.

In contrast to Hobbes's nightmare of a general state of nature, in which an unceasing war of all against all raged, the scene of horror in Addison and his Whig compatriots' writings existed specifically in the alternative political arrangements of England's neighboring countries: in France, Italy, Spain, and much of Germany. When Addison wrote fervently of a slavery that must be abolished, he wrote concretely to motivate troops in an actual ongoing liberating war against what he termed "*European* Slavery."[8] This form of nearby, potentially encroaching or invading slavery was marked—from the Whiggish point of view—by the absence of representative, republican government and also by heavy restrictions on individuals' and corporations' rights to do business and use the profits as they pleased. "Riches and Plenty are the natural Fruits of Liberty," Addison wrote in *Spectator* 287, "and where these abound, Learning and all the Liberal Arts will immediately lift up their Heads and flourish."[9] Distributed wealth might not be exclusive to liberated societies and might not guarantee political emancipation, but while admitting this,

Addison declared faith in the virtuous circle: a politically liberated citizenry would produce the wealth that would in turn produce increasing political emancipation.

This second tenet of Whiggism—the virtuous circle of wealth creation—bred a conflict within the early British Enlightenment discourse of liberty that evinces itself in Addison's silence on heavy British participation in the slave trade. Almost from its beginning, the light of new modern British freedom so touted by the Whigs was critiqued for what and whom it left in the dark. Colonial subjects, women, non-English people, people of other races, castes of servants, and slaves all provided the hidden and coerced labor that belied much of the naturalness or truly liberating effects of Whiggish economic ascendancy. Addison's emancipatory efforts are troubled and shadowed by the plight of the groups mentioned above during the same decades when Addison and his readers were empowering themselves against conservative, Tory, aristocratic interests and people.[10]

The Whig discourse on liberty during the early eighteenth century thus had an importantly aporetic aspect. Grounded in classical legal theory, it performed a substantial and often convenient disconnect from certain then-present imperial, colonial, and economic practices. Elizabeth Maddock Dillon writes: "The enduring and intractable contradiction of the eighteenth-century Anglo-Atlantic world appears in the simultaneity of the growth of doctrines of political liberty and popular sovereignty, together with the advent of systems of enforced labor, enclosure, and violent dehumanization in the form of race slavery."[11] Though continuing and strengthening a neoclassical British discourse of liberty inherited from the previous century, Addison and many of his contemporaries were publicly reticent about increasing British participation in modern African chattel slavery, even while they administered state colonial ventures and profited from investments directly connected to the Atlantic slave trade.

ADDISON'S FEW WORDS ON ATLANTIC CHATTEL SLAVERY

Addison's writings kept the expanding cruel phenomenon of British slave-trading and slave-owning largely offstage, separated by the distance of oceans. He mentioned African chattel slavery in print very rarely and more or less anecdotally as part of the exotic mix of barbarism and civilization that characterized life in "our American Plantations." In *Spectator* 215, to note a rare instance, he related a disturbing and apocryphal story about two enslaved

Black men in the British Leeward Islands who murdered the woman of their mutual affection (also an enslaved Black person) in a confusing mix of passionate love and fidelity to their friendship. The fate of the murdering lovers, who died of self-inflicted wounds, was taken as an example of "Savage Greatness of Soul" mixed disastrously with passions "not regulated by Vertue, and disciplined by Reason." The horror fable proved the necessity of providing everyone, enslaved African people included, with a liberal education: the lovers' "Temper of Mind . . . might have produced very noble Fruits, had it been informed and guided by a suitable Education." Addison therefore counted it "an unspeakable Blessing to be born in those Parts of the World where Wisdom and Knowledge flourish," though he emphasized the need to expand educational opportunity in Britain.[12] Published on the morning after the annual Guy Fawkes Bonfire night, the grotesque fable may have been read as an allegory of unenlightened religious factions fighting over the nation and the right church, destroying all three parties in the process. In this sense, the essay functioned as part of Addison's general campaign to establish religious toleration, universal education, and nonviolent domestic "sympathy as a counter to zeal."[13]

The grisly colonial story was preceded by what was Addison's most direct appeal against the violence of racialized slavery: "What Colour of Excuse can there be for the Contempt with which we treat this Part of our Species; That we should not put them upon the common foot of Humanity, that we should only set an insignificant Fine upon the Man who murders them; nay, that we should, as much as in us lies, cut them off from the Prospects of Happiness in another World as well as in this, and deny them that which we look upon as the proper Means for attaining it?"[14] In context, the appeal builds on Addison's previous suggestion that British or European "Plebeans" and enslaved African people in the New World share a common nobility and tragic oppression: both are prevented from higher achievement by the injustice of their being denied an education. The message of reform and reconsideration stands in place of a clear call to end the practice of plantation slavery, and the essay's praise of enslaved Black people known through "frequent" hearsay to be so loyal to their masters that they commit suicide upon the death or change of their masters ambiguously muddles the picture of tortuous plantation life. The larger implications of the essay and of Addison's general thought seem bent against slavery and racist thought as dehumanizing practices. But a careful contemporary reader of *Spectator* 215—Addison's strongest comment on Atlantic chattel slavery—might have been left with the impression that a milder, more enlightened, and humane form of plantation slavery could rectify the moral problem to which the author was calling attention. Why did Addison fail to call clearly and unequivocally for the abandonment of the slave trade and the emancipation of enslaved people in the colonies?

In his discussion of recent critical readings of this essay, Brycchan Carey argues that Addison's relative silence on the African slave trade is partially explained by the nonexistence of an organized antislavery movement in Britain in 1711. The energy for such a moment did not materialize earlier because Britain was perceived as "just one minor participant in a universal slave trade rather than its main protagonist"; this perception only changed after the 1713 Treaty of Utrecht, through which Spain awarded Queen Anne and her realm the previous French monopoly on shipping enslaved people to its American colonies. The critical consensus Carey analyzes agrees that Addison displayed a typical colonialist mindset in his call for European education of non-European people but that he was also typical among progressive, popular writers of his time and place in his overall failure to stake out a repeated and unambiguous stance opposed to plantation slavery. Carey notes, however, that *Spectator* 215's plantation horror story would later reemerge in some of the century's most influential antislavery literature, which also sought to motivate their readers with the idea of converting enslaved African people into enlightened Christians.[15]

Ideas about slavery in general, race, and British colonial enterprises shifted dramatically in Addison's century and even more so afterward. One aspect of the common historical mindset in the early eighteenth century is, fortunately, particularly alien now to modern readers: the idea of enslavement as a normal, ubiquitous phenomenon to which all people were potentially subject. In his broad transhistorical study of slavery, Orlando Patterson argued that slavery has been more the universal norm in human experience than our current thinking would have us believe.[16] Before the advent of modern abolitionism in the mid-eighteenth century, the remarkably charged and atypical English discourse of slavery, which will be examined below, assumed slavery as relatively common *outside of England*. A survey of plays in the first half of the seventeenth century, for example, finds that, in keeping with "English letters in the period, the social phenomenon of slavery is neither censured nor condemned; it is simply displayed as an unappealing dimension of Christian experience in Christian but non-English lands."[17]

Addison's failure to distinguish chattel slavery as a particular historical atrocity can be partially explained as an effect of the general global, transhistorical ubiquity of slavery as a practice to which all were potentially subject. It can also be explained in the specific local context of the average British citizen's relationship to slavery gradually changing after the 1713 asiento from one of victimhood (via feudal structures and the threat of foreign invasion) to one of perpetration and profit (via racialization and colonial enterprise). On the other hand, Addison's relative silence on non-European slavery becomes more troubling when one considers that the peak of his public career took place around the years of the asiento, in which he held high-level political posts giving him substantial power and expertise in colonial affairs. Indeed, Addison's elite family and social circles connected him directly with American plantation ventures and the trading companies that provided those plantations with slave labor. His brother, Gulston, died in 1709 in Madras, where he had briefly served as the local governor and president of the British government, an appointment he likely owed to Joseph's support.[18] Two years before, Steele had inherited a Barbadian plantation with two hundred enslaved people from his deceased first wife.[19] We can expect, in other words, that Addison would have had more than common knowledge about the breadth and depth of British involvement in the transatlantic slave trade and, therefore, greater responsibility to inform the public about its horrors.

His satirical allegorical pamphlet, *The Trial of Count Tariff*, did in fact attack the 1713 asiento treaty, whose terms the presiding Tory ministry had negotiated. The pamphlet positioned Addison clearly *against* those—including Daniel Defoe—who advocated for the profitability and correctness of the newly opened slave trade. What the asiento offers to the British nation, he writes, is fraud and "worse than nothing."[20] In the pamphlet's argument, the entire scheme of importing foreign labor into the British colonies should be abandoned since it will come to no good—it is an elite, corrupt enterprise, foisted upon honest workers and common people, and tantamount to the British being seduced into taking over the known moral atrocities of the violently imperial Spanish. The *Trial*'s humorous satirical tone and its failure to develop a clear moral stance against the slave trade on the basis of the suffering of enslaved people leave in place an unsettling ambiguity about Addison's stance on the treaty. His moral and economic case against the asiento and the delusive greed it inspired, after all, is largely about the new trade's impact on *British* people.[21] It may indeed be a tragedy of history that Addison did not do what he might have done to more quickly set up abolitionist consciousness and an awareness of the expanding evils of Atlantic slavery. At the time, however, his pamphlet might have made the economic and moral argument with the best chance of timely political success in preventing the expansion of the British slave trade, even if he was not ultimately successful at blocking the treaty's ratification by the Tory-dominated government.

In discussions of Addison and Steele's work, historians like Joseph Roach have pointed out the harsh irony in Whiggish celebrations of exceptional British liberty articulated during years when British merchants were making unprecedented profits through the forced labor and tyrannically controlled lives of African people. Some historians believe that the fervor with which British Whigs and later white American patriots demanded and celebrated liberty arose in part out of the desire to repress and keep at a distance intolerably cruel racial politics, which had led directly to much of their new material prosperity. The noise of chains, guns, and whips from backstage demanded loud speeches and songs of freedom front and center. Roach quotes Toni Morrison's succinct formulation of this argument: "Nothing highlighted freedom—if it did not in fact create it—like slavery."[22]

Discussing the war veteran Steele's identification of the theater as a producer of a "free-born people," Roach argued that early-eighteenth-century England, in fact, remained in constant contact with racialized slavery. For Roach, the quintessential sites of Addison and Steele's enlightenment project, out of which their notion of a reformed theater sprung, were the London coffeehouses where patrons read and "refreshed themselves with stimulating beverages extracted from the labor of West Indian slaves." Roach pointed to advertisements for the sales of slaves in *The Tatler* as evidence for the tight imbrication of slavery and domestic, sociable sovereignty in Augustan England.[23] The theater scholar Robert D. Hume, taking issue with Roach's argument that Addison and Steele's thematization of freedom was powerfully shaped by unconscious racial guilt about slavery, pointed out that there was only one known advertisement (in the context of many hundreds of ads overall) for a slave sale in *The Tatler*.[24] That advertisement read: "A Black Indian Boy, 12 Years of Age, fit to wait on a Gentleman, to be disposed of at Denis's Coffee-house in Finch-Lane near the Royal Exchange."[25] In a purportedly comprehensive survey of "all the newspapers of the twelve years of Anne's reign," the Victorian historian John Ashton also reported finding only one advertisement pertaining to the sale of a slave. Although Ashton did not cite his source, the wording of the ad that he gave is notably similar: "A Negro boy about 12 years of age, that speaks English, is to be sold."[26]

The evidence suggests that the booming business of racialized slavery entered the newspapers of Addison and Steele only in a very few instances. But in support of Roach's general contention about the tight connection between the consumption of colonial slavery and the production of English liberty discourses, one of those instances (in *Tatler* 245) testified to the strong visual presence of Black servitude in the British Augustan milieu. That *Tatler* number, written by Steele, begins as a satirical advertisement about a female (presumably white English) servant escaping from a fictional (white English) lady. The point of the faux advertisement is a lengthy description of what the escaping servant stole, revealing in a mocking way the lifestyle and possessions of the private woman. This is followed by a postscript: a fictional letter printed by the sympathetic editor from a "Black-moor Boy" who complains of being made by his lady to wear a collar and a turban and being esteemed no more than a parrot even though he has been baptized by a chaplain.[27]

Ashton, in his influential history of the social life of that time, wrote that early eighteenth-century London was a city populated by many servants, among them Black slaves. His research revealed ads seeking runaway slaves in the newspapers of Queen Anne's reign and evidence that slaves in London were indeed often made to wear collars.[28] Young Black servers (known as "blackamoors") often worked inside coffeehouses in eighteenth-century London as "walking advertisements" for the colonial wares of the house. Within a crowded, competitive market, some coffeehouses had names that referenced these exoticized, racialized servers (e.g., "The Black Boy Coffee House" or "Black Mores Head") or mentioned the names of colonial places, as in the "Jamaica Coffeehouse" (established 1674) near the Royal Exchange. Indeed, by the early eighteenth century, there was a sizable number of Black people in London, many of them mendicants, street entertainers, or chimney sweeps.[29] During a visit to London in 1710, a German traveler wrote in his diary that "there are, in fact, such a quantity of Moors of both sexes in England that I have never seen so many before."[30]

The relatively rare enslaved Black person encountered by the white Augustan in England may have triggered guilt and a selfish desire to escape from that guilt by rhetorically and hypocritically emphasizing liberty.[31] The strength of this response could well have been tied to the reminder it would have given them of the nearness of their own fate in a monarchical and aristocratic regime to that of an abject slave. Slavery in general was still strongly associated in the British imagination with feudalism, Europeans, and the lower rungs of a robust English servant class and those below them. The passion with which middling writers like Addison and Steele and their readers embraced discourses of liberty and freedom was probably strongly derived from a sense of the historical fragility of their relative class privilege and the fear of slipping (back) into a position of slavery that race would not have excluded.

Relatedly, Ashton mused on the oddness of "the somewhat inconsequent behavior of those times, keeping black slaves with one hand, and redeeming white ones from Barbary with the other." But the hypocrisy was explained for him partially by the fact that "the poor whites" whom the British government emancipated from slavery in North Africa "only changed their method of slavery, for they were draughted into the navy, and in the long war that followed, there was very little hope of their release." As such, he related the 1702 anecdote of former white slaves at a service in St. Paul being told to deliver thanks to the government for their deliverance, directly before being marched back onto navy ships and sent to war.[32]

The discursive reciprocal imbrication of British slave trading and British experiences of North African enslavement can be read in popular treatments like *Robinson Crusoe*, which demonstrate the then-present tendency to treat slavery as an amoral fact of life in the wider, seafaring world. The less exotic, felt proximity of white working- and middle-class existence to slavery can be read in the sequence of *Spectator* 214 and 215, the first of which has Steele highlighting the difficulties of working people who must find and rely on patrons to survive, and the second of which is Addison's essay on the plight of Black plantation slaves discussed above. The infamous 1710 ad for a slave sale in *Tatler* 132 is likewise contextualized by a detail in that day's main piece: a story about Bickerstaff enjoying the camaraderie of his club, which ends with his being picked up by his maid at ten o'clock at night with a lantern.[33] The casual expectation of such late-night service reveals a thick London culture of servitude, in which racialized slavery was a relatively small, exoticized component. The fragile Addisonian bubble of middling English liberty, in which coffeehouse patrons could practice the sociable debates of individual, imperfect sovereignty, was a bubble largely predicated on—and everywhere potentially confronted by—class distinction. Guilt was often closer to home than the colonies, and the conceivably imminent bursting of the privileged middle-class or bourgeois public sphere was likely to have been accomplished by people of the same skin color wearing a different type of dress.

In general, slavery in Addison's writing referred to life under feudalism and absolute monarchy, very roughly the English system before 1689 (excluding the violently turbulent Commonwealth period) against which the Whigs organized themselves as a party in favor of more balance between monarch and parliament. Given that recent historical situation, the present liberty of Addison's Britain indeed felt exceptional and under threat not only from domestic sources but also from potentially invading or influencing Catholic monarchical forces on the Continent. Addison described French, German, and Italian people as slaves, equating, as he did in *Spectator* 287, slavery with unenlightened life under a despotic government. As one moved further from Britain, the picture grew proportionally bleaker: "Above nine parts of the World in ten are in the lowest State of Slavery, and consequently sunk into the most gross and brutal Ignorance. European Slavery is indeed a State of Liberty, if compared with that which prevails in the other three divisions of the World."[34] Addison and his compatriots viewed slavery as a worldwide reality; British expansion in the world came both with the jingoistic, progressive hope that their country would prove a force of international emancipation and with the reality of their patria becoming further entwined in the global norms of business, which included slave trading. Whiggish opinion about the asiento and British involvement in the slave trade was divided in part because of fears that leaving the Spanish-American slave trade monopoly in the hands of Louis XIV would strengthen his bids for territorial conquest. Closer to home, the Whigs worried reasonably about "Country Party," Tory, and Jacobite plans to dominate the newly formed South Sea Company: the leading ministers of the government, Harley and Bolingbroke, planned to use the company to build a new territorial British empire in South America as a bulwark of power and wealth for the landed aristocracy against the domestic Whiggish social "revolution" that had been funded through wartime deficit spending. Against this fear of imperial French "universal monarchy" and a resurgent British aristocracy, the Whigs believed they must rapidly construct a counterbalance, "an empire that was commercial, maritime and free."[35] How free was "free," and for whom, were questions that risked delaying the urgent construction effort.

Addison's concrete published reflections on slavery led discursively to support for universal education, battles against feudal powers in Europe, and anti-Catholic politics, as well as to his general contention that "the making of one Person more than Man, makes the rest less."[36] From our twenty-first-century perspective, the confusion of his terms, between the status of a feudal subject and that of a modern slave, points to a seventeenth-century conflation of feudal tyranny with general slavery in English political disputes. That rhetorical conflation, whose history is outlined briefly below, was part of a struggle between a feudal system and a more democratic, capitalist system. The course of that struggle over the eighteenth century would allow the state of serfdom, gradually disappearing from Europe, to then become rhetorically disentangled from slavery, a state of being increasingly racialized and de-Europeanized.

Particularly before 1713, when Britain became identified as the Atlantic's leading slave-trading power, the British reader's concept of slavery seems to have been tied to recent historical memory of the seventeenth century and ongoing, unwon struggles against the seemingly permanent realities of feudal and monarchical systems in Europe and parts of the British Isles.[37]

The modern construction of race and racism during the early eighteenth century was fueled to an important degree in Britain by the temptation of British subjects to turn a blind eye to the "offstage" enslavement of Africans practiced by colonial planters and seafaring merchants in order to insure (in a literal way) their own freedom and escape from feudal, oppressive systems.[38] Addison and his compatriots played what we now consider a historically ambiguous role in this regard by keeping the latter active struggle against feudal slavery and the historical violence that Europeans and British people inflicted on each other very much "center stage," while discursively repressing "exotic" colonial slavery. The Whiggish habit, however, of fervently but selectively advocating for expanded liberty in this manner had a long history in its own accord. In its struggle for societal power, the Whig movement of resistance and liberation tied itself strongly to the "ancient" English tradition of exceptional resistance to slavery, dating back to the Norman Conquest and drawing perpetually on classical Greek and Roman thought.

The persistent problem of defining who could and who could not be a slave had shaped Western law, values, and institutions since seventh-century BCE Athenian legislative attempts to categorize their large slave populations. Although conquered and abducted foreigners were generally the first slaves, slavery in the ancient Western tradition knew no stable boundaries defined by physical characteristics or ethnic origins. After the fall of the Roman Empire, slavery remained common in Europe and was a fate that could befall anyone whose land or village was invaded. At least 15 percent of the population of Western Europe around 950 CE was enslaved: a total of 3.39 million enslaved people, with an annual slave trade in all of Europe of around 90 thousand people. This number declined gradually with the increasing organization of stable, large, Christianized kingdoms and empires during the High Middle Ages.[39]

The link between liberation from slavery and the process of long-term, large-scale political organization and identification—prototypical for modern nationalism—was forged in Britain by the Norman Conquest. Slavery was well established in Britain at the time; the 1086 Domesday Book records that slaves were 10 percent of the total population. They were acquired through trade, through the punishment of certain crimes, through parents selling their children during times of famine, and through successful wars and invasions. Because slavery had died out in France, however, partly due to the influence of the Church, John Gillingham notes that "the Norman Conquest was the first in the history of Britain that did not result in more slaves for sale."[40]

Mr. Spectator's initial self-introduction has him born "to a small Hereditary Estate, which, according to the Tradition of the Village where it lies, was bounded by the same Hedges and Ditches in William the Conqueror's Time."[41] His opening genealogical formulation evokes a long patriotic heritage of British liberty revolving in part around William I's simultaneously outlawing the export of slaves and establishing the "Norman Yoke" of French feudal lordship.[42] Following the Battle of Hastings in 1066, the new "Roman" invasion was cemented not just by a Norman king but by a French-speaking and Latin-writing ruling elite. The honorific literary and behavioral regime that this elite would establish developed through the centuries into the aesthetic code of courtesy that Addison would remix with academic knowledge and bring down from the aristocratic *cieux* as the groundwork for an emancipated middle-class public discourse. The early eighteenth century thus inherited a British identity and evolving, unwritten political constitution shaped by the tension and cooperation between local, Celtic, and Anglo-Saxon traditions and centralized, (French) imperial ecclesiastic and chivalric social organization. A rhetorical war over slavery and authentic freedom was thus not new to the time. It had been already long encoded into the cultural double helix of British DNA by the Norman neo-Romanization of England and the attendant colonial conflicts between indigenous "gothic" populations and a courtly Continental elite. The historical oddity of William's "liberating" invasion lent a core idiosyncrasy to British identity.

The historical rhetoric aside, the actual legal and practical distinction between free and slave in England before and after 1066 was often riddled with complexities and myriad local differences. Slavery and its associated brutalities continued in Britain regionally even well after the Norman Conquest, being gradually replaced by feudal serfdom. Overall, people in Britain during the medieval period became less subject to wholesale abduction and individual or mass sale to foreign owners. At the same time, they became, in general, more tied to the lordly, stable organizers of the local economy.[43] The difference between being a serf and being a slave was not always clear, meaningful, or identical everywhere in England. The general distinction, according to Gillingham, was that whereas "serfs could in effect be sold . . . as a package which included their families and the ground on which they were tenants," slaves "could be separated from their families and bought and sold as individual items."[44] The sovereignty of the lord in the postslavery Anglo-Norman period, then, began to be tied a degree less to pure military might and a degree more to a local populace, who in turn became legally recognized as belonging to definable families ("blood") and particular territories ("soil").

By the early seventeenth century, the patriotic conception of Britain as a land with a historically exceptional relationship to slavery was well entrenched. In their struggles with James I and Charles I, early seventeenth-century parliamentary leaders consistently referenced this traditional nationalistic discourse of liberty and slavery, tying it to such bedrock Roman legal authorities as the *Codex* of Justinian, which asserted that "the fundamental division within the law of person is that all men and women are either free or are slaves."[45] During the Commonwealth period, Milton heightened this discourse through his influential pamphlets defending Parliament's execution of Charles I, becoming the period's most famous propagandist and earning the secretaryship of foreign tongues under the Council of State. Addison, who effectively repopularized Milton partly by depoliticizing and aestheticizing him for a less regicidal age, was to be the next English man of letters with a similar professional role and impact.[46]

In his 1649 *The Tenure of Kings and Magistrates* and *Eikonoklastes*, as well as in his 1651 *Pro populo Anglico defensio* addressed to the people of Europe, Milton followed recent parliamentary tradition in arguing that a people's freedom required vigilance against both active and more insidious forms of tyranny.[47] Quoting Cicero's fourth *Philippic* in the *Defensio*, Milton wrote, "What cause of waging war can be more just than that of repudiating slavery? For the most wretched thing about this condition is that, even if the master happens not to be oppressive, he can be so if he should choose." Slavery, even under the conditions of liberality, was corrosive and fatal to a society. This was a reassertion of a then-common classical argument that had as its basis what Quentin Skinner identifies as the ancient or classical understanding of liberty: "Not being subject to a master." In counterpoint to Hobbes's vision in the *Leviathan*, Milton's *Eikonoklastes* extended the state of chattel slavery to the collective figure of his nation: under Charles I "all Britain was to be ty'd and chain'd to the conscience, judgement, and reason of one Man."[48]

The seventeenth-century British discourse on slavery that Milton voiced called on a long neoclassical tradition to condemn slavery not only as a moral and legal wrong but also as a degenerating force that a great people must throw off themselves. The combination of the two ideas demonstrates the early modern conception of slavery as a passively pervasive, threateningly universal reality of human civilizations, against which every proud local population had the duty to be on guard.[49] The following decades would show how this conception, admirable in its local historical context, would lend itself to the developing reality of vigilantly liberated but nationalistically myopic people "outsourcing" slavery to foreign populations—an iteration of an old classical republican paradigm on a larger imperial scale.

OFFSHORING SLAVERY

The neoclassical discourse of slavery and British exceptional liberty that Milton and then early eighteenth-century Whigs like Addison inherited took shape originally as an emancipatory discourse within the House of Commons well before any large-scale British entrance into the modern transatlantic slave trade. Around 1610, the primary association of British subjects with African slavery would likely have been the dread instilled by many stories of Europeans being taken as slaves by North Africans. During the early modern period, hundreds of thousands of Europeans were so enslaved, usually as a result of capture on the seas, with thousands alone taken between 1609 and 1614. Slaving raids from North Africa on mainland Britain remained a rare but contemporary, feared reality.[50] Though this form of African slavery probably remained prevalent in the imaginations of most British commoners, by the time of Milton's writing, most of his literate, politically engaged audience must have been at least somewhat aware that England had recently entered a high-volume trade in slaves of African origin.

This dramatic though untrumpeted entrance of England into massive slave trading was strategically permitted and to a degree ordered by Milton's patrons, the same parliamentarians who had permanently crippled absolute monarchy and the feudal system in England. A wave of emigration, fueled by hopes of economic gain and escape from religious and political persecution in Britain, had buoyed the colonial plantation economy in the early seventeenth century with an increasing supply of indentured servants.[51] In the 1640s, however, the prior "Great Migration" reversed itself as a stream of New Englanders moved back to England to join the side of the Parliamentarians in the civil wars. This large trend also significantly reduced the voluntary emigrants willing to risk a transatlantic journey and the harsh working conditions of the island plantations in pursuit of a better future. Those would-be laborers transferred such previous cross-oceanic fantasies to the belief and hope that the political situation in England would improve; they were surely helped in the resolve to stay and fight rather than chase profit and freedom abroad by the many horror stories that had filtered back from colonial workers, who had often found themselves trapped in deadly conditions of de facto slavery with even their assumed legal protections and right to return as citizens stripped away.[52]

The simultaneity of this decline of voluntary migration to the Caribbean and the booming of the plantation sugar economy—both coincident with the English Revolution—created a crisis of overseas labor supply. In this context, the practices associated with "involuntary migration" and penal slavery rapidly matured into a labor-supply system for Atlantic colonies and especially for the sugar plantations of Barbados, where the death rate for laborers was extremely high. "Spiriting," "barbadosed," and, later, "kidnapping" entered the English language as terms for being abducted and shipped into forced colonial labor, highlighting the frequency of these practices, to which all classes of people were subject but to which the masses of the poor were more frequently victims without recourse to justice.[53]

Because even these practices were not enough to meet their voracious labor demands, Caribbean planters began increasingly to rely upon enslaved African people to compete with each other and maximize their profit. The Dutch and the Portuguese were the chief providers of these newly sourced enslaved laborers. Would-be English Atlantic merchants in this environment of high pressure, risk, and profit potential felt stifled under Charles I's rigid system of royal trading monopolies, providing Cromwell and the parliamentarians a crucial opportunity to champion the "liberation" of commercial interests. African chattel slavery presented a powerful means to increase overall English prosperity, build incentive for an anti-monarchical movement, diminish colonial planters' previously strong support of royalism, and fulfill for common British people the promise of a Commonwealth in which British slavery would be reduced or even abolished.

The word "slavery" was used on all sides of the brewing conflict to describe the loss of political liberty that would follow the victory of their opponents.[54] Sugar planters in Barbados, traditionally loyal to the monarch, feared that parliamentary rebellions would lead to their own enslavement—a revolutionary reversal of fortunes. When empowered Parliamentarians called upon colonial plantation owners to justify their purchase of African slaves, the planters' reply linked "their right to continued access to slave labor to the rights of freeborn English men." Although the Parliamentarians' main point was less revolutionary than economic—to question the loyalty of plantation owners doing business with non-English traders—the planters' defensive "rhetoric assumed the audacity of treating an English man as one would treat an African, and created not simply compartments but a hierarchy, placing English (and other Europeans) over non-English others."[55] The exchange represented an early moment in the formation of a new ideology tying together modern racism and slavery by positing an unthinkable wall between liberated English identity and commodified slaves of other races. Racialized slavery became an economic tool used to sidestep violent and potentially cataclysmic, domestic political disputes.

The English Civil War could find a peaceful end—more quickly than the war tearing apart central Europe at the same time—because of this new tacit agreement to increasingly move slavery offshore, under the cover of race. The Parliamentarians won economic dominance by opening a new industry that had been stifled by royal tyranny, while the colonial planters liberated themselves from an association with feudal slavery by establishing race—not merely law, geographical isolation, and tradition—as a crucial criterion for who could be enslaved and who could enjoy liberty. As a result, English involvement in the African slave trade to the Caribbean and North America grew from the mid-1640s to 1660 from "a scarcely existent practice largely controlled by the Dutch . . . to a booming commercial undertaking increasingly in English hands."[56] The high volume of the British Atlantic slave trade began around 1640, with approximately 30,000 African people shipped for each of the following decades. This rate doubled in the first decade of the Restoration and jumped again to around 115,000 in the decade of the Glorious Revolution. In the eighteenth century, the volume of the British slave trade tended to increase steadily from decade to decade (with a dip around the American Revolution), peaking at 385,000 in the 1790s and finally ceasing in 1811. The total estimated number of enslaved African people shipped across the Atlantic by British ships between 1550 and 1810 was 3.3 million. Of these, approximately 10 percent were sent to mainland North America, while 90 percent ended up in the Caribbean, where the rate of death was much higher. In the same time period, combining numbers from ships under any flag, only about 11,000 enslaved African people were shipped to Europe.[57] This discrepancy between the colonial presence of slavery and its relative invisibility within Europe helps to explain how an older, classically inflected discourse on slavery persisted in England until merging with abolitionist discourse in the middle of the eighteenth century.

The complexity and contradictions of the Whig discourse of liberty grew in large part out of the brutal political struggles of the Commonwealth period.

In order to stabilize his regime during the 1650s, Cromwell pursued an aggressive "Western Design" that challenged Spanish dominance in the American colonies and particularly in the West Indies. His government sought to strengthen the British-controlled economies and workforces in the Caribbean by actively encouraging the African slave trade and the selling of thousands of Irish Catholics, military prisoners, and England's criminalized poor into bond slavery. He and his allies ended the royally granted monopoly of the Guinea Company, which had previously carried on only a limited trade in West Africa, mostly focused on gold, exotic wood, and other nonhuman goods. The company itself and its new competitors were encouraged to increase their efforts and capitalize on English sugar plantation owners' demand for slave labor for the good of England.[58] This nationalistic economic realpolitik fused the struggle against monarchy and feudal slavery to the expanded practice of Atlantic chattel slavery by making the latter a central part of the Commonwealth's revolutionary foreign policy, which aimed to aggressively defend "England against any threat of universal monarchy, be that Dutch (Protestant) or Spanish (Catholic)."[59]

As an "emancipatory" imperial strategy, Cromwell's Western Design kept the fate of Africans and criminalized British subjects in the dark while staging a British colonial moral defense of indigenous Americans against Spanish atrocities. Addison's poet-hero John Milton played an important role in this complex pamphlet theater—for instance, through his likely coauthorship of the 1655 *Declaration . . . against Spain* and through the support of his nephew John Phillips's 1656 translation of Bartolomé de las Casas's *Brevísima relación de la destrucción*, retitled *Tears of the Indians: Being an Historical and True Account of the Cruel Massacres and Slaughters of above Twenty Millions of Innocent People*. The Commonwealth government used the "Black Legend" of exceptional Spanish cruelty to justify aggression against Spain and New World Spanish interests in the name of avenging the blood "of the poor *Indian* . . . since God has made of one Blood all Nations of Men for to dwell on the Face of the Earth, having determined the times before appointed, and the Bounds of their Habitation."[60] What looks like an anticolonial argument turned on the idea that the cruelty of the Spanish invasions and genocides stemmed from Spanish disinterest in sustainably settling the conquered lands. The British would do better by justly occupying land with the consent of the native people there. While silently pursuing an unprecedented expansion of British slaving practices, the Cromwellian Commonwealth's virtuous protoglobalist rhetoric loudly presented Native Americans as distant siblings and surrogates of the emerging revolutionary, democratic citizen within intra-European political discourse. The actual direct deadly consequences of the new British positioning on indigenous American (and Irish) lives would remain unseen; the *Declaration,* however, boosted the project of European legal democracy by establishing "a new account of territorial sovereignty—one that is no longer authorized by God (from above), but one that is legitimated on the basis of territorial occupation and popular consent (from below.)" This was the beginning of "Westphalian sovereignty" organized around the right of spatial, territorial powers, not an "overarching politico-religious authority (Catholicism)."[61]

The schizophrenia of revolutionary "emancipatory" colonial schemes going hand in hand with massive increases in enslavements contributed strongly to the Commonwealth's eventual overthrow and the restoration of the monarchy, via popular outrage against the tens of thousands of British subjects who were kidnapped, deceptively lured, or "spirited" away to join the now steady (but less thematized) shipping of enslaved people from West Africa to Chesapeake and Caribbean plantations. Many of Cromwell's most effective critics were returned British émigrés, who had formed effective networks and strategies to struggle against "political slavery and the rise of slave societies" during the antinomianism crises that shook New England in the late 1630s and early 1640s. These very early English ex-colonial protoabolitionists spoke out against the international slave trade, being among the first to "challenge the ancient idea that freedom of some could be built upon the enslavement of others."[62] While their actions showed the very early stirrings of general abolitionist thought, the more direct political consequences of their revolt against Cromwell strengthened the hand of Charles II and his allies.

The restored king, of course, would not pursue a policy of general, global abolitionism but would rather see in the fall of his executed father's archenemy the need to more firmly accelerate British shipping of enslaved African laborers so as to grant reprieve to any restive, nearer-to-home subjects. Once established on the throne, Charles II quickly reasserted monarchical authority over Atlantic commerce, forming the Royal African Company and granting the direction of this company to his family associates. He continued the basic imperial economic strategies of the Interregnum government while expanding the slave trade and increasing political control over the colonies. The "Merry Monarch" and his ministers effectively verticalized the entire British economy and in particular the colonial plantation economy, driving the Dutch out of the bulk of English colonial business, including the selling and transportation of slaves.[63]

THE TURN-OF-THE-CENTURY WHIG
DISCOURSE OF LIBERTY AND SLAVERY

Throughout the Restoration, enslaved people's labor grew in importance as a source of English material liberty. The first British "comprehensive slave code," passed in Barbados in 1661, established a strong new precedent of legal and cultural separation between enslaved Africans and English subjects. For the Whigs who would inherit the diminished revolutionary energy of the failed Commonwealth, such a distant colonial slave code quietly bolstered the local effort to transform the recent tragedy of civil wars into the comedy of prosperous, national reunification: the invention of racially outsourced slavery led to domestic economic gains across the political spectrum. As long as the modern kind of racialized slave remained "a shadowy figure who inhabits a land far away from England and does not threaten accounts of English liberty in the metropole or the colony," the rise of a Whig opposition and its associated networks of middling people could perform itself as the natural flower of liberty, reason, and balanced self-assertion.[64] Their rise could also be more easily tolerated by their conservative, Tory adversaries, whose tendency toward a more libertine, ludic political mood was supported by their own growing colonial profits.

To depict the era's actually conflictual English domestic politics as a historical wink-wink game of rhetoric between privileged people, however, would be highly misleading. When the Whigs emerged as a fledgling opposition in the peace following a failed revolutionary period, the slavery they railed against was the one from which history up to that point had offered no enduring salvation. Lasting victory against the very real and entrenched, internationally supported monarchical, feudal, and dogmatically religious system—whose roots and pervasive mechanisms of punishment, censorship, and forced labor reached back to the origin of civilizations—remained highly unlikely and depressingly unprecedented.

The racialization of slavery, by creating or affirming a large, special class of people who could not be enslaved, returned to an ancient idea of slavery as an exceptional, violent encounter between people of different places, a result of the lawless encounters of international war. One of the dialectical results of this process was the strengthening of antislavery conviction inside limited geographic and cultural boundaries, prototypically the modern European nation-state. In those emerging political bubbles founded as zones of exception from slavery, transhistorically impactful and revolutionary calls like Milton's to general boundaryless freedom could be increasingly published, promoted, and read. The Whig discourse of liberty, in a difficult and ugly historical sense, was one part of a larger international emancipatory movement that worked in uneven and often breathtakingly cruel steps toward pushing the universal possibility of being subjected to slavery away from reciprocally expanding legal definitions of citizenship.

After Milton, John Locke became the key philosophical formulator of Whiggish ideas about citizenship, slavery, and liberty. In his *Second Treatise on Government* (chapter 4, "Of Slavery"), Locke defined the "perfect condition of *Slavery*" as "nothing else, but *the State of War continued, between a lawful Conqueror, and a Captive.*"[65] Locke held that slavery in society could exist only when a person who had been captured in the state of war failed or was prevented in his duty to resist false ownership to the death. The slave kept alive by his master, in Locke's description of the situation, maintained consent: "For, whenever he finds the hardship of his Slavery out-weigh the value of his Life, 'tis in his Power by resisting the Will of his Master, to draw on himself the Death he desires."[66] An individual's never-ending, just duty to resist enslavement was based upon Locke's tenet that no one but God could own the life of a person—because it was God who leased a life to the individual, under the condition of its good, borrowed use. "The *Natural Liberty* of Man," Locke wrote, "is to be free from any Superior Power on Earth. . . . The *Liberty of Man, in Society,* is to be under no other Legislative Power, but that established, by consent, in the Common-wealth."[67] Locke's charging the souls of enslaved people with responsibility and agency over their ignoble terrestrial situations was a local call to duty for feudal subjects: philosophy lent formal audacity to the dangerous resistance against the oppressive conditions of mastery, under which English people had lived for thousands of years. The heft of Locke's arguments formed a durable bulwark against the perversion and cruelty of slavery in an enlightened modern society.

The thick, brave sociality of English liberation-fighters, however, did not reach across oceans to distant enslaved people. Moreover, the extension of natural human sympathy as English, African, and indigenous American people encountered each other in foreign places was now increasingly proscribed by codes of racial categorization serving the interest of colonial profiteers. In that abetting context, what was a moral imperative for Locke's European readers to resist their own enslavement could be cynically twisted into a racist, partial moral absolution for modern chattel slavery's financiers, silent propagandists, and perpetrators. Through the mechanism of racialization, the guilt of distanced slavery could be repressed by being projected onto legally and affectively abandoned racialized others: the continued enslavement of strangers became, through this darkened, nihilistic backdoor of emancipatory logic, their own fault. The pained and cruel, half-reasoned extension of Locke's enlightenment formulation grew out of an ugly economic and political reality from which Locke, like many of the Whigs, benefited: Locke himself invested in the Royal African Company and a group of "Bahamas Adventurers," both heavily involved in slavery. He also likely helped his employer Lord Ashley (the first Earl of Shaftesbury and a founding father of the Whig party) draft the "Fundamental Constitution of Carolina," which upheld British freemen's "absolute power and authority" over African slaves.[68] No English party was likely to survive the time's crucial battles over resources without significant access to the disproportionate profits coming from enslaved labor—the fate of large political alliances and the careers of their favored philosophers depended, as usual, on what share of the local economy they could control.[69] With regard to investments in the slave trade and keeping in mind Locke's definition of slavery, many of the Whigs continued the general direction of Cromwell's Western Design: *Pax Quaeritur Bello,* "Peace is sought by war."[70]

In the preface to her 1706 *Reflections upon Marriage,* the Tory Mary Astell touched satirically on Whiggish hypocrisy by using Locke's reasoning to arrive at the conclusion that English women were "born slaves." Judith Drake, another Tory writer, had concluded similarly with more pointed, literal argumentation, drawing in her *Essay in Defence of the Female Sex* a parallel between Black slaves in "Western Plantations" and women, who were not born free and remained prisoners all their lives—"natural" slaves.[71] Through their analogical argumentation, the Tory early feminist writers created a mirroring, ideational alliance that posited English women and enslaved colonial laborers as each other's surrogates in a persistently feudal or neofeudal reality. Plantation slavery could be kept out of mind through the invisibility of exoticized distance; domestic enslavement by gender was rendered invisible by its utter everyday generality. In this sense, Drake and Astell rhetorically renationalized and on-shored slavery in order to theatrically highlight and defamiliarize the ongoing "state of war" waged through enchaining gender roles and misogynistic legal traditions. The high-flying Whiggish universal codes deployed in the enlightened war against feudal slavery hid in their own wide shadows the entangled modern slaveries of English women and racialized others.

Astell and Drake's critiques strategically desentimentalized gender-based oppression in English culture and, by the same token, exposed the cruelly wishful, half-examined misconception that a life lived under a system of chattel slavery could be thought of at all as an individual choice. Richard Steele worked influentially with this same mirroring alliance in the opposite Whiggish mode of heightening sentimentality that he and Addison perfected. Like Addison's *Spectator* 215, Steele's *Spectator* 11 foregrounds wet eyes, natural affection, and the sentimental duties of loyalty and love over dry Lockean ratiocination. Steele's essay relates a traveler's tale about an indigenous American woman who rescues an English adventurer and enjoys a seemingly happy romance with him, only to be sold into slavery by him when they arrive in Barbados, in spite of the fact that she is pregnant with his child. The told-tale is framed as an esteemed young English woman's rebuttal to a suitor's misogynistic speech.[72] The rebuttal allegorically and affectingly thematizes English women's experiences and fears in a structurally sexist society and thereby portrays the oppression of women and colonial slavery as abominable, greed-induced failures of English men in their duty to love. Steele's rendition of the tale of Inkle and Yarico was one of the most significant and impactful early attempts to create imaginative identification of British readers with a North American slave. Picked up repeatedly through the century by other artists and writers, it became a standard in abolitionist literature's attempts to elicit distant empathy by depicting enslaved individuals aesthetically as tragic, betrayed lovers.[73]

In the interest of emotionally motivating readers, the larger trope of sentimentalizing slavery in the eighteenth century tended to ambiguously deemphasize the racial and ethnic otherness of enslaved people as well as the actual conditions and politics of their enslavement.[74] The mirroring of enslaved plantation workers, defrauded Native Americans, and oppressed English women as betrayed subjects-in-need-of-liberation dialectically produced the problematic clichés of the suffering woman, indigenous person, and enslaved African person as tragic surrogates for European men, who were caught up in their own personal tragedies and collective anxieties about persistent class-based oppression. As Felicity Nussbaum has shown with respect to the fetishization of the suffering theatrical woman in the eighteenth century, Toni Morrison has demonstrated the distorting turn that even such well-meaning, sentimentally tragic figurations produced in the literary imagination vis-à-vis enslaved Black bodies: "The slave population, it could be and was assumed, offered itself up as surrogate selves for meditation on problems of human freedom, its lure and its elusiveness. This black population was available for meditations on terror—the terror of European outcasts, their dread of failure, powerlessness, Nature without limits, natal loneliness, internal aggression, evil, sin, greed. In other words, this slave population was understood to have offered itself up for reflections on human freedom in terms other than the abstractions of human potential and the rights of man."[75] The parallel rhetorics of sentimentalization and desentimentalization affectively and logically entangled the people on the otherwise attentively excluded "frontiers" of the war for liberty, as surrogates for each other. Through the same mirroring mechanism, women, slaves, and indigenous people became living literary and theatrical effigies for the white Englishmen who saw the aestheticized tragedy of their own possible return to feudal powerlessness figured in them. This tragic, imaginary spectatorship of unemancipated effigy-others thus paradoxically fueled the engine of liberation that drove English men toward colonial and patriarchal mastery and enrichment.

As the Whig movement expanded beyond its very elite beginnings, building philosophical and political alliances were not enough: affective ties of mass brotherhood and sisterhood—the oceanic feelings that could give charge to universal law—became increasingly important. The consequential change in Whig discourse in the post-Lockean generation, exemplified by Addison and Steele's husbandry of the middling public sphere, was characterized by a move away from elite, legalistic philosophical dialectics and toward the sentimental allegorical tale as the edifier of individual moral conscience. Bridget Orr writes that "one of the most important questions raised by *The Tatler* and *The Spectator* is the extent to which their sophisticated evocation of pity (for betrayed women, for exploited indigenes) can be seen as creating the means of critique of or (by contrast) facilitating commercial and colonial empire."[76] Addison and Steele's related, frequent failure to provide a clear and specific statement of policy against British involvement in the slave trade reveals their partially anxious and partially self-interested complicity in then-existent networks of power. By the same token, it may express their realism about their own situations as relatively dependent reformists subject to crushing political and financial censorship. Addison and Steele had tremendous success with the goal they prioritized: the cultivation of a large local, imagined, felt, functional community of readers with a strong bent toward progressive, cosmopolitan politics and the character and intelligence necessary to sustainably accomplish the actual work of comprehensive emancipatory reform. The later abolition movement reached its eventual success on the strength of the moral and empathetic middle-class liberalism that they helped weave into existence. The idea that they or anyone could have met with the same success or been otherwise instrumental in bringing an earlier end to the practice of colonial slavery by more insistently and specifically thematizing its abomination remains a question for historical speculation and future strategy deliberations.

As it was, Addison and Steele bolstered their published opposition to colonial exploitation and the greedy politics that drove the slave trade with sustained encouragement of general identification with African and indigenous people. The different modes of this advocacy in Steele and Addison's work speaks to their different beliefs and fields of action. For Steele, the priority lay on building the social scene of the nation as a family of tender, conscious lovers: the enslaved and oppressed would be effectively emancipated when they were affectively integrated into a network of common feeling. His Inkle and Yarico paper lets sympathetic, concluding tears over the love-fate of (enslaved) noble women slightly occlude his tale's implicit critiques against the legal and economic structures that encouraged slave trading and colonial exploit.

For Addison, the historian-preacher's son and Saturday newsprint sermonist, philosophical curiosity and clarity were still the "king's road" to correct action and perspective; the nurtured individual soul was the trying place and only true source of moral choice and emancipation. Addison was a cosmopolitan, Christian moral realist steeped in the Platonic idea of the immortal soul's betterment through countless lives and cycles of reward and punishment. The chances of an actual moral outcome on the mortal human scale depended almost entirely on Providence. Nonetheless, his historical brand of religious, balanced realism held that moral action and practicality were not opposed, even from a selfish point of view: it was not mere rhetoric when he admonished exploitative terrestrial imperialists to mind the afterlife pain they would endure for their present crimes against the rule of equality. The other half of his balanced "secular" performance of life saw the critic Addison working dually as a public propagandist, which required him to realistically maintain strong social and professional ties with powerful, sharply opinionated colleagues and patrons, even as he sought to cultivate a moral middle in society, a bulk of nonreactionary, reflective people who would settle disputes progressively through conversation and policy rather than allowing society to slip yet again in the direction of unpredictable civil war.

Spectator 55 and 56—a suggestive but unmarked sequence that the Blooms identify as among the papers most clearly expressing Addison's authentic, private moral indignation against racialized slavery and conquest—exhibit the way that he balanced his different public, professional, and writerly roles.[77] Both essays strongly condemn imperial avarice in general terms. The obvious target of that condemnation was the ruling Tory government, which was speedily attempting to agree a peace treaty with Louis XIV to conclude the War of Spanish Succession and thereby quickly secure the benefits of Atlantic trade dominance (including the asiento) for the nation and their own partisan cronies. Addison and his fellow Whigs believed that this Tory maneuver amounted to submission and potential recapitulation to European absolute monarchy. The Tories had recently swept into power at the successful height of an ideologically inspired war—near the moment of Britain's first Protestant royal succession planned and dictated fully by an act of Parliament. By bringing the war to a "premature" end, the new alliance of Queen Anne and the Tories threatened to rob the martial effort to liberalize Europe (through increased British might) of all its gains, transform the modern war of emancipation at the last moment into a traditional war about material resources and access to slaves, and leave in place a feudal monarchical-aristocratic order for the foreseeable future.

Against such dire threats both moral and locally political, the pointed critiques of *Spectator* 55 and 56 decrying imperial, European avarice can seem mild, abstract, and too indirect. *Spectator* 55 takes the allusive, allegorical mode of critiquing Tory foreign policy for having lost touch with both the natural enjoyment of plenty and the real needs of poverty, leaving only avarice and luxury to drive each other on to greater crimes.[78] The "Vision of Marraton" in no. 56 playfully builds sympathy and respect for indigenous American moral integrity before briefly and obliquely suggesting the English Tory government's moral equivalence to the hated Spanish imperialists of the Black Legend. The essay relates in embellished, imaginative detail the supposedly true account of an Iroquois prophet's vision of an afterlife paradise, concluding with a glimpse into hell: "Several Molten Seas of Gold, in which were plunged the Souls of barbarous *Europeans,* who put to the Sword so many Thousands of poor *Indians* for the Sake of that precious Metal."[79]

The timeliness of these essays in the politics of 1711, when Harley and Bolingbroke were actively negotiating with Louis XIV's regime, points to Addison's aim of disrupting obsessive Tory ambitions to gain access to French territory and Latin American mines. The dynamic, partisan struggle also highlights how "political economic conflict, rather than mercantilist consensus, shaped the British empire," as Stephen Pincus has demonstrated.[80] The partial heirs to the politics of Cromwell and Milton, Whigs opposed a Spanish-style colonial method of "conquest, forced conversion, and enslaved labor" that they "regarded as morally deplorable."[81] The damning conclusion of Addison's "Vision of Marraton" echoes Milton's impassioned polemics in rhetorically linking the legendarily infamous Spanish model of greedy, bloody imperialism to the Tories' plans. The link was realistic enough, given the central Tory belief, espoused by leading political pamphleteers like Charles Davenant, that wealth was finite and based upon the spoils of empire. In the Queen Anne–era Tory economic world-picture reconstructed by Pincus, power was a race to extract as much as possible as quickly as possible and ship it back to the feudally arranged, hierarchical centers of dominance. Military invasion, annexation, and logistics, aided by slave labor, were the necessary, most efficient tools in a zero-sum, winner-takes-all competition with the Dutch Republic and other European powers. The alternative Whig theory of value and wealth, formulated influentially by John Locke, held that wealth was created by labor and the development of good taste and was thus potentially infinite. Against what Defoe termed the "preposterous jealousy" of the court and metropole against the colonies, Whigs advocated a politically and economically integrated union, emphasizing the northern, nonplantation colonies as sources of wealth and industry and consumption of British manufactures. Whigs wanted an "empire of commerce and labour, not an empire that sought to monopolise raw materials." As Addison put it in *Spectator* 2, through the mouth of his prototypical self-made successful merchant, Sir Andrew Freeport, "It is a stupid and barbarous way to extend dominion by arms, for true power is to be got by arts and industry."[82]

Whiggishly placing the value on "commerce, not conquest"—employment and trade rather than ownership—Addison suggested that political, imperial corruption and exploitation led to personal, existential suffering. By contrast, the encouragement of industry and trade went hand in hand with faithful, religious optimism and virtuous "circulation within a providential natural order."[83] His famous panegyric on the Royal Exchange, *Spectator* 69, provided an influential modern formulation of the citizen-of-the-world motif and evinced his ideological commitment to global trade as building "a kind of additional Empire." The essay, moreover, exalts trade as a means to international peace, an activity encouraged and necessitated by divine providence's differential distribution of resources around the world.[84] In keeping with his positive poetics of cheerfulness as a means of encouraging the downtrodden and their communities, celebratory essays like *Spectator* 69 attempt to enroll readers in a lightly satirical, good-humored reverence for the imperial business of trade and profit. Given the known historical shadows of such a scene, critical readings question Addison's failure to muster a clear and specific public call to action and opposition against the expansion of British slave-trading and colonial violence. More generous modes of reading Addison's efforts underline instead the ways his papers—in the context of ongoing political struggle over control of the state and its empire—opened a general critique of colonial greed and exploitation, slavery, racism, and unequal education, expressive of his belief that moral action was motivated primarily by the individual's realistic concern for their own fate beyond worldly appearances.

If politics was not just brute power contestation, the ethical bend depended on empathy, which for Addison had a strong grounding in the belief that the suffering inflicted on a distant other was a suffering inflicted more locally, on the self and the immortal soul.

THE COMPROMISED *PAX ADDISONIA*

The power of the people as we imagine it was still a fledgling, theatrical enterprise in early eighteenth-century Britain; a large part of Addison's career was an exercise in effectively staging it. As a cheerleader in this respect, conscious of the importance of good humor and positivity in sustaining a growing, energized group, Addison self-consciously shaped his papers with the light touch of Horatian satire, avoiding critiques either too sharp or too extended. As George Saintsbury put it, Addison's darts were free from poison: "They did not even cut or pierce very deeply; but they seldom missed their mark, and they always flashed as they flew. Moreover their flashes illuminate a curious, various, and interesting world."[85] That only partially and momentarily lit-up world was the one Addison helped to discover through observational horizontality and empiricism, through validating the literature and experience of the common people.[86]

Even in his high tragic mode, the effort was to show how a morally reformed society of the future might begin to constitute and get along with itself in the present, taking the model of virtuous actors in the complex, heroic past. In a last printed critical discussion of *Paradise Lost,* Addison praised Milton for avoiding the narrowness of ancient poets who made their heroes principally countrymen of their own (Greek and Roman) readers, stirring basic patriotic identification. Milton instead "has been more universally engaging in the Choice of his Persons, than any other Poet can possibly be. He has obliged all mankind, and related the whole Species to the two chief Actors in his Poem. . . . We behold in him, not only our Ancestors, but our Representatives."[87] The modern neoclassical paradigm, for Addison, moved away from the restricted pathos of locally sacred ancestor cults in the direction of the staging of universal representatives. His *Cato* drew toward a final tableaux depicting a new interracial family as the fated inheritors of Roman virtue and, implicitly, English liberty. Modern critics (as will be discussed in chapter 6) tend to notice that the anticolonial diatribe of the North African rebel Syphax is one of the play's most intelligent, persuasive, and passionate speeches. What they often fail to notice, perhaps because of the underappreciated positivity and sophistication with which Addison portrays the Prince's sublimated internal and political conflict, is that the surviving Black Numidian Prince Juba is the tragedy's moral and intellectual center, modest, loving, and moderate as he is. Through the thematization of his Africanity and non-Roman cultural background, Addison figured Juba as the model modern neoclassical citizen: in the mirror of balanced virtue, he represented the audience's position of empathetic and ambiguously admiring spectatorship from which their own separation from the tragedy of the Roman past could be contemplated.

All of this theatricality—of distant, entangled, mirrored identities and a nascent middle-class performing, but just performing, sovereignty over policy through its public opinion—was part of a societal development in the era epitomized by the "colonial relation." Characteristic of this relation, according to Dillon, was "the often occluded interdependence of two scenes—that of British liberty and that of racialized, enslaved labor and violent dehumanization."[88] In analyzing the development of popular sovereignty during the period, she emphasizes the gathering of an audience at a playhouse and their validation of onstage scenes that often challenged the status quo. As Dillon notes, this growing seeming power of a "performative commons" organized around gathering audiences and responsive, representative scenes was shaped under pressure as a replacement for the disappearing commons of universally usable land that was being extratheatrically enclosed and privatized in Britain.[89] The urban middle class that formed itself around Addison's works, who looked to the colonies and the representative freedom or invisible labor of colonial others for their own liberation, had, in a paradoxical sense, no choice but the scene of feudal emancipation. The older feudal communities built around the commons, in which many of their ancestors had lived and worked, were disappearing as the land was forcibly cut up into a greater number of smaller, privately held properties and partially transformed into grander representative neoclassical landscape gardens worthy of performatively postfeudal aristocratic ostentation. The lure of cosmopolitan identification, of a promising national and already postnational theatrical commons, worked in tandem with the marketing of colonial work opportunities. As betrayed lovers themselves, abandoned with nothing after centuries of largely unpaid labor, displaced feudal subjects without even yet a class of their own were compensated for new rootlessness with an offer to buy into the theatrical church of being modern and exceptionally British. The price was belief, wages spent on entertainment, the willingness to travel, and sacrificed protest against either their disappearing ancestral communities or the future's imperial avarice and slave codes set up, nominally, in the name of their new privilege. The new deracinated denizens and sometimes citizens of this lower- and middle-class theatrical commons had, after all, little choice but to functionally participate in the slavery economy if they were to participate in the general economy at all; they were bribed for their complicity and energetic work perhaps with the show of great expectations, but, more importantly, with an actual place and livelihood, somewhere, doing something—and likely not often a real or automatic improvement of their ancestral situation, all things considered.

In this lens, the general colonial expansion of slave labor gave a second life to the feudal structures and aristocratic and monarchical networks against which the Commonwealth and many of the Whigs were fighting. From a cold, economically deterministic point of view, the growth of abolitionism among later bourgeois and middle-class people had exactly to do with institutional slavery's powerful effects in preventing them from seizing a greater stake in the profits and administration of industry and commerce. Early liberal writers like Addison worked against the divide et impera strategy of internationally active, top-level profiteers by cultivating a domestic middle-class solidarity that included an imaginative identification across the colonial distance of racialized fates simultaneously integrated into one growing system while more severely separated by harsh new slave codes and specifically racist nationalisms. To make a global "people" with universal rights out of deracinated laborers forced into an expanding, brutally hierarchical system for the true, mortal benefit of a very few was a project that Addison, under the pressure of historical exigency, helped to start, and that we still struggle to imagine, feel, and effect.

That work necessitates bringing the colonial relation of peculiar intimate distance into awareness.[90] The stiltedness of sentimentality and the sometimes awkward politeness of condescending satire are traces in Addison's texts of his efforts to educate himself and his class of British men and (more distantly for Addison) women in being cosmopolitan citizens and speaking subjects. This was a newly minted theater of society, imperfect: the reading middle class empowered to sit in the sovereign seat and gaze on society's cast of equals—themselves, in their intimacy. Ridout discusses a surprising figuration of that new sovereign theater critic in *Spectator* 235 where Addison has Mr. Spectator and others puzzling respectfully over the "Trunk-Maker," whom many have noted sitting in the upper gallery of the theater, expressing his approval of performances "by a loud Knock upon the Benches, or the Wainscot, which may be heard over the whole Theatre." This double of the slippery white Mr. Spectator turns out to be "a large black Man, whom no body knows." The adjective "black" in the writing of the time—still before the modern discourse of race—had a vague, polyvalent meaning: he is, in Ridout's analysis, a manifestation of *The Spectator*'s "political unconscious."[91] The Trunk Maker and all he performatively observed and professionally packed away (for transport across oceans or long storage) was an apt symbol for the shadow of Addison, the taste-maker. In our more "angelic" moment within the flowering Addisonian Great Chain of Being—with its interconnected, widened social perspective technologically enabled by prosthetic global video feeds and identificatory, everyday onscreen avatars—the Trunk-Maker is still a compelling counter-figure for our spectatorship, now minutely clicking its private and aggregate approval: in the critic "whom nobody knows" sits a reflection of ourselves theatrically staged as distant people, here condescendingly granted the "say" of power, here left in the dark and out of the story.

Addison's was a hyperconscious discourse of diplomacy, the kind that his Juba employs. It was one that welcomed with good though public humor first sketches of the naturally affected and often stiff, uncomfortable encounters of distant strangers, made proximally intimate primarily by the rough, violent, churning inhumanity of empire and secondarily by the counter of literature, newsprint, and theater itself.

The contest between English feudal aristocracy/monarchy and bourgeois/middle-class democracy was a very real, momentous, and bloody conflict, in its time without a certain outcome. That the economy became more diversified, and that the British and American societies came to stand behind universal abolition, was the consequence of the eventual victory of middle-class forces within the context of aristocratic-monarchical imperialism. Addison helped to locate the affective grounds for this future, limited sovereignty of individuals and the people as a whole by encouraging positive, sentimental identification with distant others. His Mr. Spectator watched without giving much notice—only interpretable strokes of general approval and disapproval—while hundreds of thousands of African people were enslaved by British profiteers. Even while his writing ambiguously formulated new modern clichés of racialization and gendering, Addison's work built an emotional alliance in support of the human universal for which Locke had provided philosophical blueprints. The imagination was the ground zero of building distant intimacy, and so Addison (as the next chapter discusses) attempted to draw philosophy into its contemplation and active construction.

At the same time, the Roman/Norman origin of British identity remained active in Addison and the Whigs' discourse: liberty—the provenance of a virtuous elect who styled themselves as emancipators of the people—had to be proven, fought for, and deserved through the yoke of one's daily, sociable behavior. In self-consciously imagining the modern emancipated self, the fantasy of feudal revolution, of finally being the master, fueled a strong seduction to recreate the slave across the distant mirror, as oneself and as an impediment to the unmastered future.

4

Addison's Theory of the Imagination

> Therefore am I still
> A lover of the meadows and the woods,
> And mountains; and of all that we behold
> From this green earth; of all the mighty world
> Of eye and ear, both what they half-create,
> And what perceive.
> —William Wordsworth, "Tintern Abbey"

THE PROGRESSIVE IMPERATIVE TO IMAGINE

Imagine the future, your personal future, what would make you happy, a better world, a goal of any sort at all, large or individual. We take this imperative of visionary wish-making for granted as a basic part of the recipe of emancipation, self-direction, and group inspiration. But it was Addison who discursively established the imagination as a universally accessible, positive cognitive faculty for the modern world, to be used by everyone to find better paths through a labyrinth of settled or abstruse facts and through difficult lives and alienated moments.

In the midst of anxiety and uncertainty, the imaginative act can be used to produce a sense of safety and sovereignty, of being *geborgen* in the world. Collectively, across the threatening political and intellectual aporias of the long eighteenth century, the theory of the imagination had a similar metafunction, becoming a paradigmatic *Lex Continui* of European public discourse, continuously developed in a remarkably collaborative fashion. The imagination became a concept through which an affirmative sense of shared intellectual history was itself built, across times and different individuals—a site of compromise and progressive, inclusive discussion and constitution. "Seldom in Western culture," writes James Engell, "has one idea excited so many leading minds for such a stretch of time.... The imagination became the way to grasp truth."[1] Discussions of the imagination trained and extended among a wider public a more rarified aristocratic and monastic mode of detachment and contemplation: aesthetic disinterestedness, which was—on the other side of the coin—an *interest taken* in beauty, ideas, and art independent of the rough, disrupting world. Moving "downward" toward common people, such a capacity for disinterestedness "encouraged contemporaries to discover in the realm of the private an unprecedented source of authority." At the same time, the "upward" movement of common discourse and judgments into public and aesthetic life "suffused the realm of the private with a distinctively if metaphorically 'public' species of importance."[2]

Addison's serial essay *On the Pleasures of the Imagination,* published sequentially as nos. 411–21 of *The Spectator* between June and July 1712, was a watershed articulation of the modern theory of the imagination, eventually establishing its author as a founder of modern aesthetics. From Addison's essay, Abrams wrote, "developed various important ideas which are usually held to be radically innovative by historians of eighteenth-century criticism."[3] The essay's promotion of a contemplative, aesthetic subject was part of a larger Addisonian effort to set up a standard of taste at some remove from an increasingly commercialized society. The multiplication of all sorts of products—including printed efforts to define culture and human understanding—demanded a new form of education for an audience of consumers.[4] Both defensive against these modern pressures and offensive against the exclusivity of previous aesthetic discussions, "taste" became with Addison a means by which everyone in a public was empowered to judge: "Discussion became the medium through which people appropriated art."[5] Addison's recommendation of critically imaginative taste, however, did not forsake either the marketing appeal of elitism or the less profane, spiritual motivations that had driven long-established schools and practices of sacred meditation. *Spectator* 409, which preceded and introduced the essay on the imagination, identified the Jesuit philosopher Baltasar Gracián as the authority recommending "fine Taste, as the utmost Perfection of an accomplished Man." Addison's drawing attention to the mysterious power of the je ne sais quoi inherent in imaginative cognition was partially an extension of his long steeping in the depths of theology and religious contemplative practices—depths from which the call to the typical Addisonian virtues of delight, cheerfulness, and beauty also emerged.[6]

Coupling so many discourses, sociological developments, and aspirations into a private cognitive practice, Addison's seminal work constructed the idea of the imagination as a "first artery joining philosophy and psychology with the arts and criticism."[7] Becoming the pivotal reference point in discursive efforts to lay a new foundation for modern experience, his validation of the imagination's combined power of fantasy and vision emerged just as the exponentially accelerating engines of image manufacture and distribution were making themselves heard. The essay implicitly began a durable cultural meditation on the modern human ability to radically re-create the world through our own manufactured images. The shared visual commons and classic ground of an anciently persisting basic terrestrial background landscape began just incrementally to give way to a more plastic, less tethered Anthropo-scene. Addison's essay created a new space to lightly, ambivalently differentiate the two. A sympathetically subtle intellectual scalpelist, his incision in the old picture of the world cut poignantly into our primal love affair with our own eyes.

MILTONIAN MO(U)RNING: THE IMPERIAL REPUBLIC OF SIGHT

Addison was a particularly sensitive witness to the power of sight. Throughout his life and, notably, in the years directly preceding the publication of his essay on the imagination, he was troubled by his own eyesight's periodic failure, usually in times of overwork due to his government posts.[8] His biographical awareness of sight's fragility resonated with the Newtonian optics' new clarification of the abstract and tenuous connection of the human creature to the universe via its eyes. Even when they performed unnoticeably, Addison knew, his two little floating theatrical globes—themselves no perfect radiant orbs—functioned as complex lenses, filtering out the most salient features of the cosmos and leaving us blind to everything but minor, local, and relatively arbitrary aberrations in the consistency of light.

Given the historical moment in human understanding and its intersection with his own biography, it is no surprise that Addison's principal attempt to contribute to philosophy came with his imagination essay. In *Spectator* 409, he alerted his readers to the fact that his "Essay on the Pleasures of the Imagination" was coming, stating that "an Undertaking of this Nature is entirely new."[9] A committed reader of both modern and ancient philosophers, Addison generally contented himself to report on others' insights, even disguising his own synthetic originality under the humility of adulatory citation. Here, though, he was not so modest. His essay would hover where few philosophers had dared to hover since Socrates (in Plato's *Phaedrus*) had proposed a direct shortcut between the pleasure of gazing on beauty and the distant comprehension of ideal forms. The disjuncture at the connecting center of human sight that Newton had posited and Addison had experienced was a corridor through which previous philosophers generally preferred to hurry, busily talking. Addison proposed to tarry precisely there.

The imagination essay was published nine months before the premiere of *Cato*, during a time when Addison held no ministerial posts due to the Tory supremacy in the late reign of Queen Anne. Everything that the Whigs had worked for since the Glorious Revolution—and really since the fall of the Commonwealth—was potentially at stake, as Anne and the Tories sought peace with France and the specter of a reconciliation with her exiled brother began to haunt the London halls of power. Addison and his political compatriots may have felt a certain déjà vu in relation to what had seemed an improbable new Stuart Restoration. As he stared at flickering pages of his old, optimistic writing, digging up drafts of unpublished essays from the 1690s to fill up the daily *Spectator* papers, Addison was likely to think of his literary hero, Milton: the Commonwealth's poet laureate had resigned himself to the fate of blindness—to "only stand and wait," as he put it in his Sonnet 19, yoked and serving in a state made by divine ordinance "Kingly" again.[10] Like Milton's radical sixteenth-century republican vision, the simulacric, long revolutionary fantasy of Whiggish Enlightenment was, potentially, almost spent.

How were Addison's new spectating middling English subjects supposed to maintain a feeling of agency, effectiveness, and security in a modern world whose direct political future was possibly so bleak, whose reconceptualized cosmos also allowed no neat and happy mirroring under a close heaven? The "haunting and almost sinister dualism" the age had inherited from seventeenth-century empiricism revealed a universe that seemed to operate according to principles that were either beyond or alien to common understanding.[11] Like an ascending royal emperor sending a few minor, rarefied angels to abstractly govern a distant, colonized terrestrial backwater, the gaze of science threatened to leave behind the primitivized, archaic scene of common sense and action. How was Addison's crucial optimism to avoid the bitter melancholy of Milton's tragic Restoration-era alter ego—the once-supreme Samson, whose divine blind fury could only find vengeance in pulling down over his own misery the Merry Monarch's palace-cum-theater?

As usual, the answer for Addison was in finding a middle, a plane of elevation that yet subtly broke the old chain of aristocratic entailment. An Addisonian modernity began with the horizontal paradigm of the imagination upstaging the vertical paradigm of the Great Chain of Being within the intellectual debates of the day.[12] The uniqueness of Addison's solution can be seen in the contrast to his more elevated contemporary Shaftesbury's own analysis of the movement from sensible to speculative pleasures. Taking a traditional view of that movement as one from the earthly below to the heavenly above, Shaftesbury's discussion in *Characteristicks* "entirely bypasses the middle ground of the imagination, which in his view is too sullied by the senses to engineer a dependable refinement of them."[13] Addison's middle ground—the imagination validated as a horizontal plane of human cognition between the senses and the understanding—became a historically crucial site of intellectual healing and reconciliation, generative of a more pragmatic public of more equal individuals.[14] Although his discursive intervention is today often discussed primarily in sociological or ideological terms, its social, political, and conceptual impact can equally be attributed to the advancement in thinking itself enabled by what Addison believed was his historical contribution to philosophy. In contemplating the weightless waters of the imagination, one becomes aware of an essential human alienation (disinterestedness), balanced between clinging to and relaxation from the objects of both perception and thinking. This philosophical idea suggested a new form of true basic human equality, even apart from political and social motivations, and a new understanding of a "kind of property," rooted in a shared vision of the world that was equally inevitable, chosen, and utterly contingent.

The aesthetic subject that Addison inaugurated was a citizen loyal to a mixed, never fully writeable, constitution. They could not, like Socrates or the Stoics, have faith alone in a transcendental world of ideas that rejected earthly forms as delusional while, on the other hand, taking them for granted as socially stable illusions from which philosophers could perpetually depart. A greater post-Newtonian estrangement from the world of senses demanded a philosophical commitment to technology and progress. As a modern, Addison's duty was to refute the Socratic assertion of a world map that would look forever mostly the same.[15] Time, a revelatory and changing force, would be neither passive nor purely natural anymore; it took upon itself the aspect of a manufacturing machine. Addison found the virtue of the imagination—a compromised landscape between sensuality and reason—to be its capacity as a reservoir of daily health and renewal among anticipated, technological paradigm shifts in the human worldview. The garden must be a bit unkempt, not given over to merely momentarily transcendent design. The human must be allowed, and not merely as a failing, to remain something of a creature.

Accordingly, Brian Michael Norton argues that Addison's essay sought to share "an art of living, one that pursues affective well-being through intensifying and enlivening our experiences of the world"; its purpose was to found praxes and "modes of experience" in daily life.[16] As such, the essay itself takes the shape of a mildly differentiated, readerly landscape. The peaks of argument, the through-line of reason, are there but tempered by an overall layout, a winding sense of order, and a good-enough symmetrical form that emphasizes the architectural gap of the middle—where the senses and the mind vanishingly meet, and the essay's formal mimesis of the imagination suggests the stony solidity of realized human art exploding into the exponential expansion of interior cognitive space.

EPIGRAPHS

The first draft of the essay, likely written between 1696 and 1698 while Addison was still at Oxford, does not include any Latin epigraphs.[17] Addison wrote elsewhere that the untranslated motto preceding each *Spectator* essay "is of little Use to an unlearned Reader, for which Reason I consider it only as *a Word to the Wise*."[18] Taken as sequence, the epigraphs above the individual installments of *On the Pleasures of the Imagination* suggest a walking tour through the essay provided by a reflective author mapping out his own earlier draft for a wiser, classically trained audience. (The second, "wiser" neoclassical optics of the essay, then, contain a textual element of autobiography.)

The motto of the essay's first installment comes from Lucretius's first-century BCE *On the Nature of Things*:

> Avia Pieridum peragro loca, nullius ante
> Trita sola; juvat integros accedere fonteis;
> Atque haurire.[19]

In English translation, it would read:

> [I travel] through unpathed haunts of the Pierides,
> Trodden by step of none before. I joy
> To come on undefiled fountains there,
> To drain them deep.[20]

In Lucretius's six-book poem, these lines begin a section of about fifty lines near the end of book 1 that then is repeated almost verbatim as the opening of book 4, the poem's second half. The repeated section expresses the poet's hope to receive a crown of flowers from the muses for pleasantly and medicinally instructing on important and difficult matters—thus loosening "from round the mind / The tightened coils of dread religion."[21] In book 1, the poet addresses the question of whether the universe is infinite or not and answers affirmatively. In book 4, the speaker sets off to elaborate a theory of images, which posits that very tiny, thin films—simulacra—flit through the universe, combine, and sometimes enter the eye and the mind, causing strange, seemingly fantastic visions.

The doubled optimism of Lucretius's speaker fits not only the tone Addison wanted to strike in opening his essay but also the Roman author's historical moment: at the beginning of the golden age of Roman literature when the Republic enjoyed unprecedented prosperity and military successes. The passage is also a notable choice because of its immediate anti-religious context and its argument for an infinite material cosmos of many worlds and scales, a cosmography similar to the one that had recently been revalidated by Newton, who privately claimed that "the philosophy of Epicurus and Lucretius is true and old, but was wrongly interpreted by the ancients as atheism."[22]

The Lucretian motto demonstrates Addison's commitment to a knowledge "detached from but also rooted in the irreducible ground of sense experience and its constitutive interestedness."[23] From this jubilantly materialist starting-off point, the essay will move rather linearly through its eleven installments, from the comedy of the senses to the tragedy of the understanding. This thematic arrangement mimics the process of reading, in which a letter, a word, and a line begin as a sense experience and transform through a process of recognition as one moves the eyes horizontally into an understanding.

The first installment of the essay in *Spectator* 411 frames and gives a general introduction to the essay's overall scheme. The opening sentences eulogize "Our Sight" as "the most perfect and most delightful of all our Senses. It fills the Mind with the largest Variety of Ideas, its proper Enjoyment . . . Considered as a more delicate and diffusive kind of Touch," Sight creates the notion of an extendable body "that spreads it self over an infinite Multitude of Bodies, comprehends the largest Figures, and brings into our reach some of the most remote Parts of the Universe." Sight allows the individual (like Hobbes's Leviathan or a fantastical Übermensch) to collect ideas without tiredness over great distances.[24] Addison announces that the departure point for his landscape tour will be the "Primary Pleasures of the Imagination, which entirely proceed from such Objects as are before our eyes." If one imagines the essay as a landscape of the imagination, on the left-hand side the depiction would be photorealistic, finely and naturalistically painted. The path from there will then lead to the center where Addison takes up the "Secondary Pleasures of the Imagination," the more abstract realm of memory, art, and writing. The essay here stays true to Hobbesian and Lucretian empirical explanation and steps ever so subtly away from Christian and Platonic notions of divine forms never seen directly on Earth but remembered by eternal souls. Addison's materialist declaration: "We cannot indeed have a single Image in the Fancy that did not make its first Entrance through the Sight."[25]

But when Addison writes in this opening that he is considering "by the Pleasures of the Imagination . . . only such Pleasures as arise originally from Sight," his insistent emphasis on *pleasures* frames the landscape he is intent on painting as something other than a disinterested, empirical materialist investigation of the nature of the imagination.[26] Pleasure was the general "Vehicle" through which Addison and Steele planned to bring philosophy to "Domestick life," but here Addison thematizes the practice of taking pleasures more specifically.[27] With its opening number published on a Saturday, the essay as a whole was prescriptive; it takes its place as the crown jewel of another, longer series that Addison developed in *The Spectator:* the "Saturday sermons." An earlier installment of that weekly series, *Spectator* 93 foreshadowed the imagination essay's overall spiritual direction through its allegory of a man with only "a little Stock to improve" who would like to use the time of his short life wisely but faces the frustrating reality of large stretches of boredom, wasted hours, and impatient waiting: "Because the Mind," Addison wrote, "cannot be always in its Fervours, nor strained up to a pitch of Virtue, it is necessary to find out proper Employments for it in its Relaxations."[28]

HEALTHY IMAGINATION

In *Spectator* 411, Addison identifies the pleasures of the imagination in exactly the location between sinking into "Negligence and Remissness" and the rigor of "serious Employments." The guiding compass of moderation—where pleasure and concern for long-term existence met—was physiological health. Adjusting the argument of Francis Bacon in "Of Regiment of Health" for a less elite and courtly audience, Addison held that "the Pleasures of Fancy are more conducive to Health, than those of the Understanding, which are worked out by Dint of Thinking, and attended with too violent a Labour of the Brain."[29] The mild use of the imagination had a restoring effect on body and mind. Not abandoning the long-held Platonic and Stoic insistence on the supremacy of understanding, Addison simply tempered that supremacy by emphasizing the analysis of pleasure. The pleasures of "the Understanding" are, he wrote, "more preferable, because they are founded on some new Knowledge or Improvement in the Mind of Man; yet it must be confest, that those of the Imagination are as great and as transporting as the other. A beautiful Prospect delights the Soul, as much as a Demonstration.... The Pleasures of the Imagination have this Advantage, above those of the Understanding, that they are more obvious, and more easy to be acquired.... We are struck, we know not how, and immediately assent to the Beauty of an Object, without enquiring into the particular Causes and Occasions of it."[30]

This raised a basic question of theodicy for a Platonist like Addison. Why would an Almighty create such a philosophically unsatisfying human system, in which the attainment of knowledge yields no greater or more transporting pleasure than that which is more easily and readily, imaginatively attained? Addison's initial bridge over the troubled waters of theodicy is characteristically moderate and minimally announced, even as it reverses orthodoxy and the direction of long controversies. Using the imagination, he argues, gives pleasure more easily than using the understanding because the Creator wants us to have an easy, universal way to attain pleasure even in situations understood to be bad; this proves (again) that the Creator is good.[31] The human is divinely designed with the capacity to produce its own imaginative pleasure even when the theater of its local cosmos in fact provides a rather dreadful show; this, in turn, supports the human capacity to grow and understand, incorporating experiences of new environments and situations beyond initial comfort zones. The imagination is a divine gift, there to support our species, its strength, its reproduction, and its speciation. In procedural analogy to Newton's moving the creation of "color" into the eye and mind and away from the actual, external milieu, Addison subjectifies some of the causation of thought and sensation by focusing on the genesis of pleasure within the opaquer room of the psyche itself.

Even "a Man in a Dungeon," Addison writes, can entertain himself with the imagination, an example that points to the balance between the imagination's function in supporting health and the understanding's function in providing realistic assessments of an individual's situation.[32] Here again the subtlety of Addison's identification with dissident, oppressed, and laboring people whose circumstances required endurance and routine regeneration shines through. More generally, his advocacy of imaginative exercise "advertises" a means to more easily acquire obvious, free pleasures for readers in a gigantically expanding market of consumer goods, full of endless possibilities to acquire knowledge but also enclosing the new middling reader in an alienating, distracting, and exhausting crush of marketed cultural objects—or pushing them into that crush's shadow: the sense of exclusion or lonely, "open-air" imprisonment coming for the person who does not or cannot buy access to a broad cultural life mediated increasingly through bought commodities and transposed into silent reading, away from the free and natural commons.[33] Addison's essay can be read as a philosophical meditation on the modern problem of grounding individual existence away from external discourses, whose inexhaustible accessibility revealed the need to train the self in establishing and maintaining a new sovereign position, even while taking breaks from the pursuit of understanding.

As such, the essay on the pleasures of the imagination performs a midpoint in a genealogy of modernity that connects Descartes in his parlor with Coleridge in his, the latter meditating on the film of soot lightly clinging to his fireplace grate in "Frost at Midnight." Descartes reestablished Platonic authority with the declaration equating *thought* with existence. Coleridge, sitting in a similar room, mused on the Romantic abandon of the soul as a fleeting stranger in an even stranger contingent landscape between the small scale of burning passion and the vast cold of eternity; the poet's bit of black soot (colloquially called a "stranger") was a fitting symbol for the individual, his understanding, and the black textual output of both. Addison's spectator, roving through the city and its multifaceted social life alone, grounded individual existence in a hermaphroditic position prior to thought—perception—and made it sociable by prescribing pleasure. The capacity to heighten perception into pleasure, a relatively simple trick of cultivating receptivity wherever one was, was proof, for Addison, that the soul was no mere sinning calculator nor abandoned stranger but an intended guest at a reaffirming divine theater.

Touching somewhat lightly on one of the more powerful concepts driving English political discourse and the sociological formation of a new class of citizens, the essay proposes an influential new version of property linked to pleasure and use rather than traditional ownership: "A Man of a Polite Imagination . . . often feels a greater Satisfaction in the Prospect of Fields and Meadows, than another does in the Possession. It gives him, indeed, a kind of Property in everything he sees, and makes the most rude uncultivated Parts of Nature administer to his Pleasures."[34] For Addison and those in the elite philosophical subsection of his audience, such a passage played on the etymological and associative links between words pertaining to comprehension and cognition and those pertaining to physical grasping or holding. The imagination as a separate mode of cognition is a kind of light, diffuse, nonexclusive enclosing, akin to participation in a public claim reversing the direction and center of feudal administration. The firmer grip of understanding, in contrast, might exclude in its narrow insistence the broader purposes of cognitive enjoyment. Although the word "polite" in this context is sometimes interpreted by present-day critics as pointing to a kind of ownership attached to bourgeois false consciousness, Addison's articulation can also be understood as an early, genealogical point in the political formation of utilitarianism, moral concepts of ownership, notions of public property, and universal rights to own and use land against settled (mostly aristocratic) holdings.[35] In the colonial rather than domestic context of the British Empire, however, the implications of the still rather light but subversive suggestion reveal themselves as differently problematic: whoever could appreciate and know how to use the land better already had a faint claim to ownership.[36] Still, in dialectical tension, Addison's suggestion theorized a process by which more people might begin to reasonably claim a sovereign position in the world, at first imaginatively, using just what they had, just where they were.

Unlike Hobbes's sovereign, who singularly merited the absolute entailment of all property, Addison's imaginative sovereign entailed no body politic but, rather, in direct Protestant fashion, the individual's productive connection to nature. Nature, converted imaginatively into a benevolent state administering to the individual's pleasures, could never be *understood* to be so in reality, at least in the Augustan discursive world. The more well-known state of nature—the reigning, overwhelming, cruel, capricious, and inhuman chaos of endless civil war and horrific, senseless suffering—could not be delightfully forgotten. It threatened to return and engulf the world as it had in the previous century during the anarchical English civil wars and the bloody Thirty Years' War on the continent. Born out of that chaotic period of struggle, the emboldened, middling, republican subject might rely on natural claims to imagine a stronger, more equal future. Yet few in the time could fail to remember the dangerous, drowning aspect of Nature's jealous grip as they went onward like Lucretius's hero in search of refreshing undefiled fountains.

THEATRICALLY MOTIVATING AND NECESSITATING THE HUMAN

The second epigraph of the imagination series, opening *Spectator* 412, passes on Martial's advice to his reader, should his *Epigrams* prove boring: read only half, *Divisum sic breve fiet Opus* ("Divided the work will thus become brief"). The epigraph alludes to the goal of pleasure and points to the small philosophical terrain of Addison's undertaking: the stage of the imagination, divided on one side from sensing and on the other from understanding. The epigraph also refers to the second installment's more immediate topic: the liminal activity of the sensing mind in differentially directing our admiring attention to greatness, novelty, and beauty in the natural world. Engulfed in a glut of potential stimuli, pleasure serves as the functional guide of our interest and attention in Addison's protopsychoanalytic theory. Stepping over the boundary of the eyes into the sensing mind, Addison confronts how our seeing and our unconscious aesthetic judgment are shaped by our reproductive needs as a species: "We find by Experience, that there are several Modifications of Matter which the Mind, without any previous Consideration, pronounces at first sight Beautiful or Deformed. Thus we see that every different Species of sensible Creatures has its different Notions of Beauty." Addison emphasizes that the eye itself is shaped to perceive some things more favorably than others, claiming in particular that "the Eye takes most Delight in Colours."[37] As Newton revealed the essentiality of color to be a lie of our peculiar eyes, Addison theorized that there was no essentiality in beauty: what looks beautiful to one species of being—what looks symmetrical or harmonious or grand or unusual—probably looks to other species ugly, deformed, or unworthy of notice. Martial's epigraph thus finally speaks, in Addison's imagination, to the role of unconsciously divided perception in making it easier for birds (and humans) to find appropriate mates and thus keep them from mating with other species, serving a divine will for the integrity or eternal forms of species.[38]

Stepping further into the interior and abstraction in his next installment in *Spectator* 413, Addison summarizes the post-Newtonian epistemological situation of natural philosophy: "We know neither the Nature of an Idea, nor the Substance of a Human Soul, which might help us to discover the Conformity or Disagreeableness of the one to the other."[39] The paper's translated epigraph from Ovid—"The cause is secret, but the effect is known"—confesses Addison's modesty in the face of explaining *how* some visions produce pleasure in a human being. Referencing Aristotle's classification of causes, Addison argues that since we cannot know the "necessary and efficient causes," it makes sense to turn instead to the question of *why* and to investigate the theological "Final causes" for the pleasure we take from certain sights. Our ability to admire greatness derives from the necessity of contemplating the nature of "the Supreme Author of our Being," who is "neither circumscribed by Time or Place"; so is our attraction to the new an internal prod toward our own effortful development.[40] Likewise, because we observe that we are motivated by beauty, we can deduce that our experience of beauty was designed by a creator who desires our survival and demonstrates goodness by guiding our survival through pleasure. "Ideas which are different from any thing that exists in the Objects them-selves, (for such are Light and Colours)," are "Supernumerary Ornaments to the Universe"—unnecessary decoration placed simply to make our experience more pleasant.[41]

The pathos of the Newtonian paradigm shift, which decisively split the classical terrestrial world from the abstract modern cosmos, lay close to the surface in the paper's description of the human actor's immersion in a divine imaginative theater:

> We are every where entertained with pleasing Shows and Apparitions, we discover imaginary Glories in the Heavens, and in the Earth, and see some of this Visionary Beauty poured out upon the whole Creation; but what a rough unsightly Sketch of Nature should we be entertained with, did all her Colouring disappear, and the several Distinctions of Light and Shade vanish? In short, our Souls are at present delightfully lost and bewildered in a pleasing Delusion, and we walk about like the Enchanted Hero of a Romance, who sees beautiful Castles, Woods and Meadows; and at the same time hears the warbling of Birds, and the purling of Streams; but upon the finishing of some secret Spell, the fantastick Scene breaks up, and the disconsolate Knight finds himself on a barren Heath, or in a solitary Desart. It is not improbable that something like this may be the State of the Soul after its first Separation, in respect of the Images it will receive from Matter; tho' indeed the Ideas of Colours are so pleasing and beautiful in the Imagination, that it is possible the Soul will not be deprived of them, but perhaps find them excited by some other Occasional Cause, as they are at present by the different Impressions of the subtle Matter on the Organ of Sight.[42]

The imagination rescues where the understanding deprives: the pleasure of seeing colors connects the newborn, modern scientific subject and the good soul of the afterlife alike to the estranged classical terrestrial world through the umbilical cord of the imagination. Being possibly forced to forsake the naturalized, immediate pleasure of seeing colors—for Addison, a step too far in the direction of an inhumane universe—suggested, conversely, the motivational system that was the imagination's divine raison d'être. Like Oedipus, a sobered-up Don Quixote, Shakespeare's Lear or Caliban, the tragic hero of Addison's tale would be cast out on a disenchanted, desolate, barren landscape the moment he would insist on too much understanding. "Could we see Nature as it is," Fontenelle had written (in a book Addison praised), "we should see nothing but the hinder part of the Theatre at the Opera."[43] The more serene path, supported by the soul's divinely created structure, guides the individual to accept being wrapped in the pleasurable scenes of the imagination. The recent "great Modern Discovery" of natural philosophy, Addison writes, drives home the point, since even the most basic, unavoidable constituent aspects of human experience, like "Light and Colours, as apprehended by the Imagination, are only Ideas in the Mind, and not Qualities that have any Existence in Matter."[44] Newton had recently utterly erased and redrawn the consequential line between understanding and delusion in an act that scientists of the future were likely to repeat again and again.

The next installment of the essay (414) steps toward a more clearly subjective yet still external phenomenon: the work of art, in contrast to nature, lacks vastness and immensity, Addison confessed, leaving it primarily reliant on beauty and strangeness to produce pleasure in its viewers. Addison's ordering of art proceeds scientifically, from the outside in, beginning with those art forms we experience in a way most similar to the way we experience nature. Here again the discussion is haunted by the Newtonian revision of vision. The later installments' Platonic spelunking into the caves of art begins only superficially—picking up on the previous installment's discussion of light—with an experiment "very common in Opticks": the camera obscura, which Addison describes as producing "The prettiest Landskip I ever saw."[45] Gardening is also considered as a special case of art and nature ambiguously mimicking or blending into each other. "Each by itself is vain" (as the translated epigraph from Horace reads), but nature and human activity meet and sublimate in the imaginative individual viewer to suggest the human her- or himself as the necessary conjunction and bringer of order.[46] Thus, the paper influentially urged English gardeners to leave more forest and uncontrolled spaces, allowing an artificial rudeness to invade their overtidy, sterile, and out-of-touch productions in the land; this would more accurately mirror the human condition.

The next installment of the essay (415) steps again in the direction of the artificial and the man-made, arriving at an art form that strikes a synthetic dialectical balance between externally and internally derived imaginative pleasure. Architecture, the last of the primary pleasures of the imagination, both encloses and projects the interiority of the imagination into the exterior at its most magnificent scale, where it is reencountered as part of the external world, the objective landscape dotted by ancient and modern cities. At the very border between internal creative human subjectivity and the physical environment it encounters, Addison muses on the curved surface of the eye and its influence on determining the pleasure we take in concave architectural forms.⁴⁷

UNDERSTANDING THE CAVE

The essay is structured as a double series with a central gap separating its consideration of the primary pleasures of the imagination (derived from objects actually seen by the eyes) and its secondary pleasures (derived from internal cognition, from what is "afterwards called up into Mind, either barely by its own Operations" or by our experience of external works of art).⁴⁸ If the essay is pictured as a landscape of the imagination, the next installment (416) ambiguously begins to show two vertically symmetrical, incrementally diverging paths. As Addison proceeds through the pleasures of artistic mimesis further away from direct sense-reaction and toward the other border of the imagination in the flanking bright light of understanding, the "heroic" imaginative subject (like Goethe's Faust in part 2 of his tragedy) follows the increasingly powerful abstraction of signification seemingly both up-and-out to the comprehension of solid knowledge and facts and down-and-deeper into the swallowing delusion of reality-replacement.

Turning to the second half of the essay's consideration of the secondary pleasures of the imagination, the epigraph to 416 again gives the wise hint: *Quatenûs hoc simile est oculis, quod mente videmus.* The line is a shortened version of two lines from Lucretius; Addison's version, translated into English, keeps Lucretius's sense but adds ambiguity: "In so far what we see with the eye is similar to that we see with the mind."⁴⁹ The motto references Lucretius's materialist theory of the simulacra in a subtle, formally witty echo of the essay's opening epigraph, which was taken from the twice-repeated "beginning" marking the two halves of Lucretius's *The Nature of Things*. Lucretius is here positing that the mind perceives images in the same way that the eye does, except that the films (simulacra) that stir the mind (in a dream) can be much thinner, leading readily to fantastic recombinations—to visions of centaurs, for example. The Lucretian Addison observes that taking pleasure in mimetic arts depends not just on a species-specific set of innate preferences, but on an act of comparison between the sensed object and the image it stirs up through memory and association. The resumed walk now quickly descends through the caverns of art and ascends toward the full, artistically bestowed Ideas of things. Addison the poetic prosaist settles, unsurprisingly, on writing as an object for his longer analysis: it is writing as an art that has the most flexibility to suggest exciting, yet highly specific, minutely modifiable ideas. This power of writing (as with other forms of art) depends on the mimetic forms that a culture has developed and on an individual's experiences with them and the world; additionally, it depends on how "perfect" the imagination is in the individual, either from birth or through cultivation of sensitivity and judgment.[50] In passages like these, one finds the crucial aesthetic turn inaugurated in Addison's theory toward the "perceiver's stance" as well as the "radical subjectivization" that will be developed at the end of the century by Kant.[51]

Settling first on the solid marble ground of classical poetry, *Spectator* 417 begins with an epigraph from Horace's *Odes* in which the poet praises his own ability to win fame and praise, not from feats in the physical world but by vividly enclosing the physical world in his verses. The installment will concern itself with the "purest" of the secondary pleasures of the imagination—those based on poetry that most directly seems to stir up delightful images and memories of real places tied to the writer's experiences. Addison only lightly here takes up the theme of the heightening, distorting psychological effects of the secondary pleasures of the imagination. Cartesian theory, he explains, shows how poetry renders its powerful effect by triggering grouped traces in the brain of pleasant places. Overall positive experiences in such places had already shaped the associated regions of the brain with wider channels "worn in the Pleasure Traces" for the passage of "Animal Spirits," in contrast to the comparatively very narrow, impassable channels for any "disagreeable Ideas." Recalling what is pleasurable through the associative memory of poetry thus triggers traces of other pleasurable sights by way of the "violent" flowing of "Animal Spirits" around these grouped regions with widened "agreeable" passages, triply compounding the effect of pleasure.[52]

As the craftsman working most intimately with the material of these internal, grouped memory traces, the poet, per Addison, "should take as much Pains in forming his Imagination, as a Philosopher in cultivating his Understanding," and he must do so by dwelling in both country and courts, becoming familiar with all of the landscapes and arts famous among his past and present peers.[53] In the inky atmosphere of the secondary pleasures of the imagination, Addison presents three classical guides, each associated with one of the three imaginative pleasures his essay proposes: Homer is the poet of the Great, Virgil of the Beautiful, and Ovid of the Strange or Novel. But the perfect master of sublime composition is a modern author, Milton, who was encumbered only by the English language, which Addison compared to brick in contrast to Latin's marble.[54]

The admired work of the blind poet Milton surfaces again and again in the essay's exploration of the secondary pleasures of the imagination, just as the first half of the essay's grand tour of the primary pleasures repeatedly touched upon the visionary work of Newton. A comparison of the pleasure induced by Milton's descriptions of heaven and hell provides the sublime example for Addison's further venturing into the imaginative interior in *Spectator* 418. Comparison itself emerges here more fully in Addison's protopsychoanalytic theory as "a new Principle of Pleasure" whereby the mind is naturally driven to compare mental and artistic representations with their objective counterparts as part of its search after truth. In other words, this "new Principle of Pleasure," beyond the previously established Cartesian pleasure principle, undergirds a reality principle, allowing a greater degree of abstraction in our imaginative experience through which we can enjoy even descriptions of disagreeable things like dung or hell (though Addison believes we would still prefer to read about a positive place like Paradise, the skillfulness of the description being equal).[55]

As it begins to approach the tragic boundary of understanding, the landscape of the imagination becomes self-reflexive. Addison considers that some pleasures the imagination takes in reading poetic description—pleasures that open "a wider and more universal" perspective than that offered by the pleasures of sight alone—seem to be more aptly the "pleasure of the Understanding." At the same time, *Spectator* 418 acknowledges that poets enhance our pleasure through falsification and the creation of distance between ourselves and a harsher world. The tragic, "more serious parts of poetry" heighten imaginative pleasure by simultaneously stirring the mind with terror and pity yet, through their very artificiality, stimulating the imagination's comparative faculty, thus granting the reader the pleasure of feeling safer and more secure than the suffering "Afflicted." The "Dangers that are past" are likened to "a Precipice at a distance, which would fill us with a different kind of Horreur, if we saw it hanging over our Heads."[56] The tragic gaze Addison locates in both poetry and history thus culturally stabilizes the "new Principle of Pleasure," the reality principle, by allowing us to mourn a simpler, more directly but more dangerously driven life: a life of purer magnificence, beauty, and rarity, and extraordinary pain. Yet in the dark or too-bright interior of its psychic court, the imagination's unrelenting drive to compare continually threatens melancholic tyranny: it can always "fancy to it self Things more Great, Strange, or Beautiful, than the Eye ever saw, and is still sensible of some Defect in what it has seen." The daydream of the poet, then, must "humour the

Imagination in its own Notions, by mending and perfecting Nature," adding flowers to meadows or, like Virgil in the number's epigraph, sweet-smelling myrrh to a thicket.[57]

In *Spectator* 419, the imaginative sojourner approaches the realm of fantastic poetry: Dryden's "Fairie Way of Writing." As the classical ground gives way to the gothic, Shakespeare's genius becomes the guiding light. "The Poet quite loses sight of Nature," and the comparative faculty of the imagination, so crucial to the readers' pleasurable experience, calls more fully on deep, childhood memories to produce the effect of realism. Addison links these memories to tales told to children as well as, historically, to the postclassical, pre-Reformation, feudal dark ages "when pious Frauds were made use of to amuse Mankind, and frighten them into a Sense of their Duty." Pity is lost as a prevailing, pleasurable emotion, while horror and terror take precedence. The readers' fuller, more childlike immersion grants them a fantasy of what it must be like to be of a very different culture or even of a very different species of spirit, to be momentarily of a kind with the "many Intellectual Beings in the World besides ourselves . . . subject to different Laws and Oeconomies from those of Mankind." Through personified allegory, Addison remarks, poetry in this further fantastic realm "represents even the Faculties of the Soul," drawing the imagination into a kind of self-feeding reflection—*mentis gratissimus Error,* "a most pleasing delusion," as the installment's epigraph has it.[58] The original literary context of the motto resonates with Addison's view of human sovereignty as supported by a divine theatricality. Taken from Horace's *Epistles* 2.2, the line describes the hallucination of a man who sat and applauded in an empty theater, believing he was hearing admirable tragedies. The man, who had otherwise been perfectly adept and upright in his life, was cured of the delusion, but the cure destroyed him.

The danger of the secondary pleasures of the imagination—their delusive ability to construct a virtual reality estranged from that of the senses—mounts through Addison's essay in the shadow as imaginative cognition approaches the light of understanding. Looking briefly again at the essay's elaborate but subtle late-Baroque doubled construction opens this thematic up to the wise reader to whom the epigraphs were addressed. *Spectator* 411 set off with a Lucretian hero to explore the primary pleasures of the imagination, derived from those objects directly seen by the eyes. In the middle of the essay, the epigraph to *Spectator* 416 again references Lucretius's doubly launched hero, who, in the middle of *De rerum natura*'s book 4, turns to contemplate the similarity of the mind's inner workings to the workings of the eyes themselves. Now relaunching the essay on the trail of the secondary pleasures of the imagination, specifically those derived from writing, *Spectator* 416 echoes 411. The next four installments likewise mirror the installments from the first part of the series, just as writing mimics the ability of the sensed world to produce the primary pleasures of the imagination. Classical poetry (417) aims at the greatness, beauty, and novelty produced by the most humanly compelling sights of nature (412). *Spectator* 418 dialectically considers the "Final" functional reason for the secondary pleasures of the imagination in the poet's appeal to the soul's comparative drive to classify, sharpen its concept of reality, remove itself from tragedy, and demand a better, particularly augmented world. This echoes *Spectator* 413's theory of the divinely ordained primary pleasures' "Final Causes" in prodding the soul toward its health and improvement. In their different ordinal domains, *Spectator* 414 and 419 both then consider art forms that most directly—with the least seeming intervention—mirror and frame the "objective" wildness of "nature": the camera lucida and the liberal landscape garden in the case of the primary pleasures of sight; the "fairy way of writing" and personified psychological allegories in the case of the secondary pleasures of writing, which take the content of memory and the psyche's own prime movements as their second "nature." The peripatetic dialectic of the first half of the essay walked toward *Spectator* 415's synthesis in architecture, the most intimate merger between an objective world of the senses beyond human intervention and a subjective will to distill and maximize pleasure, to produce out of the cosmos a fitting, easy, and restorative landscape and dwelling place. If the scheme just outlined holds true, the mirroring architectural plan of the essay would suggest that *Spectator* 420 holds the synthesis of Addison's dialectical consideration of the secondary pleasures of the imagination.

The epigraph to that penultimate installment of the essay is again drawn from Horace. Addison quotes line 100 of his *Ars Poetica*, "Quocunque volunt mentem Auditoris agunto," which is a modified version of Horace's original: "Et quocumque volent animum auditoris agunto."[59] The modification in the Latin speaks to exactly the dialectical tension building up as the essay approaches the imagination's (right-hand) framing border with the understanding. The original refers to poetry's power to "bear away the soul of the auditor whithersoever they please."[60] Addison's modification of the original replaces *animus* (soul) with *mens* (mind), stressing the ranging of the mind (in the imagination and understanding) in contrast to the embodied soul's more fixed and earthbound reality in mortal life.[61] Moving further into the abstraction of writing, the imaginative landscape grapples with those "who are obliged to follow Nature more closely"—that is, "Historians, natural Philosophers, Travellers, Geographers, and, in a Word, all who describe visible

Objects of a real Existence."[62] Addison notes that his chief concern in the paper is not with the *veracity* of these writers but, rather, with their ability to move the imagination. Veracity, however, is exactly the effect that categorizes these writers as a group who (supposedly) try to match their output to nature itself. As the interior capacity of the imagination to propose and envision alternative, complete worlds grows more pronounced, it approaches the act of world-making that comes with understanding. Nonfictional or scientific writing—at the very frontier of the imagination and the understanding—strives to provide the synthesis between the psyche's inborn (or unconscious) content or inclinations and its memory and new experiences: its learning, conclusions, or *Bildung*. As a kind of writing that proposes a real picture of the world with a veracity equal to or even greater than the picture we take from our senses themselves, scientific writing's status in relation to the secondary pleasures of the imagination is indeed analogous to architecture's status among the primary pleasures. Put simply, scientific writing provides the believable and dogmatic blueprint into which we fit our human experience. By pleasing both our imaginative inclinations and the somewhat opposed reality testing of our memory, the most impactful scientific writers charm us out of the effort of comparison. They weave our diverging interests and passions tightly into a single narrative thread so that the "Reader becomes a kind of Spectator," engrossed and thereby a witness to truth rather than an aesthetic contemplator of mimesis and sense.[63]

Pushing the borderlands between the imagination and the understanding further, the essay's climax synthesizes Newton's distantly stretched cosmos and the darkly dazzling pathos of Miltonian flight. Addison singles out "the Authors of the new Philosophy" as those who most "gratifie and enlarge the Imagination." Reading of their discoveries,

> we are filled with a pleasing Astonishment, to see so many Worlds hanging one above another, and sliding round their Axles in such an amazing Pomp and Solemnity.... But if we yet rise higher, and consider the fixt Stars as so many vast Oceans of Flame, that are each of them attended with a different Sett of Planets, and still discover new Firmaments and new Lights, that are sunk farther in those unfathomable Depths of Ether, so as not to be seen by the strongest of our Telescopes, we are lost in such a Labyrinth of Suns and Worlds, and confounded with the Immensity and Magnificence of Nature.[64]

But here the shadow sense of the number's modified motto returns: the modern scientific depiction of unmanageable scales now widens a chasm between what previously could have been considered one mode of cognition on a gradual continuum—imagination and understanding. Lost and confounded, the scientifically intoxicated mind races and revels in a pluriverse of massively shifting, folded scales; it "might yet carry it farther, and discover in the smallest Particle of this little World, a new inexhausted Fund of Matter, capable of being spun out into another Universe."[65]

In the essay's focus, the creatively exploding black holes of infinite scales stem first from the letters of imaginative scientific writing, which carry the reports of observations through new glasses and the new hard mimesis of natural-philosophical calculus. Contemplating the ambiguity between the readerly, escapist pleasure taken in imaginative writing and the satisfied certainty of understanding centers attention, again, on "the Body of Man" and the inevitable comparative balance it gives to the Soul's experience of wildly differing scales, upward and downward. The climax of the imagination essay is, thus, a telling example of what John O'Brien claims was "at the heart of *The Spectator* project": a "stubborn desire to retain and refigure the human body" that worked against the cultural direction of "virtualization and disembodiment" reflected in "the corporate authorship of the periodical and the emergence of print at this moment."[66] As a newly theorized form of cognition, the imagination is allied with the soul in its conjunction with the body. "I have dwelt the longer on this Subject," Addison writes,

> because I think it may shew us the proper Limits, as well as the Defectiveness, of our Imagination; how it is confined to a very small Quantity of Space, and immediately stopt in its Operations, when it endeavours to take in any thing that is very great, or very little. . . . The Understanding, indeed, opens an infinite Space on every side of us, but the Imagination, after a few faint Efforts, is immediately at a stand, and finds her self swallowed up in the Immensity of the Void that surrounds it: Our Reason can pursue a Particle of Matter through an infinite variety of Divisions, but the Fancy soon loses sight of it, and feels in it self a kind of Chasm, that wants to be filled with Matter of a more sensible Bulk. We can neither widen nor contract the Faculty to the Dimensions of either Extreme: The Object is too big for our Capacity, when we would comprehend the Circumference of a World, and dwindles into nothing, when we endeavour after the Idea of an Atome.[67]

Ever the progressive, Addison confessed an agnosticism about whether one day, "perhaps, the Imagination will be able to keep Pace with the Understanding, and to form in it self distinct Ideas of all the different Modes and Quantities of Space."⁶⁸ In his own age and experience, however, the healthily modest, limited imagination provided the nutrition for the practically embodied soul, where reason provided the charts and projected routes for the mind in its self-liberating, imperial adventures.

LUCRETIUS AT SALMACIS

The hero of the essay's opening epigraph—the optimistic Lucretian poet—would have run boldly into the refreshing, clear pools of infinite space, confidently connecting the material world of the senses with the beautiful result of inspired understanding. Addison's essay runs instead into a swampy mire in its final installment, which functions in the double structure just analyzed as an appended synthesis, a concluding foray into understanding itself. The last motto, from Ovid, closely echoes the opening motto, from Lucretius: it reports the boy Hermaphroditus's joy at the onset of his adventurous journey: *Ignotis errare locis, ignota videre / Flumina gaudebat; studio minuente laborem.* Almost twenty years before, Addison had translated these lines: "[He] sought fresh fountains in a foreign soil; / The pleasure lessened the attending toil."⁶⁹ Perhaps not incidentally, that translation was among Addison's first published works, his 1694 version of the tale of Salmacis and Hermaphroditus from the *Metamorphoses*.⁷⁰

On the reflected surface, the striking resemblance between the first and last mottos suggests the frame of ideal classical symmetry. Both epigraphs feature a would-be hero wandering eagerly through a wilderness populated by divine female guardians of the pure, clear waters the hero seeks. A note of labor creeps into the latter, but Hermaphroditus's fate is unmentioned. Indeed, Addison, as he reached the tragic modern boundary of the imagination with understanding, was characteristically discreet with what is, after all, a provocative and even disturbing conclusion. His words to the wise kept the second optics of his essay tucked away in Latin allusion, plainly and meaningfully available only to those already used to wrestling with the abysses of complex philosophy and long history.

The tale from Ovid that Addison used to deconstruct the classical frame around the imagination at the end of the essay concerns the child of Hermes and Aphrodite. Hermes, the messenger of Zeus, is associated with the pursuit of understanding, particularly understanding through letters and interpretation, an association that survives in the etymology of "hermeneutics." Aphrodite, the goddess of beauty and sensual love, is associated with the pleasures of the senses. When their fifteen-year-old son, Hermaphroditus, leaves his homeland in search of new fountains, he finds a particularly clear river where a vain and indolent nymph, Salmacis, lives. The virgin Hermaphroditus rejects her flattering attempt at seduction, and she pretends to leave only to wait until he, naked, enters the water. A scene of struggle ensues, during which Salmacis rapes the boy (or at least holds him very tightly—like a sinuous snake to the talons of an eagle until it folds around his head and wings, like ivy to the trunk of a sturdy oak, like a polypus with sucking tentacles . . .)[71] In the midst of this action, Salmacis prays to the gods to be forever joined with the boy. The gods grant her prayer, grafting the two together under one skin. When Hermaphrodite emerges from the waters and feels his relaxed half-male body, he cries out to his parents and implores them to make any male who enters the waters of Salmacis only half-male upon his emergence.[72] This strange request is, of course, granted, completing Ovid's explanation for the famous feminizing effect of the waters of Salmacis—a well-known ancient bathing destination in modern-day Bodrum, Turkey.[73] Drawn from the same tale, the epigraph of the third installment of the essay (discussed above) had already thematized this effect in regard to the primary pleasures of the imagination: "Causa latet, vis est notissima," translated by the younger Addison as "The cause is secret, but the effect is known."[74]

The echo of the Lucretian starting epigraph by the final motto taken from Ovid alludes historically to the change from an ascending golden age of Roman republican glory in rational discovery to an artistically falling and dangerous Caesarian age of coded, satirical, imperial metamorphoses—the latter being the same age in which Jesus of Nazareth was crucified, forty years after Cato's suicide. His own death marking the end of the golden age of Latin poetry, the Augustan Ovid looked back on Lucretius with nostalgic admiration and the will to see his work perpetually resurrected in the human imagination: he called Lucretius "divine," asserting that his verses "will perish only / When one day gives the world over to destruction."[75]

Poetically, moving from Lucretius's positivistic, infinite quest to Ovid's myth, the bold statement of truth and fearless exploration transforms into a cautionary tale about a beautiful but naive young man who in his reverie falls into a trap. The same quest, perhaps even the same water, but the passage in Ovid is shadowed by the offstage scheming of the nymph Salmacis. A popularizer of Epicurean Platonism, Lucretius's philosophical vision had been confident, republican, optimistic, expansionary, and empiricist. His own fate as a mythic historical figure, however, was charged with Hermaphroditic overtones: this avant-garde preacher of atomism and evolution was rumored to have been driven mad and then to suicide by a love potion. In the recent English theatrical history that would have still haunted Addison's childhood decades later, the waters of Salmacis had featured famously in the last royal masque of the Stuart court before the Civil War and the Interregnum. The would-be royal martyr Charles I himself appeared in Inigo Jones and William Davenant's *Salmacis Spolia,* a star turn that served as a historical warning about the refreshing waters of flattering theatricality turning into a delusive trap.

Addison's psychological and historical acumen gave the essay's concluding synthesis its brilliant pathos: be it republican or kingly, an overconfident belief in the projective fruits of human understanding looks basically the same as a potion-induced imaginative reverie. Understanding's attempt to conceptually grasp the imagination becomes in the essay's last installment an equivalent reflection of imagination's attempt to pleasurably bathe in the landscape of expanded understanding. The fresh and particularly clear waters that both Lucretius's and Ovid's would-be heroes seek out stand metaphorically in Addison's use for the refreshing visions promised by both cognitive faculties, with the ambiguous threat of pleasure's embrace lurking beneath the surface, equally narcissistic and alien.

HERMAPHRODITIC EPISTEMOLOGY

By emphasizing and closing with an allusion to the myth of Hermaphrodite, Addison put his essay in the tradition of Platonism's suspicion of artistic reverie and imaginative completion. Simultaneously, he hinted that—like Plato after Socrates's death and the onset of Athens's decline, like Ovid after the fall of the Roman republic and Lucretius's rational freedom—the generation of poets after Milton and Newton may have found that the enlightened waters of an expanded, imperial field had a dark undercurrent. To the classically trained reader, the space of the essay is marked off as an immersion in the Platonically ambivalent imagination, between the young hero's exuberant approach (the rhapsodic possession of the naive artist or the triumphant comprehensive explanation of the sophist) and his changed exit, now internally caught in an earthly, serpentine, and feminizing snare (the mortal error of the unreflective sensualist or sophistic disciple.) The self-conscious framing employed by Addison suggested his awareness of the difficulty of staking a serious philosophical inquiry on the value of imagination proper given the imagination's general association with delusion and misleading, ill thinking: much of philosophy concerned itself, naturally, with the work of dispelling false illusions to arrive at clear, virtuous sight.

Addison's new philosophical position validated the imagination as a necessary, hermaphroditic type of cognition between sense and understanding. As a cognitive capacity, he suggested that it was akin to understanding in being a dangerous but refining water. The peril and refining capacity in both cases are linked but opposite in causation. The water of understanding can carry someone with too little regard for their self, human comforts, and limits far out from land into the freezing cold drowning wastes; the water of the imagination, on the other hand, tempts the sensualist and the narcissist away from their intended quest into some little flattering pond, in which enticing, gripping refreshment is given at the secret price of corruption (by some entrapping other). Making the two faculties substantially more equal in status, importance, and potential harmfulness for the human soul, Addison allusively brings the delusive "evil demon" that haunted the Cartesian project of distilling rational thought into close proximity with the feminizing water nymph, Salmacis. Although the allusion carries in it the sexist classical and Platonic trope of "bad" feminization as a corrupting trap (Diotima's foundational influence set aside)—and although the Addisonian countercurrent against that sexism is far too weak for we modern discursive swimmers—the gesture of the essay's final hermaphroditic synthesis resonates with Addison's desire to moderate and integrate in his own writing the separate spheres of traditionally domestic, feminine and traditionally adventurous, masculine concerns.

Spectator 421 steps to the most abstract realm of the imagination, furthest from actual sight toward conceptual visions based upon the memory of things seen. Here the essay considers critics, moralists, and intellectual writers, who, as it were, take a second dip in the waters of the imagination from the dryer realm of understanding. The synthetic weave of the final installment speaks to the cross of criticism, balanced sharply and correctively between the realms. Addison valorizes the pleasure of allegories, metaphors, and similitudes, which speculative writers draw from "the visible Parts of nature" to give their writing more impact: "By these Allusions a Truth in the Understanding is as it were reflected by the Imagination; we are able to see something like Colour and Shape in a Notion, and to discover a Scheme of Thoughts traced out upon Matter. And here the Mind receives a great deal of Satisfaction, and has two of its Faculties gratified at the same time, while the Fancy is busy in copying after the Understanding, and transcribing Ideas out of the Intellectual World into the Material."[76] The liminality of liquid surfaces—the play between which cognitive faculty is reflected for which—poses the questions of whether mimesis belongs primarily to the imagination or the understanding and of whether the movement into understanding is a descent into the darkness of the mind (and text) or an ascent out of the captivating muddied waters of sense-pleasure. In the twilight scene of modernity "works of the imagination refine the senses, making them also cognitively accessible" even while "they domesticate the understanding, making it figuratively available to our materiality."[77]

The essay's thematic approach to the border of imagination and understanding is also its inevitable, sly approach to self-reflexive criticism. Addison, of course, was one of the quintessential "Polite Masters of Morality, Criticism, and other Speculations" about whose work the last installment concerns itself. The third paragraph of the paper, which we know the later Addison added to his earlier draft, uses characteristic subtle but poignant self-irony to both preserve the light, glimmering surface of the essay's conclusion and allow the full shadows of the essay's pathos to emerge most clearly, almost touching the open air. "Allegories, when well chosen," it reads, "are like so many Tracks of Light in a Discourse, that make every thing about them clear and beautiful. . . . But we often find eminent Writers very faulty in this respect; great Scholars are apt to fetch their Comparisons and Allusions from the Sciences in which they are most conversant, so that a Man may see the Compass of their Learning in a Treatise on the most indifferent Subject." The criticism of the learned satirical essayist turns lightly on his serially extended essay itself, which from its starting installment took the form of one of his famous "Saturday sermons." Addison confesses that he has "heard many a Sermon that should only have been preached before a Congregation of *Cartesians*."[78] Readers of the second optics of the essay—of its chain of classical allegorical guides figured forth by its Latin mottos and its long meditation on the modified Cartesian-Platonic world-picture revised and dissected by Newtonian science—are put on notice that Descartes's evil demon is about to burst out of the water. The skillful speculative or poetic writer's "Talent of affecting the Imagination . . . has something in it like Creation; It bestows a kind of Existence, and draws up to the Reader's View, several Objects which are not to be found in Being. It makes Additions to Nature, and gives a greater variety to God's Work. In a word, it is able to beautifie and adorn the most illustrious Scenes in the Universe, or to fill the Mind with more glorious Shows and Apparitions, than can be found in any Part of it."[79] Something *like* creation, theatrically embellishing good sense and adding diverting variety to natural providence, begs a devilish question, which the final passages of the essay inconclusively take up, considering how the imagination can be filled just as easily with painful "Distaste and Terrour."[80]

In an essay that consistently plays with the oscillation between framing form and content, the suddenly thematized pain of the imagination signifies the essay's coming to its end: the imagination and the essay's structural shrinking within itself as it molds into the desire of understanding. Quoting Virgil's untranslated Latin (from book 4 of the *Aeneid*), Addison alludes to two classical scenes: Pentheus so overwhelmed by fear that he sees two suns and two Thebes, and Orestes flying over the stage in a vain attempt to escape the fright of his mother's ghost. Both scenes, strongly allegorical in themselves and in Virgil's brief allusion to them, provide literary examples of the horrifying fate of "a Distracted Person, when his Imagination is troubled, and his whole Soul disordered and confused."[81] In the rippling mise en abyme of Addison's concluding allegory, the understanding's twilight confrontation with the utmost interior limits of the imagination produces a phantasm, indeed, of two suns, two Apollonian systems, two civilizational eras and two world pictures, premodern and modern, pre-Newtonian and post-Newtonian, imaginary and understood. The fright of Orestes, who has killed his mother, stands in for the fearful alienation of the modern subject confronted by a cosmos of dead matter, from which he has emerged, the violent, rather isolated victor and criminal. "*Babylon* in Ruins is not so melancholy a Spectacle" as such a subject, Addison asserts. His allusion builds another wall of Babylon, containing the secondary pleasures of imaginative writing between the first allusion to those walls in *Spectator* 415 and 421, where those secondary pleasures threaten to break down along with writing's claim to heavenly truth, the fall of Babel's Tower.[82]

The pivot to formal, positivistic conclusion beyond the two lights on Babylon's ruins is (Addison seems to admit) rather abrupt: he offers "only" the consideration "what an infinite Advantage this Faculty [the imagination] gives an Almighty Being over the Soul of Man, and how great a measure of Happiness or Misery we are capable of receiving from the Imagination only."[83] The ambiguous punishing, guiding Almighty Being carries the ghost of Descartes's evil demon and the imaginatively versed propagandist. Addison's two concluding figures—the distracted man, and he "who knows all the ways of affecting the Imagination"—conjure up the potential equivalence of the too-tight grip of the understanding and an immersive delusion, both of which can disconnect people from their actual environment.[84] The first, distracted figure represents, for instance, the scientist in the moment of "Eureka," running through an alienated scene apparently blind to any reality but that in his imagination. The second figure of the (Cartesian) Almighty manipulator, who can "make Scenes rise up before us and seem present to the Eye," stages in shadow the author and subject of propaganda, the fraudulent preacher or pious worshipper of a false religion, or the historical prophet or subject of a closed paradigm of knowledge, a complete cosmological system, a unified theory. Addison disquietly ended his essay with a sentence considering the latter's fate as, reasonably, the universal mortal fate, subject to a creator who "can so exquisitely ravish or torture the Soul through this single Faculty, as might suffice to make up the whole Heaven or Hell of any finite Being."[85]

By reconsidering the essay with the second, wiser optics of its Lucretian-Ovidian frame as an imaginative landscape itself laid out for our consideration rather than an essay pushing us inevitably toward the understanding's firm teleological conclusions, the final gesture of the essay is less troubling than it is painterly. If a certain direct, nonaesthetic mode of reading still insists on the essay serving as a script for the tragedy of understanding, then the essay-as-sermon preaches resigned admiration, directing us back in any case to mild enjoyment as the elective sign of received grace. In the Addisonian condition of providential theater, the moderate cultivation of limited imaginative pleasure would seem to be the sustainable heavenly path to make it, in a good mood with a fit psyche, to the end of the show. The central stretches of that middle road accentuate vistas on humane architecture and course windingly through the hospitable, well-structured tunnels of classical poetry. With the reality of sensual touching, insisting on the body, the hermaphroditic paradigm of the imagination breaks the narcissistic mirroring of writing and the understanding. It reveals an equality between the quest to immerse oneself in understanding and the gripping desire for imaginative pleasure: drive and subject, the act of cognition produces a new synthesis, a new kind of human, that reveals, in turn and again, the essential human contingency of understanding.

MODERN METAMORPHOSES: THE ACCELERATING HISTORICAL PAGEANT

Almost exactly a century before Addison translated the tale of Salmacis and Hermaphroditus (and may have near concurrently written his first drafts of his imagination essay), Shakespeare had penned *A Midsummer Night's Dream*, likely at least partially inspired by Ovid's *Metamorphoses*.[86] The enchanted forest where Shakespeare's characters underwent metamorphoses was ultimately ruled over by monarchical sovereigns, human and fairy. Typical for Shakespeare's plays, magical transformations were dispelled by the end of the action, restoring the (all too) human, presented repetitively in that poet's work as an eternal, known nature. Shakespeare secularized and diminutized the enchantment of Ovid. The earthly theater of metamorphoses was largely a complex distraction for the repetition of the same.

Addison's response to the libertine, monarchical theatrical culture of the Restoration, on the other hand, recovered a different strain from Ovid in which metamorphoses were permanent and historical. If Shakespeare's oeuvre presented the allegory of metamorphoses as a useful way to contemplate, feel, and structure fates that repeated within the eternal human experience, Addison's oeuvre presented the allegory of metamorphoses to contemplate, feel, and structure agency in a cosmos and in a living kind of body that often changed form, evolving at a scale beyond mortal individual experience.

In Shakespearean drama, regardless of what the bard's real political beliefs were, adequate worldly authority almost unfailingly reasserts itself by the end of every work. For Addison, carrying the Miltonian revolutionary legacy through and beyond the treacherous, sheering narrow between Hobbes and Locke, Newton had established the unnatural aspect of any belief in worldly authority. The modern progressivism that Addison helped to establish offered hope in the vacant place of transcendent authority: faith that the almighty creator of each individual's Ovidian theater of metamorphoses signaled goodness by making pleasure accessible through the self-cultivated use of the imagination, even in the direst, ugliest circumstances. The sovereign in Shakespeare's cosmos apportioned theater as a distraction and clarification of permanent conditions; in Addison's cosmos, the creator assembled a theater of limited, individual sovereignty as a means to enable necessary evolution.

The imagination, as the module of earthly, bodily bound evaluation dismissed by Platonists, was for Addison and his eighteenth-century readers the reasonable sovereign balance to an understanding that newly exposed its own lack of sovereignty via the unsettling paradigm shift of Newtonianism and its postulation of flimsy eyes designed for the highly contingent terrestrial environment. Pleasure and health, the aims and criteria of this second, imaginative verification system, made life and, thus, philosophy possible on earth, among humans. If human life and its thought were to advance and expand—if the large middle of human beings was to be welcomed into the space of public thinking—modes of evaluation that placed pleasure and health as salient goals would need to be elevated. In this dialectical sense, the Addisonian imagination became a critic of scientific, explanatory, and philosophical writing. It was the newly empowered cognitive house of commons that would critically collaborate with the formerly transcendent sovereign, the understanding, to judge and decide about the scenes of terrestrial life and, therefore, to fashion a now broader and more powerful assent, a stronger synthetic sovereignty.

In its deliberations, Addison's imagination provided a reserve, an extrahistorical position for the human soul, from which paradigm shifts in understanding could be anticipated. The imagined history of human understanding, driven by the development and use of new technology, was understood by the aesthetic soul to offer a menu of existentially different epistemological conditions. On offer was not only the standard menu of that history but also the pleasure of choosing to contemplate a scene outside that menu that could just as well belong to a future, a forgotten past, or an unknowable present. With the modern imagination, the middling classes could themselves become the critics of reality, pleasurably and discursively evaluating the present state of the world in comparison with other arrangements, aiming to optimize enjoyment.

Recent critics have argued that Addison's use of the phrase "A Man of a Polite Imagination" signified his validation of a very particular, elitist, and/or conformist bourgeois aesthetic subject.[87] Seminal in general for the modern European aesthetic discourse (partially through its French reception), *On the Pleasures of the Imagination* indeed underwrote the later formulation of art for art's sake and the particular blend of taste, class, detachment, and freedom such a formulation entailed. But Addison's polite aesthetic "club" remained in his own writing an open society, connected by socially interested urban and countryside flaneurs. Addisonian art appreciation foregrounded art's broad social and theological/existential utility: it validated and helped to construct a middling subject position capable of reflection, doubt, critique, and pleasure in many conceivable circumstances, loosening proscriptions around what kind of readers could reasonably feel themselves addressed. Addison's view of emancipation here can be separated out from Locke's earlier liberal view. While Locke's liberal subject held a practical property only in his body and had no further claim to property except that made through labor, pleasure granted the Addisonian, republican citizen a virtual property in "every thing" he saw.[88] Addison's formulation risks deemphasizing labor and the struggle over material ownership, but it does so to expand and even potentially universalize the "stakeholders" entitled to feel themselves as owners, regardless of their material means or present historical circumstances. The Addisonian idea of expanded latent equality based not just in law but in existential feeling helped to drive the development of a modern liberal subject over the following two centuries.

On the other side of the same coin, the imagination essay's dual optics praised open nature and turned attention toward shared, general human taste, warning against rarefied self-quarantining and delusive escapism in closed rooms or overcultivated thoughts. The warning was emphasized through its cautionary hermaphroditic frame, which spoke specifically to readers whose erudition included, indeed, the elite classical education of the kind increasingly becoming "bourgeois." The later aesthetic discourse, gradually "liberating" itself from Addison's more general religious, philosophical, and social project, became a means to demarcate a "free," unique private experience, elevated or cordoned off from mass public society, from religion and certain less tasteful social or political affiliations.[89] But Addison's essay was rooted in the deeper religious urge of rerooting: it urged imaginative exercise "as a spiritual experience, not simply as a mental-hygienic one or a preparation for moral improvement."[90] No mere spiritual escapism, either, the Addisonian approach to the imagination presented a paradigm shift in philosophy, changing the proper aims of the philosophical subject and the species to which he and (with an emphasized new discursive inclusion) she belonged. Hybridized between local embodied feeling and the disidentificatory freedom of reason, this new subject was both practitioner and construction of the imagination's positive power of world-creation—*poesis*—which Addison newly emphasized against the imagination's ancient association with dangerous false visions and passively infectious mimesis.[91]

The danger of false visions and infectious memes, however, remained: the strengthened modern call to imagination prepared private citizens to invest in particular visions of the future, which often came with their own stocks, bonds, and pension schemes.[92] As with the bubble of art-for-art's-sake, the bubbles of financial speculation overdriven by greed were not necessary correlatives of Addison's republic of imaginative citizens, although they historically followed. A healthy, balanced use of the imagination, to the contrary, affirmed the necessity to survive and resist the hoarding and mania of bubbles by remaining mentally independent inside of overheated social and historical scenes. Addisonian aesthetic thinking meant a cultivated mix of alienation and absorption, not overselling or being oversold. Having a "kind of Property" was more important than legally holding property because the healthful aim was to increase imaginative pleasure itself. "Addison," as William Walker notes about his periodical essays in general, "criticizes people who sell things for profit and get people wanting and thinking things, who set fashions, so people will buy more, because they make the world ugly."[93]

The later paradigm of bourgeois aesthetics would distort Addison's milder, meditative landscape by extracting an ideal of aesthetic mastery through which all of Nature could be made to perform for the subject—"the chance force of natural objects becomes an effect designed to produce pleasure," as Neil Saccamano's analysis of Addison's essay puts it. Yet the essay's figuration of "an agent able to touch the subject" through Nature, whereby "the eye becomes the canvas of a painting" posited God as that agent. Thus, when Addison's imaginative "subject actively assents to its passivity in this encounter" with Nature, the effect of being a masterful audience-member *at* a divine show was meant indeed to be dwarfed by the meditatively following realization of being an actor hopelessly immersed *in* a divine theatrical architecture, *inside and out:* the hermaphroditic Newtonian subject was now unable, scientifically, "to separate itself from nature so that it could call and represent nature as other."[94]

FINDING DIDO: THE ESSAY AS A LATIN POEM

If the essay presents a landscape of the imagination, the Latin mottoes can be taken as an overlaying map and legend. The second installment's epigraph containing Martial's advice to make the work brief by dividing it (*Divisum sic breve fiet Opus*) takes on another meaning if one uses it as a clue to attend to the essay's classical-language map. As analyzed above, what Addison is after is not the old shortcut of masterfully dividing understanding—whereby sensuous experience can be simply conceptualized, dismissed, and abandoned—but a new mixed constitution. Particularly important to the form of the essay, then, are the untranslated classical language quotations mixed into the body of the essay itself. Signaling Addison's identification with Virgil, Horace, and the Augustan golden age of Roman literature (between Lucretius and Ovid), the in-body passages of classical verse can be read as a collage poem composed largely of quotations from the former two Roman authors with two key exceptions: a modern Latin stanza of unmarked authorship (identified by scholars as Addison's own verses), and a very short snippet of Homer's Greek. The essay's scattered Latin poem performs as Hermaphroditus, dipped into the watercolor of the imagination and thereby unexpectedly gripped and disruptively hybridized, on his way to codifying "eternal" knowledge of the world.

Very briefly reading that poem in its sequential order, the first stanza from the anonymous modern hand in *Spectator* 412 resonates metapoetically as the faithful pledge of the plume-wielding author (the "feather'd Husband, to his Partner true," in a later translation) to his own time, kind, and historical, species-specific sensoriolum. Alongside the self-ironic display of enclosing perceptual limits—even biologically determined ridiculousness—are the writerly pathos of obsessive masculine, spousal rescue and commitment: "We often see the Male determined in his Courtship by the single Grain or Tincture of a Feather, and never discovering any Charms but in the Colour of its Species."[95] In his drag as Clio, the muse of history, Addison the Latin poet presents in the essay's next untranslated sequence a succinct classical image of civilization's progress, beginning in the timeless golden age loved by writers (414's lines from Horace's *Epistles* and Virgil's *Georgics*). Stepping inside the walls of Babylon (the secondary pleasures of the imagination), the poets' classical images proceed to evoke the tyranny of kings (the magnificent Ur-Father of 417's Homeric "Jupiter") followed closely by the mix of eros and might in the reign of urban matriarchs and political princes (the "Queen of Love" and her beautified young conquering son in 417's Virgilian Venus and Aeneas). The poem then turns in *Spectator* 418 to a scene of primal tyrannicide borrowed from Virgil's multilayered narrative of Hercules slaying the monster Cacus, a foundational moment for a new Rome. The image of Cacus's carcass and "extinguished eyes" carries not simply the layer of Virgil's hope for an Augustan Roman restoration after Caesar's murder and the civil wars but also, for Addison and his readers, the gruesome memory of the previous century's liberating regicide and the severed head of Charles I, the last truly sacrosanct English king.[96] The bend of history toward a different vision of sovereignty is marked in *Spectator* 419's Horatian admonition that fauns brought of the forest onto the stage should not be made to speak with either the obscenity of the street or the high oration of the court. Addison's mission as a reformist dramaturg of the middle style and body politic is clear; through a contrasting, ironic reference to Buckingham's *The Rehearsal* (a 1671 parody of Drydenian heroic tragedy), 419 juxtaposes Horace's rhetorical instructions directly with the bawdy, aristocratic irreverence of the Restoration comedy.

The essay's final Latin allusions to Orestes and Pentheus in *Spectator* 421 throw a telling classical relief over the entire essay, courtesy again of Virgil, Addison's poetic role model and Dante's pathbreaking guide through Hell and Purgatory. Saccamano points out that, in its well-known original context, the quoted passage from the *Aeneid* takes the double-visioned Pentheus and the mother-frighted Orestes as simile figures for the distraught Dido, who descends into madness after being abandoned by her lover, Aeneas.[97] Virgil's account of the latter lovers' separation resonates strongly with the tale of Salmacis and Hermaphroditus to which the installment's motto alludes. Virgil has Mercury (the Roman Hermes) convince Aeneas (the son of Venus, the Roman Aphrodite) to obey Jupiter's divine command and abandon Queen Dido for Italy in order that he might escape Juno's love trap and continue on his destined heroic journey to found Rome. The traumatic hermaphroditic separation ends in Dido's suicide as she curses Aeneas and Rome with Carthage's perpetual enmity.

The essay's Latin poem figures Dido, then, just under its surface, as a personified emblem of the classical imagination: an abandoned Salmacis, seductively but unsuccessfully gripping the heroic understanding on its race to eternal acts. In the *Aeneid,* Virgil had added the fictional tradition of Aeneas's dalliance with Dido in Carthage to the influential historical account of the Aeneas myth that Cato the Elder's *Origenes* had related two centuries before. Virgil's work established Aeneas's legitimate right to found Rome while giving him a legendary presence in Carthage—Rome's perpetual enemy-in-the-mirror, for whose destruction Cato the Elder had long urged, with eventual success. The new narrative signaled the opportunity for a restored, reintegrated Augustan Rome to overcome Dido's curse after its destructive civil wars. Practically, the new Roman Empire would strengthen itself through a reintegration of Dido's Carthage in its new status as Rome's most important African colonial city, having been refounded by Julius Caesar during his North African campaigns against republican forces.[98]

The historical analogy for Addison's time is made more evident by tracing the way the classical civilizational history of the essay's Latin poem mapped onto the previous century of English history. Out of a history of mythic "magnificent" and terrible kings (performing, like Henry VIII, the earthly role of Jupiter), the seventeenth century had begun in London under the waning reign of Elizabeth—a famously self-styled virginal "Venus" even in her last years. Her successor, James I, was the son of Mary Stuart (another, rival "Queen of Love"), fashioned as an Aeneas-like new Scottish Augustus, founder of Great Britain as an ascendant empire in the line of Troy and Rome, patron of Shakespeare's Roman plays and Inigo Jones's innovative architectural classicism.[99] Charles I's mid-century beheading represented the defeat of Cacus-like tyrannical, sacral kingship. In the Restoration period, the opposition Whigs began to form a coalition drawing from the political energies of a gradually emerging class and discourse of middling people, coalescing as if from the wilds of fauns. The political scene of Addison's 1712 essay had indeed two tragic heroic political parties contesting to guide and stand in for Queen Anne's government, fearful of the potentially undoing jealous wrath of Anne, wrestling as she was with the Dido-like situation of abandonment in the shadow while ambitious Tory and Whig leaders charged ahead toward their own visions of triumph and empire.

Committed to the mildness of peace and efficacy in his time, Addison the middling stylist—the Virgilian Latin poet and "feathered husband" of his society and its transition to a mixed republican-monarchical empire—was haunted, like Orestes, by the returning "ghost" of the sacred Queen, whose power the Whigs had previously constrained and guided. Like Pentheus, he saw clearly the two suns and two Londons of diverging Tory/Jacobite and Whig/Hanoverian-Succession futures. But, as in classical literature, the layer of the particular political time to which Addison was committed fell into the archetype of myth and long-debated, deeper forms. With the sun of Newtonian understanding pulling away from the earth, the longer consistency of human cognition belonged to the classical earth-centered sun of mixed, aesthetic thinking. The politics and the epistemology were the same.

The larger gesture of the essay repeats the appeal of Ovid's *Heroides* to recover and reglorify the maligned and abandoned heroic feminine counterparts of classically masculinist paradigms of understanding. That Ovidian work's epistolary form emphasized the territorialization of its feminine subjects against its more epically journeying, deterritorialized masculine heroes. The dichotomy is congruent with the split between the all-too-human imagination and the alienated, transcendent understanding that Addison attempted to synthetically heal. Like the mythic Aeneas, driven on by Mercury's certain admonishments, the doubting subject of modern science wished to be done with the past's tyranny, to escape into a future of pure understanding and into New Worlds unmarred by long histories of feudal subjugation.

In book 7 of *Heroides,* seeing her lover's ships depart, Dido equated Aeneas's betrayal of love to his betrayal of his divine mother and prophesied that he would never find better conditions to take up a happy sovereignty than those he found with her in Carthage: "What is achieved, you turn your back upon; what is to be achieved, you ever pursue. One land has been sought and gained, and ever must another be sought, through the wide world."[100] At the dawn of Britain's own Augustan empire of expanded colonialist venture, Addison's Ovidian essay resonates with his own nationalistic advocacy of greater cosmopolitan integration at home and abroad (discussed in the previous chapter), lest adventuring colonial Britons be haunted by Dido's curse: "Should you arrive at the place you wish, you will be but a stranger." The spiritual and political bent of Addison's writings cheered British mercantilism and "liberating" war efforts in the same tone that they cheered the astonishing progress of modern science, a tone that often moderated itself with the cautionary frame of Dido's warning to Aeneas: that, abandoning love and his maternal nature, the promised land of sovereignty would continue to recede from his sight until the very end of his life.[101]

Like the recovered perspectives of Ovid's heroines, the Addisonian imagination held in view the epistemological landscapes (or "natures") abandoned by paradigm shifts in understanding. It thus provided the human capacity to stably reintegrate and mourn each departing heroic, masculine system of knowledge by serving as a reservoir for all the scenes such systems had presented to the eye and the psyche, past, present, or potentially future. As such a stabilizing cognitive faculty, the imagination attained an ultimate and more active role, becoming the imperfectly sovereign judge of systems and paradigms.

The passionate flattening obscenity of the twentieth century—with its heroic will to discover a transcendence and universality beyond history, its final splitting even of the secret court of the atom and its schizogenetic, suffocating embrace of the human animal in scientific anthropology and the secular religions of health and self-optimization—invented terms that help us to speak more plainly about the psychoanalytic theory encoded within the nuanced Baroque allusions of Addison's middling theory of the imagination. Carl Jung, one of that century's most impactful *Aufklärer* of the imagination, wrote also of the masculinized ego's tendency to repress its deeper, historical belonging in the world. Jung saw this tendency expressed in the widespread archetype of the arriviste hero slaying the feminized/phallic serpent, splitting her into two parts: "From one half he makes the heaven and from the other he makes the earth."[102] A typically unannounced revision of the last Latin line in the essay anticipates Jung's prescription for emancipation without "distraction" in a post-Newtonian reality, in which the classical fantasies of heavenly flight and nostalgic return are equally alienating. Changing Virgil's "Cum fugit" to "Cum videt," Addison subtly transforms the tragic actor Orestes, *fleeing* his mother's ghost, into a spectator-actor, *seeing* his mother's ghost. For Jung, this decision to stay, face, and perhaps even converse with the unconscious was the crucial way of breaking the delusional grip of the historically constituted, fearful "complex" individuals experience as their falsely sovereign ego-identity.[103]

Addison's brave modern turn historically connects a little-noticed hermaphroditic discourse of the imagination stretching from Montaigne to Jung. Montaigne's well-known essay on the power of the imagination, which Addison must have contemplated, centers on the imagination's ability to cause and alleviate what are now called psychosomatic symptoms or events. Particularly, in his typically ribald manner, he focuses on tales of the imagination's ability to form and control penises, retelling Ovid's myth of Iphis (a woman whose desire to marry another woman causes her to grow a penis) and exploring the role of fantasies, fears, and emotions in producing impotence or its unwilled opposite.[104] In comparison, Addison's essay is a case study in sublimation, potentially also in the sense of sublimation as a style of censorship.[105] Where Montaigne thematizes the different (unconscious) desires of organs, the tight yet dualistic communication of the mind and body, the physical "ejaculative" power of eyes (especially women's eyes) to send darts of pain to others, and the equivalent medicinal power of tales, ceremonies, and anal suppositories, Addison's imagination is hermaphroditic but hardly sexual, a committed, lawful critic abstracting and refining higher pleasure inside the skin of a receptive body with modern absorptive—not ejaculative—eyes.[106] Between the two texts, a certain reversal of gendering direction is at issue: Montaigne's imagination forges penises in female bodies and controls penises in men, Addison's catches the alienated masculine body and merges with it, an ambivalent act of feminization that the bulk of the essay suggests is a healthful, reconstituting act.

Hermaphrodite was classically associated with the invention of marriage, Salmacis with civilizing and taming "the savage mind of men."[107] He/She was in this sense a positively integrating, nontragic mirror figure for Pentheus, the doomed (Apollonian) civilizer and founder of Thebes, whose ban on Dionysian worship resulted in his being torn apart by his own aunts and mother. In its comparative carnal discretion, perhaps the Addisonian aesthetic imagination's hermaphroditic sublimation performs the constricted "cultural," polite sexuality of the sycophantic middling subject in a repressive aristocratic culture. Perhaps it is an artifact of Addison's own (secret) branding as a hermaphrodite in his dangerously sexually restrictive time—his turning to the utopia of sight and its more invisible, promiscuous power to "touch."[108] Jacques Lacan influentially argued that sight has a special relation to the human feeling of sovereignty since we enter the world as uncommonly "premature" animals with uncoordinated limbs: our sense of power and wish fulfillment comes first through our eyes' ability to reach and exclude what our limbs cannot.[109] This special relation between sight and sovereign wish-pursuit is likely strengthened in those who are legally and culturally proscribed from ever reaching sexual "maturity," whose sex organs, in Montaigne's sense, are impeded or never medicinally assisted by the strong songs of culture to phallically act out their own desire. For people of "cultivated" imagination, images—including letters—hold in themselves the archaic memory of embracingly adaptive landscapes seen before their fuller conjunction with a harsh spoken law and the alienating symbolic matrix of linguistic abstraction: the necessary infantile, "most pleasing delusion" that Addison philosophically revalidated for all of our occasional indulgence, the same theatrical delusion that many of the most powerful figures in our little sensoriolum never seem to have to relinquish in the slightest, even until the final curtain draws over their lives.

Whatever the reason for Addison's special sensitivity, his skillful articulation of it resonated with larger cultural currents. Imaginative sovereignty was no absolute sovereignty nor any real mastery; such a claim of absolute sovereign spectatorship belonged only to Providence. Wherever that Providence was, everywhere and invisible in the new far-reaching telescopes, he regarded, as *Spectator* 237 put it, "the whole System of Time and Things together, so that we cannot discover the beautiful Connexions between Incidents which lye wildly separated in Time, and by losing so many Links of the Chain, our Reasonings become broken and imperfect."[110] In the "future State" of the soul, for which Addison hoped, one of its greatest pleasures would be "an enlarged Contemplation of the Divine Wisdom in the Government of the World ... from the Beginning to the End of Time." The paradise of the hereafter would present "a Scene so large and various as shall then be laid open to our View in the Society of superior Saints." In contrast, the current state of the soul must be acknowledged to be limited: "In our present Condition, which is a middle State, our Minds are, as it were, chequered with Truth and Falshood; and as our Faculties are narrow and our Views imperfect, it is impossible but our Curiosity must meet with many Repulses. The Business of Man-kind in this Life being rather to act than to know, their Portion of Knowledge is dealt to them accordingly."[111]

In this regard, Addison held Seneca to be "a greater Authority" than Plato: Seneca affirmed the central virtue of Stoic theatricality in a contingent human world in which Adversity was "the Poet of Honour." The audience was the Creator; for the Roman—Jupiter, whose great pleasure was to see the acting of Cato "amidst the Ruins of his Country preserving his Integrity."[112] Like Dido, unable to keep a hold on Aeneas, Cato was both a paragon of a virtuous but abandoned history and a cautionary, erring actor unable to mourn a passing scene. The two North African self-martyrs call to mind the autobiographical thread in Addison's revision of his imagination essay, one root of his spiritual, synthetic neoclassicism being in his father's seventeenth-century comparative religious scholarship on North African communities. As the conceptual constitution of matter changed fundamentally in the understanding, the imagination held the lifelong set, where so much persisted in its old appearance. Lancelot, the father, had gone to North Africa and studied the way that differing religions perform themselves in the world. Joseph, the son, went there in his imagination to contemplate how to bring together his own religion with the world he actually encountered, the living trinity received through history, described by natural science, and wrestled with in day-to-day politics.

On the Pleasures of the Imagination gave one element of the sought-for North African synthesis, displaced on another shore from which Rome could be contemplated, not unlike the general geographical Orientalist relation of Europe to its holy lands of religious origin. The second optics of the essay formed a mirror in which the Carthagian Queen Dido was silently reflected, even while the essay's surface optics, blending in to the punctuated daily installments of *The Spectator*, carried her appeal as an invisible underside of Addison's ambitious, sinuous line of text—aspiring to a two-gendered readership, a fuller modern hermaphroditic public, attached and attracted by shared affect and advancing science.

Cato would provide the second mirror of reimagined North African heritage and synthesis. The revised neoclassical poetics reflected in that tragedy were already apparent in Addison's theory of the imagination. The particular modernity and a possible "offshore" origin of Addison's revisions are hinted at in his account of one of the most significant meetings of the young critic's life. In a letter to his father's direct ecclesiastical superior in Litchfield, just after he relates Malebranche's telling him about his efforts to add a third "equally true" theory of colors to Descartes and Newton's theories, Addison shares the details of his conversation with the aging Boileau, the most famous critic of his era. Sitting in Paris, London's rival "New Rome," Boileau discussed Corneille's tragedy on the death of Pompey in Egypt—a final turning point in the Roman civil wars that set up Cato the Younger's hopeless situation in Utica. In this context, Boileau remarked to Addison that Aristotle "proposes two passions that are proper to be raised by Tragedy, Terror and Pity, but Corneille endeavors at a new one, which is Admiration."[113] Pity and Terror—these would remain the necessary emotions to spark tragic mourning, to move on. But becoming modern required a different quality of persistence and commitment on earth, alongside mourning. It demanded the staying power of admiration, the aesthetic relation to the imagination and the landscape it presented: an alienated yet holding pleasurable attraction and identification with the heroine-hero-and-country figured in the mirror, even as the framed stage set wobbled—its contingent construction revealed—and the whole bright enlightened scene was gripped and drowned in the dark vortex of mere local greed and desire.

5

Staging a Shadow King

Addison's Theatrical Politics

> When I observed very many men to mistake grosly in point of manners,
> I thought we were to help and inform their judgements; chiefly that
> they might live gloriously, and attain to honour. Now, dear Child, I will
> teach thee how thou mayest order thy behaviour.... Fit thy self: for the
> pleading place; or, to the present occasion.
> —Cato, preface to his *Distichs,* 1659 Hoole translation

STATELY CONTEXTS AND RHYMED POLITICS

The pinnacle of Addison's career as an author coincided with a historical peak of partisan tensions around a potentially very dangerous royal succession. Rather than being coincidental or simply synergistic, the events in the theatrical and political worlds turned out to be the same: the 1713 premiere of Addison's only tragedy, *Cato,* symbolically inaugurated a long era in which the head of state would come to be chosen—increasingly not through military maneuvers, claims to divine right, engineered revolution, or even elite legislative consensus, but through a contest of virtue decided by popular acclaim.

As the site of a sublimated agon between factions that sixty years before might have opposed each other on the battlefield, the theater at Drury Lane on the opening night of *Cato* consolidated a new body politic away from the monarch's body and court. This was a mixed body of commoners and aristocrats whose internal, passionate feuding over allegorical interpretation was held and shaped by the architecture of the theater and Addison's dramaturgy, leaving at center stage the ambivalent effigy of the true patriot: Cato. The rhetorical and performative contest that night was implicitly about everything (e.g., religion, law, morality, power, wealth, prestige), yet the singular tragic effigy's rightful claim to centerstage was not in question. The question was rather who that familiar, uniting, heroic effigy—Cato—symbolized in real, political life, and which faction would have the numbers to declare that their opinion was *the* real answer, consensus.

The *event* of Addison's tragedy—remembered through anecdotes, criticism, literary and journalistic allusions, the mass printing of the play script, and frequent revivals—was in this sense constitutional for the coming more democratic British nation and the ongoing, serial event of the US presidential campaign. Like the somewhat amorphous checked executive power of the US president, the unwritten British constitution consists of conventions that use various texts written at different times and in different places as a repertoire of legitimacy. These conventions were themselves often forged out of significant events, if they do not simply repeat the events ritualistically or theatrically at various scales and levels of formality and improvisation. (From this perspective, William the Conqueror still periodically declares the will of a new government to end the injustice of slavery, and Abraham Lincoln still eulogizes the fallen of domestic massacres as patriotic martyrs.) Texts from some of these events—like the Magna Carta or the US Constitution—survive parallel to the conventions themselves, but simply reading the texts is not enough to understand the working of the governing, performative institutions or serial occasions. If one has not seen, heard, or read Addison's *Cato,* one cannot fully understand the DNA of the American presidency. But seeing, hearing, or reading Addison's *Cato* after 1713, one cannot understand how this dramatic text played such a large role in political history without understanding the context of its premiere. While the next chapter will consider the text and premiere event itself more in depth, this chapter fleshes out the political context of Addison's staging via a consideration of his own political career and imbrication in the long English dance of theatrical and monarchical representation.

Addison, Macaulay influentially wrote, "climbed higher in the state than any other Englishman has ever, by means merely of literary talents, been able to climb."[1] Eventually attaining the position of secretary of state, Addison represented the heights of a particular and ultimately short-lived bubble in English political history when the public poet-statesman was something of the norm. Rulers always need propaganda and flattery, and those with energetic and subtle enough minds to work themselves into high networks of power are wise to magnify their own public persona (and harmlessly dispose some excess ambition and thought at the end of the day) through literary pursuits. But the Augustan poet-statesman in particular represented the will of competing factions to more thoroughly shape or reshape the direction of English society and government at the beginning of the eighteenth century. Addison's prose was well suited for the task, since the basis of power was shifting (still rather slowly) away from the singular monarch's court and the rarefied houses of aristocracy toward the middle-class home and the urbanized networks of the general populace.

After the Stationer's Company monopoly lapsed in 1695, "the proliferation of newspapers and periodicals," as Peter Thomson writes, "had brought affairs of state into the street. More than 8,000 political pamphlets (not including books and broadsheets) were published in the first fifteen years of the eighteenth century." Politics was gradually becoming an affair of print and masses, and Queen Anne—whether strategically or as a subject of her time—represented the transition: "The age of the mighty monarch was over: Queen Anne was quite as 'middle class' as William and Mary had been."[2] Since the Triennial Act of 1694 had mandated a general election every three years, large, complex public campaigns were becoming a regular part of British life, demanding the corresponding increase in political writing.[3] Different sets of political interests financed different poets, and the salient political divisions of the era—Tory vs. Whig and Country vs. City—were reproduced in literary and theatrical culture. Battles in print to determine political taste and consolidate loyal readerships also took on more indirect, secondary guises: disputes "over immediate political questions played out through discussions of literary form and poetic tradition."[4] Before the era of polling and popular voting, sales of pamphlets and periodicals could influence opinion on large scales and indicate which parties were in favor and which stances on certain issues were likely to garner support from the citizenry.

Joseph Hone writes that, in general, the "earlier ideological battles" of the republican period "were still raging." Indeed, as Stephen Pincus summarizes, "party politics permeated everyday life in the early 18th century."[5] Nevertheless, a large number of the politicians and writers of the period undertook a historically conscious, extrapartisan effort to reinforce a moderate frame around political discourse and thereby avoid the conflagration of the civil wars that had plagued the previous century: "By the start of the eighteenth century earlier conflict between republicans and royalists had developed into a differently nuanced set of arguments between supporters of hereditary and elective monarchy."[6] Part of the danger of the time, however, was that the terms, feelings, and beliefs at play were not all as analytical and secular as later readers might be tempted to read them. What is today thought of as a political distinction overlapped significantly with the era's ongoing religious disputes: divine-right, hereditary monarchy went along with what was for Protestants the "political threat" and "tyranny binding individual conscience to the pope."[7] In the view Addison expressed in *Freeholder* 54, for instance, what we now dryly call "Protestantism" was still "the Reformed Religion," which served as an essential political-spiritual "Over-balance for Popery through all *Europe*."[8] Not failing to imagine the disasters should the "opposite" factions prevail, Addison nevertheless worked against the balancing disaster of renewed cultural regression and war of "all against all"; he played a leading role in encouraging the overall, urgently patriotic process of taming the former violence of domestic political and religious zeal into "civility and sociability."[9] Though sometimes guilty of the age-old rhetorical trick of attributing partisanship only to the other side, he maintained long friendships and working relationships with Tories (including the incendiary Tory hero and sermonizer Henry Sacheverell) and preached a belief that a person's belonging to one party or another was due primarily to the accidence of circumstances and social life rather to "any essential Distinction."[10] *Spectator* 125 employed a typical Addisonian mix of registers to advocate political moderation as necessary to avoid civil war. Plutarch, Addison explained, "derives the Malignity of Hatred from the Passion it self, and not from its Object." The laziness of confusing the matter, inflaming the animonisty, would ultimately tear into an individual's own closer social fabric. According to Addison's gloss of Plutarch, "A Man should not allow himself to hate even his Enemies, because, says he, if you indulge this Passion in some Occasions, it will rise of it self in others; if you hate your Enemies, you will contract such a vicious Habit of Mind, as by Degrees will break out upon those who are your Friends, or those who are indifferent to you."[11]

The slip, of course, between domestic peacemaking and foreign warmongering has never been hard. Conforming to a trope of imperial histories, the previous domestic warfare in Britain had been and continued to be partially put on hold through offshoring. In Continental Europe, Britain entered the War of the Spanish Succession. Its self-touted role in that conflict was to defend religious freedom and check the growing power of

Louis XIV, who stood to gain control over the Spanish throne and empire via his grandson's accession there. Louis XIV harbored James Francis Edward Stuart—the younger, Catholic half-brother of Anne—and supported his hereditary and gender-based claim to the English throne. The English Bill of Rights of 1689, which had barred Catholics from sitting on the throne, legally excluded his succession. The mighty French military across the channel had been historically a regular threat to English sovereignty, and Louis XIV's aggressive designs in Europe made a Jacobite restoration seem highly probable without active military resistance. Thus, as Hone argues, the War of the Spanish Succession had a proxy function as a "War of the British Succession."[12]

Representing the liberalizing, democratizing party in the English politics of the time, Whig authors helped drive the expansion of political discourse toward the larger reading public and away from more rarefied spheres. They tended to take on the role of wartime panegyrists in strong support of English military involvement in the War of the Spanish Succession. For them, political and military events were central subjects for poetry. This stood in contrast to what David Womersley identifies as a general Tory position that the role of politics was to create the conditions under which a more independent sphere of "literature either flourishes or declines."[13]

One of Addison's first published forays into English panegyric verse was his 1695 "A Poem to His Majesty." His characteristic moderation can be read in the way he fills the role of the Whig poet praising the warrior-king, William, while also urging calm: "When now the business of the field is o'er, / . . . let the muse / In humble accents milder thoughts infuse." Somewhat self-effacingly, the young poet argued that he must leave it for others to adequately describe William's martial deeds, citing the classical delay between heroes and their poets: "One age the hero, one the poet breeds."[14] Nonetheless continuing to extol William's martial virtues, Addison referenced the king's royal, ancestral house, the House of Nassau, and its Continental position as a mediating dynasty in the balance of powers:

> The race of Nassaus was by Heaven designed
> To curb the proud oppressors of mankind,
> To bind the tyrants of the earth with laws,
> And fight in every injured nation's cause.[15]

The poem celebrated a somewhat contradictory Whiggish agenda: Britain was to be, under their dual Dutch-English monarchy, exceptionally cosmopolitan and acquisitively liberating. British ships, when they were not busy with war, were to "fetch uncontrolled each labour of the sun, / And make the product of the world our own." The new scale of imperial war stretched even poetic sovereignty:

> Who can run the British triumphs o'er,
> And count the flames disperst on every shore?
> Who can describe the scattered victory,
> And draw the reader on from sea to sea?[16]

The last lines of the poem thematize the profound alienation stemming from the scale of violence in a war waged—as Addison's speaker would have it—for good: the laureled monarch emerges from a landscape of "whole heaps of dead."[17] The double strategy of Whig poetry was evident. On the one hand, the poem praised imperial war for opening up and liberalizing trade opportunities for the British and keeping Catholic absolutism at bay. On the other hand, the poem described war as a nightmare and reminded its domestic audience of the greater need for peace, calm everyday life, and lawful, polite behavior. Without the latter reminder, still passionately factional British audiences might forget the horrors of civil war and take politics away again from the manageable realm and dead heaps of printed letters.

ROYAL STAKES: VACANT EFFIGIES AND THE THEATER OF SUCCESSION

A series of deaths at the turn of the century signaled a new era of British politics and letters. In Spain, Carlos II's 1700 demise threw Europe into the crisis that broke into war the next year. The poet laureate of the Restoration, John Dryden, also died in 1700, only some weeks before the young Prince William, the last obvious Protestant successor to his mother, the future Queen Anne. The eleven-year-old prince's death prompted the passing of the 1701 Act of Settlement. The 1689 Bill of Rights that had accompanied the accession of William and Mary had officially demoted the former strong sovereign monarch to "a King in Parliament."[18] The Act of Settlement now further asserted parliamentary authority over the monarchy and named the Electress Sophia of Hanover (a Protestant granddaughter of James I) as heir to the throne in the event that William and Anne both died without further issue. James II died in France a few weeks after the passage of this act, whose full title— "An Act for the Further Limitation of the Crown and Better Securing the

Rights and Liberties of the Subject" made clear the Whiggish intention to see "the old style divine right monarchy thus finally disappeared into a welter of clauses and sub-clauses of parliamentary law."[19]

Tories and Jacobites, of course, usually had another view of the direction of history and Anne's right to reign: they could swallow the 1701 Act as a compromise because the force of English tradition would continue to assert itself in a hereditary succession of the monarch, over the top of noisy legal justification.[20] When William III died the following year, Anne—the eldest surviving child of James II—became the first female singular sovereign in England since Elizabeth I. Her coronation meant a triumph for Whig politics in extending the peaceful, parliament-approved mechanics of dynastic succession after the Glorious Revolution. It remained an ambivalent triumph since her direct, hereditary claim to the throne theoretically needed no Whig approval or Dutch military invasions to carry legal weight under the old paradigm of divine right monarchy.

The beginning of Queen Anne's reign coincided with Addison achieving a high, fairly stable position within national administration and networks of cultural patronage. In 1704, he "took his seat in the Kit-Kat Club," which, though "charged by its enemies with godlessness and republicanism, was at once the most distinguished and the most powerful politico-literary society in England."[21] The next year, 1705, would see him appointed undersecretary of state for the South under Charles Hedges, a moderate Tory; Hedges was succeeded the following year as secretary by the Duke of Marlborough's son-in-law Charles Spencer, the Earl of Sunderland. Addison's official political career was a good example for the way in which the English state was developing away from a government centered around a royal court toward a robust bureaucracy of professional administrators. As undersecretary, he obtained significant responsibilities and power over English affairs with France, southern Europe, and the New World "plantations."[22] Smithers described the new position thus: "The office of Undersecretary had grown during the seventeenth century from a mere secretarial post to a position of executive authority. As the Secretaries of State themselves became concerned with major policy which had formerly been a royal preoccupation, so the Under-Secretaries took over from them its day-to-day execution. This process was accelerated by the succession of Queen Anne, who left to her ministers a greater degree of responsibility than their predecessors had ever possessed."[23] The detailed business of government expanded, and the monarch vacated more and more arenas of decision. Whig ministers like Addison were happy to expand their influence over these somewhat abandoned but still vested interests of the royal state.[24]

Though one Whiggish political current moved in the direction of making politics more bureaucratic, mechanistic, and professionally invisible, another political current sought to mobilize larger and larger groups of people to push policy-making in the "right" direction. Theater was a highly effective mode of such popular political event-making during Anne's reign, which was shadowed from its beginning by the momentous war. Especially during the winter—when soldiers, officers, and high government officials mingled in London while waiting for the summer's renewed Continental campaigns—a play often functioned to performatively gather the diverse elements of political alliances, articulate a vision of the culture that guided or would guide those alliances, and provide a charged opportunity for unity, celebrations, and public visibility.[25] Plays typically ran for only a few performances, and their advertisements tended to deemphasize their literary or "authored" nature: British Augustan drama was constituted by ephemeral, impactful, and often highly political events.[26]

Even as a medium of short-lived events, however, the theater had long been woven tightly into the fabric of official British political institutions and particularly into the organization and performance of monarchy. Both theater as an art form and the monarchic cult respond to collective human desires for artificially extended or immortal life. Monarchs in their theatrical function—as with properly theatrical figures in their long historical and political function—embody, structure, and adaptively accompany our contemporary experiences at the same time that they, often uncannily, threaten or promise to have lived or to go on living beyond the scale of our human, mortal lives. Theater and political institutions of official representation like the monarchy both deal strongly in superhuman effigies and ghosts.[27]

From its beginning, Queen Anne's reign was particularly haunted by the foreboding triple death—of person, monarch, and royal Stuart line—that would be her own inevitable demise. Her vivacious Continental rival and would-be successor Sophia, the Electress of Hanover, was both happily fertile and agreeably Protestant. Without surviving children, Anne's famously flickering health, in contrast, heightened and performed the political anxieties surrounding which foreign "usurper" would mount the throne upon her death: either the legally sanctioned German aristocrat, or her half-brother, the exiled and legally excluded Catholic Stuart Pretender in France. The series of rather drastic parliamentary interventions in the monarchical succession over the previous two decades weakened the sense of inevitability, let alone divine right, that had ideally attended the orderly historical progress of English kings and queens. At Anne's accession, the new lack of both a warrior-king (William III) and dynastic certainty opened up an opportunity for the theater to supply the public yearning for compensatory effigies. The relation between monarchical and theatrical culture took on, in this respect, a valence similar to that which had existed during the golden age of Shakespeare and Elizabeth I.

A century before, the Virgin Queen's rule and theater had been haunted not only by comparison with actual historical kings but also by the many living aspirants (e.g., faraway, close, Catholic) whose real presences were doubled in a dangerously censored media environment by Shakespeare's fictional historical kings. In like manner, Anne's government and theater were haunted not just by the Hanoverians and the Jacobite Pretender but by a Whig military champion crucial to her war efforts on the Continent. The Duke of Marlborough was a popular hero and highly successful general who went into self-exile at the end of 1712, when the Tory ministry succeeded in disgracing him and convincing Anne to remove him from his post at the head of her army. Roving the Continent with loyal armies, being received with high honors in court after court, Marlborough shaped and haunted British domestic politics throughout Anne's reign. He was a strong supporter of the Hanoverian succession (out of favor among many powerful Tories), but he was in regular touch with a nephew who was James II's illegitimate son, raising (probably very unwarranted but nonetheless real) suspicions that he might turn coat and support a different kind of coup. Domestically, in those latter years of Anne's reign, another powerful man of uncertain allegiances led the Tory party. Even as he served on the Queen's privy council as secretary of state, Lord Bolingbroke carried on secret negotiations with the Pretender and officials from Louis XIV's court that eventually came to center on a plan, supported by many other Tories, for a popular uprising to restore the Stuart monarchy after Queen Anne's death and the proclamation of George I.[28]

Alexander Pope and other sources tell us that at the 1713 premiere of Addison's *Cato,* a competition began between rival Whig and Tory factions as to which could applaud the loudest. It would be flattering to the playwright and to the status of art in general to think that the two factions were simply entering into such an applause competition to prove which of the two could better appreciate poetic genius. The competitive objective of the applause had much more to do with which faction could lay claim to the high patriotism modeled on stage and which could be pinned down allegorically as the disloyal party of traitorous tyranny.[29] In this context, Lord Bolingbroke famously summoned Barton Booth, the actor who played the heroic Cato, to his box at the conclusion of a performance in order to give him a purse of fifty guineas for "defending the cause of Liberty so well against a perpetual dictator." The "dictator" Bolingbroke seemed to allude to was taken to be the exiled Duke of Marlborough, who had aspired to the Caesar-like post of "Captain General for life" and been supported by the Whigs in his fervent desire to continue the war.[30] Whigs in the audience, meanwhile, would clearly associate the offstage, threatening Caesar of Addison's tragedy with Louis XIV and his puppet, the Stuart Pretender. From his position in the audience, Bolingbroke attempted—and to a degree succeeded—in making a performative intervention that greatly affected the bipartisan way in which the theatrical event was subsequently received and discussed.

The premiere of *Cato*, then, staged a major crisis of monarchical legitimacy in Britain. Moreover, because of Addison's unique political and cultural position, the theater at Drury Lane where *Cato* played became the site of a new kind of ludic campaign. Through this campaign of mass acclaim, dangerously different desires for the political future of the nation met and competed over a larger philosophical and aesthetic consensus that was safely abstracted and displaced into a staged Roman context. Whigs and Tories alike declared for Cato and against Caesar as the spiritual head of state par excellence. The question of the day became who could most convincingly claim the mantle of Cato in real life.[31]

ANNE'S REVIVAL OF ELIZABETH'S MIRROR: THE THEATRICAL ONTOLOGY OF THE ENGLISH QUEEN

The Lord Bolingbroke who attended Addison's tragedy, Henry St John, was a man who conspired to replace a monarch, George I, with another whom he believed was more legitimate: the would-be James III. The tale of his well-known paratheatrical interpretative reversal, performed from his box seat during an intermission of *Cato,* resonates with the theatrical ghost of another Bolingbroke. A little more than one hundred years before, the usurping Bolingbroke of Shakespeare's *Richard II* had also used public, succinctly reversing wordplay in his insidious moves to depose a ruling monarch. That character's successful action served as a theatrical inspiration for Essex's Rebellion, a failed coup against Elizabeth I led by one of her favorites and preceded by a specially commissioned performance of *Richard II* by Shakespeare's company.[32] This famous incident and Elizabeth's self-identification with the deposed *Richard II* point to the close relationship between court politics and the theater in Elizabeth's reign, which marked the full emergence of the modern English theater.[33]

The last Tudor reign of Elizabeth was a mirror and a model for the last Stuart reign of Anne, just as the golden age of Elizabethan theater acted as a mirror and a model for the silver age of English drama a century later. In both reigns, theaters and the debates their productions inspired served as shadow courts and parliaments, allowing public articulations and contests about heated topics to take on the ludic and protective cover of allegory and aesthetic displacement. The energy that might otherwise have gone into active plotting or military organization could be funneled into the playhouse, where felt allegiances to the reimagined figures of the past could temporarily bind together microcosmic bodies politic that shared hopes pinned on alternative futures. During both Elizabeth and then Anne's reign, the theater in this sense paved the way for Parliament to seize a larger share of the theatrical function and authority of *Dignitas* in the subsequent reign of a foreign king.

Anne well knew from her own family's travails in the previous century and from the distant mirror of Elizabeth about the difficulties a sole-ruling female monarch faced in effectively wielding the traditionally patriarchal, godly Dignitas of national identification. Like Elizabeth, her reign would be plagued by charges of illegitimacy and worries about her lack of a direct heir. She would counter the extra gender-based threat against her power by tolerating and even encouraging—also like Elizabeth—a hermaphroditic theatrical identification of her reign with kingly warriors. In Queen Anne's case, the shadow body politic of the nation was divided (not very neatly) between those who would have the nation drawn back in the direction of a divine-right monarchy and aristocratic oligarchy, and those who would have it progress in a republican direction. The challenge for a monarch in such a context to legitimately represent a unified nation while redefining her role as head of state was considerable.

Reappropriating the potential of public art to stage alternative, shadow sovereigns, Anne pursued a strategy that had effectively allowed Elizabeth to increase her popular authority. Hannah Smith has documented how Anne and her handlers used archetypal images to legitimate her power, drawing heavily on the biblical figure of Deborah as well as Elizabeth herself.[34] Anne took Elizabeth's motto, *Semper eadem* ("Always the same"), suggesting not just stability and even-temperedness—good qualifications for the job of monarch—but also a nostalgic, performative consistency, a powerful Queen with staying presence among a world of changing images and theatrical kings.[35] Even in her attempt to perform the warrior and martial monarch, Anne echoed Elizabeth, who had also drawn on Deborah: she was depicted as a "heroic queen who restored honour to the nation, as the people's princess." Pointedly, like Elizabeth, she was truly English, neither ambiguously French like the Jacobite Pretender (or half-Spanish like Elizabeth's sister Mary had been), nor a product of complex, negotiated invasion and immigration like her Dutch predecessor and her Hanoverian successors. Anne was the balanced real present, in all its antitheatrical lack of glamour but ultratheatrical immanence. The many portraits of her that survive even feature a noticeable and perhaps strategic "lacking in majesty to the point of being almost bourgeois," certainly a different aesthetic than the dramatic painted representations of Elizabeth.[36] Anne was almost the same as her spectators, not only the subject of representation but also its consumer. No theoretical or strategic purist, however, Anne continued to perform the "king's touch" as a means to cure scrofula, projecting an image of benevolence as well as an aura of sacral, eternal kingship that would come to an important historical end in England with her death.[37]

MARKETING THE MARLBOROUGH MAN

Seeking to distance themselves from the civil wars and associate themselves with Louis XIV's aesthetically courtly style of power, Anne's uncle and father, Charles II and James II, had generally avoided a soldierly identification. In marked contrast to his predecessors, William III's supporters had bolstered his authority after the revolutionary settlement of 1689 by "stressing his ability to perform the long-established kingly role of the nation's military leader."[38] Anne, following her sister (Mary II) as a demonstrably pious Protestant and deferential, feminine wielder of power, could not charge the battlefield nor indulge in the French style of theatrical, libertine royal display that her father and uncle had made famous in the Restoration. As a royal protobourgeois, she could attempt to show leadership through "personal morality and through promoting the piety of the nation. . . . But this was, in effect, an extension of the traditional and complementary role of the queen consort [similar to her sister, Mary's, chosen role]."[39] After brief attempts to present her chronically ill husband as the military successor of William III ended in failure, John Churchill, the Duke of Marlborough, emerged as the successor to William's kingly role as military general. Echoing the classical myth that Spenser (among others) had used to cast Elizabeth as a celestial virgin goddess who would restore a golden age, Congreve captured the symbolic split image of Anne and Marlborough in his ode from 1706: "Again *Astraea* Reigns! / Anna Her equal Scale maintains / And Marlbro wields Her sure deciding Sword."[40]

The staging of a second royal body—the effigy of the warrior-king hero of the Glorious Revolution—was a strategy pursued by the Whigs sometimes synergistically and sometimes antagonistically with Anne's own self-staging strategies. In a mark of her antilibertine style, Anne seldom attended the theater itself, leaving a vacuum into which the Whiggish professional politicians who also filled up her ministerial posts poured their efforts. The Kit-Cats, among others, took over the role of the earlier Stuarts as collective patrons: they attended theatrical events as a group, funded productions, and financed the building of a "Whig" playhouse, the Queen's Theatre in Haymarket, designed by Vanbrugh and opened in 1705.[41] Directing the Mint through Isaac Newton and Charles Montagu, the Whigs were also well positioned in Anne's reign to control the influential two-sided imagery of coins and commemorative medals. Montagu had led the Treasury's Great Recoinage and brought in Newton, who took an unexpectedly active role in supervising the manufacture of coins as warden and then master of the mint. The use of medals for propaganda was tied to the origin and identity of the Whig party and its oppositional tactics.[42] Addison in part showed his later-generation Whiggishness (as well as his loyalty to Montagu) through his well-known enthusiasm for numismatics. In his *Dialogues upon the Usefulness of Ancient Medals,* he argued that "there is a great affinity between Coins and Poetry, and that your Medallist and Critic are much nearer related than the world generally imagines."[43] Passionately elevating "one of those arts of peace" that Addison believed led nations and their people to greatness, Newton embraced the role of medalist as poet and critic. He and his colleague John Croker designed the 1702 coronation medal for Anne, which depicted her as Pallas Athena, the favorite daughter of Jupiter, hurling thunderbolts at a supine four-armed giant with snake legs, symbolizing Louis XIV and James Francis Edward Stuart. The legend labelled her as "UICEM GERIT ILLA TONANTIS": vice-regent of the thunderer. In his official explanation of the medal's imagery and legend, Newton wrote that William had been the thunderer, a warrior-king.[44] The Cambridge physicist turned London currency administrator, who made consistent efforts during his tenure at the Mint to regularize and systematize coin and medal output, was consciously extending the iconography of William and Mary's coronation medal. That medal had depicted Jupiter throwing a bolt of thunder from a cloud to hit Phaeton, the recklessly doomed son of Helios who was associated with the fleeing James II.[45]

The rhetoric of Anne's coronation medal slyly played on the established Elizabethan doctrine of the king's two bodies in several ways.[46] First, it picked up on the notion of the English sacral monarch as a vicar of God. Second, it followed the tradition of representing the monarch's sacred position as mediated through the Roman pantheon—the Christian God was also evoked in his classical aspect of worldly power, as Jupiter or Jove. Third, it represented Anne on the obverse as herself (her "body natural") and on the reverse as an immortal playing in an allegorical, dramatic scene (her "body politic"). Fourth, it showed the new Queen in the established gendered position of filling a role that at the same time exposed a lack—the lack of the dead and future king who could be Jupiter or the thunderer himself. Newton's notes explained that the legend of the coin identified Anne as "God's Viceregent and K. W.ms Successor." In the phrasing of Newton's description, the immortal Pallas-Anne continued "the Scene of the last Reign" by waging a just war against a tyrant whose many hands were grabbing and incorporating entire "bodies politic."[47] Though granted the status of a classical goddess, the Queen's body in Newton's design fits a general Whig strategy of staging Anne as slightly secondary, functional, and reliant on some other higher authority, be that either an absent, fatherly warrior or parliament. Her most important role: domestic continuity.

While Newton's coronation medal suggested that Anne's legitimacy was backed up by William III's spiritual revolutionary body, Addison was employed to poetically stage the *future* incumbent of that particular heroic kingly effigy. In 1704, Addison, up to that point under considerable financial anxiety, was commissioned by the lord treasurer (Sidney Godolphin) to compose a poem celebrating Marlborough's war-turning victory at Blenheim. As reward for doing so, he was appointed as commissioner of appeal in excise, directly succeeding John Locke, who had recently died. *The Campaign* was published in a coordinated media campaign on the day that Marlborough returned in triumph to London. Until the twentieth century, it enjoyed a prime place in the British literary canon.[48]

Two years before he took the commission to eulogize Marlborough's victory, he had opened an early draft of his "Letter from Italy" with an extended sardonic stanza disgustedly satirizing poets gearing up to write clichéd lionizing poetry about the heroic bloodsheds of the coming war's conflagration.[49] He cut that opening from the "Letter" before its publication, and the self-aware critique of ambitious, bloodthirsty poets chomping at their bits is also absent from the surface of *The Campaign*, for obvious reasons. Yet the idea perhaps survives in the shades that make the latter poem notable for its early formulation of a modern sensibility in regard to war—an often contradictory mixture of alienation, inverted pastoral imagery, a sense of innumerable nauseating repetitions of carnage, and the glorification of violence in the name of a new, more peaceful international order. The modern war, echoing Cromwell's slogan, was not waged just for national glory but to end both war and its unnatural extension: slavery. The split perspective is encapsulated in the opening stanza: "Rivers of blood I see, and hills of slain, / An Iliad rising out of one campaign."[50]

Anne, in ingenious Whig fashion, is praised as the director of many nations with the English King's body split between head and arms:

> To Britain's queen the nations turn their eyes,
> On her resolves the Western world relies,
> Confiding still, amidst its dire alarms,
> In Anna's councils and in Churchill's arms.

The Whiggish praise for the hereditary Queen is further rhetorically qualified by the claim that she merits accolades because she encourages a culture of meritocracy:

> Thy favourites grow not up by fortune's sport,
> Or from the crimes or follies of a court;
> On the firm basis of desert they rise.[51]

Recently returned from his grand tour of war-torn Europe, Addison's view was markedly cosmopolitan when it came to the mockery that death and battlefield violence make of national rivalry: "Nations with nations mixed confusedly die, / And lost in one promiscuous carnage lie." The chaos of disorientation, where even national identification falls apart, helps to summon, on the other hand, an archaic need for an orienting figure on horseback. Addison addresses his hero directly: "Europe's destiny depends on thine." Marlborough rides into the ravaged and riven scene, a patient peacemaker and decisively violent general, both "good and great": "Unbounded courage and compassion joined, / . . . make the hero and the man complete."[52] A man of modernity and law, Marlborough is rational, not hungry for unnecessary slaughter or dominance. Even as he witnesses the victory of his army, "The leader grieves, by generous pity swayed, / To see his just commands so well obeyed."[53] In the midst of a hellish landscape—of "floods of gore" and "Mountains of slain"—Marlborough is welcomed by oppressed foreigners as the "deliverer."[54] His "easy greatness" in either "camp or court" marks him as near-divine, like Achilles or Aeneas, "the great father of Almighty Rome."

Addison's speaker declares him, in a line that was likely not easy for Anne to swallow, "the British chief."⁵⁵

"Blest by rescued nations as he goes," the kingly Duke guides a war that frees foreigners to "taste the sweets of English liberty."⁵⁶ British patriotism and exceptionalism are grounded in comparative liberty. The foreign war becomes a lesson for its soldiers on the virtue of their homeland. In southwest Germany,

> Our British youth, with inborn freedom bold,
> Unnumbered scenes of servitude behold,
> Nations of slaves, with tyranny debased,
> Their Maker's image more than half defaced,
> Hourly instructed, as they urge their toil,
> To prize their queen, and love their native soil.⁵⁷

An immensely famous passage of the poem grants Marlborough an angel-like sovereignty. Waging a righteous battle to shake a "guilty land," the general divinely and even serenely directs an exercise of shock and awe, likened to a famous recent storm (which Defoe had memorialized in his 1704 *The Storm*, sometimes called one of the first works of modern journalism).⁵⁸ Marlborough:

> In peaceful thought the field of death surveyed,
> To fainting squadrons sent the timely aid,
> Inspired repulsed battalions to engage,
> And taught the doubtful battle where to rage.
> So when an angel by divine command
> With rising tempests shakes a guilty land,
> Such as of late o'er pale Britannia past,
> Calm and serene he drives the furious blast;
> And, pleased the Almighty's orders to perform,
> Rides in the whirlwind, and directs the storm.

The scale and rapidity of protoindustrial war, however, exposes the fraud of the poetic tradition, as "troops of heroes undistinguished die." Apart from the singularly captivating Marlborough, the characteristic British soldier is distinguished and dignified en masse by a modern, emancipated pride: "With native freedom brave, / The meanest Briton scorns the highest slave."⁵⁹

The Campaign exhibits an emphasis on Marlborough rather than Anne that was typical for Whig poetry.⁶⁰ Addison, according to Joseph Hone, "vests military authority exclusively in Marlborough. The queen barely features. Limiting the poetic authority of the queen and heightening the sublime power of the general purveyed a distinctly Whiggish message."[61] As with Elizabethan poets and playwrights, Addison played in a heightened way with the doctrinal language of power. His verses grant the general not just the heroic might of arms but the vicar's head, miraculously illuminated in his directions by direct communication with the Almighty. Abigail Williams notes that the conclusion of the poem features "a deft reversal of the idiom of divine right... Anna is royal, but Marlborough is 'god like.' The queen may be granted the custodianship of the nation, but it is the duke who comes closest to divinity... the angel riding the storm."[62] That the storm is identified with one that has recently shaken the British homeland leaves a suggestion that it might be the Duke who could direct politics as well as foreign wars toward a future of heavenly peace and away from a past of slavery and shaking, civil discord.

Hannah Smith argues that Anne did much more than merely tolerate the Whig staging of the general as a kingly martial leader. Indeed, "Anne colluded in the creation of Marlborough as a quasi-royal," elevating him to a status nearing an imperial prince and gifting him "the royal manner of Woodstock as the site of Blenheim Palace."[63] This strategy and indulgence had its limits, however. In the year after her coronation, Newton's mint had struck a medal that pushed the political envelope a bit too far by featuring a crowned female figure kneeling, giving three keys to Marlborough on horseback, with the Latin legend SINE CLADE VICTOR, meaning "A conqueror without slaughter." In its direct context, the medal celebrated Marlborough's fairly bloodless victories over Bonn, Huy, and Limbourg.[64] But, despite the obverse's standard portrait of Anne as Regina, the reverse and its legend seemed to stage a symbolic repetition of the Glorious Revolution, Marlborough indeed as the second coming of William III. Newton had to defend the medal against potentially dangerous charges of undue flattery by saying that the depicted victorious figure did not represent Marlborough, but any "small armed force." As John Craig has written, however, the problem remained that the medallion showed "the surrender of the three cities as tendered to a solitary horseman." Afterward, Anne's government required that all medal designs had to be approved by the Treasury, leaving one of Anne's more trusted (Country Whig) ministers, Robert Harley, to exert substantial control over the images printed by the mint for the next decade.[65]

Addison also likely tempted the limits of royal favor with his 1707 libretto for *Rosamond*, his only attempt at opera. Dedicated to Marlborough's wife, Sarah Churchill, with whom Anne had a famously close friendship plagued by jealousy and competition, the opera was set on the grounds of Marlborough's new palace at Woodstock Park.[66] The elaborate Drury Lane staging celebrated the construction of that heroic residence, called Blenheim Castle after the same famous victory that Addison had feted in *The Campaign*. The climax of the opera featured the Whig architect and impresario Vanbrugh's design for the castle as a dramatically revealed backdrop for the onstage King's prophetic vision of a triumphant British future. Altogether, the opera's short run at Drury Lane functioned as part of a patriotic publicity campaign for "an incipient tourist industry" growing up around the new palace grounds, which was already a site of national significance.[67] Woodstock Park had been the reputed home of Chaucer and, as the libretto related, it held the bower where King Henry II had legendarily kept his beautiful Welsh paramour, Rosamond Clifford, hidden away from the jealous wrath of Queen Elinor.[68] Much later, Woodstock Palace had been the place where Mary I kept her Protestant half-sister, the future Elizabeth I, imprisoned while she and her advisors deliberated about whether or not to put her to death after Wyatt's Rebellion. Vanbrugh's Blenheim, whose grounds were designed to preserve the ruins of the palace and famous bower, was planned as a symbol of Whig aspiration, a new order headed by a grand coalition of poets, statesmen, and generals.[69]

Brean Hammond reads *Rosamond* as an allegorical celebration of the 1707 Act of Union, which merged Scotland and England and their prospective parliaments, creating the United Kingdom of Great Britain. Addison's heavy use of the terms "British," "Britain," and "Britannia" within the opera may point to this intention, as does also his referring to Elinor as "Britannia's Queen." To the tune of Thomas Clayton's much-maligned score, Addison mixed the known legend, taken from a popular ballad, with political allegory—a familiar mode of relating the Rosamond legend. Hammond reports that "in the precursor treatments of the story with which Addison was familiar, there was an established tradition of adapting it to contemporary affairs of state."[70]

The first act of the libretto establishes a dramatic situation, articulated by Rosamond, that was allegorical for England's political situation at a time when the country was polarized over the war's continuation and when Anne was often furious about the political impasse: "At home thou seest thy queen enraged, / Abroad thy absent lord engaged / In wars, that may our loves disjoin."[71] The libretto continued Addison's staging of Marlborough as a kingly warrior and rightful shadow monarch to Anne. The angels in act 3, scene 1, put him on a par with Henry V, equating the victory of Blenheim with that of Agincourt. True to the legend, Addison's version has the jealous Queen Elinor discovering Rosamond in the bower and offering her either a dagger or a bowl of poison with which to end her life. If Elinor was Anne, Rosamond would be Sarah, a Whig champion and powerful woman in her own right but subject to Anne's jealousy against her and her threateningly kingly husband, who—like the opera's King Henry—was lavishly feted as a hero whenever he returned to England from victories abroad.

Addison's libretto changes the tragic end of the ballad and medieval legend by having the Queen at the end of act 2, scene 6, reveal that the poison she offered to Rosamond would not kill her but only put her into a deep sleep, time enough for her to be whisked away to a convent. The vengeful, tricky, yet merciful queen, standing over the unconscious body of her rival, sings:

> When vanquished foes beneath us lie,
> How great it is to bid them die!
> But how much greater to forgive,
> And bid a vanquished foe to live![72]

Addison's complex message seems to urge patience, moderation, tolerance, and balance on the part of the romantically mismatched Queen when confronting her rivals, the celebrated denizens of Woodstock/Blenheim. The end of the play has the King promising to return to the Queen, who in turn agrees to let Rosamond go on living in a secluded convent—surely not the future that the opera's dedicatee, Sarah Churchill, imagined for herself, though not too far from her fate in Anne's later reign, when she fell out of Anne's favor and eventually went into Continental exile until the Queen's death.

Addison's libretto mirrored the tensions inherent in the coalition between Anne and the Whigs, both of whom relied on the war hero Marlborough. Anne's reliance was more pointedly ambivalent, but she only decisively turned against the recently named prince of the Holy Roman Empire—whose towering ambitions were well known across Europe—after he urged his appointment as captain-general for life in 1709.[73] His Caesar-like demand failed, and Anne continued to tolerate his stature and power, strategically using his image, fame, and martial ability to balance the lack of a military king that haunted her reign. But her wariness had grown, and she ultimately kept Marlborough in check, dismissing him from service in 1711. That move gave new hope to Tory Jacobites that perhaps the Queen's affections were moving in the direction of her banished half-brother, against the Hanoverians. At this moment, Addison again performed the political insider working in the public sphere, helping to guide the public's perception of Marlborough as a sympathetic figure with a regal stature: his essay on fame, in *Spectator* 256, was published a week before the Queen dismissed her princely general and is relatively transparent in that context as a defense of Marlborough against Tory attacks.[74]

As events developed, Marlborough's dismissal was a dramatic endgame to the upheaval Anne initiated in 1710 when she replaced, somewhat autocratically, most of her Whig ministers with Tory ministers, thus showing her remaining power to pilot the ship of state.[75] Although she presented a calm public face, she was known in political circles to be quite jealous and strategically protective of her singular status, developing a strong and decisive envy against competitors and associates like Sarah Churchill or the charismatic Electress Sophia, the older but devilishly healthy potential successor to Anne whose children and grandchildren were in any case the designated usurpers of the Stuart hold on the throne. "Like Elizabeth," Edward Gregg wrote, Anne "could bear no thought of an heir, of eyes and thoughts diverted from the setting to the rising sun."[76] In spite of the Act of Settlement and her professions in favor of the Hanoverian future, Anne seems to have cultivated a degree of suspense around whom she would ultimately support to inherit the crown. Perhaps, as Elizabeth was known to have done, she used this shrewd means to center power and speculation about the nation's political destiny on her personal decision. Avoiding the optics of a settled future sovereign that might replace her, the Queen's policy was to oppose state visits or premature arrivals in Britain by the Hanoverians (as well as, of course, any visits by her half-brother, the Stuart Pretender).[77]

Historians debate the extent to which Jacobitism, a never emerging historical potentiality, threatened Britain's stability in the period as a viable alternative future to the Hanoverian succession. Jacobitism is usually presented from the triumphant position of Whig historians as "a series of disconnected, small-scale and unsuccessful rebellions." It may be that the ease of this presentation is due to the fact that Whig dominance during 1689–1760 resulted in the strategic destruction and nonpreservation of Jacobite documents from the historical archive.[78] Still, many historians argue that, in retrospect, "there was never a real chance that the Pretender would be restored."[79] Even early critics and historians of the period sometimes suggest that the anxiety that circled around a Jacobite restoration—supported by Louis XIV, performing himself as a modern imperial Caesar—amounted to political delirium. Commenting on the support for the first production of Addison's *Cato,* Samuel Johnson, for instance, wrote sardonically: "The time however was now come when those who affected to think liberty in danger, affected likewise to think that a stage-play might preserve it."[80]

Other historians caution us that the Hanoverian succession and the permanence of its settlement were not by any means foregone conclusions. The historian Howard Erskine-Hill wrote that "the Jacobite diaspora abroad was an enormous, international and influential network of people" including powerful aristocrats, high churchmen, and military brigades.[81] But even if hindsight is granted clarity about the real relative strength of the Hanoverian versus Jacobite movements, such clarity can be misleading when it comes to the mood at the time—delirium or not. Gregg noted that "by early 1714, when the Queen had less than nine months to live, it had become an article of faith for both Jacobites and Whigs that the Queen desired to overthrow the Act of Settlement of 1701."[82] This was partially due to Anne's estrangement from the House of Hanover, which had recently publicly criticized her decision to seek peace with France: "Relations between Great Britain and the Electoral court were at their worst between 1712 and 1714."[83] In sum, politically involved people during Anne's reign, as Erskine-Hill argued, "really did confront a twofold situation, needing to remember that two communities of allegiance bore upon Britain, each nourishing certain hopes, promising rewards, and threatening penalties up to and including proscription and death. There was a frontier, political and psychological as well as geographical."[84]

One could even read a political meaning into Addison's statement in *Spectator* 10 about the need for daily psychological vigilance, given his crucial role as a Whig propagandist in preventing Jacobite arguments from taking hold among the populace: "The mind that lies fallow but a single Day, sprouts up in Follies that are only to be killed by a constant and assiduous Culture."[85] Addison had served as a special envoy to the Hanoverian court during his European tour and again with Vanbrugh and Montagu in 1706.[86] Besides these apparent efforts to shore up the Protestant succession of a Parliament-approved monarch, one of the main projects of Whig culture during the reign of Anne was to interrupt the formation of nostalgia, inertia, and tradition around the mystical body of the king—a formation that might summon forth another Stuart restoration. In the place of the royal ex-pat, James Francis Edward Stuart, the Whigs offered the future-oriented, progressive vision of a talented general on horseback whom Addison immortalized as a sovereign angel riding through the storm of civil war, defending a free society overseas against a new Continental Caesar and pointing the way to a universal, emancipatory peace.

The intense mixture of politics, literature, and theater in Whiggish lives of the time is partially explained by the activity required for such a resistant cultural agenda, since the arts were traditional magnets and magnifiers of monarchical court culture. These energies were sharpened by the impending end of Anne's reign, prompting Addison and a group of Whig writers to form the Hanover Club in 1712, with the goal of supporting the Hanoverian Succession in the public through a steady output of works and pamphlets.[87] As during Elizabeth's reign, the question of the rightful heir to the Stuart throne (or, more pragmatically, the question of what one could realistically expect of the nation's political future) was a confusing one to answer. John Byrom, a well-known poet of the time, captured the mood well:

> God Bless the King!—I mean the Faith's Defender;
> God bless—no Harm in blessing!—the Pretender.
> Who that Pretender is, and who that King,
> God bless us all! is quite another thing.[88]

Some evidence suggests that the Whig bias in eighteenth-century history leads contemporary historians to underestimate what may have been the real chances of a Jacobite restoration. In the same year (1708) that he published a pamphlet, *The Present State of War,* to urge a peace-inclined British public to continue and even expand the war on the Continent as a matter of self-defense against French absolute monarchy, Undersecretary Addison was busy monitoring and coordinating the military defense against a real French-backed invasion of Scotland by James Francis Edward Stuart. Later that year, Addison was made secretary of the Irish government (under lieutenant governor Lord Wharton), taking on high responsibility for another often explosive front zone in the struggle between Catholic and Protestant political factions and societies.[89] In London, his former boss, Charles Spencer, would continue as secretary for two more years until being dismissed by Anne at the beginning of her 1710 purge of the mighty Whig Junto. Aggressively responding to this move against his son-in-law and his own commanding position over British politics, Marlborough sent Anne a copy of a circulating medal showing the Pretender's head on the obverse with the British Isles on the reverse "so that She may see the hopes he has." The sending of the medal was a warning to her not to end the war before he had declared victory over the French, lest Louis XIV retain enough power to aid a Jacobite restoration. But the act was likely to dually signify for Anne the continued need to move against Marlborough's own kingly "hopes" by rejecting his request to become captain-general for life and dismissing him outright the following year.[90]

The Preliminary Articles of September 1711, an agreement between France and England that set the stage for an end to the war, were negotiated on the English side by Anne's new chief ministers, among them Robert Harley and

Bolingbroke. The articles effectively worked out a separate peace between the two powers that broke with Britain's Continental allies. The talks reached their success "on the basis that a Jacobite restoration would be the ultimate result."[91] In 1713, when George Berkeley wrote to Percival about seeing *Cato*'s premiere, his high praise of Addison's tragedy was directly preceded by an account of recent, urgent gossip about which of Anne's high ministers (particularly Harley) might support the Jacobite cause, a repeated significant concern in his correspondence during those days.[92]

Bolingbroke was prevented from possibly seeing his Jacobite plans through from within the Privy Council when he was dramatically exiled from royal favor in the intense, intrigue-filled politics climaxing in the last week of the Queen's life. Seizing power four days later upon Anne's death, the Whig-led regents put Addison in place as his immediate administrative successor. Bolingbroke—falling further from grace after the accession of George I and a pivotal general election lost by the Tories—fled to France, where he served as secretary of state to James III during the failed 1715 Jacobite rebellion.[93] Given Bolingbroke's stature, position, and political skill, his trajectory alone would suggest that the fear of a Jacobite rebellion was not much exaggerated. After all, even Johnson's critique that the stagers of *Cato* were affecting "to think liberty in danger" must be read in the light of Johnson's admitted Jacobite sympathies.[94]

As with Elizabeth, the suspense about Anne's choice for her succession lasted until her death. The speculation even gained an afterlife in rumors about some closely guarded papers found in her chamber after her death. Minutes from August 4, 1714, record the first meeting of the lords regent at which Addison—restored to political office at his highest rank yet—attended as secretary. The last years had seen the peak of his literary career with *The Spectator* and *Cato* during a time when most high Whig ministers were excluded from the government. The minutes of that meeting, taking place in the crucial stretch of time between the death of the last Stuart monarch and the arrival in England of the first Hanoverian, George I, record that a "secret packet" discovered in Anne's quarters was burned in accordance with instructions affixed by the Queen to its cover.[95]

Her twentieth-century biographer, Gregg, recounted that the Hanoverian envoy in London, Hans Casper von Bothmer, was present at the burning and noticed "that some sheets on the fire were written in French by a large, clerical hand." Bothmer concluded that the package contained the letters from James Francis Edward Stuart to the Queen. Gregg found this conclusion unlikely, instead suggesting that the papers "were the Queen's letters from Prince

George of Denmark," her husband. But there is room to speculate that the strongly pro-Hanoverian lords regent, by burning Anne's packet of letters, committed the phoenix of divine right kings finally to ashes: Bolingbroke had written secretly in March 1714 to Charles François de la Bonde—the French ambassador to London—that a will leaving the Crown to her brother might already exist, hidden in a "secret packet" that the Queen "kept on her person or, at night, under her pillow."[96]

The mystery surrounding this secret packet and Queen Anne's private decision about her successor dramatically highlights the changing balance of power between the British monarchy, state ministers, and Parliament. The restored Whig Junto that exiled Bolingbroke upon Anne's death and fixed Addison in his stead staged a royal succession in line with their long planning, forceful propagandistic efforts, and previously passed laws. It was made to look, as it often does historically, inevitable. However, Addison and the Whigs' contributions to staging a kingly *body politic* riding parallel to Queen Anne's reign were one part of stabilizing a new performed constitution of balanced sovereignty between traditional, inherited monarchy and the advancing, still avant-garde anointment of authority by democratic acclaim. The orderly, inexorable Hanoverian succession was a theatrical rather than a natural political result.

Addison's public efforts—exemplified in *The Campaign* and *Rosamond*—fit within a broader Whig strategy of lionizing the Duke of Marlborough as a figure of royal stature and preparing the public for the accession of a Whig-approved and Whig-invited, martial male body once Anne's problematically legitimized rule came to its end and left Sophia's proven line of sons to inherit the throne. On the same day that Addison attended the meeting where it was revealed that Anne's secret packet had been burned, Marlborough and his wife, Sarah, made a festive, near-royal entry and parade through London to their house in St. James. Having previously timed their arrival from the Continent in England for the day on which George I was officially proclaimed as king, Marlborough's London progress was accompanied by more than two hundred gentlemen with horse contingents. People thronged in the streets, proclaiming: "Long live King George; long live the Duke of Marlborough." Certain "enemies and enviers" censured "his making such a magnificent Entry, while his Royal Mistress was hardly cold," but his supporters argued that it was necessary to shore up opposition to the Pretender.[97] With the energy and pageant of the exiled magisterial general's return to London underwriting the promised accession of George I (who would not arrive in England until later that month), a certain period of Addison's theatrical work approached a successful end: the haunting kingly body politic of Anne's reign was drawn home to be reintegrated into the dual body of the coming Hanoverian king. Addison, in this regard, had been a public artist working in a long history of theatermakers dramatizing to political effect the "second" body of the English monarch. "No eighteenth-century moulder of public opinion," writes Karl Axelsson, "was as proficient and attentive as Addison in diagnosing the displacement of political authority and exploiting a mistrust of the body politic as an enduring and natural entity of truth."[98]

The next chapter will consider Addison's 1713 staging of *Cato* with this theatrical-political background in mind. A drama of succession, the theatrical event and the play itself were the "crowning" achievement of Addison's multifaceted, performative public career. The neoclassical tragedy's success led to the playwright reaching the top of the British government as a secretary of state, while symbolically representing the "liberty" of a British imperial future and capturing the assembled people's factional but newly empowered will to determine who would be sovereign over the theatrically opened modern era.

6

Addison's Cato

> Ritual theatre ... establishes the spatial medium not merely as a physical area for simulated events but as a manageable contraction of the cosmic envelope within which man—no matter how deeply buried such a consciousness has latterly become—fearfully exists.
> —Wole Soyinka, *Myth, Literature, and the African World*, 1976

ACTING THE KING'S BODY: THOMAS BETTERTON

Coins and poetry—in the service of political impresarios like Addison and his Whig colleagues—could be ideal tools to create and institute a doubled official or semiofficial reality. But it has always been theater that specializes as an art form in the slippage between representation and the real. Because of its liveness and its consequent need for repeated enactment by living bodies, the theatrical tradition encourages double vision through recycled characters, recycled narratives, and the reuse of houses, properties, and actors.[1]

In *Tatler* 167, Richard Steele linked this special doubling effect of the theater to the aims of Whig politics, declaring that "there is no Human Invention so aptly calculated for the forming a Free-born people as that of a Theatre." Steele's argument directly reversed the Platonic argument that theater should be banned from an ideal Republic because it discouraged the youth from having a sense of "oneness" with themselves, disrupting their belief in their organic birth from the land as unified individuals. Instead, Steele held that theatergoing was a valuable antidote and training ground against the dissoluteness of a fragmented social world. Oneness must be trained and cultivated, and the actor served as a model citizen in this respect. In Cicero's account, Steele reminds us, the classical Roman actor Roscius was an exemplar of virtue and grace for his contemporaries and "used frequently to say, *The Perfection of an Actor is only to become what he is doing.*"[2]

What Steele was in fact doing by citing Cicero's praiseful quotation of Roscius was eulogizing the most famous actor of his own age, Thomas Betterton, and thereby defending and praising the theater for its role in the proper course of politics. "Free-born" refers in Steele's usage to the special brand of English exceptionalism (discussed in chapter 3) that supposedly had long exempted people born on the island from a world generally plagued by slavery. Theater, Steele argued, uses pleasure to "naturally" shape those prereflective lovers of liberty "who are too unattentive to receive Lectures."[3] At a more reflective level, Steele's musing suggested the provocative idea that to be free is to be born theatrically. In Roscius's argument with Platonism, theater is akin to a mirroring baptismal font: to be the perfect actor is to choose one's birth—similar to the way in which Socrates wished to choose the birth myth of Athens's guardians—and thus to become the doing of one's chosen actions.

With the last sacred English monarch childless on the throne, unfit by gender conventions and ailing health to be imaginarily the confidence-inspiring, warrior-king, eulogies to the actor Betterton became something of a miniindustry inside the cultural project of providing surrogate, nostalgic images of heroic kingship. Joseph Roach writes that "some Englishmen came to see Betterton, or at least the Betterton created by the hagiographic accounts, as a shadow king, a visible effigy signifying the dual nature of sovereignty, its division between an immortal and an abject body, and the ultimate symbolic diffusion of the former into a body of laws."[4] Roach argues that Charles Gildon's 1710 *The Life of Mr. Thomas Betterton, the Late Eminent Tragedian*—perhaps the first book-length theatrical biography—leaves the reader with the impression "of a single public life standing in for an epochal memory (Betterton came in with the Stuart Restoration and exited in their dynastic twilight.)" Gildon's narrative "invites comparison, in the Plutarchian tradition of parallel lives, between what Steele called 'the Imaginary and the Real Monarch.'"[5]

Steele wrote in his *Tatler* eulogy that Betterton's performances of Shakespearean kings had led him to reflect that the actor and the actual kings he had impersonated shared the same ultimate fate, their bodies now buried together in the grounds of Westminster Abbey. Gildon's biography set Betterton up as the monarch of the theater, a "mimic state." Betterton had worn the aura of Shakespeare's heir: he had learned how Shakespeare guided his actors in creating the roles of Henry VIII and Hamlet directly from William Davenant, who, rumor held, was Shakespeare's illegitimate son. Via "the secular sanctity of Shakespearean stage business," Roach writes, "in public memory Betterton's action became synonymous with kingly dignity."[6] The theater and Betterton's theatrical body had become the safeguards of the behavioral secrets of true and legitimate kingship, originally historically imagined by Shakespeare against the foils of Elizabeth and James I's controversial live performances.

In the sunset of Betterton's theatrical reign, Addison and Steele's establishment of a regular mass discourse about the theater and its actors shared a conjoined birth with the daily output of the "fourth estate," the popular press that would comment upon, investigate, and balance the other power centers of the modern administrative state. The two theatrical and journalistic friends thereby furthered the original Elizabethan movement of debates about statecraft and representation away from the royal court and the halls of government proper and into the theaters. If in Shakespeare's age the theaters functioned partly in the context of inns where people waited and trained to be *at court,* coffeehouses began to function in Addison and Steele's age as places where people waited and trained to go to *the theater.* The encounter with Betterton the impresario and actor gazing out from his elevated, central stage had become perhaps as vestedly auratic as the encounter with the real Queen herself, still tasked in those days with "playing" an absent king.

Roach asserts that Betterton's funeral "constitutes an epitomizing event in the early development of a particular kind of secular devotion . . . in which the body of an actor serves as a medium—an effigy" central to a modern style of ancestor worship, "the secular rituals through which a modernizing society communicates with its past."[7] A historical shift in these rituals can be seen by comparing the continually staged Shakespearean *texts* of "ancestor worship" for which Betterton's body was an important kingly metaeffigy during Anne's reign with the new Augustan theater's *use* of the corporate metaeffigy, be it the actor (Betterton) or the playwright (Shakespeare). Shakespeare's plays tended to present a mimic state that was complicated and fractured but held together at a larger scale through might and some general tendency toward order. A large part of the reflected theatrical interest in his theater seems to have lain in the intrigue, dubious split identifications, and political controversies that the complicated plots bore out. The neoclassical theater of Addison's age, on the other hand, strove rather toward an ideal of unity: selling Betterton as a mimic monarch and Shakespeare as a national bard were two attempts to metatheatrically stage a figure of national identification that would transcend even the post-Shakespearean wounds of recent civil wars.

Betterton's theatrical funeral, Roach wrote, "eternalized an effigy dedicated to those who would otherwise remain anonymous to one another in the fictive kinship of race and nation."[8] The long Shakespearean revolution had been—after the civil wars, the regicide, the Glorious Revolution, and the Act of Settlement—successful enough that the coin reversed. The popular theater itself became not the necessary site providing alternatives to official, heavily enforced unitary identification but instead the necessary site of providing the orientation of that *lost* unitary identification. Even our contemporary reception of Shakespeare is, of course, partially shaped by the British Augustan attempt to rebrand "the Bard" as a central author of virtuous themes and a transcendent source of national unity.

Following Roach, Jane Goodall sees in the funeral cult of Betterton "the beginnings of a democratisation of Presence, through the mediation of the actor who plays the sovereign and is at once the king and the common man."[9] Yet the significant energies that went into staging the shadow king-actor of Queen Anne's reign relied on Betterton's exceptional status as a performer in a short, Kabuki-like lineage connecting him directly to Shakespeare. Importantly, as Roach notes, Betterton could become a lionized "national effigy" because—via his association with Davenant—he served as a living bridge to the now distant theatrical culture before the Interregnum.[10] He offered, in short, what no lineage of seventeenth- and eighteenth-century English monarchs could: a supposedly unbroken, theatrically patrilineal inheritance, mystically and charismatically tinted as such inheritances often are.

Holding open a space in which different kings from different pasts could haunt and march and campaign with potentially greater backing from Parliament, the Elizabethan theater had played dangerously off of a performatively ingenious monarch and her powerful court. Against the backdrop of the comparatively much-diminished, untheatrical court of Queen Anne—a parliamentary-approved monarch—the theater of Addison and Steele's time became differently charged as a prosthetic reservoir of sacral, national identifications. Whig theater-making after the Hanoverian succession would famously develop the down-to-earth sympathetic merchant as its modern hero par excellence. The stately Whig theater of Addison's age, however, was busier selling unifying compensatory kingly figures.[11]

The coffeehouse, in its turn, inherited part of theater's older social role as the site of debate, contrasting identifications, and disappearing tragic and comic scripts matched to the political controversies of the day. In *Spectator* 49, Steele depicted the coffeehouse as just this kind of representative theater, the varied clientele of a single day performing with their diverse agendas, ages, characteristics, interests, and outlooks a modern body politic that defied capture in a singular, human-shaped effigy. The paratheatrical literature of Addison and Steel used the speed and economy of newsprint to stage "the power of effigies like Betterton to imbue time with narrative," to anchor and phantasmatically populate a new buzzing, quotidian discursive network that flooded both public and private spaces.[12] If older courtly literature and drama had found their double in the cagey, complex, artful, and long-enduring masks of the successful monarch, newsprint found its double rather in the skillful, professional actor himself: a performatively flexible effigy able to continually and rapidly invite and shed different roles and identifications, thus projecting and absorbing different possible futures for the nation at the speed of modern financial exchange.[13]

Steele's eulogy to Betterton points to a subtle but important difference in how he and Addison—the two copublishers and friends—approached death and identity in general. Reflecting on the kingly actor's historical burial service at Westminster Abbey, Steele professed a belief that "the Distinctions amongst Men [are] ... meerly Scenical," ending in a death that obliterated societal divides.[14] Addison's own walk through Westminster Abbey a year later, on the other hand, inspired him to develop a three-tiered contemplation of the afterlife. His *Spectator* 26 begins with a degree of horror: diving below the settled ground underneath which Steele had more discreetly left his rotting actor and monarchs, Addison digs up the terrestrial underworld as a jumble of formerly separate people mixing promiscuously. Moving up to the second, more ordered, terrestrial level, the still chaotic assembly of variously styled memorials in the abbey reveal a national problem: the need to adopt more reasonable standards for memorializing their dead. Finally, Addison's Spectator looks upward and forward to the heavenly day when all people from all times, enemies and friends alike, will be contemporaries appearing together on a celestial plane.[15]

The imagined glance back from the afterlife on the artificial distinctions between individuals in this mortal life bred in Addison, like Steele, a certain sorrow over the pettiness of painful and violent earthly scenes. But Addison's view was not that those distinctions were "merely" scenical; indeed, the second, terrestrial stage where identities should be commemorated in a common yet orderly fashion seemed to allow not, as in Steele's general afterlife, the falling away of all distinctions, but the coming together of a new and true community at a higher, heavenly level. The difference is subtle but maps reliably onto their distinct approaches to drama and politics, which will be discussed in chapter 7 in terms of Addison's emphasis on sociability versus Steele's stress on a fuller sociality.[16]

While Steele's views often aligned with a more radical version of Whiggism, Addison's fell in line with Locke and the moderate Whigs.[17] In *Tatler* 161, Addison developed a dream vision that allegorically showed his general balanced view through its depiction of the goddess Liberty sitting enthroned between a fearsome Commonwealth and a benign Monarchy.[18] At times, he could come off as a strong adversary to monarchy altogether: his 1708 tract in favor of continuance with war against France, *The Present State of the War,* declared France the greatest enemy of the British, in part because French "pursuits of universal Monarchy" would "fix them for ever in their animosities and aversion towards us."[19] But in fact he pragmatically advocated a limited monarchy and could prove quite deferential and solicitous of royal favor, praising and supporting William III and Queen Anne, visiting the court of King Frederick William I in Dresden, and maintaining close contact with the Hanoverian court in order to help ease the eventual Protestant succession.[20]

Although his tragedy *Cato* would become a rallying drama for later antimonarchical movements and affect, its politics at its moment of premiere were more complex. Already articulated in Addison's revision of the Cato myth was something more than a typical, strategic Whig balancing act between the ghosts of the failed Commonwealth and the strong Tory, royalist half of the country. That balancing act—modulated after 1710 by the Whigs' fall from power and the resurgence of Tory and Jacobite power—could alone explain a key shift perhaps evident in Addison's earlier drafts of *Cato*'s first four acts compared to the later drafted act 5: the last act moderates the militancy of classical accounts of Cato's death and emphasizes the republican hero's fatal mistake in reasoning.

Addison's friendliness to a balanced monarchy, and especially to that of the future Hanoverian kings, was long established. His Cato came off looking milder and more problematically human than the classical defiant hero, marrying his daughter not to Brutus but to an admiring foreign king spiritually identified with republican Rome. In *Cato,* he utilized the anxieties around Anne's succession to stage a new model of middling paternal sovereignty uniting the sentimental father, ruling over and defending his private sacred house of love from the reaches of a tyrannical state, with the evolving cultural role of a theatrical monarch, an actor (like Betterton) invited by the people less to wield political might than to culturally and aesthetically mirror the passing, human-scaled era of his historical subjects. Addison shaped his modern self-sacrificing paragon for the age that marked its ascendancy via a massive performative incursion into the sacred national cathedral to mournfully install a new kind of revered national saint: the people's beloved regal actor.

THE ROMAN TRILEMMA AND THE "GLORIOUS ANSWER" OF 1713

Addison's *Cato* is a historically paradigmatic drama. However, because it was staged in 1713 London yet set in the last days of the Roman Republican Senate's North African campaign of resistance to Julius Caesar, the specificity of its historical representation is difficult to grasp. The play performed and goes on performing the end of an era, the passing of a code and reality of social organization into obscurity and even incomprehensibility. When Cato died in Addison's version of his historical death, the long Roman Empire ended and the short British eighteenth century began.

The nature of catharsis is usually understood in terms of grief: an audience at a tragedy cries or feels pity, horror, or remorse over the death of a hero, over a defeat with which in some way they can identify. Catharsis in this sense is, since Aristotle, understood to be therapeutic and pleasurable. In *Spectator* 418 (see chapter 4), Addison formulated the modern solution to the problem of tragic pleasure: people at a play take pleasure in seeing awful things and suffering people not only because of a tragedy's classically theorized affect-purging effects but also because their spectatorship produces a secretly enjoyable awareness of distance between the dying hero and their actual presence in a safe seat, watching an intricate piece of art.[21] Usually it is assumed that the audience member experiencing this pleasure of relative safety experiences it in reference to their own position seated in the auditorium, but the social nature of human beings also suggests that the relative safety of the tragic actor in contrast to the impersonated character creates or at least facilitates a large degree of the spectator's pleasure. The character can safely and repeatedly die in the body of the actor, a basic but alluring bit of magic and reassurance that brings theater into close contact with the most serious of human rituals.

Tragedy as an art form relates to grief in both its painful, "negative" aspect and its "positive" aspect—the recognition of one's relative safety in comparison to the mourned person, object, or constellation. The end of grief, after all, is also a celebration of freedom: a new time when fresh dreams and connections can begin. The tragic theater not only mimics the phantasm of an old social order; it also performs the shrinking of an old scene into a small corner of the city, its closing, and perhaps even its being forgotten, clapped and swept away as brighter lights go up and a thousand new conversations begin. What was once an enclosing reality can now be visited in a picture box, if and when one wants. It was exactly this forgetting that Socrates opposed in *The Republic* in arguing that theater should be banned from the ideal city, his allegory for the philosophical mind: forgetting would mean an alienation of the self from the self via an alienation of the self from its scenes. A philosopher must, in Socrates's view, prepare to die, but theater was a fantasy of dying yet remaining that bred twin, tearing-apart desires to escape from and stay in worldly existence. The world—a trap—was to be, for Socrates, the one theater the immortal soul would gradually discursively miniaturize and strive to escape as it widened its gaze toward a larger, consistent truth.

The twentieth-century German poet Gottfried Benn wrote that, in terms of historical change, only an hour had elapsed from Homer to Goethe, while from Goethe to Benn's own time a full day had come and gone.[22] Lost in the sweep of Benn's metaphoric description of rapid industrial disruption were perhaps more local perspectives such as the difference between Socrates's Athens and imperial Rome—also a large disjuncture if one considers how greatly the density of Rome and its military and organizational reach must have affected the life-feelings of its citizens compared to those of classical Athenians. Cato's historical death was emblematic for the last gasps of an effective societal organization that did not entirely break the mold of the Athenian republican city-state. The completion of Pompey's theater in 55 BC—superficially disguised as a temple to Venus to comply with a city ban on permanent theater buildings—and the triumph of Julius Caesar in 49 BC reflect, in the Socratic perspective, two sides of the same transition of sovereign souls into massively centrally organized subjects: the theater was the tool that urban populaces used to grieve and hold onto the rapidly shifting scenes of accelerating imperial life, over which they no longer had much control, let alone overview.[23]

In this analysis, it is no surprise that Cato would reemerge as a theatrical hero at the historical moment of London's transition into a large imperial city, increasingly alienated from the agrarian life of most of the British Isles. Cato embodied for Romans and their followers the defiant but defeated Republic. His theatrical death in 1713 London came to symmetrically signify (in the eventual post-Jacobitism historical hindsight discussed in the previous chapter) the promised rebirth of republicanism and the end to the sway of European tyrants in the guise of sacred (Roman) kings and queens. *Cato* succeeded as a cathartic event to an extent matched by few plays in history, and it did so by triggering and expressing not only pity and terror but also the celebratory joy of a populace that was deeply politically divided but nevertheless living in a moment of national triumph. The centuries-long, transatlantic emulation of Cato inspired by the Drury Lane production and Addison's printed play text was not simply a call to vigilance against despotism; it was a more complex vision of completed, transformative grief that opened the way for newly unleashed, innovative, and imperial ambitions. The performative event's mournful or anxious patina was at least partially a sublation of the guilt and fear that would shadow those heightened modern ambitions' competitive and violent means.

The argument just presented depends upon an understanding of the transformation of the British relation to Rome, which the play itself performed, in effect partially causing the increased difficulty succeeding generations have in grasping the significance of Addison's play to its original hearers. Put simply, *Cato* performed the theatricalization of Rome in the British reality. Addison's audience grieved a militant local past in Cato's death yet celebrated a victory: because they had stood up to and cornered the old Roman Catholic order, via its most powerful agent, Louis XIV, a new system of ethics, governance, and power could be stabilized, expanded, and decided upon by them. If they were united—within the factionally divided theater of the nation, by the goddess of love, as it were—the Roman paradigm would be supplanted by the globalizing British empire.

The British nation had been up to that point a hermaphroditic construction of ancient, colonial Roman organization and autochthonous, gothic tradition. For centuries, the literature and law of England had taken Latin and Roman texts as the ultimate authorities. The long moment of modern Britain's birth was the moment it simultaneously rejected Roman control and began to set itself up as Rome's new mirror. The paradigm of Rome presented the trinity of republic, empire, and church as a trilemma of how to mediate between tyranny and liberty. The modern British constitution, worked out through strife, civil war, and compromise between the reigns of Henry VIII and Queen Anne, settled the trilemma in a new form: constitutional monarchy held in balance by a strengthened parliamentary system, a domestic state church accompanied by expanded religious freedom. Addison's tragedy marked the triumph of Whiggish reform in these respects and its settlement into custom and law. The model of Roman Republican (Commonwealth) martyrdom was restaged as a theatrical figure to be safely grieved and even, eventually, forgotten. The era of civil war was declared over with England's successful exit from the War of Spanish Succession.

England had triumphed against absolute monarchy, Louis XIV's Caesar-like tyranny, and religious dictatorship. By taking pains to prevent a partisan reading of his play, Addison displayed his ambition to house the echoes of civil warfare within the confines of a theater where the resounding applause of partisan factions would be transformed into a ritual of unified clapping away the old Roman ghost.[24] The success of *Cato* was the beginning of a new national sovereignty, inaugurating an era of empire and transforming the military contest over who should be head of state into a theatrical contest of acclaim over who should stand for a time on the stage that unconquered Cato had left perpetually open.

THE FAMILIAR CATO

By the time *Cato* premiered, Addison was famous for uniting England in a joint, daily readership. The texts that he, Richard Steele, and their collaborators produced were organized around a fictional, corporate person who stood in as a sovereign, rational everyman.[25] Though modern consumers take it for granted, the kind of daily mass reading that did not depend on a religion, party, trade, or specific site (other than the city of London as a whole) was a new experience in the world. For readers of the time, the most analogous reading experience was likely to have been in their school years or in a religious service, with the difference that now their simultaneous pedagogical or religious community was spread out throughout the city and country and united through a collective, pleasurable attachment to the fictive body of Mr. Spectator.[26]

Mr. Spectator, then, had a founding media effect on the minds of English people that would be difficult to reproduce, since it was the first of such an effect of timeliness, dailiness, and mass mimesis. The reading and theatergoing public was trained over years to think like Addison, to accept his mode of articulation and characterization as natural and routine. This mass effect of public mind-shaping—in England, Europe, the Americas, and the globalizing media landscape of journalism and general prose—may even continue today in a way that makes it hard to recognize historically.[27]

As developed in previous chapters, the Addisonian discourse was characterized by a popularization of the era's world-shaking scientific discoveries and a corresponding effort to build a moderate, rational consensus around proper behavior, commonplaces, religion, philosophy, and wide-roving criticism of art, literature, social life, and politics. The everyday life of the reader was described as both the fount and object of crisp, rational, modern conversation and reflection. When a reader of *The Spectator* met a reader of *The Spectator*—which was probably the general case of most London social interactions among literate people—a thinking, rational character was meeting a thinking, rational character. The London world was becoming for the first time populated by scientists of life, highly discursively coordinated and subject to daily textual updates.[28]

Following Stuart Sherman's landmark work, Christine Mazurkeywycz argues that Addison and Steele's texts had a profound influence on the modern mind that is difficult to recognize because they impactfully helped to inaugurate the regime of modern history and time-consciousness—organized around economic interest, prose, and daily scale—in specific contrast to the newly expanded, extreme scale of scientific, cosmological time: "If only by organizing time formally through daily publication, *The Spectator*'s schedule brought with it then a nascent time consciousness, cultivating a set of behaviors that are historical manifestations of the early periodical and its implicit promotion of imminence—the idea that tomorrow will surely happen, that the future is certain."[29] Mazurkeywycz argues that Newton's traces, via Addison, can be seen in the English readership's adoption of a new habitus of daily manners and customs. In *Principia*, Newton had made the distinction between eternity (or what he named "duration") and relative or clock time—time in the human sense, a sensible measure of duration made by motion.[30] "Time," under the influence of *The Spectator*, "was no longer something to understand or explain. Time was rather something that you did. Time was mimed, cut out, and organized into a burgeoning middle-class ideology."[31] Generally, because of the shaping influence of the Addisonian voice and perspective for Londoners of the era, the first audiences of *Cato* were more strongly conditioned in their reception of the play than simply by the author's fame. They were likely to have experienced a somewhat uncanny effect of a play produced as if from the depths of their own collective mind—as if the entirety of Twitter or Facebook were to be incorporated into a person, and that person were to author a film.[32]

Addison and Steele had guided the English public into a deepened engagement with classical figures as a way of simultaneously connecting with elite cultural discourses and becoming more modern. Stoicism, Roman analogues, and the Platonic tradition were familiar to the masses of *Spectator* readers. Cato, in particular, was already a corporate figure in a stronger sense: he functioned as a primary voice of conscience for European schoolchildren. Education at the time was steeped not only in Roman literature and principles but also in the personalities, conflicts, and examples of Cato and his famous contemporaries. The introduction to Conyers Middleton's 1741 life of Cicero gave a typical picture of the deep personal relation that the era's schoolchildren developed to such classical figures: "The scene of it is laid in a place and age, which are familiar to us from our childhood: we learn the names of all the chief actors at school, and chuse our several favorites according to our tempers or fancies; and when we are least able to judge of the merit of them, form distinct characters of each, which we frequently retain through life. Thus Marius, Sylla, Caesar, Pompey, Cato, Cicero, Brutus, Anthony, have all their several Advocates, zealous for their fame, and ready even to quarrel for the superiority of their virtue."[33]

The understanding of contemporary political disputes in Britain was driven by analogies with Rome's period of civil war. Ayres writes that "the classically framed discourse of virtue and liberty . . . sanctified the [Glorious] Revolution by analogy with hallowed classical precedents and guarded it by ceaselessly warning of dangers which had destroyed liberty at Rome and might conceivably do so in England."[34] Already by the early 1600s, stories from the late Republic and early Empire had provided English writers and readers with a mirror through which anxieties and debates about constitutional liberties could be symbolized: there was in that time "a rapid increase in the production of printed literature on Roman themes," including translations into English of classical texts. Marcus Porcius Cato the Younger was central to the events surrounding the fall of the Republic and the establishment of the Empire under Augustus, and the majority of translated Roman texts in the seventeenth century dealt with this theme and time period.[35] Cato "was interpreted as a historical commonplace to which educated men made passing reference in the course of wider rhetorical endeavours."[36]

But Cato was more than a historical figure. From the medieval period through the eighteenth century, he spoke directly to English and European schoolchildren as a moral and practical authority on life. The *Distichs of Cato,* a book of proverbs structured as a teaching dialogue between father and son, existed in antiquity and was "the major pagan gnomic source-book of the Middle Ages." Akin to a European Confucius, Cato's apocryphal advice in 4 books of 57 monostichs and 144 couplets was used as a standard primary textbook for Latin education and often translated. Barry Taylor reports that, "like Solomon, Cato came to be credited with any ancient saying of unknown authorship."[37] Schoolchildren referred to the book and its wisdom simply as "Cato." On a par with the Bible for teaching basic proverbs, literacy, and eloquence, spawning many imitations, "the *Distichs of Cato* were a byword for elementary education well into the early modern period."[38] James William Johnson summarizes Cato's cultural authority as a wise man, political exemplar, and moral paragon for the British Augustan Age: "Wherever he turned in his perusal of the intelligible world of the past, the English Neo-Classicist found ample proof of the greatness of Cato. No other ancient hero had such complete and impeccable credentials as he."[39]

Addison's tragedy merged two towering ghosts of cultural authority, Cato and the spiritual king. His literary, theatrical, and political work had actively participated in loosening the body politic of the king into print, debate, coinage, and the theater in general. This cultural achievement—freeing the body politic of the nation from the body of the monarch so that it could become an assignable abstraction of the assembled—drove the celebratory, patriotic applause at *Cato*'s premiere. If one listened to the simpler sound of Drury Lane on the night rather than for the meaning of the applauding factions contained therein, one heard a house resounding. Cato was an obvious effigy for the assignation of a spiritual head of state; he had been so since his self-martyrdom in the literatures of Rome, medieval Europe, and the Renaissance.[40] This comedy of marriage, between Cato and a political organization that could at last free itself from Caesar's Rome, was anticipated in Addison's text and expressed in its historically revisionist, somewhat tragicomic form and ending.

THE FORM OF THE PLAY

Cato is a neoclassical blank-verse tragedy built around contrasting and complementary pairs, proceeding in perfect Aristotelian manner from sunrise to sundown. The central pair whose primary conflict shapes the action of the play is Cato and Caesar. Cato is the leader of the exiled Roman Senate, whose remaining members (along with some fifty auxiliary members cobbled together from the local Roman expat population) have fled to the North African city of Utica. Caesar, who by the play's temporal setting in 46 BC had defeated his chief rival Pompey, never appears on stage but is an ever-looming, threatening figure. At the beginning of the play, he is already on the march to seize Utica and complete a near-certain victory over the Senate's Republican forces; by the end of the play, his drums can be heard loudly offstage.

A closer look at the text of the play reveals how Addison adapted the mythic historical tale into a unifying fantasy for his audience and their very particular political and cultural situation in 1713. Cato's first entrance in act 2 stages him as the legitimate authority over a threatened but free people, poised to make the ultimate decision about the fate of Republican Rome. Addressing the theater audience, the duplicitous Roman villain Sempronius opens the act, proclaiming, "Rome still survives in this assembled senate!" Lucius, the archetypal loyal friend and advisor of the play, heightens the anticipation declaring that "Cato will soon be here, and open to us / The occasion of our meeting." To the sound of trumpets and Lucius's hale, invoking "the guardian gods of Rome," the general, leader of the senate, and mythical childhood patriarch then emerged, declaring,

> Fathers, we once again are met in council.
> Caesar's approach has summoned us together,
> And Rome attends her fate from our resolves:
> How shall we treat this bold, aspiring man?[41]

The text of the scene that follows features opposing speeches by Sempronius and Lucius, the arrival and speech of Caesar's representative, Decius (heralded by Cato's son Marcus), and Cato's formal responses. There is no indication of other characters being present on stage or a reference to their reactions. The suggestion seems to be that Cato and the three other senatorial speakers are throughout addressing the British audience directly as the assembled senate in its colonial exile, the last leaders of the Republic. To decide the fate of Rome would have been a flattering task for a British audience, one that corresponded with two pending political changes over which the audience in April 1713 would indeed have felt called to decide—if not as members of Parliament, then as opinion-holders in the new theatrical Addisonian public. The Treaty of Utrecht had been signed a few days before, controversially ending the War of the Spanish Succession and leaving Louis XIV, James Francis Edward Stuart, and the Papal States in a strong position relative to what many Whigs and the exiled Duke of Marlborough wanted. *Cato's* debut and the theatrical Cato's calling the Roman Senate into session thus coincided with the natural timing of a long and successful war's ambivalent ending and celebration. Compounding this shift in European politics was the uncertain succession of the ailing Queen Anne, whose court had been dominated by Tory ministers since she and then the electorate had thrown the pro-Hanoverian Whigs out of power in 1710. At the time of the premiere, the approaching Caesar offering unsatisfactory terms of surrender to the exiled Republican Senate was ghosted by the living agents of Continental power, offering contrasting styles of peace and strengthened cooperation to the British nation: the Duke of Marlborough, Louis XIV, the pope, the future restored James III, and/or the future Hanoverian George I.

Under these circumstances, Addison's Cato poses himself as the rational, balancing voice of the assembled Senate, the executive in a state of exceptional emergency. He tempers Sempronius's (false) appeal to patriotic and militantly republican defiance as well as Lucius's plea for the recognition of defeat and the avoidance of further bloodshed through surrender. He urges what seems to be a middle path, waiting without surrendering to see if Caesar approaches with better terms. In a theme that cuts through Addison's poetics yet is often missed by more recent interpreters of *Cato,* Addison's protagonist is deceived by his own rational, empiricist procedure: one side of the balanced equation is tainted by the utterly deceptive testimony of Sempronius. Cato's suicide, his tragic mistake, in this reading stems directly much less from his zeal for liberty or from his rigid virtue as it does from Sempronius's effective deception. Sempronius intelligently but traitorously throws Cato off balance by staging a false, distracting, and exaggerated wing of parliamentary debate, clothing—as he tells Syphax—his "feigned zeal in a rage."[42] Behind his performed Stoicism, as a virtuous leader successfully manipulated by a cunning villain, Addison's Cato embodies a similar dramatic archetype to Othello: destabilized by his Iago (Sempronius), the sublime public man loses all trust in his philosophical bride, the world.

Yet the play was animated for its original audiences by something more than a tragic outlook on human dealings or even the grandeur of tragic destiny. *Cato* as Addison wrote it and staged it was a Protestant passion play. Like Judas Iscariot's betrayal, Sempronius's unbalancing actions ultimately work to fulfill the play's opening prophecy of Cato as a unifying sacrificial figure of peace. In the play's first lines, Portius had already declared to his brother, Marcus, that "our father's death / Would fill up all the guilt of civil war, / And close the scene of blood."[43] That sentiment of Cato as a sacrifice to peace frames the play. Lucius proclaims in his closing speech that the body of Cato should be laid before Caesar so "that it may stand / A fence betwixt us and the victor's wrath; / Cato, though dead, shall still protect his friends."[44] The metaphor, of course, has shifted slightly from one of Cato filling up a wound to one of him as a protective bulwark, but taken as a single figuration, it is a familiar and highly Christian trope: the rebellious leader who, by being rendered unto Caesar, pays the community's spiritual debt of guilt, appeases retributive wrath, and allows for a healing peace.

Addison's intent in writing a passion of Cato could be interpreted as a gesture toward atheism, in the sense that establishing the alternative moral authority of Greek and Roman figures allowed authors to sidestep the preeminence of the church and its canon. In Catherine Edward's words, "The classics served as a marker of social distinction but also offered alternative models of authority, with the power to justify practices which had little or no sanction in Christian ethics."[45] Because religious plays had been largely banned since Queen Elizabeth's proclamation of 16 May 1559 (in the name of protecting public peace from inflamed creedal rioting), the stage had an established cultural role in showing alternative spiritually significant figures acting their parts.⁴⁶ Modern tragedy acted conventionally to an extent as a secular surrogate for the community's formerly unified witness to Christian passion.

But the tremendous energy and enthusiasm around *Cato*'s reception suggests that Addison tapped into a stronger vein of religious feeling than mere secular displacement. As established in previous chapters, Addison's religious faith was sincere and attested to in many of his writings and deeds, beyond what would have been necessary for a public man, including his final historical defense of the gospel, the incomplete *Evidences of the Christian Religion* (published by Tickell in 1730). More specific to Addison's religiously tinted intentions in producing *Cato* was probably the political dimension of Protestantism at the time, still a protest against the authority of Rome, still a movement attempting to solidify its long-term safety and freedom under the threat of ongoing religious wars and persecutions that might return Europe to a despotic theocracy. *Cato* marked a lasting victory in that struggle for firm establishment, which remained significantly a military struggle. The conquests of the Duke of Marlborough had cornered France, Rome, and Catholic Spain and strengthened a northern European (German, Dutch, and English) alliance of Protestant states that would be further cemented if the Hanoverian succession were shortly to be successfully effected. Cato was a political Christ whose martyrdom, by being free of religious dogma, affirmed a moderate Protestantism: the oblique separation of private religious devotion from politics and public culture.⁴⁷ Addison's Cato died for the sake of affirming a fence between state politics and private life and the mind: he protected a new kind of family and collectivity. From a more secular future to which such an affirmation eventually contributed, we may misread the affirmation itself as primarily about political freedom; in its context, it was dangerous, spiritual, and sincerely theological. The play resonated, for instance, with St. Augustine's well-known praise of Cato as the best of Roman pagans for connecting national achievement to the widespread practice of virtue in the home.⁴⁸ Historically, it reperformed the sense of Dante—a poet much admired by English Protestants—in placing Cato as the warden of the island of Purgatory, to whose shores the path-breaking medieval poet arrives at dawn on Easter Sunday, seeking liberty with his guide Virgil after his descent into hell.⁴⁹

The play's writing history may show traces of a shift in Addison's conception of how and where true, satisfying, *modern* liberty was to be found. Addison probably drafted the first four acts of *Cato* in the 1690s; he showed drafts of the drama to Dryden while still at Oxford in 1694.⁵⁰ That decade was marked by a revival of interest in Milton's work and the language of republicanism; it was also a time of the Whigs' maturing into a ruling party and distancing themselves from the religious zeal of nonconformists and other religious sectarians—owing not insubstantially to the effective satires that Dryden as the age's poet laureate pointed at the Whigs for their connection to the Puritan cause. The version of Rome that Cato is fighting for is referred to twice in the play as a "commonwealth," the translated term for *res publica* that would have reminded British ears of Cromwell and Milton. If one reads the first four acts as a play from the 1690s, *Cato* could read as a paean to the failed Commonwealth and a call for its renewal within the conventions of the heroic drama.[51] The Tory laureate Dryden, in that case, would have been a politically odd addressee but one fitting Addison's consistent literary ambition—not only with *Cato*—to urge the transcendence of party politics.

The end of act 4 could very well have been the end of a complete tragedy, with Cato bidding his friends farewell twice (alluding to his impending suicide but keeping it neatly offstage) and speaking a last funeral oration over his son Marcus's corpse:

> The conqueror draws near. Once more farewell!
> If e'er we meet hereafter, we shall meet
> In happier climes, and on a safer shore,
> Where Caesar never shall approach us more.
>   [*Pointing to his dead son*]
>   The firm patriot there,
> (Who made the welfare of mankind his care,)
> Though still, by faction, vice, and fortune, crost,
> Shall find the generous labour was not lost.[52]

Such an ending, in the 1690s, would have celebrated the triumphant and defiant return of republican energies through the settlement after the Glorious Revolution. The "Roman" Commonwealth would be reborn on the "safer shore" of England, after the abdication of James II and as a consequence of William III's hopefully victorious struggle against France's long-reigning Sun King.

James Malek, drawing attention to the evidence that Addison wrote the final act of *Cato* only shortly before its premiere, argued that the fifth act's emphasis on Cato's flaws demonstrated a change in Addison's conception of the appropriate material for tragedy. Malek influentially critiqued earlier critics' idea that Addison's play presented Cato as a flawless man to be emulated. Between the completion of acts 1–4 and act 5, Malek argued, Addison came to believe that a tragedy, rather than presenting a perfect Senecan hero, should rouse the terror of the audience by depicting someone whom the audience more resembled.[53] More interesting for the argument that will follow is the question Malek raised about the meaning behind Addison's *hesitation* to write an act 5 (if indeed he had a plan for such an act before 1712) and to stage the drama at all.

The staging delay could have had more mundane reasons in the life of a busy author, such as a tortured perfectionism, a dissatisfaction with or fear about the play he had written when held up against his hopes for such a tragedy.[54] But the intervening decade of history and world experience may indeed have changed Addison's view on Cato, the tragic, or the appropriate kind of play to present to his public. Similarly, the final act may bear the largest traces of Addison's adjusting the play to fit the particular, more narrow, time of its staging.[55] Certainly, as later scholars have agreed, act 5 emphasizes the mistaken aspect of Cato's suicide. Arguing against earlier interpretations that more singularly read *Cato* as presenting an exemplary hero for political purposes, many later scholars tend to underline Cato's *overall* flawed nature in Addison's depiction. Against the notion that the play is political and not primarily interesting dramatically, they emphasize the consistency of complications in Cato's supposed monolithic virtue and the other characters' reactions to it. As such, they tend not to elaborate on any breakage between the first four acts and the fifth, rather seeing the flawed depiction of Cato as fairly consistently interwoven into Addison's tragic depiction.[56]

In the following argument, I will attempt to integrate these various strains of *Cato* interpretation. Following the arguments of the scholars whose work was just discussed, the politics of *Cato* are appropriately read as deeper and more nuanced than those of partisan contest or state representation. Cato had always been a flawed yet exemplary hero: Steele, in his 1701 *The Christian Hero*, had echoed St. Augustine's disapproval of Cato's suicide as motivated by a heathen longing for fame and success.[57] Addison's depiction of Cato's flaws points to new societal configurations with regard to domesticity, economics, privacy, public performance, race, love, gender, empire, and religion. As a text, Addison's *Cato* (along with the rumors of its pressured final drafting) carried a sense of timeliness and was a response to the politics of the year of its premiere. With the addition of the final act and its staging as an event, *Cato* became a play about the impending succession, the ambivalent victory over France and Rome signified by the Treaty of Utrecht, and the possibility of a new peace on the basis of domestic love, which would demonstrate the establishment of a more cosmopolitan, democratized, bourgeois, and imperial future for Britain.

Addison the classical scholar would have been well aware of the highly significant revisions of the Cato myth and history that his version featured in contrast to the Latin sources. Perhaps most notable among these revisions were a pair surrounding the moment of Cato's death. Addison omitted the famously horrific sequence in which a physician stitches Cato back together after his first stab at suicide fails. In the tale from Plutarch, Cato awakens and foils the physician's intention by defiantly tearing out his own bowels.[58] In Addison's version, the physician is absent, and Cato dies a rather peaceful, "good" death surrounded by his family and friends, even stating repentantly in his last moments that "a beam of light breaks in / On my departing soul. Alas! I fear / I've been too hasty."[59]

The mistaken "hastiness" of Cato's death, alluding to his status as a last pagan martyr before the Christian revelation, is emphasized by Addison's second large historical revision: the arrival—in the moment just before Cato's offstage self-stabbing—of an invitation from Pompey's son to leave Utica and head a recently successful campaign against Caesar's forces in Spain. Although, according to Plutarch, the news of Pompey's son's victory in Spain did reach Utica in the lead-up to Cato's suicide, Cato himself spoke about it days before his suicide with no mention of traveling to Spain.[60] The invitation and its timing, with the promise of victory, were Addison's dramatic invention. The play, in an echo of Shakespeare's *Julius Caesar* (where a mistaken Cassius kills himself in imitation of Cato just before Brutus and Young Cato arrive with good news), leaves the audience with the impression that if Cato had hesitated a few seconds more, Caesar would not have triumphed, and perhaps the Roman Republic might never have fallen.

Several critics argue that this dramatic historical revision demonstrates Addison's ambivalence toward Cato and the Stoics.[61] From the perspective of classical philology, however, Philip A. Stadter argues that Addison's revisions betray an opposite intention: one of "cleaning up" Cato's death in order to make his suicide look less unreasonable and more pitiable for a Christian audience of his era.[62] Indeed, Addison's oft-expressed admiration for Cato and the Stoics was not diminished by his reasonableness in regard to every human being's imperfection. In a comment much cited within the critical discourse surrounding *Cato,* Addison called Stoicism the "Pedantry of Virtue" and described Cato as possibly ranting when (in Cicero's depiction) he claimed that only a virtuous man could be handsome. His criticism of Stoicism, though, is exceedingly mild in context (*Spectator* 243), and even Cato's extreme idea of physical and moral beauty converging is presented with subtlety in support of Addison's main point: that virtue is not just a duty but has underappreciated qualities of beauty and loveliness.[63] The use of such comments as proof that Addison had a negative overall opinion of Stoicism is unfortunate, since his overall regard for Stoical thought was high. In fact, a few days before, in *Spectator* 237, he had written that Seneca was a higher authority than Plato — both, of course, being for Addison extremely admirable human beings.

The simple point is that Addison was not an extremist. His interpretation of Cato and others of great stature was nuanced and in line with Montaigne's essay on the same famous Roman martyr, where he argued that those who would detract too much from great actions do so out of envy rather than honest criticism.[64] Addison believed it was important to properly honor greatness in human action, while acknowledging that any acquaintance with a great person came with seeing significant flaws.[65] In *Spectator* 548, from late November 1712, he wrote:

> Our Goodness being of a comparative, and not an absolute Nature, there is none who in strictness can be called a Virtuous Man. Every one has in him a natural Alloy, tho' one may be fuller of Dross than another: For this reason I cannot think it right to introduce a perfect or a faultless Man upon the Stage; not only because such a Character is improper to move Compassion, but because there is no such a thing in Nature.... The most perfect Man has Vices enough to draw down Punishments upon his Head, and to justifie Providence in regard to any Miseries that may befal him. For this reason I cannot think, but that the Instruction and Moral are much finer, where a Man who is virtuous in the main of his Character falls into Distress, and sinks under the Blows of Fortune at the end of a Tragedy, than when he is represented as Happy and Triumphant. Such an Example corrects the Insolence of Human Nature, softens the Mind of the Beholder with Sentiments of Pity and Compassion, comforts him under his own private Affliction, and teaches him not to judge of Mens Virtues by their Successes. I cannot think of one real Hero in all Antiquity so far raised above Human Infirmities, that he might not be very naturally represented in a Tragedy as plunged in Misfortunes and Calamities.[66]

Rather than building up an image of perfection or representing Cato as a figure apt for scathing critique, Addison's revisions to the Cato myth leave the hero admirable and construct the stage tragedy as a passion play. Cato, a sacrificial figure who reaches an apex of human virtue and reason and who in the end falls miserably and darkly below divine transcendence, nevertheless by his error forges a providential direct link between Socrates and Jesus of Nazareth. The chain Addison drew created a short, religiously tinted progression of enlightenment working in history toward both the eventual failure of the Roman Empire and the virtuous birth (in Addison's hope) of Newtonian Britain as a new, independent empire of liberty and peace.

Kantorowicz noted that nothing becomes staler faster than political mysticism.[67] Nevertheless, as Kantorowicz proved, the unpacking of mystical constellations sheds important light on past theatrical cultures and their relation to the mysticisms of our disenchanted modernity. The reading above—which will be supported by further evidence from Addison's play text—helps to expose the energy behind *Cato*'s reception in its time by revealing a key difference between the Shakespearean and the Addisonian theater scenes. Both tragedians emphasized the element of timeliness in creating tragedy. But, whereas for Shakespeare, the difference of news arriving one moment too late exposed an element of horrible, nihilistic, structural absurdity in life and particularly in the order of political representation, for Addison the same slip in timeliness revealed a providential order beyond the scope of human reason.

By comparing the political dimensions of Shakespeare's *Julius Caesar* and Addison's prequel, *Cato*, in terms of the dramatic employment of timeliness, their different dramaturgical approaches to the fall of the Roman Republic can be shown to anticipate the different historical tasks facing the English/British nation and its political system. Shakespeare's tragedy of Caesar (or Brutus) looks into the abyss of regime change and civil war with only a small light of hope (embodied by Brutus's young servant, Lucius) for anything meaningfully better around the bend. Addison's single tragedy, on the other hand, revises the meaning of Cato's resistance to tyranny as a call for a lasting peace: after regicide and civil war, domestic peace was the next step in a long struggle toward a new imperial age. The basis for that historical destiny was provided by an innovatively stable political-cultural system that balanced formal sovereignty and individualistic liberty while largely offshoring the conflicts of the old time—in fantasy, to classical Rome and, in reality, to the overseas world beyond settled, daily, English life.

THE FUTURE REGAINED: ADDISON'S *CATO* AS A PREQUEL TO SHAKESPEARE'S *JULIUS CAESAR*

The problem with Brutus, in Shakespeare's *Julius Caesar*, is that he cannot sleep. His young servant, Lucius, who exhibits rather the opposite of this problem, is tasked at his first appearance in act 2 with bringing his master light in the middle of the night and readying the study. But Brutus's sleepless mind—instead of retiring to books—broods on the death of Caesar.

The trope repeats in act 4, after Caesar's murder, on the night before the fateful Battle of Philippi, during which Brutus will imitate Cato in taking his own life. Lucius appears again, tasked with playing music to allay his master's nighttime distress. The boy cannot keep himself awake, the music fails, and the ghost of Caesar appears to threaten Brutus. Lucius, whose name Shakespeare plays with by associating him with light, not only symbolizes the gentleness of enlightenment—for which the insomniac Brutus yearns but from which he remains estranged—but also evokes through his name the memory of Brutus's famed ancestor, the Lucius Junius Brutus, who defeated the Tarquin kings and founded the young Roman Republic.[68]

Brutus's insomnia has its origins in Cato's defeat, and he and his conspirators will ultimately find Cato's rest in self-martyrdom. Shakespeare uses Lucius, the personification of Brutus's and Rome's dissociated innocence and mild pleasure-taking in learning and arts, to develop through his dialogue with Brutus the theme of a disjuncture in time. At the beginning of act 2, Brutus in his private Edenic orchard calls to Lucius, unable to discern the time of night "by the progress of the stars." When Lucius appears and disappears again to light the candle in Brutus's study, Brutus declares, "It must be by his death," going on to develop how "his" crowning "might change his nature":

> It is the bright day that brings forth the adder,
> And that craves wary walking. Crown him that,
> And then I grant we put a sting in him
> That at his will he may do danger with.
> Th' abuse of greatness is when it disjoins
> Remorse from power.[69]

Though it is obvious from the larger context and Brutus's tortured, obsessive contemplations that the beginning of this speech refers to Caesar, there is something jarring about the ambiguity of his first utterances after Lucius exits; the only "he" that has appeared and been named in the act up to that point has been Lucius. The progress of enlightenment, its imperial nature as successful cultures and cities begin to "crown" proven learning, is revealed in Shakespeare's tragedy to encounter a fatal paradox: the settledness of order and peace is poisonous to the republican cultural habitus that originally produced the possibilities of enlightenment. Brutus acts out this paradox by repeatedly calling to his "better light" yet repeatedly again falling into tortuous thoughts of regicide and dissent that prevent him from concentrating or calming himself with books, study, or music. The time of light's crowning is at hand, but Brutus is drawn to nighttime vigilance and disturbed by a sense of growing disjuncture between reality and the man-made order of Rome's time.

In Lucius's subsequent reentrance, Brutus contradicts his earlier berating of sleeping by ordering him: "Get you to bed again, it is not day." Immediately, though, Brutus changes the scale of time's disjuncture from hours to days by asking Lucius to look in a calendar and confirm that the next day will be the first of March, when in fact it will be the ides of March. David Daniell has pointed out that, in such scenes sprinkled throughout the tragedy, Shakespeare's play with time and calendars being out of joint was even more complex, given the date of the tragedy's premiere and the division of Europe's timekeeping systems along Catholic and Protestant national lines. Catholic countries had adopted Pope Gregory's calendar reform in 1582, while England and other countries in revolt against Rome's authority had continued with the Julian calendar, originally introduced as a dictated reform by Caesar in order to regularize the old Roman calendar's relation to the astrological year. Daniell argues that the evidence suggests *Julius Caesar* was written for the opening of the Globe Theatre, and its premiere was scheduled for the astrological vernal solstice. This would have been on 12 June, a full nine days before its associated holiday (21 June) on the English calendar. The high tides on such an astrologically significant day would have made it especially auspicious for a theater opening, since the crowds coming by boat would not have had to walk over an extended stretch of the Thames's muddy banks to arrive at the show.

The natural date and Caesar's date had been brought into line by Pope Gregory, but in England, people who might have wanted to celebrate the astrological midsummer by attending a play would have felt the whip of Caesar's tyranny over time because the day was a workday. In Caesar's Rome, Daniell argues, the calendar reform had increased the sense among the populace of his will to tyranny. Shakespeare dramatically exploits the unnatural, tyrannical tie between Caesar and his contemporary audience's alienated experience of time throughout the play. The republican conspirator Flavius directs his opening admonishment to the commoners celebrating Caesar's triumphant return on the streets as if addressing the audience. Hinting playfully at the continued, complex dispute over Caesar's time versus astrological, Catholic time in Elizabethan London, Flavius chastises: "Hence! home, you idle creatures, get you home! / Is this a holiday?"[70] Brutus's stated inability to discern the hour from the night sky, in this context, would have continued a metatheatrical irony, since the open-air Globe was lit by the afternoon sun, so anyone searching the sky for stars to tell the time of night would have been very confused indeed.

The time of day in the theatrical context depended on the actor's declaration in the same way that the date and time depended on Caesar's revisionist decree in Rome.[71]

This alienated confrontation between the ghostly world of theater and the continuance of Rome's direct influence over British institutions and experience was likewise performed by the premiere date of Addison's *Cato*. The natural date for a passion play in the Christian calendar was Good Friday, which fell in the English calendar in 1713 on 3 April. The theaters, of course, were closed for such a high holy holiday. England in 1713 still used the Julian calendar, but most other Protestant countries had adopted the Gregorian calendar since the time of Shakespeare's writing *Julius Caesar*—accepting a difference between Roman tyranny and that of nature, the former of which it seemed increasingly unwise to resist, given the reality of the latter. England was virtually alone among its allies in celebrating Good Friday on 3 April that year. In the Gregorian calendar that same day had a date eleven days later: 14 April. Many documents in Britain at the time printed both the European and the British dates for such important dates, and cosmopolitan people of letters and diplomacy like Addison, Steele, and their circle would have been highly conscious of the dating divide.[72] *Cato*'s premiere, then, on 14 April of the British Julian calendar marked the slippage of time over the centuries between Cato's death and his theatrical passion, eleven days after that years' commemoration of Christ's crucifixion. It also marked Britain's exceptional distance—and latterly remove—from Rome.

Many of the details, and even much of the language, of Shakespeare's Caesar drama were taken directly from Sir Thomas North's 1579 translation of Plutarch's *Lives*.[73] That is not the case with the character Lucius, who as Shakespeare's invention subtly frames much of Brutus's dramatic destiny. Addison's Lucius is also more or less his invention: though there were historical figures with the common name Lucius playing minor roles occasionally in the general Cato myth, only one (Lucius Caesar, a spokesperson for the three hundred Roman men acting as senators in Utica) could be any basis for Addison's character, and Plutarch notably sends him on his way well before Cato's death.[74]

The dramaturgical function of the elder statesman and loyal friend Lucius in Addison's prequel is similar to that of the sleepy young servant Lucius in Shakespeare's. Both characters ghost by their names (and their respective age or youth) the reason and innocence of the old Republic, founded by Lucius Junius Brutus. Both are human mirrors to their tragic counterparts, offering redemptive light and a new connection to natural time that belie an urgent sense of disjointed historical destiny. The "lightness" of both characters is more or less dismissed by both Brutus and Cato, hell bent as they are in performing self-destroying resistance to tyranny. Ironically, modern critics tend also to disregard the importance of Lucius in Addison's drama, even though he gives the play its final speech and twist in meaning. This disregard may be indicative of a tendency to read *Cato* superficially: Lucius is dismissed as a character because Cato largely dismisses his counsel. But in the play this dismissal is Cato's fatal error, effected by Sempronius's treachery and causal for the hero's general falling out of balance. In reading *Cato* superficially—because the text itself does not offer certain signs of nuance and depth for modern readerships—twentieth- and twenty-first-century critics miss a larger tragic point. *Cato* is a drama *about* highly performative people at their world's closure attempting to communicate about their inner lives while simultaneously fulfilling the demands of virtuous public leadership; their doomed situation yet requires their militant adherence to form if any hope for victory is to remain.[75] Addison's tragedy marks the (tragic) apex of English cultural theatricality, before readers and audiences became increasingly accustomed to mass culture and the private reading of novels, before pleasure and observation shifted away from bodies and faces on stage and toward the silent, long exploration of hidden emotions and psychological meanings spelled out in prose on blank pages.

Modern readers—shaped historically by three centuries of novel-reading and industrial culture and by the last century of accelerating mass media consumption—make an odd assumption when they assume that the theatrical taste and discernment of British Augustans were not significantly more advanced than their own. Moreover, they make an absurd assumption when they, like many of the last century's critics writing on *Cato,* assume that eighteenth-century audiences and readers were so impoverished in their theatrical imaginations that they took the rhetorical displays of Addison's characters at face value, as if they spoke at all moments directly from their inner, performative souls.

More psychologically nuanced readings of Addison's only tragedy could place it in a cultural history of the unconscious, since the complex providential drama it reveals works through the protagonist's specific unawareness of the reasons for his primary action. Cato's suicide is clearly marked in Addison's text as justified by a hasty misreading of Plato, the hastiness owing to his intellectualized repression of a tremendous disappointment over Sempronius's betrayal compounded by grief for his slain son. The crucial break in Cato's resolve and Stoic pose comes in act 4, scene 4, as he speaks with Lucius after the revelation of Sempronius's treachery. At first, Cato seems to maintain his Stoic worldly masterfulness, saying, "Trust me, Lucius, / Our civil discords have produced such crimes, / Such monstrous crimes, I am surprised at nothing." A long dash indicates an unusual rupture in his rhetoric, followed by perhaps his most unguarded line in the play, "O Lucius! I am sick of this bad world! / The day-light and the sun grow painful to me."[76] Leslie Radford describes this moment as the failure of Cato's Stoic faith in reason, where the truth symbolized by the Apollonian sun becomes itself bad: "To Addison and his audience, clearly Cato has come to the first premise of Christianity, that man is born into sin, to which heathen Stoicism must succumb."[77]

The moment also marks the breaking out of the suicidal plague, the emergence of the adder into Rome's bright day that Shakespeare's Brutus bemoans. The transmission is direct, since we know that Brutus, the rumored illegitimate son of Caesar, admired his uncle Cato above all Romans and studied to imitate him, marrying Cato's daughter, Portia, his first cousin.[78] The relation between Shakespeare's Brutus and Addison's Cato would have been more than textual and historical for *Cato's* original audiences. Barton Booth, the famous actor who played Cato, also played Brutus in a production of *Julius Caesar* that was performed regularly at Drury Lane in the years around *Cato's* premiere. Booth had appeared as Brutus on Easter Monday of 1713, the week before *Cato* opened, and would reprise the role again on 4 May. The version of *Julius Caesar* staged in the early part of the eighteenth century was the one altered by Davenant and Dryden, in which 128 lines were cut and 28 added to "make Brutus more sympathetic and heroic," a better analogue to Addison's Cato.[79] Booth, a well-known Tory, had taken over the role of Brutus from Betterton shortly before Betterton's death, almost coincidental with the Tories' rise to supremacy in Anne's cabinet. Adding another theatrical doubling effect for the audiences at Drury Lane was the fact that Caesar and Sempronius were played by the same actor (John Mills), as if the ghost of Caesar from Shakespeare's play went back in time to foil Cato's virtuous stand and break his Stoical faith.[80]

Addison's tragic hero recovers most of his Stoic pose after the uncontrolled confession of his inner turmoil and grief to Lucius, who was played by the same actor (George Powell) who played Shakespeare's Cassius, Brutus's chief coconspirator. Beginning with John Dennis, critics writing in opposition to the overwhelmingly favorable reception of Addison's work in its time have pointed to Cato's quickly following reaction to his son's death in the same act as unnatural and somewhat monstrous.[81] Yet these kinds of interpretations (even echoed by some of the modern defenders of Addison's tragedy in the midst of their arguments that the play was *not* intended to valorize Cato) seem to share an assumption that the text was not made to be well acted or to be seen by audiences steeped in a culture of theatrical and social observation before the rise of the novel. When informed by Portius, his other son, of Marcus's death, Cato, playing the part of general in a siege, does at first remark only, "I'm satisfied."[82] But the scene is laden with pathos, and a clued-in audience member or reader would understand Cato's role as an experienced general and father. Previously alerted to the danger Marcus faced, he would have seen in Portius's stricken face upon reentering the scene the immediate truth of Marcus's death. Indeed, there would be no pleasure in the play for audiences if by mistaken interpretation or acting, Cato's interruption of Portius—before he announces the news of Marcus's death—did not convey that the general-father already understood the death and had begun his Stoic performance of commander in chief over the parental shock. In the midst of "a true golden age of the acting profession in England,"[83] Addison could have safely assumed that an actor of Barton Booth's stature would perform Cato's interruption of Portius not as preposterous maudlin Stoicism but as a more character-appropriate admonishment and correction of Portius's dangerously public display of sensational despair.[84]

A closer look at the pivotal scene reveals some of Addison's smoothed-over dramaturgical complexities. When Portius breaks into Cato's tense waiting with Lucius and Juba (two important political leaders) exclaiming, "Misfortune on misfortune! grief on grief!," Cato sternly corrects him, referring to the fallen "passionate" brother Marcus: "Hah! what has he done? / Has he forsook his post? has he given way? / Did he look tamely on, and let 'em pass?" The pathos-laden irony here seems often lost on a modern readership: forsaking his post and looking tamely on is exactly what Portius—previously the performatively more patriotic, Stoical, and duty-filled son—has done. According to his own previous report to his father, he allowed Syphax to escape and catch his brother off guard. Portius chose, instead of fulfilling his obvious and urgent martial duty to protect his brother, to report to his father. His well-established virtuous admiration of his father, in contrast to his martyred brother's seemingly more rebellious spirit, is revealed as a darkly ironic shirking of responsibility that brings to the surface a shadowy vein of providence and his own repressed desire. Portius's failure to live up to his own high standards of virtue effects (unconsciously) exactly what a more devious villain in a love plot might have planned: Marcus, his rival for the beloved Lucia, is killed, freeing his path to connubial bliss. The end of the play's sentimental tone might occlude that dark twist, but the subtle dramaturgy of desires' rebellion against duty fits Addison's larger gesture toward an uncanny providential breakthrough of love in transformatively creating a new era of peace.

These are the kind of late Baroque complexities and intricacies that gripped the attention of Addison's eighteenth-century sociable audience and drove the burgeoning business of theatrical commentary. The political nature of the pamphlet war that developed over varying interpretations of the play may suggest that the theatergoers of Addison's time were incapable of imagining tragedies that were *not* significantly about national politics.[85] Indeed, Samuel Johnson reported about the premiere that "the whole nation was at that time on fire with faction."[86] What survives of the time's printed theater criticism has a strong bias toward political interpretation—a bias that might be exaggerated in the archive, since the growing but still somewhat nascent business of mass printing tended to be controlled by a relatively few hands, who had a competitive political interest. Actual theater audiences were a much more diverse group than the rare few writers and publishers.[87] Therefore, while the play is often interpreted as having fed upon the political passions of the day, it seems wise to entertain the balancing view that these passions fed upon the play's dramatic achievement. Political pamphleteers, after all, wrote theater criticism in order to harness the tremendous energy around a sophisticated theater scene for their causes. Moreover, reliable authorities indicate in private letters from the time that the interest in Addison's tragedy transcended political interest: John Gay reported that "Cato affords universal discourse, and is received with great applause,"[88] while George Berkeley remarked that it had "introduced the greatest ideas of virtue and religion upon the stage with the greatest applause, and in the fullest audience that ever was known."[89] Colley Cibber wrote that the play was an unprecedented box office success, filling houses every day for a month and bringing in a financial windfall equivalent to two normal seasons.[90]

In his investigation of the reasons for the popularity of *Cato,* Lincoln Faller found that epistolary discussions of the play suggest that the play's many repeat hearers had reactions to it that were highly nuanced and sophisticated in contrast to the more superficial reactions of modern readers, professional critics among them. Some of the former, like Lady Hervey writing to her husband, report indeed of a heightened political pressure to attend the play: "'Tis I find made a mighty party business, for my Lady Cooper told me three or four days agoe that I must needs be there; but why I cant tell, for both sides agree in the liking of it."[91] Faller concludes, however, as Lady Hervey's last line might hint, that the popularity of the play had to do with a genuine dramatic interest and identification with its characters on the part of diverse members of the audience, under the influence of the then-dominant conventions of heroic drama.[92] If one assumes an audience who, living in a theatrical social world, are adept at theater-watching and listening and accustomed to peering through conventions of theatrical expression in order to discern nuanced characterizations and subtle plot-changing events and articulations, the play reads very differently. When Cato, in other words, pronounces only his satisfaction in Marcus's manner of dying, it is doubtful if Addison could have imagined that we would hear only what he pronounced. His deeper feelings are, of course, emphasized in the rather extensive public speech he next gives at the end of act 4 over Marcus's corpse, in which he urges the large number of assembled to follow the example of his son in committing their grief to Rome rather than to any individual. Briefly settling the remaining coalitional business of the seemingly failed resistance, the representative general-father, then concludes by imagining for Marcus an afterlife rewarding to his self-sacrifice.

Picking up his pen to compose act 5, Addison juxtaposed Cato's act 4–ending public declaration of confidence in Marcus's triumphant immortality with an image of Cato sitting alone in his bedroom, reading Plato, trying to convince *himself* of the truth of an immortal soul. Addison further dramatically emphasized the public/private split in Cato's self-representation through another significant revision of Plutarch. Whereas in Plutarch Cato debates his conclusions at length with two philosophers—one Stoic and one Peripatetic—and reads *Phaedo* twice, Addison features the grieving father alone in act 5, scene 1, already with his sword at his side, quickly summarizing one of Socrates's arguments.[93] The soundness of his reasoning, concluding to agree with Plato that the soul is immortal, is undermined immediately by an outbreak of despair about the possibility of happiness in the world: "But when! or where!—This world was made for Caesar, / I'm weary of conjectures—This must end 'em."

A human emblem of justice, balanced between the sharp instrument of death at one hand and the instrument of law and life ("Plato's Book on the Immortality of the Soul") in the other, Cato in the end resigns himself to a lethargy that he does not understand, ending his intellectual exploration and giving in to nature's call to sleep. His unconvincing and Platonically incorrect conclusion in favor of suicide is left half formed but indicates an assurance that he will live forever, in any case. He seems to leave the ultimate action to chance: before falling into slumber he states an indifference toward the "choice to sleep or die." His reasoning has converted death, perhaps, into just a form of temporary sleep. But equally, following the sense of the young Lucius in Shakespeare's play, sleep is the choice not to overtax nighttime reason with fateful decision.[94]

Raising dramatically ironic hopes of a good outcome, the elder Lucius of

Addison's drama reports in the last scene of the play that the sickness of sleepless decision-making seems to have broken. He tells Marcia that he has seen her father in his chamber: "A kind refreshing sleep is fall'n upon him." Cato is "stretched at ease, his fancy lost / In pleasing dreams," from which Lucius hears Cato, smiling, cry, "Caesar, thou canst not hurt me."[95] Shakespeare's Brutus comments about the young Lucius at the beginning of act 2: "I would it were my fault to sleep so soundly."[96] Echoing in theatrical time Brutus's later imitation in historical time, Addison's Cato is, like Brutus, driven to tragedy by the vexation of insomnia: he wakes a moment too early and kills himself just before Portius arrives to announce the victory of Pompey's son in Spain and the fresh wind of hope.

Cato's flawed timing matches the statement he makes over Marcus's body at the end of act 4 that, "whate'er the Roman virtue has subdued / The sun's whole course, the day and year, are Caesar's."[97] If thorough and virtuous reasoning had subdued his grief and convinced him to live, he would have become not the mythic Cato but one of Caesar's subjects. Formally, Cato's act 5 closet monologue of Platonic contemplation is marked as problematic because the tragedy is built around dialogue and characters holding each other in balance: besides Cato in this monologue, only the villains Sempronius and Syphax develop monologues of any length, revealing their inmost thoughts and plans. Breaking the formal decorum of social life by entering the concealed space of private, unchecked thought and observation is consistently presented in the play as exceptionally dangerous. In an exception that proves the rule, only once in the play is such a breach successfully reintegrated into the social fabric. It is that exceptional breakthrough that sets a tight new climactic clock running, which leads to Marcus's death, Cato's isolated error in timing, and the play's final almost tragicomic synthesis of that error into the advancing providential dawn of a new era.

That one reintegrated social breach takes place in act 4 when Juba—the noble prince of Numidia who, like Shakespeare's Brutus, admires Cato and loves his daughter—encounters and defensively kills his living mirror image. By accident, Juba surprises the Roman villain Sempronius, who has disguised himself as the Numidian prince as part of a plot to kidnap and rape Marcia. The scene of two British actors dressed as North African princes (one as a Roman disguised as a North African prince, the other as a North African prince ghosting the historical familial role of Caesar's noble assassin, Brutus) is suggestive of many readings, but two interrelated visual stories stand out. In one, Juba kills a false version of himself. In a second, a North African kills a villainous Roman stereotype of a North African.[98] Having protected an unwitting (offstage) Marcia from Sempronius's rape attempt, Juba exits to report Sempronius's treachery, leaving Marcia to return to the stage to discover what appears to be Juba lying murdered on the floor.[99] Juba, reentering the scene and listening unseen, at first only hears Marcia confessing her love over the body of Sempronius and, in his momentary isolation, is tortured into near-madness by the mistaken thought that Marcia loved Sempronius.

Marcia had previously affirmed her Stoic duties to deny love in a time of crisis and to love only as her general father directed.[100] At the apparent sight of Juba's corpse, however, the restraint on her liberty to love and the control of her sexuality by the patriarchal Roman structure breaks decisively: "Oh Juba! Juba! Juba!" she exclaims, to the unseen's Juba ecstasy and relief. The outburst of love relieves him from his perilous monologic isolation.[101] Juba and Marcia's reunion over the revealed dead old Roman's corpse foreshadows the blessing of their union at the end of the play by a dying Cato. It also allegorically reveals Addison's belief that a modern renewal of Republican Rome's promise depended on the new, "natural" coalitions of international, cosmopolitan liberalism triumphing over rigid patriarchal traditionalism and false, racialized, parochial nationalisms.[102]

The moment of love's breakthrough in act 4 is also the breakthrough in the love triangle between Marcus, Portius, and Lucia. Syphax, flying from the scene of his conspirator Sempronius's killing with troops intent on breaking through the city gate to join Caesar's forces, is killed by Marcus, who then is overwhelmed and killed in turn. At roughly the same instant that Marcia frees herself from her father's militant order to live as a true lover, Cato's male namesake Marcus dies rashly offstage as a patriot in the Republic's defense. "Let Caesar have the world, if Marcia's mine," Juba declares, invalidating Cato's tragic time.[103] Cato had previously rejected Juba's suit for Marcia's hand in marriage by declaring, in a line that would echo in real-life political agons for the next centuries, "It is not now a time to talk of aught / But chains or conquest; liberty or death."[104]

By dismissing Lucius's honest call to end bloodshed, as well as his subsequent pleas for Cato to preserve his life to help his family and friends during Caesar's coming regime, Cato commits himself to the false balance set up by Sempronius. He is trapped in an old, poisoned, dying time. In his hesitation, while he indulges the somniferous pull of unreasoned nature rather than the dictates of rigorously reasoned virtue, the community of the sentimental comedy gathers: two pairs to be married and a loyal friend to be the second, contract-administering father. As Radford puts it, "It is while he sleeps that hope floods his house."[105] Cato's accident of perfectly ill-timed awakening, in

Addison's version, makes his self-martyrdom responsible for Caesar's victory, just as Shakespeare made Cassius's mistaken imitation of Cato's suicide (in act 5, Scene 3 of *Julius Caesar*) dramatically responsible for Antony and Octavian's victory at the Battle of Philippi. Granting Cato a much milder death scene than Plutarch did, Addison ahistorically allows Cato to play the part of the benign sentimental father, blessing the love-matched couples, who have previously worked it all out themselves.

After his final moment of doubt and corresponding witness to a new enlightenment of the world, Cato dies in prayer, and Lucius, the light-bearer, sets Cato up rhetorically as a fence between Caesar and their new domestic world.[106] The complexity of Addison's hermaphroditic aesthetic is restored: the tragedy performs the tragedy of tragedies, drawing a providential, hermeneutic thread between Socrates's Athens, Cato's Rome, Christ's Jerusalem, the Roman church's Europe, and, finally, Newton's Britain. Marking an end to a culture of immanent theatricality and the dawn of an industrialized society of printed and mediatized simulacra, *Cato* speaks from the triumphant moral apex of an old order's historical defeat about the dangers of reason in isolation, without the saving heart's breakthrough.

The comedy of bourgeois life, with its self-conscious sentimental readers, is one of the renewals that Addison's tragicomic tragedy anticipated for the theater (in spite of his earlier essayistic protests against the "monstrous" invention of "Tragi-Comedy").[107] The other, of course, was the correction of time via the theatrical shrinking of Rome: the present of 1713 was no time for a second passion of militant Catos but rather a time to peacefully celebrate a historic British victory—over Rome and its allies. For Britain, the long-plaguing question that that "shining" classical civilization posed to its modern imitative subjects—what sort of resurrected Rome to serve, church, empire, or republic?—could be again synthesized in the singular rising modern nation-state: Roman service was owed to Britain as church, empire, *and* republic.

The last act of *Cato,* then, performed a metatheatrical, historical fence between the old age of aristocratic, tragic neoclassicism and the first glimmers of an age to be characterized by the novel and more prosaic sentimental heroism in the service of bourgeois selves, families, and national empire.[108] Shakespeare's Young Cato had appeared in act 5 of *Julius Caesar* only to mark the blooming plague of self-martyrdom and then promptly to die on the fields of Philippi. In the revised British Augustan prequel, he might yet be saved from doom through an (ahistorical) enlightened marriage to Lucia, if he heeds his father's last advice to retire to the country. The role of passionate self-sacrificing son was, in Addison's play, already fulfilled by his ahistorically present, passionate brother Marcus. After seeing *Cato* at Drury Lane, a young British Portius might well be inspired to seek a future away from the high pitch of urban political battles and take a provincial seat. From there, he could calmly and patriotically vote for moderate Country Party representatives and imbibe his cosmopolitan culture from newspapers, Fielding novels, and the occasional London sojourn, during which he could watch with delightful, nostalgic irony the latter playwright and novelist's Tom Thumb farce, *The Tragedy of Tragedies*.

With moderate Anglicanism and religious toleration, a strong Parliament, and a chosen, limited, Protestant Caesar drawn from abroad, the vacant spiritual effigy of Cato would soon be filled by the person whom the people assembled saw fit to interpret into the role, be it queen, king pretender, prince, or prime minister.[109] With Addison's Cato, the divine right king died. A timely, modern, limited notion of sovereignty had been established; an imperial, cosmopolitan nation was dawning—one that could reproduce its cities, order, and consensuses with a technological speed that began to put into question whether "Rome" might indeed be built and rebuilt in a day. The Addisonian imagination was of liberated individuals and a free nation restored to healthful sociability and everyday commonality by the breaking through of providential, natural love. His quintessentially modern Cato myth showed the way forward: the tragedy of reason's overwrought scales and law gave way to the tragicomic, historical self-sacrifice of one time's paradigm for the renewal of another.

THE BIRTH OF TRAGICOMEDY IN THE TEMPLE OF VENUS

According to Pope, Steele's marketing strategy of politicizing the play in order to pack the house successfully transformed *Cato,* against the wishes of its author, into "a party play." At the premiere, Pope reported that "the numerous and violent claps of the Whig party on the one side the theatre, were echoed back by the Tories on the other."[110] Testimony in sources like the letter from Lady Hervey to her husband quoted above shows that active party supporters came to feel that their attendance at *Cato* was a political and patriotic duty. Addison, Pope wrote, "sweated behind the scenes," worried during the premiere that the politicized and factional audience's "applause proceeded more [from] the hand than the head." In the same letter, though, Pope pointed to evidence that the play was popular beyond the political crowd: "The town is so fond of it, that the orange wenches and fruit women in the Park offer the books at the side of the coaches, and the Prologue and Epilogue are cried about the streets by the common hawkers."[111]

Pope influentially claimed that the love scenes in *Cato* were added on after the main writing to suit popular taste and, as such, had nothing to do with the plot. As many scholars have argued, any careful reading of the play shows that Pope's claim (though resonating with Dennis's famously savage criticism) cannot be true: the love plots are deeply woven into the texture of the play and form a crucial part of the play's meaning, leading as they do directly to Cato's self-sacrifice.[112] One of Addison's earliest biographers, Robert Shiels, even believed that Addison's "lovers are the most sensible, and address each other in the best language, that is to be found in any love dialogues of the British state." (Shiels was particularly impressed by Marcus's line in act 3, scene 1, "A lover does not live by vulgar time," suggesting indeed the difficulties of understanding different historical paradigms of romance.)[113] Pope's critical assertion nonetheless fits into a strong masculinist and/or militaristic vein of reception for the play, one manifestation of which became the 1764 staged revision, *Cato without the Love Scenes*.[114] On American shores, the same vein of reception can be seen in *Cato*'s appropriation for the "iconic self-dramatizations of George Washington, Patrick Henry, and Nathan Hale," among other later revolutionary actors.[115] These real-life, soldierly emulations of Cato later in the century also carried the valence—as Jason Shaffer argues—of attempts to stage Addison's tragedy without the love scenes.[116]

For Addison, however, the lovers and their marriage destinies had everything to do with his play's suggestion that modern Britain was the Utican gathering place from which the true Roman republican spirit would be reborn in exile. The modern reincarnation of that spirit depended—like *The Spectator*—on an expanded, actively political public, one-half of which were women. *Cato*'s love plots wove women's presence, their militant and political stances, and their life decisions into a classical narrative from which they were largely absent. Evidence from the time in letters and occasional verses suggests that women indeed felt moved and involved in the play's patriotic call for Britain to free itself at last from the tyranny of kings through which Rome and then all of Europe had suffered for 1700 years.[117] The terms of the Treaty of Utrecht kept Rome and much of the Continent under the sway of that tyranny, but Britain would become the leading European nation, one that could finally offer "a safer shore / where Caesar would approach no more" to those who felt a spiritual kinship to Cato.[118] The British public adopted Cato as something of a father to their modernizing, early twilight quasi-Republic. Pope, admitting a great admiration for Addison's dramaturgical feat, declared that "Cato was not so much the wonder of Rome itself, in his days, as he is of Britain in ours."[119]

Ironically, Addison's revision of the myth granted Cato his godlike status in the providential theater of Europe because of a series of errors, starting with the trust he bestowed on the duplicitous Sempronius. Stumbling off the high pedestal of moral and intellectual near-perfection, he became a victim of his own too-hasty pride, taking his last uncertain gasps in the first twinkling light of Caesar's star and the coming Christian era. Addison's *Cato* performed the failure of both Roman Stoic reasoning and the cultural paradigm of tragedy to provide a convincing, sublime path to the heights of virtue. Indeed, in Addison's retelling of the Utica myth, the future truly opened when Cato's error in trusting Sempronius forced Juba into the role of defensive hero, killing the villain in order to save Cato's daughter, Marcia. Cato's own mistake about Sempronius's true nature was then echoed in Marcia mistaking Sempronius's corpse for Juba, prompting a shocked grief that momentarily broke the "vulgar time" of Cato's war and allowed the united next-generation family to confess and assert their hearts' desire.

Stilted as they may be, the love scenes were crucial to *Cato* in part because the emancipation of women and colonial/racial others was rehearsed through the comedy of Marcia and Juba's betrothal, a new alliance forged between more equal citizens.[120] The united cosmopolitan family tableaux was, in fact, one of Addison's major revisions to any classical telling of Cato's history. The historical Marcus Portius Cato's daughters were in Rome with his wife, Marcia; only one of his sons—whom Plutarch names "Porcius"—traveled to Utica with him. Addison, however, surrounds the doomed Cato with three children, the two of his invention (Marcia and Marcus) bearing differently gendered variations of their father's first name. Addison's tough but loving Marcia takes the place of Cato's famous historical daughter Portia, the coal-eating wife of Brutus. Utterly absenting Cato's wife from the fictionally enhanced family milieu, the tragedy artificially emphasizes the issue of Cato's singular "will" as well as his spiritual marriage to Roman Liberty.[121] One thread of suspense and competition in the play revolves around which of the three children will inherit, via their father's final word and nod of approval, the right to represent the Republic's virtuous future.

The complex and often subtle Addisonian maneuver of modernizing via hermaphroditically splicing previous discourses comes to the surface again with Cato and his three heirs. Marcus, the doomed, fictional heir of militant Cato's hot-headed masculine honor, zealously converts his romantically wounded pride into a hasty, self-sacrificing patriotism. His impatience yields his quick martyrdom via a deathly colonial conflict with Syphax. On the other hand, Marcia, the feminine heir of Cato's first name and his struggle between passion and stoical self-mastery, is spurred by the evident breakdown of the protective Roman patriarchal structure to cede the ground of her action to a love both passionate and rational. She gains a new kind of sovereignty by softening her stoical paternal obedience and charting a novel course with a foreign prince, Juba. Marcia's more self-determined future in a "modern," international republican-monarchical marriage marks her as Cato's active political heir, in a sense ghosting the historical Portia. Her decision likewise encourages her friend Lucia to marry her brother, Portius. Carrying Cato's second name, Portius is marked in the play as inheriting the private side of the aristocratic patriarch, who hailed from an ancient family with a long "enlightened" tradition of retiring when possible to the countryside to cultivate wine as citizen-observers of the capital city's dangerous and corrupting politics.

The other half of Marcia's avant-garde power couple, the Numidian monarch, Juba, is likewise given a dramatic role at profound odds to his historical role as a political ally of the Republic who followed Cato's lead in suicide shortly before Caesar seized Utica.[122] The ambiguous symbolism of Juba killing his shadow self (the would-be Roman rapist and traitor Sempronius) confirms and synthesizes his decision to reject Syphax's politics of anticolonial, race-based warfare. Addison highlights this decision via Juba and Syphax's preceding elaborate debate, in which Syphax gives some of the play's most passionate and convincing speeches, criticizing the extravagance of Stoicism, the hypocrisy of Roman virtue, and Juba's potential betrayal of his own people through his loyalty to Cato and the Romans.[123] With Juba taking the position of virtuous, assertive assimilation against Syphax's violently separatist and nationalistic strategy, the debate is an early staged instance of a "classical" debate about the best and most appropriate means for an oppressed racialized group to attain power and/or equality. Juba's shaping choice was further emphasized for *Cato*'s original audience by the fact, as Laura J. Rosenthal points out, that the actor dressed as Juba gave the play its prologue: "Cato himself ostensibly may occupy the center, but the Numidian prince frames the play." As the play's opening figure, it is Juba who "suggests the transformation of the British people before him into Romans precisely at the point of their mourning Cato: the author, he insists, 'calls forth Roman drops from British eyes.' Cato will die, but Juba will remain to direct the community's grief."[124]

Moreover, it is Juba who (in act 4, scene 4) directly inherits the active political legacy originally meant for Cato's son and namesake. When Portius informs his father that Syphax is attempting to flee with Numidian troops through the gate being guarded by Marcus, he relates that he merely "called to stop him, but in vain" before coming to tell his father. Cato admonishes his performatively dutiful and rational son with his missing sense of urgency; in this same moment, he marks Romanicity with the valence of a theatrical role, implicitly suggesting that Portius is failing to fulfill the requirements of his inherited citizenship: "But haste, my son, and see / Thy brother Marcus acts a Roman's part." In the unfolding artificial contrasts and progressions of Addison's late-Baroque dramaturgy, it is Juba who then enters to apologize and express shame about his national/ethnic group's failure to perform their duties as good Roman allies. Cato responds by bestowing on him what a moment before he found dramatically lacking in Portius—"a Roman soul." He declares that "Falsehood and fraud shoot up in every soil, / The product of all climes— Rome has its Caesars," but Juba "has stood the test of fortune / Like purest gold, that, tortured in the furnace, / Comes out more bright, and brings forth all its weight." Later in the scene, after seeing Marcus's corpse and being urged by Juba to live and challenge Caesar, Cato states his belief that Juba's virtues will "one day make [him] great."[125] Inheriting the high praise and Roman destiny that in Cato's next lines are withheld from Portius and eulogized in the martyred Marcus, the way is free for Juba to marry into the family. Cato's hale to his future son-in-law rhetorically transforms the idea of Roman citizenship into a code of virtue among exiles, over which Roman men themselves have no special claim, especially after Caesar's victory and Sempronius's treachery. "The definition of a Roman," as Ellison writes of the scene, "becomes dissociated from both place and race."[126] Combined with Cato's shortly following declaration that "Rome is no more," Addison's play suggested that "Roman" virtue belonged to the future of its Republic's spiritual imitators, to non-Romans on global shores (perhaps also to non-British Protestants assuming the British throne, if Anne would identify with Cato and set her heart's desire on George I as her successor).[127]

Rosenthal similarly sees the message of the tragedy in the tragic fate of characters who "adhere to a nation, while others develop the internally divided subjectivity of cosmopolitanism."[128] Armistead likewise interpreted the intricately interwoven denouement of *Cato*'s two-plot structure as signaling that the "action involving political faction and Stoic honor moves inexorably towards death," the last calamitous events of an "era of faction, military exploit, and stern, sterile morality." In contrast, the "socio-civil plot" moves "toward the opposite pole of union, peaceful love, hope, and vitality."[129] The renewing marriage of outward cosmopolitanism and a future of domestic peace give the play what Lisa A. Freeman labels its "almost tragicomic conclusion."[130]

That conclusion matched an optimistically Whiggish vision for Great Britain's destiny: the *celebration* of Cato's death has to do (per Rosenthal) with "the passing of an era of 'civil discord' that opens up the possibility for Juba and Marcia's transracial and transnational romance, for they can gain permission to marry only at Cato's deathbed."[131] Near his last breath, Cato suggests that his opposition to the marriage had only to do with defending republican values: "A senator of Rome, while Rome survived, / Would not have match'd his daughter with a king."[132] Addison's nineteenth-century hagiographic biographer, Macaulay, found Cato's approval of the Marcia-Juba union dramatically awkward and extremely unlikely along historical and xenophobic lines.[133] But, in Addison's own theatrical Whiggish circles, Prince Juba's depiction as an ideal Roman participated in a familiar trope linked to revisionary poetic justice. In the 1690s, for instance, Charles Gildon (Thomas Betterton's future biographer) had celebrated such morally appropriate revisionism in Shakespeare's historically unlikely, "anti-racist" elevation of Othello.[134] If we read *Cato* as a play draft from the 1690s, the marriage of Marcia and Juba reads as an allegorical celebration of the Glorious Revolution: the union of the Dutch Stadtholder William and the English Stuart princess Mary had cut across close-to-home "racial" and national lines to renew the promise of liberty via the power of militantly virtuous royals.[135]

Staging Cato pronouncing the end of a nativist Rome whose spirit was set free for others to inherit, the British Augustan theater could simultaneously mourn a past and look into a future of domestic peace, imperial cosmopolitanism, and virtuous, republic-loving patriot kings. Of course, the optimism of Addison's vision uncannily presented a shadow. The marriage of Marcia and Juba, which Rosenthal interprets as the symbolic solution to the play's tragedy, also historically resonates with domestic England's newly strengthened tie to African chattel slavery via the asiento contract of that same year.[136]

Domestically alone, Addison's vision was a risky gambit. His double call for peace and defiance of foreign tyranny was quickly and influentially interpreted by Tories as justifying the continued exile of Duke of the Marlborough and, possibly, another Stuart Restoration. Addison remained, of course, a clear and staunch Whig supporter of the Hanoverian succession, Marlborough, and the entrenched, institutional resistance against restored Catholic or monarchical supremacy. However, his journalistic efforts, and especially his writing and promotion of *Cato* as a nonpartisan play, had partially belied his ideological commitments in order to draw a polarized civil society into a single house. A higher aim of solidarity and national community shaped Addison's public work because he knew—as he wrote in *Freeholder* 34—

the human importance of bringing people together to "mutually rejoyce in the same agreeable Satisfactions." He believed that "when People are accustomed to sit together with Pleasure, it is a step toward Reconciliation."[137] To combine that reconciliation with progress required, in the end, not just momentary coffeehouse camaraderie or theatrical pleasure but also sustainably institutionalized compromise. *Cato*'s Whiggish politics were thus not to be read "within a revolutionary milieu, but as a rhetorical display of republican political ideas designed to consummate, to reform and perfect, an emergent transition to constitutional monarchy."[138] Perhaps as he listened to the competing applause of party factionalists to hear whether they applauded out of conformity and competition or out of genuine feeling and thought, Addison was listening not only for signals about his own fate as an admired playwright but also to hear whether the balance of the assembled representational nation would allow narrow political enmity to be broken by the eros of national community. Only the latter force might keep the sovereign liberty of domestic republicanism alive in spite of the inevitable arrival of *some* foreign Caesar, be it a Tory-backed Stuart or a Whig-appointed Hanoverian.

The splitting of Cato's legacy among his children that the play performs was the end of tragedy as a dominant form—a "happy" end effected through the workings of Providence rather than through the supremacy of the deciding mind and its virtue. It was reminiscent in its call not to Shakespeare's more nihilistic perspective in *Julius Caesar* but to the perspective developed by Addison's literary hero, Milton, in *Samson Agonistes*. The latter tragedy seems to head classically toward a well-reasoned confrontation of the strong, proud individual with a harsh fate stemming from a previous fatal error—his giving into the temptation of love. But, in its final turn, the blind Samson suddenly breaks with his own reasoning, choosing because of an inner signal from God to appease the ruling court by appearing as a spectacle at the feast celebrating their god, Dagon. The messenger who relates Samson's fate at the end of Milton's closet drama reveals that the feast was held in a "spacious Theatre," where virtually the entire body politic of the Philistine regime gathered to see the captive Samson. There, on his divine mission, he performed one final feat of strength: tearing down a main pillar of the theater, crashing the roof over the assembled government.[139] The liberation of his people that Samson thus effected fulfilled the particular kind of tragic role that Milton marked out for his hero on the play's title page. There, Milton chose the Latin word *lustratio*, "a purification by sacrifice," to translate Aristotle's κάθαρσιος (catharsis).[140] Milton's Samson sacrifices his life to bring down the house of the "Sea Idol" Dagon, allegorically collapsing the theater of Hobbes's Leviathan, becoming the Protestant republican martyr the blind Milton may have wished for in the libertine Restoration age of the theater-loving Charles II.

In *Cato,* Addison combines a Senecan individualistic and a Miltonian historical, republican notion of providence to provide his own, quintessentially modern theatrical solution to the problem of theodicy. The Latin epigraph for his printed tragedy comes from chapter 2 of *De Providentia,* where Seneca explains the seemingly contingent misfortunes of human life as owing to the gods' spectatorial pleasure in watching how challenged individual humans will act their parts in tragic real-life dramas. Cato was for Seneca the paragon of virtuous acting due to his repeated gesture of self-sacrifice after his initial wound failed to bring about his death. In a passage just after the section that Addison used as his epigraph, the Stoic philosopher wrote: "I would like to believe that this is why the wound was not so telling or effective—it was not enough for the immortal gods to look on Cato only once. His virtue was kept back and called upon again that it might display itself in a more difficult role; for to seek death once does not require so great a soul as to seek it again. Surely the gods looked with pleasure on their pupil as he escaped by so glorious and memorable an end."[141]

By modifying the biblical scene of Samson's death in *Judges* to present the Philistine temple as a collapsing theater outside of which the common people survive as spectators, Milton displaced the Senecan theatergoing gods and transcendental providence into the witnessing people and the providential progress of history.[142] Addison, in turn, merged these two providential models of tragedy. The repression of Cato's second gory disembowelment provided the theatrical opportunity by which he could indeed be "called upon again" to die in the representational service of history and its modern paradigm change. This time dying as a milder, blessing patriarch—praying for forgiveness to a singular, good god—Cato performs his end for a diverse family and its mirrored British public, bringing down the tragic theater of the lonely Stoic warrior-king, a corporation sole. He sacrifices his own status as an effigy of highest virtue in the interest of transforming history and the future into the new time of a surviving, liberated community (without the need for a second, militant uprising and disemboweling civil war). This tragic destruction of tragedy marks Addison's drama as a passion play, a tragedy that in its epochal completion and metatheatrical transgression consubstantiates as comedy, ambiguously abolishing its own form.

Cato's hastiness, like Samson's abandoning his well-developed reasoning, works in Addison's drama toward a providential plan. The ambivalent light breaking through at the end of Cato's life—does it signify Caesar or Christ's reign, Cato's salvation or just the realization of his mistake?—represents a rupture in history much greater than the life of even its most exemplary individuals and their struggle to understand and perform virtuously. Love makes a terrible mistake redemptive. This enlightened perspective may have been one learned directly from "Cato" in the twelfth distich of his second book: "Seek not by lot, what God's intentions be, / He knows without thee what to do with thee."[143]

Addison's shepherd-like Cato creates a new fence in history, protecting the domestic comedy of sentimental life, an Enlightenment re-creation of the Greek ideal contrast between *bios* (a form of life that can become political life, led by the head of the household) and *zoe* (natural life, relegated in society to the interior of the household).[144] Love in the Catonic flock was no longer the predatory weakness driving society into the ruin of division via the passionate tragic engine of aristocratic, honorific conflict. To love in the new theater and literature of the coming century was restored as a virtuous ability required of the head of household and his protected household members. The modern British nation, a theatrically extended family, thus re-formed in spirit the classical model of a republican theater: the original site of Caesar's murder at the hands of Cato's surviving allies had been Rome's first enduring theater, Pompey's "temple" dedicated to Venus Victrix—to the victory of love.

Addison could risk bringing his tragedy to the public—could even risk the sacrifice ("lustration") of Cato as a symbol of antiquated revolutionary, militant republicanism of the kind that had indeed banned theater and its love scenes during the Interregnum. He could do so because the premiere of his play was now part of a larger societal transformation well underway: the forging of a nation of private Catonic households, a cosmopolitan society of smaller, fenced-off, partial sovereignties. Like the exiled Senate in Utica, the English bourgeois society of *Spectator* readers would become the true, long-awaited heirs of the noble Roman spirit and the deciders of that faraway city's legacy and imperial fate.

ADDISON AND THE ENGLISH CONSTITUTIONAL SCENE CHANGE

Perhaps because Cato remained a too-dangerous political rallying figure for any standing regime, the Romans themselves left us no extant Cato drama. Even Seneca did not provide a model for Addison's much later realization, despite his praise of Cato as the planet's most worthy theatrical attraction: "Behold! Here is a spectacle worthy of a god's regard as he looks upon his works; behold, here a contest worthy of god—a brave man matched against ill-fortune.... I do not see, I say, what nobler spectacle Jupiter would find on earth, should he wish to turn his attention there, than the sight of Cato, after his cause had already been broken more than once, nevertheless standing erect among the ruins of the state."[145] It was this passage from *De Providentia* that Addison had printed in Latin on the title page of his drama. Cato the "ideal Roman" and spiritual father of the failed and future Republic gives way in Seneca's vision to Cato the semidivine archetype of the tragic human actor. A phoenix sacrificing himself to close and preserve a past scene by becoming its embodiment and climactic symbol, this quintessentially theatrical Cato defiantly in the same moment outlives the catastrophically falling set of his own era to birth a new incarnated future.

Cato the tragedian standing in the ruins of the commons (*publicas*) had as a figure a valence beyond the overtly political: he became in Addison's modern vision a symbol of the self-realized death of a classical system of understanding. Playing witness was now a collective of theatrical spectators, surviving together through the epistemological paradigm shift of Newtonianism and the accompanying new technological-scientific order. That valence is unlikely to present itself immediately and affectively to contemporary readers, who are several centuries away from the initial abyss-openings of modern science. But it was suggested at the most inward moment of Addison's play as Cato made his decisive turn toward self-martyrdom and expressed the militant resolve against Caesar that would rise up again and again as the eighteenth century moved toward revolution. His reasoning, captured in one of the century's most famous soliloquies, clearly came not from Plutarch but from a very modern kind of Platonism mixed with a pathos-laden reception of Newton and the developing science of massive scales. Alone in his chamber after reading *Phaedo,* Cato addresses his own proto-Romantic soul:

> The stars shall fade away, the sun himself
> Grow dim with age, and nature sink in years,
> But thou shalt flourish in immortal youth,
> Unhurt amidst the wars of elements,
> The wrecks of matter, and the crush of worlds.[146]

The same British audience earlier called upon to listen and deliberate, taking up the role of senate-in-exile, is now haled as the pagan general-father's most intimate mirror in the chaos of the universe: his witnessing, surviving soul.

The new physics of immeasurable scales threw the old ordered paradigm of earthly reasoning into absurdity and left Cato, like his British compatriots of 1713, a subject of Providence's will. In private, where the mind could not "be always in its Fervors," they and he were "weary of conjectures," seemingly unable to rely on anything but internal instinct, self-aware moles trusting the poor senses with which they were born. Like the modern British audience watching him enact his famous choice now as cautionary tale, Cato's wrestling with Plato's aged words performed the estrangement inherent in neoclassical nostalgia for antiquated models.[147]

Addison might have advised—and he did, through the love plots—that Cato stick around, be more conventional, and daydream about arcadian landscapes instead of waking immediately to horrific, reactive thoughts about Caesar. Certainly, it was the advice that Addison had his fatherly martyr ultimately give to his surviving son Portius, the same advice that St. Augustine criticized Cato for not also adopting for himself.[148] As it was, the historical Cato was mourned by the people of Utica, who assembled immediately in front of his house, where "with one voice they called Cato their saviour and benefactor, the only man who was free, the only one unvanquished."[149] Plutarch focused his narrative on two famous images of Cato that reveal the fallen republican hero's hermaphroditic classical figuration as a civic savior. In the first—the gory death scene painted for Caesar's triumph parade and later celebrated by Rousseau—he has been sitting for some time in Utica, drawing together and gestating the old age's philosophy and the last moments of the Roman Republic inside of him, while his anxious family awaits the birth of his decision.[150] When his violent self-delivery goes wrong, and the doctor arrives, he rips open his own belly and holds up his guts for everyone to see, the stillborn child of the old era, the Republic that, cornered, still seizes and decides its own destiny. In the second "immortal" image of Plutarch's narrative, a restored Cato, carved out of stone, stands with sword raised as a monumental statue protecting the shore of Utica, signaling forever defiance against tyranny.[151]

Addison adapted his Cato to the framing revelations of seventeenth-century glass and mathematics, which had demonstrated a cosmos radically larger and stranger than thought previously and had relegated terrestrial order to a necessary but mere contingency. The bourgeoisie were ready to learn that sovereignty belonged to no singular person nor to any single hermetic system on earth. In correspondence with this new learned existential humility, instead of a gruesome suicide and abortion and the accompanying granite pose of a warrior general, Addison made the final hermaphroditic poses of Cato mild. Distilled as an archetype, Father-Cato wielded less a defiant sword than a pen, settling the private contracts and accounts of his last will in his dying moments. Mother-Cato's life ended with a sanitary yet fatal, modern Caesarian section that was simultaneous with her gift to the world of a surviving pair of happily married bourgeois couples. Having purged themselves of a militancy that demanded a post of honor above love, those two latter bound couples performed the (as yet undiscovered) DNA of the colonial, bourgeois future: half undefeated, cultivating a private household of love that flees across seas, unable to break finally free from the siege of Caesars and the threatening mass outside their privileged, semicollective walls. The era became the generation. Rupture became progressive increment.

The Cato myth and its effigy as Addison moderated and revised them loomed large in the background against which the next generations' sentimental father and republican mother were figured. *Cato*'s immensely popular first run was interrupted only by the increasingly urgent pregnancy of its female romantic lead (a Jungian theatrical-historical coincidence that uncannily added live comic pathos to the general father's suicide as he blessed his daughter's quickly arranged marriage and Caesar threatened to burst through the city gates).[152] Subsequently, the play "became the main conduit for the Cato legend throughout the eighteenth century."[153] In his *Letters Concerning the English Nation,* Voltaire called the drama "a Master-piece" and declared "the illustrious Mr. *Addison*" to be "the first *English* writer who compos'd a regular Tragedy and infus'd a Spirit of Elegance thro' every Part of it." The rationalist literary grandfather of the French Revolution further opined that "Mr. *Addison's Cato* appears to me the greatest Character that was ever brought upon any Stage."[154] Indeed, the printed tragedy's unprecedentedly rapid breadth of popularity across Europe and in colonial North America spawned many major revivals over the next hundred years as well as translations and direct imitations in Italian, French, Irish, German, Polish, and, finally, Latin.[155]

THE PEOPLE'S KING

The theatrical, liberating warrior-king that had ridden as a shadow of Queen Anne throughout her reign—the mystical effigy whom Marlborough had distantly embodied in his Continental exploits and Whig-feted homecomings, the same effigy to whom Betterton had given live, fleshy presence nightly at his theatrical mimic court—retired into the Drury Lane death chamber of Cato in Anne's last days. As Cato, the sacred king's body politic died in a sterile, theatrical manner, becoming a purely culturally contested effigy. Who was Addison's Cato, after all, in the allegory that everyone came again and again to see? His death was the performative birth of the bourgeois order, which made itself visible as a loose collective of *Spectator* readers, paying for tickets to see the uniquely successful drama throughout the century in order to claim their right to vote in the contest over which party could name the living, real-life surrogate for the last unifying Roman republican spiritual leader. The Hobbesian, kingly, British corporation sole (Cato) divided into a grand coalition of free middling households—an artificial body of nuclear family cells, balanced between imperial cosmopolitanism (Marcia and Juba, moving to the city) and an ancient, pastoral scene of domesticity (Portius and Lucia, retreating to the country).

Cato was the drama of succession, of one theatrical age to the next, accompanied by a paradigm shift in monarchs. Real catharsis is no mundane, easy-to-manufacture medicine; in the neoclassical paradigm, an effective tragedy was the rare apex of artistic achievement, not just the accomplishment of one author, production, or year, but of a people, an age, a civilization, an entire aesthetic regime. Written and staged in the dark days of Addison and his Whig colleagues' potentially permanent exclusion from power, Addison's everywhere extolled triumph catalyzed a real-life reversal of fortunes. When Bolingbroke fell and entered exile, Addison would usurp his position and responsibilities, becoming secretary to the lords chancellor just after Anne's death. In this position, he would oversee not only the military suppression of Jacobite rebellions and invasions but also the transitional ceremonies of Anne's funeral and George I's arrival in England and installation in power.[156] "In literary England," Smithers wrote, "he had become the oracle, the successor to Dryden, universally admired and respected. He was a squire in the country, a parliament man in town, the familiar companion of the great in society, the lion of the coffee-houses. With the highest honour both as a man of affairs and as a man of letters, he might feel he personified the ideal of Roman citizenship."[157] Equally, though, as a "Roman" citizen, he performatively accomplished a singular synthesis that heralded the reformed body politic of the kraken-like modern nation-state, via achievements in literature, theater, bureaucratic administration, colonial and military management, diplomatic statesmanship, and middle-class advocacy.

At the time, Pope and Steele both quoted Addison's own lines to express their admiration and recognition of his public standing after *Cato:* "Envy it self is dumb, in Wonder lost, / And Factions strive who shall applaud 'em most."[158] In their original context, Addison had used those lines (45–46 in *The Campaign*) to praise the partnership of Anne and Marlborough and the Queen's "meritocratic" style of governance: she and her favorites constituted an ensemble-sovereignty of talent, to which—Pope and Steele's praise implied—Addison was now raised. As a latter-day "Renaissance man" or early unitary performer of the modern administrative state, Addison had achieved a level of wide cultural esteem reflected in Swift's ironic comment "that if he had proposed himself for king, he would hardly have been refused."[159] A few years later, when Addison was appointed secretary of state, the prone-to-envy Swift sympathetically congratulated him with a compliment that turned the sentiment of Addison's panegyric to Anne and Marlborough on its head: now a high official at court, Addison was a "prodigious singularity," since he owed his "Rise entirely to Merit."[160]

That validation came from a poet who had previously abandoned his Whig colleagues for the inner sanctum of the previous Tory government under Bolingbroke's watch. Addison's accomplishment was a small source of political hope, something worthy perhaps of the regard of Cato, whom Swift esteemed "to have been the wisest and best of all the Romans."[161] In the eyes of one the world's greatest satirists of courts and power, Addison had achieved what his Portius, in an oft-quoted passage early in the tragedy, had declared as his intention:

> I'll thunder in their ears their country's cause,
> And try to rouse up all that's Roman in 'em.
> 'Tis not in mortals to command success,
> But we'll do more, Sempronius; we'll deserve it.[162]

7

Cato's Coda

Death after Tragic Fame

> His compositions are but a noble preface; the grand work is his death.
> —Edward Young on Addison

THE SEPULCHRAL LAMP AND THE LIGHT OF DAY

Forty years after the death of his friend and literary benefactor, Edward Young confessed the wish that drove his *Conjectures on Original Composition:* that "a monument more durable than those of marble, should proudly rise in this ambitious page, to the new, and far nobler *Addison,* than that which you, and the public, have so long, and so much admired."[1] The "you" was the novelist Samuel Richardson, to whom Young addressed his 1759 book-length epistolary essay. *Conjectures on Original Composition* would contribute significantly to two diverging main currents in literary history. On the one hand, it became, via immediate Continental translation and reception, a significant text in the development of the Sturm und Drang movement, Goethe's literary thought, and what would become German Romanticism. On the other hand, Young's account of Addison's death—the climactically revealed raison d'être for his essay—became a main source for later Addison hagiography, the attempts that began with Addison himself to celebrate the large virtuous effects that his labors rendered in England and beyond.

A split Addisonian *Geist* haunted the subsequent nineteenth century via the darker vision of Romanticism and the moral pedantry of middle-class philosophy and Victorian realism. In the climax of his own monument to and departure from an earlier age of authorship, *A Portrait of the Artist as a Young Man,* James Joyce self-consciously performed the Modernist gesture of re-collecting the fractured light of everyday secularism, religion, politics, science, classicism, Romanticism, and realism—all the divergent mainstreams of Addisonian Enlightenment. The middle of *Portrait* shows the young Daedalus's thoughts half-overtaken by the strident voice of a preacher, who admonishes him to consider the example of the death of "the great English writer," Addison.[2] The sermon pushes Daedalus to experience the "whole wrath of God" aimed against the sin in which his soul is festering. Daedalus—as Addison had—eventually rejects the call to a deathly priestly vocation, heeding instead a call to Europe and a destiny as witness to the sensuous, ceaselessly recreated world. Lucretius's exuberant pre-Ovidian/pre-Hermaphroditic adventurer through a world of strange and unknown waters is restored. Joyce went to find himself as a writer in the same Paris and Italy where, two centuries before, Addison had visited Boileau and mused on Ovid's old stomping grounds, making the transition from Latin poet to modern neoclassicist.

In Joyce's *Portrait,* the fall of the young artist's soul into the swampy mud of shame and self-disgust is precipitated by the opposed sacrosanct height of Addison as a saintly, dying, authorial figure. Via the famous epiphany scene at the end of chapter 4, however, the artist-soul's authentic Modernist rescue and restoration reperforms the fuller structure of the Addisonian imagination, against its institutional, moralist reduction.[3] Like the nymph who captured Hermaphroditus, the mermaid- and bird-like girl in the water manifests as an external mirror of the young perambulating poet's soul. The structuring ur-paradigms of nature, contingency, and classical tradition merge seamlessly in the "emerald trail of seaweed [that] had fashioned itself as a sign upon the flesh" of the girl's bare legs. Liberated from the darkened cloisters and the reproving clerical voice, the "Heavenly God" that Daedalus cries out to "in an outburst of profane joy" restores the artist as spiritual truth-giver and the diverse, cosmopolitan world as the object divinely ordained for higher contemplation.[4] Addison's actual discourse—his attempt to affirm the middle of quotidian existence as the source of sublimity—is freed from its death in his name.

The vision of the young girl as anima repeats the essential Addisonian trope: Daedalus's soul can take wing only insofar as he forgoes the false but seductive higher sublime of feudal dogma for the lower-but-best-possible sublime of necessary entanglement in the refreshing, contingent waters of nature, the city, and sociability. Addison's twentieth-century "death" as a well-known author covers and reperforms in literary history the paradigm of his Cato, whose ambiguous act of liberation through death paradoxically created and ended his status as a towering moral paragon.

Addison was paradigmatic for a writer and cultural worker seeking to create and foster a "middle." The previous chapter discussed how he moderated Cato's death to situate the pagan "saint" between secular and Christian martyrdom, between a dying model of singular, patriarchal, masculine leadership (the king) and a rejuvenating benevolent, cosmopolitan, sentimental paternalism (the bourgeois father). The evolution or responsiveness of the Addisonian discourse did not end with *Cato* but continued through the revolutionary period to the end of the century. Between mystical, hegemonic union and disenchanted, contingent anarchy, between religious scripture and art-for-consumption's-sake, the monumentalized Enlightenment law and political praxes of the later eighteenth century had much to do with Addison's achievements as a writer and public man.

The beginning of this book discussed the disappearance of Addison's fame from the Romantic period onward as partially the result of a failure of later readers to sense the darker pathos and real, dangerous political conflicts that had haunted his work in his own time and century. Like a programmer who develops and implements a code that is easily, quickly, and freely replicable, Addison's unprecedented success contributed to his later invisibility as an original artist and politician. But his impact was not just at the "literary" level. Axelsson writes that "the purposeful act of constructing the reality of society was, for Addison, to be compared to a moment of artistic creativity, and the body politic to be likened to an original work of art."[5] As middling people really liberated themselves against uncertain odds and threatening situations, what was for Addison an assertion of sense, sensibility, taste, and the common became itself law, hegemonic culture, and entrenched political culture. Again his reformulation of the Cato myth resonates: Addison's was not a work designed to tower above life austerely, a permanent measure and sublime critique of life's tragic failure to manifest the highest that could be experienced. Rather, it was a work pitched pragmatically at making life better, more peaceful, and more reasonable for a future of more represented people. As such, much of the felt pathos that the Addisonian discourse addressed gradually fell away with its success.

The author of *Night Thoughts,* Edward Young, is still read as a guide to the abysses that discomfited the sleepless Enlightenment.[6] As such, and as an intimate of Addison, his *Conjectures* reveal the context of darkness in which the Addisonian construction was originally conceived, the swallowing, infinite

Newtonian space of the eighteenth century's "overwrought" legalistic, imperial cultural achievements. Already seventy-six at the time of writing *Conjectures,* Young announced at the beginning of the essay an intention to guide the reader toward "a monument . . . in which is a hidden lustre, like the sepulchral lamps of old."[7] Addison had pointed to Cato pointing to Plato pointing to Socrates as the best teacher of how to prepare for death: in Socrates's teaching, wisely preparing for death was the ultimate aim of philosophy. Young, in turn, pointed to Addison: *Cato,* in Young's argument, was a rehearsal for Addison's own performed death. "*Addison taught us how to die,*" he wrote.[8]

Already in his time, Young claimed that Addison's reputation had suffered because so many had praised his writing's style, instead of drawing attention to its substance and effects. In language that echoes the often-surprising hermaphroditic structure of the Addisonian discourse, Young declared: "On subjects the most interesting, and important, no author of his age has written with greater, I had almost said, with equal weight: And they who commend him for his elegance, pay him such a sort of compliment, by their abstemious praise, as they would pay to *Lucretia,* if they should commend her only for her beauty."[9] For Young, the proof of Addison's philosophical weight lay not in his textual performances but in their test: the difference he made in his world, and how he in fact lived and died.[10] Bringing his reader (the novelist Richardson) to his reason for writing the foregoing essay, Young tells the story of Addison's deathbed scene, a story he says he first heard from Tickell — tears still in his eyes — just after Addison's death. The dying statesman, barely able to compose himself in agony after a long illness he could not shake, had called his stepson, the young Warwick, into his chamber and commanded him to "see in what peace a Christian can die." With the long withheld story now related, Young declares that this was his "chief inducement for writing at all . . . the *monumental marble* . . . to which I promised to conduct you . . . the *sepulchral lamp.*"[11]

Young builds on the story to critique the "*age of authors,*" which crowns the head but not the heart. In Young's view, the post-Addison literary age regressed into favoring the fame of talent over the nobility of fear-reducing actions and performances. Before the reign of Addison's fame, the sway of those who had prioritized sublime wit over benevolent speech and action had destroyed society's peace and health. The reforming, philosophical, saintly Addison was not just England's physician but "*Europe's Addison.*" Against the claim of literature to immortality itself as a highest value, Young posited that for Europe's modernity "the *dying Addison* far outshines her *Addison immortal.*"[12]

Death, as it always had for philosophers, exposed human existence to its necessary theatricality. If truth were to come at all out of human mouths, it would come from people looking steadily into the void; if virtue were to be manifest from human actions, it would be continued by another person willfully taking up its part. Addison was the summit of modern philosophy because he was not merely an author but an actor in the abyss. "All listen," Young wrote, "when a death-bed speaks; and regard the person departing as an actor of a part, which the great master of the drama has appointed us to perform to-morrow: This was a *Roscius* on the stage of life; his exit how great? Ye lovers of virtue! *plaudite.*"[13]

The command to applaud echoed and anticipated another long theme of Addisonian reception: the sense that high stakes surround a public demonstration of Addison-appreciation. Between a literary Christ figure (in need of faith and resurrection) and a clothier dressing up Cato, Marlborough, and George I in dignified British Augustan form, Addison became a paradigm for a literary taste that one *should* strive to attain. The Addisonian effigy was the latest in a series of philosophical-political effigies that, like Russian dolls, each contained the previous—Addison, Cato, Plato, Socrates. All four exemplary figures shared a certain austerity and coldness as well as an uncomfortable kitschy exaggeration in their most sublime moments (reminiscent of the painted unfleshy surface of said Russian dolls). All four performative, self-allegorizing, discourse-founding effigies were surrounded by a heavy crowd of partisans, acolytes, fans, readers, and dedicatees *warning* that much would be lost if one did not strive faithfully to absorb the virtue of their example. Addison, dying, became the first eighteenth-century Catonic effigy, the Socratic effigy—already an ambiguously displaced, secular, atheistic, or simply humbler, Protestant figuration of Christ.[14]

Lawrence E. Klein summarizes the novel figure Addison cut in his time, and how he was received in the later part of his century, as a new moderation between cosmopolitan urbanity and spiritual shepherd: "Addison was the embodiment of polite worldliness, a model for comporting oneself in a polite culture. At the same time, the figure of Addison had a strong Christian inflection, pointing in an otherworldly direction. Among their purposes, Addison's writings mediated the Christian word; among its modulations, Addison's personality could be taken as saint-like."[15] The debate over the worthiness of his achievements in what Young labeled "the age of authors" was increasingly pitched against him. The arena was wrong. Addison and his admirers—in a partial kinship to readers in our age of subjectivity and authorial death—argued that his textual performances were only one part of the Addisonian act. "His own ideal," Klein writes, "was Ciceronian; literary endeavour was one feature of a larger ambition to be a great public man—a feature that was subordinate to and instrumental for achieving that public role."[16] Cicero, that outspoken contemporary admirer of Cato, died for his politics. Addison did not judge his own age as the proper time for martyrdom but rather for the modest hard work of peaceable compromise, where possible. Some may argue with Steele that he was seduced to compromise too much in becoming in the end a married, aristocratic, monarchical propagandist: a social role in which he quickly indeed fell mortally ill. But for Addison, this was how a philosopher of his age wisely died—into an enlightened, nontragic subjectivity, weaving the fabric of progressive generations.

Philosophy as a satisfying larger discourse perhaps never recovered from its divorce from the high stakes of religion. But as its energies through the Addisonian turn were bent increasingly toward the arrangements of average people's lives, it gained by the century's end what Socrates had dreamed for it: the place of kingship. Debated, contemplated policy began to rule over the human state, and kings were increasingly confined into neoclassically codified, cultural life-performances. With this achievement, the Addisonian legacy could die along with tragedy, in the separate realm of art, because what was needed in the conditions of enlightened democracy was not sublime, singular genius (performative, political, or literary) but, ever increasingly, reasonable prose, the sociable cooperation of the many. Addison's project of bringing sociable philosophy into the common conversation had begun to subtly open up and shift cultural and political arrangements that had long seemed fated and eternal. It succeeded even against a historical backdrop of failed—though more pitched, passionate, and violent—struggles against those unyielding arrangements.

HÄNDLING THE KING

Looking holistically at all of Addison's actions or "performances," one discovers a rare, comprehensive combination of contributions and interventions in many separate fields coalescing in a first manifestation of the modern nation-state. Simultaneous changes and developments in literature, political philosophy, theater and theatrical action, bureaucratic administration, military effort and organization, social discourse, scientific understanding, market participation, statesmanship, propaganda, coinage, and middle-class advocacy all helped to foment the dominance of the nation-state as an organizing entity of modern life, citizenship, and subjectivity. This new kind of state was not primarily the nation-state of rights for middling people but rather the renovated nation-state of middling people's own manufacture. At a pivotal early moment of that manufacture, Addison played a signal role in producing the invisible coordination and progressive leaps across separate communities of activity that contributed to the modern nation-state's seemingly organic, natural birth. A hard-working artisan and conceptual artist of the functional middle-class nation, he was an essential node in the system of transnationally cooperating middle-class people.

His rise to unprecedented cultural power for someone of his original station was part and parcel of larger developments resulting in and from the British state's triumph over its European imperial adversaries. Something more than general trends, however, attended Addison's particular Ciceronian focus on the attainment of high office in the State Ministry. Smithers remarked that, even after *Cato*'s success, Addison was not contented with "literary glory, of which he already enjoyed more than any Englishman living... but thought first of his political distinction."[17] In the prologue at the opening day of the Theatre-Royal at Drury Lane, the day after George I's 1714 public entry into London to succeed Anne, Steele laid bare the political motivation that drove their theatrical endeavors:

> At length, *Britannia*, rescu'd from thy Fears,
> Renew thy Joys: Thy promis'd King appears...
> While you were zealous for your Soveraign's Right,
> For Him We made our *Greeks* and *Romans* fight.
> Oft as the Muse some God-like Hero drew,
> Or set a virtuous Patriot to your View;
> So oft we warm'd you in the BRUNSWICK Cause,
> And fix'd a generous People to their Laws.[18]

The moment of triumph—art as legislator and political coordinator of an unprecedented, peaceful, international dynastic change—was one in which Steele's close collaborator also reveled. But Addison's main theater of action at the time was the larger world of public ceremony, in which he had taken charge of stage-managing Queen Anne's funeral and King George I's arrival in England, as well as coordinating many details of the coming coronation.

But the Hanoverians were not passive showmen. Their entrance as grand monarchs had been prepared in good measure by their kapellmeister, George Frideric Handel, who had been drawing elite London audiences away from Addison and Steele's Drury Lane since 1711 with his magnificent Italian operas. The lasting success of the German immigrant's first such opera, *Rinaldo*, proved the box-office appeal of a different kind of theatrical nostalgia—this one for Continental opulence and a musicalized neofeudal sublime, distantly aggrandizing the romance of high chivalric honor. The Queen's Theatre in the Haymarket was the site of this regathering of genteel operatic taste, and Handel's third Italian opera there—*Teseo* (*Theseus*)—pitted neoclassical arias fashioned around mythic Greek heroism against the vernacular, political declamations of Addison's Roman *Cato*.[19] The competition for hearts, minds, and eyes between the two genres and venues throws Addison's efforts into an important, paratheatrical relief: chivalry did not die with 1713's polite modern Cato, and the coming rule of the Hanoverians would certainly not amount to an end to the entrenched, courtly form of royal European power in England. Even as his tragical triumph abetted his sharp political ascendancy as a crucial agent in the Hanoverian machine, the competition from Handel's opera seria about a prince restored from foreign exile must have bedeviled Addison.

Italianate opera had long been a vexing foil for Addison and perhaps particularly for his *Cato:* an operatic version of Cato's last days that he saw in Venice may have irritated him enough to inspire renewed work on his own draft tragedy.[20] In any case, his record of that theatrical experience in his *Remarks on Italy* became only a first instance of his pronounced tendency to bash Italian operas in print ("The poetry of them is generally as exquisitely ill, as the music is good").[21] His own attempt at starting an English tradition of more reasonable opera librettos with *Rosamond* had failed, even though critics generally applauded his lyrics. Handel, on the other hand, succeeded in making the Italian form into a popular and treasured part of English cultural life, in spite of Addison and Steele's stinging critical attacks.[22] To see his *Cato* potentially outshone by the operatic herald of the king he hoped would bring him back into the inner sanctum of power might have thrown a shadow on the optimism Addison had about the political future that he was helping to create. As it was, Cato defeated Theseus at the box office by good measure, but the proud Continental refrains from the rival theater signaled some bitter passages for Addison ahead.

Despite performing his job as secretary to the regents ably, and in spite of the many years of preparing and bolstering the Hanoverian succession, Addison did not at first receive the high position under the newly installed king that he and his allies expected.[23] Charles Montagu, then lord treasurer, had promised to see Addison named secretary of state, but George I did not approve the recommendation. Instead the king heeded advice to check the power of Montagu, a highly effective and often divisive political fighter, despite the Whig leader's recently professed resolve to quit partisanship and "make King George, the First not the Head of a Party, but the King of a glorious united Nation."²⁴

Something of the wariness that the newly arrived George I may have felt toward his Whig kingmakers—not only directed at Montagu—can be understood by reading the panegyric verses that Addison published shortly after the coronation. His poem "To Sir Godfrey Kneller" extolling the artist's portrait of George ran through four editions and proved very popular.²⁵ In the simplest reading, the poem's ekphrasis admiringly describes the felicity with which Kneller depicted the new ruler as a virtuous king transfigured through the Olympian pantheon as Jove. The public gesture of magnificent praise was echoed, in this simple reading, by Addison's subsequent verses to the Princess of Wales, Caroline. That poem from November 1714 finally bestowed on Caroline (the king's daughter-in-law) the dedication of *Cato* that Anne, the last Stuart queen, had requested but failed to win from the playwright. Both of these publications fit with the surface of Addison as an admiring Hanoverian partisan, who had since 1703 served as a special envoy between England and that blessed, fruitful, Protestant German family's court.²⁶

But the poem celebrating George I as a virtuous Jove contained a few difficult lines that allowed another level of interpretation. It was, after all, not a panegyric truly dedicated to George I but, rather, to the artist's "delusive Hand," which presented an awing image to a seeing "we."²⁷ It was not enough for the royal sovereign to sit in majesty. The speaker of the poem—perhaps hoping for the job of trip director—gave the king a necessary itinerary: he should make a progress through the land so that, somewhat ominously, "crowds" would "grow Loyal as they Gaze[d]." George's coronation had been marked by a large number of Jacobite riots throughout south England.²⁸

In the poem's trickiest section, Addison wishes the king a long reign through an unusually complicated and somewhat backward formulation. Listing the English monarchs since the Restoration, the speaker (addressing Kneller) arrives at George, the first of the Brunswick House and proclaims:

> O may fam'd BRUNSWICK be the Last,
> (Though Heav'n shou'd with my Wish agree,
> And long preserve thy Art in Thee)
> The Last, the Happiest *British* King,
> Whom Thou shalt paint, or I shall sing!²⁹

An uncareful reader might arrive quite naturally at the thought that Addison was wishing George I to be the last British king. Of course, the meaning is otherwise, although the generally quite careful poet lets the "wrong" meaning ambiguously linger across several lines, even repeating "The Last" and in the meantime clarifying that he does not wish *Kneller* an early death. George I is wished, indirectly, a long reign so that Kneller (the artist whose preservation is parenthetically prayed for in language echoing that traditionally used for the king) might never paint another in a long line of portraited Restoration monarchs. But one could be forgiven for stumbling over the awkward passage or wondering why Addison, often so smoothly sycophantic, did not more overtly espouse in that passage—or, indeed, anywhere in the poem—his belief in the long continuance of British monarchs after George I's assuredly long life.

The jewel of the poem is the penultimate stanza, which parallels Kneller's painted Restoration monarchs listed two stanzas previously with the sculpted pantheon centered around Phidias's famous sculpture of Zeus (renamed Jove), one of the seven wonders of the ancient world. The last stanza leaves the work of art triumphant in itself, a painted king or sculpted king of gods. There is, perhaps, something troubling in that final stanza's assertion that the work of art awes even the artist—Phidias's "art was at a stand" because he dared not risk creating more after finishing his masterpiece. This suggestion of the artist being conquered by his art would echo with a curious parallel italicization in the fourth stanza to the end and in the penultimate stanza. Italicization of proper names in those two stanzas maps each British monarch to an allegorical Greek deity. *Pan* (*Charles* II) was "wont to chase the Fair," while *Thetis* (*Anna*) "the troubled Ocean's Queen" mourned her "short-liv'd Darling Son." George, however, "the Last, the Happiest *British* King" becomes

> He, whose Thunder slew
> The *Titan-race,* a Rebel Crew,
> That from a Hundred Hills, allie'd
> In Impious Leagues, their King defie'd.[30]

Again, a troubling subtext haunts the official meaning that a fortunate George triumphs over an impious conspiracy of Jacobites: the parallel structure of italicization alone would match the freedom-loving *British* with the conquered *Titan-race,* suggesting an ambiguous peril for George I's new reign (if he should decide to rule delusively "over" the British rather than ruling "as" a Briton himself).

From the perspective of a freshly arrived foreign king, such a public poem between artists staged his relatives, his predecessors, and himself as objects of art—simultaneously deified and miniaturized—for a watching, potentially rebellious public "We." Moreover, it echoed Dryden's 1694 poem to Kneller by ending with an idea of painting's limits as an art form: unlike theater, painting remained still, and unlike poetry, painting could not speak.[31] The German-speaking king who came to power through the work of deifying, native public artists could not survive politically with portrait painters alone. And the foremost political poet of the age was now, in the same volume, dedicating his famous tragedy not to the king but to the wife of the king's son, who had set up a rival, oppositional court. Addison's dedication of *Cato* to Caroline again held out the implicit power of poets ("the tuneful tribe") via an offer that the poets would now turn to less revolutionary topics and instead "teach the nation their new monarch's praise, / Describe . . . Caesar's power with Cato's virtue joined." Pointedly, however, that poetical service was offered to the princess, to whom and to whose children the future belonged, via the assurance "of successive reigns."[32]

Bitterly indeed, with George's accession Addison was returned to his post as secretary of the Irish government under Lord Lieutenant Sunderland. Trickier court politics and his personal ambitions to one side, his appointment confirmed his previous success in that difficult Irish role and demonstrated his potential as a manager of fraught overseas relations for a foreign imperial monarch. George subsequently saw the wisdom of further availing himself of those skills by employing the highly esteemed playwright, journalist, and poet as commissioner of trade and plantations in 1715. The death of Charles Montagu in the spring of that year had paradoxically increased Addison's employability by diminishing the threat of his faction's ministerial dominance. Behind the offer of that lucrative new post (earning one thousand pounds a year) was an understanding that Addison would undertake efforts to bolster the popularity of the imported king, whose favorability with the public had significantly fallen without the enthusiastic prop of his former Whig public relations team. As something of a professionalized mercenary, then, Addison began to write the biweekly political newspaper *The Freeholder*, from December 1715 through June 1716. The reward for him was a change of class: his increased income and higher position gave him footing to marry the widowed Countess of Warwick, Charlotte Myddelton.[33] Leaving middling for Myddelton, Addison became a new aristocrat.

"The brilliant but brief period of alliances between poets and statesmen . . . was now drawing to a close," Smithers wrote of the time after the death of Montagu, Addison's close political patron and Newton's intimate friend.[34] Addison had already turned his attention slightly away from the common city milieu toward growing and enclosing his own large private estate at Bilton. After his marriage in 1716, he entered more fully into the mold of professional politician (and estate-holding courtier), a role he would not long enjoy in good health. *The Freeholder* essays responded directly to the Jacobite rebellion of 1715. Instead of philosophy down from the heavens, *The Freeholder* "brought politics out of cabinets and parliamentary committees and the all-male society of the coffee-houses, and into the circle of the family tea-table." The speaker was an "English free-holder of forty shillings" identified with the House of Commons.[35] Incessantly attacking and ridiculing the Pretender and his followers, *The Freeholder* appealed to Britons' sense of loyalty in an attempt to rally them to the king, who was, in turn, presented as a bulwark against foreign subversion and invasion. *The Freeholder* demonstrated Addison's clearest structural political thought and its overall emphasis on a constitutional balance of powers. At the same time, it more baldly displayed his acquired expertise as a political propagandist.

For the knowing reader, though, Addison continued to use neoclassical motifs to self-consciously perform the artist's role in staging a monarch as a chosen servant of the people. *Freeholder* 2, for instance, is preceded by an epigraph from Pliny's *Panegyricus* and follows the Roman author's formula in that work for how a new appointee might praise a king in such a way as to program his behavior and policy.[36] After extolling the legislated heir's qualifications for high office, Addison wrote that "What gives us the greatest Security in the Conduct of so excellent a Prince is, that Consistency of Behaviour, whereby He inflexibly pursues those Measures which appear the most Just and Equitable."[37] The king, in other words, is well qualified for his job of public service because he models forth the lessons of *The Spectator;* he is, in essence, a performing, utilitarian human service-machine, an exemplary, working citizen of the nation. *The Freeholder* is a monument of the historical articulation of divided-powers constitutionalism and the simultaneous apotheosis of the national monarch as a (neoclassical) sentimentalized, mass-consumer product.

In April 1717, Addison's service to the king was finally rewarded with promotion to the top of the administrative state. In a few years, Addison's fellow Kit-Kat Whig Robert Walpole would transform British politics through his ascendency and long tenure as the first "prime minister," reaching the new peak of nonroyal power that had eluded Charles Montagu. But in 1717, the two secretaries of state were still the principal ministers. Newly appointed as the secretary for the Southern Department, Addison took on the higher administrative load of the two secretaries and was in charge of colonial affairs, including Ireland and the Americas—the latter referred to functionally as "the Plantations." Smithers notes that his new seals of office gave him "unrivalled access to every department of governance, for the Secretaries of State were more than ever before the clearinghouse through which all business must pass, and were in frequent contact with the king himself."[38] Indeed, Addison's power as secretary was augmented by the fact that the king spoke French and German but little English and frequently returned to his home in Hanover. At a crucial moment of empire-formation and colonial transformation, then, the author of *Cato* became to a significant degree the author of British imperial policy. Among the tasks that fell to Addison's charge was the effort to bring colonies and particular colonial legislatures more firmly under the crown's authority. This centralization strategy included revising and printing chaotic Plantation laws. His brief tenure as the highest representative of colonial governments to the king and other high ministers proved to be a particularly busy time for affairs that touched on the colonies and the chartered trading corporations.[39]

In Europe, Addison the secretary carefully sought to foster the new, fragile peace through balancing various national and imperial powers, forging more durable and stable alliances. One can hear the resonance of Young's assertion that Addison was "Europe's Addison" when one considers that it was he who, in this sensitive time after long, engulfing wars, managed complex negotiations between the Triple Alliance (England, the Dutch Republic, and France), the Holy Roman Empire, Prussia, and Spain. Addison's work helped to lay a historical framework for a cooperating, cogoverning Europe, an effective balance of powers. As secretary, in spite of a constant Jacobite threat, he oversaw a reduction in size of the British army.[40] Working closely with his French counterpart, the Abbé Dubois, he made further strides to peace by negotiating the groundwork for what would become the Quadruple Alliance of 1718 between France, the Dutch Republic, and the Hapsburg Empire. Those negotiations helped to established a lasting peace with France and an effective counter in Europe against Spain's imperial ambitions. The Anglo-French alliance of 1716 had been a "diplomatic revolution"; the Quadruple Alliance was yet another revolution that ended the bipolar nature of European diplomacy.[41] It "marked the highest point in British prestige and the greatest advance of British diplomacy up to that time." During Addison's tenure, Britain became "the foremost diplomatic power in Europe."[42]

Near the pinnacle of British politics as a powerful secretary of state, celebrated as a literary figure across Europe, and newly married to a wealthy countess, Addison became a defender of the balanced system that his work had helped to settle. Through his pro-government writing in *The Freeholder*, he developed a firm political stance that signaled a genuine embrace of the more restrained, theatrically representational monarchy of George I and especially that promised by his son, the future George II.[43] His last play, *The Drummer*, whose first run in 1716 was presented under anonymous authorship, featured a character modeled on Homer's Odysseus, returning to England after a long absence. His name, Sir George, celebrated the happy appellation shared by both England's patron saint and its new line of Protestant kings. Read this way, the comedy's plot was an allegory for a peaceful transition to a domestic, apolitical monarchy, where the retiring George was to chase away the two warring parties vying for his wife's heart and hand, one party of which was dressing up as a ghostly Pretender in an effort to frighten and drum away the other.[44] It also, in a slightly different valence, staged a sentimental, allegorical homecoming and happy conclusion for the spiritual character of the rightful warrior-king, whose arc moves through all three of Addison's dramatic works and follows the broad career contours of the cunning General Marlborough—the important patron who had returned just after Anne's death from his Continental exile.

As a dramatic poet, Addison left behind one opera libretto, one tragedy, and one comedy. Had he lived into the age of Walpole, perhaps he would have had a farce in him. As it was, his last play finished a metatheatrical dramatic arc from gothic English opera based on a folk ballad through the high rigidity of Roman neoclassical tragedy to those two traditions' happy marriage in Englishified Greek pastoral comedy, the epic life of myths made sentimentally, regressively domestic. It glimpsed perhaps at the fantasy of a new English Orphic age in which Addison could have led an expanded Country Party from his new grand house in Kensington. But the high dream of a republic of letters developing at a moderate pace toward an expanded sociable world of reflective, privileged egalitarians had something of a wake-up call in the box office failure of his comedy, which (without Addison's name attached) could run for only three performances in his lifetime.[45] The particular milieu of domestic optimism and balance that Addison's work had helped to achieve was on the verge of being outstripped by other agendas for the progress and use of time.

CORPORATE DIVIDE

Part of the mystical concept of the king's two bodies holds that civil discord manifests as an illness inside the king's body. The corpus—political, literary, and theatrical—of Addison's work represented and helped to create a new public culture and mixed sovereignty. It effectively, incrementally challenged monarchy's divine right to supremacy over the state, the nation, and the people of Europe and the Americas. Via busy, demystified administrative and distributional efforts, Addison and his colleagues took over much of the state's center. Active across so many different spheres of society and meaning-making, Addison's moving body itself performed much of the new, more diffuse political orchestration that guided an island populace toward reformed democracy—a seriously ludic, representational politics—and proportionally away from threatening civil war over a literal king's body.

No wonder, perhaps, that Addison's final illness coincided with the return of an uglier partisan power politics in the fall and winter of 1717, when the rivalry intensified between the courts of George I and the future George II. The new royal, intergenerational, father-son conflict would structure the progress of British politics for much of the rest of the century. Rising to the top of the state, Addison had found himself, now an aristocrat, for the first time in the party of the past, working for the aged father; the modern engine of time that he had helped to set up accelerated past him. More agile, fully specialized professional politicians like Walpole and literary writers like Pope could keep pace and balance atop the newly established, spinning spheres of public life, unencumbered by Addison's neoclassically holistic breadth and philosophical bent. Proliferating magazines and specialized public personalities matched the accelerating range and speed of fashion and its dissemination of new tastes and new products throughout the post-Addisonian century.[46] The paths and tentative trails he had helped to establish turned into dedicated thoroughfares and streaming highways.

In another sense, time did not move fast enough for Addison: the bubble of sociability inside of which the world might be quickly and rationally re-negotiated burst into new partisan, dogmatic socialities and tyrannies, of many sorts. By moving forward too slowly in the direction of expansive but middling sovereignty, British politics regressed again away from philosophical inquiry and sped toward terrestrial action for its own sake, following its own momentum. In March 1718, illness forced Addison to resign his secretaryship, and he retired to his wife's "princely" estate, Holland House in Kensington, where he attempted to recuperate and work on his never-finished treatise *Of the Christian Religion*.[47] Lewis Theobald's 1713 companion biography to Addison's tragedy in a sense gave the formula: the "Celerity and Vastness" of the new order's successes forced the weary late Renaissance man and overtaxed modern state administrator, like Cato, to "shut his Eyes against the Victor, and make his Retreat to the friendly Arms of Death, *ne Tyrannum Videret;* least those sacred Opticks which were only bless'd with Scenes of [British] Liberty should be blasted with the Sight of" a market economy transforming itself into a corporate "Caesar." The age of Walpole unleashed imperial greed, and the joint-stock nation became a reckless "Inslaver."[48]

Steele had written in his 1701 *The Christian Hero* about the unsuitability of Cato as a hero, given his antisocial manner of death, which left his friends and family without the help they might have needed to endure and overcome the new age of tyranny.[49] In the last year of his life, the ailing Addison would indeed disappoint the man who had been his friend since their school days, for thirty years. One of the more famous political splits over the direction of the period's reforms turned out to be the tragic friendship-ending split between the two newspapermen who had collaborated in print roughly since Addison had Steele appointed as the government's gazetteer in 1707.[50] The politics of the feud, as I will describe, are telling enough, but a deeper consideration of the separation—as Addison the lonely but sociable individual prepared for death—suggests a background aesthetic and philosophical difference between the two that, at least from an Addisonian point of view, reveals something essential and determining about the intimate friends' differing existential perspectives on life.

Steele's essays and plays present a comedy of conscious characters perfectly melding into a new sovereign societal scene. He performed the comic imagination, an optimism that continues in the "bright" side of neoliberalism with its message of potential frictionless integration between individual drive, maximized functional productivity and achievement, and worldly, progressive social/technological reality. In *Spectator* 370, Steele wrote: "All that is done which proceeds not from a Man's very self is the Action of a Player. For this Reason it is that I make so frequent mention of the Stage: It is, with me, a Matter of the highest Consideration what Parts are well or ill performed, what Passions or Sentiments are indulged or cultivated, and consequently what Manners and Customs are transfused from the Stage to the World, which reciprocally imitate each other."[51] Both men shared an interest and several projects in using print and theater to engineer good "Manners and Customs" and emotional moderation into the populace. But Steele, while espousing a reciprocal imitation between world and theater, believed that there was a "true" performance of a role that had the observable social world as the ultimate trying ground. Addison, on the other hand, advocated a stricter Stoicism, in which the individual theater of the world, observed from the inside by the imperfectly sovereign soul, was ultimately judged by an Almighty audience interested in the performance of singular people. The external mortal context—the entire sensoriolum and the body in it—was, finally, akin to a clapboard illusion: truth and apparent social performance could not, for Addison, be made reliably agreeable.

The difference between the two friends and collaborators manifested in their strategies for the progress of politics. Steele believed principally in the necessity of a growing egalitarian scene of people of lesser means who would overwhelm the old monarchical and aristocratic structures. Addison's alternative Whig vision foresaw transcendence rather from the inside out, the Stoical assertion of individual sovereignty as the force that would cause all of society's roles to be occupied and thus changed by singularly, rationally, and faithfully acting philosopher-citizens. For Addison, the middle between the opposed, dangerous delusions of solipsism and groupthink was both ideal and existentially realistic: even Socrates sought social confirmation in his last minutes and then fell silent, becoming for his gathered friends a visual spectacle. "We should be only so *far sociable*," he had written in *Spectator* 576, "as we are reasonable Creatures." Too little independent "Singularity" like too much mental isolation led to violence, shared frenzy, and disease.[52] Addison's model of sociability emphasized the willed choice inherent in "-ability"; it put less faith in the redemptive power of purely social solutions than Steele's staging of the world did. A belief in the "good" inevitability of a certain individual reserve and unknowability matched his greater political advocacy of conserving or making a disinterested, partial sacrifice to multiple, alienated traditions of political representation—not throwing the power of sovereign decision into one flattened stage set and house.

The gulf in friendship mirrored a larger gulf that would open in British history after Addison's death, coinciding roughly with the end of silver's monetary dominance and Walpole's golden ascendance as the first prime minister. Via dueling anonymous pamphlets, Steele and Addison had an acrimonious public spat over the proposed 1719 Peerage Bill, which would have increased the membership of the House of Lords by six members and then permanently barred any new members except those inheriting the seat upon the death of another. Steele vehemently opposed the bill while Addison supported it on the side of the government. Steele believed the bill would increase the power of the House of Lords over the House of Commons. In his series of *Plebian* pamphlets, he made the case, increasingly pointed against Addison and the latter's corresponding *Old Whig* pamphlets, that supporting the Peerage Bill amounted to abandoning basic Whig principles. Addison argued that the bill provided a necessary check on the power of a (future) king, who might control another branch of government through his power to appoint new members of the House of Lords. His argument called for venerating the tradition of the House of Lords as an independently mighty part of a tri-balanced system. Steele saw in Addison a new selfishness—his old friend had just married into the aristocracy—and a betrayal of the progressive spirit. Addison saw in Steele's hopes for a watered-down peerage and increased equality between the Houses a dangerous reempowerment of the monarchy, as with Caesar's rise in Rome.[53]

The government's reform did not pass in 1719; Britain would muddle through with the constitution of balanced estates—monarchy, two separate houses of Parliament (one ancient and hereditary), the courts, and the press—that Addison had worked to politically and theatricality forge. When Addison received a string of visitors to Holland House paying their last respects, Steele was not among them. The year following his death saw the government removing Steele from his position in charge of the theater at Drury Lane as retaliation for his consequential opposition to the Peerage Bill. But the near future belonged to the social theater of his 1722 *The Conscious Lovers,* which loosely adapted the slave-turned-Roman-playwright Terence's *Andria* to celebrate young, urbane intelligence and the new networks and reformed political solutions through which proceeding generations would overcome rigid traditions and old dramatic traps. Steele staged a social world that continued to expand, a world whose complexity provided the opportunity for clever, virtuous individuals to negotiate novel contracts and sidestep anciently scripted fates through sharper, more innovative communication. Bevil Jr., one of the heroic eponymous *Conscious Lovers,* believes in his father's wisdom and goodness and sets about successfully negotiating the obstacles of a complicated love plot without ever disobeying his father or the moral rules of society.[54] It was an optimistic vision indeed from a playwright with profound sympathies for his fellow war veterans, many of whom had recently lost much of their promised government pensions in the crisis of the South Sea Bubble. Steele, however, had reason for his optimism: Walpole had rapidly ascended to high power on the basis of his effective management of that crisis and had already in 1721 reinstated Steele, his ally, as the manager of Drury Lane.[55]

The historic financial bubble that burst in the year after Addison's death had prompted Steele to write and publish his last journal, the *Theatre,* partly to take on the politicians who had removed him from office, the same who had set up the dangerous and unprecedented frenzy of stock speculation. The fictional author of that journal had been Sir John Edgar, whom Steele identified as the prefiguration of Bevil Jr.'s benevolent father—his comic "noble father" alternative to Cato.[56] Through Sir John, Steele's paper had argued that the *absolute* property rights of those who purchased the government's wartime annuities—a supposed retirement boon for veterans—could not be alienated by the new administration (and sold to the South Sea Company). Implicit in the argument was Steele's advocacy of a social sovereignty of the many against an elite, monarchical sovereignty enclosing the many. Steele's pamphlet from the same year, *A Nation a Family*, proposed a different solution for the national debt crisis: a French tontine model. In Steele's comedy of the state, the tragic paradigm of the king's two bodies could be transformed into a "nation as a family, with the King as its patriarch" and an immortal "Body Politick" divided into smaller, mortal subcollectives (tontines) of ten investors. Steele thus sanguinely imagined an egalitarian reorganization of society and the national economy on the familial scale: in John O'Brien's gloss of Steele's vision, "the political-economic becomes like the theatrical; the business of the state mirrors the business of comedy."[57] Steele's proposal, ignoring the already available hard biopolitical statistics that would have been crucial to a workable tontine design, partially masked a high-stakes class struggle through a dramaturgy of sentimental family politics: the radicalism of Cato was replaced with a fictional scene of kind, rational fathers presiding over communal living rooms, replicated cell-like across the national social body.[58]

The South Sea Company had been chartered in 1711 in anticipation of the asiento contract with Spain. Stocks in the Tory-dominated company initially performed disappointingly in spite of the company's exclusive monopoly on the supply trade to the Atlantic plantations—including the slave trade—which had been wrested from French control. But in the latter part of the decade, a policy pushed by James Craggs the Younger (Addison's successor to the secretaryship) and Craggs's father to convert government annuity debt—much of it owed to war veterans—into South Sea Company stock caused a tremendous rise in the stock's value.[59] The rapid speculative inflation and collapse in 1720 summoned forth not only Steele's responses but also a long-lasting and influential reincarnation of Addison's tragic hero as a more radical, openly militant oppositional figure. On the other side of the Whiggish middle now ghosted by the deceased Addison's still popular works, John Trenchard and Thomas Gordon's series of *Cato's Letters* often called for violent revenge against the conspiracy of the South Sea Bubble under the hallowed Roman martyr's name. When the *London Journal* series was canceled (probably because of a bribe to the editor from Walpole), *Cato's Letters* moved to the *British Journal*. There, from 1722 until 1723, its identifying header featured "the same Roman medal that had headed Addison's print editions [of *Cato*] of almost a decade before": an oppositional corporate brand.[60]

Gordon and Trenchard's Cato was an effigy for what would become libertarianism; it drew from the political radicalism of the old Addisonian hero, Milton, taking away the polite literary mask under which Addison had helped to revive Cromwell's poet laureate. Printed subsequently as a popular book, *Cato's Letters* was "widely held in the libraries of prominent families in colonial America," where Anti-Walpole/"Robinocracy" literature was devoured with a reading lust rivaled only by that for the likes of the Bible and *The Spectator*.[61] One of the first American newspapers, the *New England Courant*, which was published by Benjamin Franklin's elder brother James, began to reprint *Cato's Letters* just eleven months after their first publication in London.[62] Through Gordon and Trenchard, "Addison's hero Cato became, in the wake of the Bubble, the signal example of an individual resisting the tide of modernity."[63]

As the bourgeoisie became a ruling class through the century, eventually rivaling and supplanting the aristocracy—by revolution in America and France—the martial side of Cato's legacy was reinvigorated. Emerging within the call of emergent, modern nationalism, the militant and ultimately retiring warrior-king of Addison's imagination became the people-uniting father-general (iterated across many nations undergoing this transnational transformation.) The more fiery, resistant version of the Addisonian/Catonic spirit flamed up offshore, in places where basic feudal arrangements remained to be challenged and modern chattel slavery exported an even harsher machinery of subjugation onto foreign, racialized populations. The real-life performed incarnations of the neoclassical father-general specialized in ambiguously leading both masses and volunteer bands of heads of households. The masses fought for basic freedom, livelihoods, equality, an escape from the long norm of cruel oppression. Under the same abstract flags, the bourgeois revolutionaries fought in part for the privacy and liberty of their own sentimental domestic empires: after the fight, following the ideal of Cincinnatus and Cato the Elder, they planned to return to their little free sociable fiefdoms to representatively farm and collect their pensions—if only realpolitik bankers like Alexander Hamilton and Jacques Laffitte could save their retirement investments from financial devastations like the South Sea Bubble. There again Addison was avant-garde: his last surviving letter—nine days before his death, when his only child, Charlotte, was five months old—was a plea to allow his wife to collect any South Sea Company stocks in his name.[64]

Seven days after his death, the government's victory at the Battle of Glen Shiel ended the Spanish-backed Jacobite Rebellion. A certain ghost of the previous century's civil war dissolved with the end of Addison's hard-working life.

More quietly, a Pax Addisonia would extend, domestically, through the next centuries, even as the retooled machine of partisanship began to roar in the age of Walpole. Theater continued strongly, but the dawning *literary* age was that of the popular novel: Defoe's *Robinson Crusoe* washed up on the banks of the Thames almost simultaneously with Addison's death. In 1720, Sarah Churchill had the ruins of the old palace at Woodstock, which Vanbrugh had preserved and *Rosamond* celebrated, knocked down. Pope would soon be satirically labeling George II an usurping tyrant (in his *Epistle to Augustus*) and lampooning Addison (in his *Epistle to Dr. Arbuthnot*) as Atticus, an admirable writer but petty tyrant of the former literary regime.[65] As the fast-moving politics churned, the opposition would soon be turning to the court of George II's eldest son, Frederick, for a symbolically collective body on which to pin hopes for a better future.[66]

Authors have a quadruple body: one human double-body like the king's double-body, oscillating between the community of readers they come to represent and the writing individual's idiosyncratic mortal life; the other a textual mirror of the twofold human first, the public writings and the private. Most of Addison's private papers disappeared around the time of his death—destroyed by his widow, his daughter, or himself—but Addison's *body politic* grew in proportion to the broken boundaries of his deceased *body natural*.[67] The missing private letters leave an emptiness inside the project of public Enlightenment that echoes: as readers of the author, we mistake what was performed theatrically for what it was like to be.

That famous process of the author's oeuvre claiming a life and even counter-life of its own had started, of course, while he still lived—one measure of the impact he had on his culture. In parallel with the March–May 1716 revival of *Cato* at Drury Lane, for instance, the "Tory" theater—Lincoln's Inn Field—had produced François Deschamps's version of *Cato*, in John Ozell's English translation. Though Deschamps's play features some strongly republican and anti-monarchical sentiments voiced by Cato, the staging of the French tragedy in its English context played to Jacobite sympathies. Cato's daughter, Portia, is sworn at the end of the play to go into exile in Spain (the Stuart Pretender's strongest military backer at that time) and do everything she can to bring down the unjustly ruling Caesar. The published version featured a comparison of the two Cato plays—dedicated to "an English Nobleman, now residing at Paris"[68]—which concludes that the French version is more historically accurate and aesthetically superior.[69] (If only the rightful succession of kings could have been determined by such critical criteria, the noble English expat in Paris would have been undoubtedly more gratified.)

Even *The Drummer* enjoyed a relatively high success when it was published and produced posthumously, Addison's name now attached. The next decades saw it performed frequently, and nine English editions, two French and two German adaptations, as well as an Italian paraphrase of the French, were published by 1800.[70] But it was the afterlife of Mr. Spectator and *Cato* that helped to inspire and give form to the political passions behind many of the larger-scale European and American movements of the Enlightenment. *The Spectator* became international Enlightenment scripture; the enormous volume of versions printed, translated, and imitated for the next two centuries across Europe and the Americas were read and cited as "bibles of enlightened behaviour."[71] Samuel Johnson—whose life from his earliest school days in Addison's hometown exhibits what Robert DeMaria Jr. has called a certain "rota Addisoniana"—several times credited Addison's periodicals as the origin of the content and polite style of modern conversation. Having inherited the papers of the latter's very preliminary unfinished dictionary project, Johnson's own landmark dictionary used approximately 4600 quotes from Addison works, at least one appearing on most of its pages.[72] In 1776, when reprinting *The Spectator* was a highly competitive, profitable enterprise, Samuel Johnson wrote in an advertisement for a new edition: "The book thus offered to the public is too well known to be praised: it comprizes precepts of criticism, sallies of invention, descriptions of life, and lectures of virtue: it employs wit in the cause of truth, and makes elegance subservient to piety: it has now for more than half a century supplied the English nation, in a great measure, with principles of speculation, and rules of practice; and given Addison a claim to be numbered among the benefactors of mankind."[73]

According to Claire Boulard-Jouslin, "The influence Addison exerted on the great Enlightenment thinkers [in France] seems to have been concealed" through a lack of citation, even when his work was directly translated in their published work, perhaps "indicating the normative power of his opinions among the *philosophes*."[74] In spite (or probably often because) of his writings' heavy critiques of Louis XIV and certain aspects of French culture, Addison himself enjoyed a high reputation across the channel as a philosophe. His popularity there stretched well into the nineteenth century, and all of the major writers of the French Enlightenment (including Montesquieu, Voltaire, Rousseau, Marivaux, and Diderot) owned his books in translation or in English originals.[75] Echoing Voltaire's high accolades (quoted in the previous chapter), the Chevalier de Jaucourt wrote in the *Encyclopédie* that Addison's "Cato is the greatest dramatic character, and his play is the most beautiful that has ever been staged. It is a masterpiece of regularity, elegance, poetry and noble sentiments."[76]

On the two dimensions of the page, Addison the essayist was Enlightenment chapter and verse, but it was his Cato who ultimately carried the performative Gestus of revolutionary eighteenth-century ardor. As De Tocqueville would later reflect: "When the revolution that changed the social and political state of an aristocratic people begins to make itself felt in literature, it is generally in the theater that it is first produced, and it is there that it always remains visible. The spectator of a dramatic work is in a way taken unprepared by the impression that is suggested to him. He does not have time to search his memory or to consult experts; he does not think about fighting the new literary instincts that are beginning to emerge in him; he yields to them before knowing them."[77] *Cato* functioned historically as a metatragedy for the aristocratic, tragic theater. It inspired parody (e.g., John Gay's *The What D'ye Call It*) and many imitative neoclassical plays, but few of the latter had any success: by imitating, they missed the metatheatrical point of the passion itself, of a paradigm and genre of history cracking. An admiring critic of Addison's play wrote:

> But *Cato* itself has increased the Evils of the present Time: how many Poetasters have since then infested the World with wild Notions of Liberty and Patriotism! What strange romantick Whims have they had of Freedom, and Independency from Power! As if, as Mr. *Dryden* says,
>
>> They led their wild Desires to Rocks and Caves,
>> And thought that all, but Savages, were Slaves.[78]

Steele's prologue (discussed earlier) at the opening of the 1714 theatrical season confessed that the fighting of Greeks and Romans staged by public Whigs was intended as a prelude to an age when those theater-makers would more directly and boldly act in the arenas of power.

De Tocqueville observed that "democratic peoples have only very mediocre esteem for learning, and they scarcely care about what happened in Rome and in Athens; they mean for you to talk about themselves, and they ask for the present to be portrayed."[79] The applause at *Cato's* premiere and its subsequent political life outside the theater proper marked in this sense a vulgarization of classical theatrical allegory—the clothing of allegory became newspaper thin along with the mystical *Dignitas* of aristocracy. (Opera performed the counterreaction.) Dipping the Roman Republic's grand martyr and schoolchildren's conscience into the new expansive theatrical commons shepherded together by Mr. Spectator, Addison knew—as he professed in *Spectator* 463—that "the Weight of Natural Parts" is "much heavier than that of Learning," that, in his quote of an old Scottish saying, "an Ounce of Mother is worth a Pound of Clergy." Never one for zero-sum agon, his formula with *Cato* was synthetic and hermaphroditic: he saw in a dream that the "Conjunction" of "Natural Parts" and "Learning," through a magical bit of Newtonian neoclassical physics, would increase both their weights disproportionally.[80] Cato was resurrected as an essential modern folk hero.

Parallel to its presence in extratheatrical cultural and political life, Addison's tragedy was read widely and "consistently performed in every theatrical season from 1713 to 1750." In the 1730s, such performances were often funded and staged as blatant attacks on Britain's first prime minister, Walpole, and his domineering machinations.[81] Mid-century translations and productions flourished alongside *Spectator* reprints and imitations throughout Europe and the Americas.[82] For the generation that would be the fathers and grandfathers of democratic revolution, as for Voltaire, Addison's was a first kind of well-designed "regular" theater, worthy as a starting place from which to learn how to make new, appropriate modern drama over and through Newtonian gulfs.[83] Voltaire even claimed that his *Socrates* (published using a pseudonym in 1759) was merely a translation of a manuscript that had started as Addison's incomplete Socrates tragedy—the highest unrealized ambition of the deceased author.[84]

Notes

Introduction

1. Westminster Abbey, "Joseph Addison." As an "ornament of Britain," Addison provided one of the early molds of modern celebrity, which, Joseph Roach argues, emerges "out of the energy released by the transformation of a utensil into an accessory." Roach, *It*, 43.

2. General George Monck (the Duke of Albemarle) played a large role in effecting the "blood-free" Restoration of Charles II, ending an era of large-scale civil violence.

3. Westminster Abbey, "Joseph Addison."

4. Tickell, "To the Earl of Warwick," xv.

5. Tickell, xiii.

6. Klein, "Joseph Addison's Whiggism," 121–24; *Spectator* 26: Addison and Steele, *Spectator*, 1:108–11. (References to *The Spectator* are hereafter to this edition.) Addison's statue memorial was paid for by a bequeath from his sister and heir, Dorothy. Westminster Abbey, "Joseph Addison."

7. Klein, "Joseph Addison's Whiggism," 124.

8. Klein, "Addisonian Afterlives," 105–6.

9. Defoe, *Robinson Crusoe*, 4.

10. Klein, "Addisonian Afterlives," 101, 112.

11. For Voltaire, see chapters 6 and 7; Franklin, *Autobiography*, 12; and Heavilin, "Love for Joseph Addison," 39–54.

12. Miller, "Strange Career of Joseph Addison," 656–57; Orr, *British Enlightenment Theatre*, 27–30.

13. Axelsson, *Political Aesthetics*, 9–10, 241.

14. Habermas, *Structural Transformation*, xvii.

15. Smithers, *Life of Joseph Addison*, 270

16. Due to their circulation within coffeehouses, it is likely that many daily copies were read by more than one person. Addison estimated that an average of twenty people read each copy. Cowan, *Social Life of Coffee*, 230.

17. Boulard-Jouslin, "Introduction," 18–19. The most complete and current database of imitative European "Moral Weeklies" is maintained by Klaus-Dieter Ertler, Alexandra Fuchs, and Michaela Fischer at the University of Graz: Moralische Wochenschriften-GAMS, http://gams.uni-graz.at/context:mws/sdef:Context/get?mode=&locale=en.

18. D. Hume, "Of the Protestant Succession," in *Selected Essays*, 297.

19. For the archival records of Addison's political work, see Alsop, "New Light on Joseph Addison," 13–34.

20. Courthope, *Addison*, 4.

21. Abrams, *Doing Things with Texts*, 17–19, 63, 138–39.

22. In one of his final essays, James A. Winn brought to the foreground clues suggesting that Addison may have enjoyed a necessarily secret same-sex love life and thus may belong to history's important cadre of covertly queer writers. Winn, "More Sensual Delights," 138–41. My own study of Addison's work and life led me to similar speculative conclusions, which lend a different inflection to many of Addison's writings.

23. Davis, "Introduction," 13.

24. For an excellent very recent exploration of Addison and his legacy, which came out only in the last stages of this book's revision, see Davis, *Joseph Addison*.

25. Young, *Conjectures on Original Composition*, 48–49.

26. Roach, *It*, 13.

27. Saintsbury, *Peace of the Augustans*, 39; Orr, *British Enlightenment Theatre*, 7–8.

28. Orr, 15, 26–27.

29. Nevalainen and Tissari, "Contextualising Eighteenth-Century Politeness," 136.

30. Mackie, *Rakes, Highwaymen, and Pirates*, 10.

31. Knights, *Devil in Disguise*, 141; Nevalainen and Tissari, "Contextualising Eighteenth-Century Politeness," 136.

32. Klein, "Joseph Addison's Whiggism," 117.

33. Henderson, "On Bourgeois Dignity," 281.

34. Klein, *Shaftesbury and the Culture of Politeness*, 2, 36–37. Axelsson, *Political Aesthetics*, 27–30.

35. Klein, 13; also 9, 12.

36. Klein, 41.

37. Rancière, *Politics of Aesthetics*, 40.

38. *Spectator* 447, 4:71.

39. McKendrick, Brewer, and Plumb, *Birth of a Consumer Society*, 1–2, 9–12.

40. McKendrick, Brewer, and Plumb, 13–16, 19–24.

41. McKendrick, Brewer, and Plumb, 29.

42. McKendrick, Brewer, and Plumb, 269.

43. The standard work on this topic (discussed in subsequent chapters) is Mackie, *Market à la Mode*.

44. Habermas, *Structural Transformation*, 19.

45. McKeon, *Secret History of Domesticity*, 359–60.

46. Bowers, "Universalizing Sociability," 151.

47. Boileau was a hero, and it was reported that Addison frequently consulted Bayle's Dictionary. Bayle was also the force behind *Nouvelles de la République des Lettres*, one of the first journals to practice literary criticism. *Addisoniana*, 1:207; Ertler, "Addison, Lecteur de Bayle."

48. Voltaire, *Letters Concerning the English Nation*, 109–11.

49. Voltaire, 143.

50. For the polyvalent general crisis of authority after the Thirty Years' War, related

Newtonian laws and figures of abstract, universal mechanics replacing anthropomorphic figures, see Sheehan, *Balance of Power*, 43–48.

51. Barbauld, *Selections*, 1:xxx; quoted in Klein, "Addisonian Afterlives," 113.

52. Davis, "Addison's Forgotten Poetic Response," 267.

53. Sennett, *Authority*, 81–85.

54. Young, *Conjectures on Original Composition*, 42.

55. Montaigne, "The Author to the Reader," in *Essays*, 12. The *Oxford English Dictionary* credits Addison's first usage of "egotism" and accompanying etymological explanation in *Spectator* 562.

56. Smith, *Empiricist Devotions*, 133, 186.

57. Addison, "An Essay on Virgil's Georgics," in *Works*, 1:156; Smith, *Empiricist Devotions*, 186. Addison's identification with Virgil was the subject of many contemporary compliments: Tickell, for instance, called him the "British Virgil" in *Spectator* 532, in "Verses to the Author" in the seventh edition of *Cato*, and in a prologue for a performance of *Cato* at Oxford in 1713. Fitzmaurice, "Coalitions, Networks, and Discourse Communities," 114n9.

58. *Spectator* 41; discussed in Zwierlein, "Grace in Deformity," 63–67.

59. Addison, *Discourse on Ancient and Modern Learning*, 14. On the text's provenance, see Broadus, "Addison's Discourse," 1.

60. Addison, 21.

61. Bloom and Bloom, *Joseph Addison's Sociable Animal*, 8.

62. Bloom and Bloom, xi.

63. See, for instance, *Spectator* 10 and 447 in *Spectator*, 1:44–46 and 4:70–73. For the relation of Addison and his contemporaries to the celebration of husbandry in Virgil's *Georgics*, see Smith, *Empiricist Devotions*, 31, 175, 184. Addison, "Essay on Virgil's Georgics," in *Works*, 1:154–61.

64. Klein, "Addisonian Afterlives," 105.

65. Macaulay, "Life and Writings of Addison," 610.

66. Smithers, *Life*, 468.

67. Johnson, "Addison," 36, 38. The twenty-first-century performative paradigm: Jon McKenzie, *Perform or Else*, 171, 176. On performance's ontological disappearance, see Phelan, *Unmarked*, 146.

68. Johnson, "Addison," 36–37.

69. Johnson, 20.

70. Courthope, *Addison*, 4, 153–54.

71. Johnson, "Addison," 38.

72. On the illusionary "effortlessness" of Addison's prose, see Parker, "Addison's Modesty," 180.

73. For Addison's punning play on the visually polished and the polite, see Winn, "More Sensual Delights," 123.

74. Addison, *Discourse on Ancient and Modern Learning*, 27–28.

75. Jost, *Prose Immortality*, 56–60.

76. *Spectator* 166, 2:154–55. See Jost, *Prose Immortality*, 63–65.

77. Power, "Coins and Circulation," 80, 89, 94; Ellis, "Time and the Essay," 100.

On *The Spectator*'s marked dailyness as constructing a new genre of literature and new modes of communal reading, see Jost, *Prose Immortality*, 44–46, 56–65.

78. Addison, *Discourse on Ancient and Modern Learning*, 10.
79. Smithers, *Life*, 11.
80. Courthope, *Addison*, 7.
81. Smithers, *Life*, 218.
82. Alexander Chalmers, *The British Essayists*, 2nd ed., vols. 6, 10 (London: n.p., 1817); quoted in Klein, "Addisonian Afterlives," 104.
83. Ellis, "Time and the Essay," 107–9.
84. Habermas, *Structural Transformation*, 43, 32. For overviews of Habermas's project and its differing critical receptions, see Ellis, *Eighteenth-Century Coffee-House Culture*, 1:xii–vii; Knights, *Representation and Misrepresentation*, 48–53; and Ridout, *Scenes from Bourgeois Life*, 79–85.
85. *Spectator* 464 and 574, 4:139, 563; Mackie, *Commerce of Everyday Life*, 5–10.
86. Miller, "Strange Career," 655. For Addison's construction of middling orders and public opinion, see Axelsson, *Political Aesthetics*, 20–21.
87. Wollstonecraft, *Vindication of the Rights of Woman*, 11.
88. Historians generally agree that a "tripartite" division of English society into something like "lower," "middling," and "upper" sorts of people was evident to many people in the seventeenth century and afterward, but that the stable (self-)identification of people belonging to a "middle class" did not really emerge until the nineteenth century. Who the "middling sort" were is notoriously difficult to define, especially when one moves between urban and provincial environments and across time and rhetorical interests. Since my focus here is mainly on emerging, eighteenth-century national and international democratic culture and politics, I use a broad understanding of who could be "sorted" as "middling"—roughly including anyone below aristocratic rank who could acquire enough material resources to potentially enter broad networks of trade for their own profit. For fuller discussions and overviews on the challenge of defining a historical middling class, see French, *Middle Sort of People*, 1–29; and Barry, "Introduction."
89. Habermas, *Structural Transformation*, 36–37.
90. Gadamer, *Truth and Method*, 1975, 34; cited in Habermas, 252n17.
91. Ellis, "Sociability and Polite Improvement,"146.
92. Ellis, "Coffee-Women," 31; Ellis, "Sociability and Polite Improvement," 151; Klein, "Coffeehouse Civility." For a succinct discussion of the varying, critical historiography of the English coffeehouse, see Ellis, *Eighteenth-Century Coffee-House Culture*, 1:xi–xxxi.
93. Mackie, *Market à La Mode*, 14, 18–25; Cowan, *Social Life of Coffee*, 236, 256, 260.
94. Klein, *Shaftesbury*, 13.
95. Habermas, *Structural Transformation*, 33. For the classic feminist critique of Habermas in this regard, see Fraser, "Rethinking the Public Sphere"; and Fraser, "What's Critical." For the "exceptional" status of the female coffeehouse "Idol" and barmaid, see Clery, *Feminization Debate*, 21–25.
96. Roach, *Cities of the Dead*, 17.
97. Ridout, *Scenes from Bourgeois Life*, 119–20; Bond, "First Printing."

98. Shevelow, *Women and Print Culture*, 140–41.
99. Clery, *Feminization Debate*, 45–46.
100. Habermas, *Structural Transformation*, 37–38.
101. Puchner, *Drama of Ideas*, 26–30.
102. "Berkeley to Percival March 27 1712/13," in Rand, *Berkeley and Percival*, 111.
103. Johnson, "Addison," 19.
104. Habermas, *Structural Transformation*, 17, 38; Siebert, "Authoritarian Theory of the Press," 20. Tonson was called the "chief merchant of the muses" and pursued a strategy of making classics out of the literary works to which he held exclusive printing rights under the Copyright Act. His partner and nephew, Jacob Tonson Jr., purchased the copyright to *The Spectator* around 1713, adding Addison and Steele's journal to a list that included the works of Shakespeare, Milton, Dryden, and Congreve. Brewer, *Pleasures of the Imagination*, 382.
105. Habermas, 25–26. The international impact of Addison's work will be discussed in subsequent chapters. Much work remains to be done on Addison's global impact in the eighteenth and nineteenth centuries. For *The Spectator* as a transnationally model periodical and discourse-starter, see Ertler et al., *Storytelling*; Doms, *"Spectator"-Type Periodicals*.
106. Miller, "Strange Career," 651.
107. Mackie, *Commerce of Everyday Life*, 14; see also 1–5.
108. Genovese, *Problem of Profit*, 11–12.
109. Powell, *Performing Authorship*, 46. See also O'Byrne, "Spectator and the Rise of the Modern Metropole."
110. Clery, *Feminization Debate*, 44.
111. See, for instance, *Spectator* 465, discussed in the context of Addison's discursive engagement with Jesuit meditation practices in Szécsényi, "Jesuit Thread in Joseph Addison's Aesthetics," 60–62.
112. Ellison, *Cato's Tears*, 170.
113. Engell, *Creative Imagination*, 36.
114. Ogée, "Nature and Imagination," 273.
115. Cahill, *Liberty of the Imagination*, 72.
116. Ogée, "Nature and Imagination," 274.
117. McKeon, *Secret History of Domesticity*, 379.
118. Arendt, *Origins of Totalitarianism*, 473.
119. Baudot, "Joseph Addison's Lucretian Imagination," 899; Anderson, *Imagined Communities*; Smith, *Nation Made Real*.
120. Engell, *Creative Imagination*, 3.
121. William Walker, "Ideology and Addison's Essays," 82.
122. Womersley, "Introduction," *Cultures of Whiggism*, 15.
123. Council, "O Dea Certe," 341.

1. Addison the Ancient Author

1. Smithers, *Life*, 242, 278.
2. Shelley, *Complete Poetry*, 326.

3. Cibber, *Apology,* 208–9.

4. Addison, *Discourse on Ancient and Modern Learning,* 2.

5. Addison, *Freeholder* 45, 258–59; emphasis in original.

6. Pope, "First Epistle of the Second Book of Horace Imitated: To Augustus," ll. 216–20, in *Major Works,* 279. It is quite possible, of course, to read a sardonic double meaning in Pope's eulogistic verses that would satirize Addison as an empty artificer of his own "natural" public: a stuffed and moulded audience anticipating the Prince's beloved puppet in Goethe's *Der Triumph der Empfindsamkeit.* In this vein, the passage might also playfully allude to Addison's relation to his publisher Jacob Tonson, for whom he likely acquired a very special kind of white paper as well as a censored book with a risqué Hermaphrodite plate in Amsterdam in 1703. Junqua, "Moment in Amsterdam."

7. Addison, *Discourse on Ancient and Modern Learning,* 22.

8. Young, "Addison and the Victorians," 316.

9. Smithers, *Life,* 270

10. Addison, *Works,* 1:81–82.

11. Addison, 1:82; Williams, *Drama in a Dramatised Society.*

12. *Spectator* 10, 1:44–45. The title of the French translation of *The Spectator* is one indication of Addison's success: *Le Spectateur ou le Socrate moderne* was published in six volumes from 1714 to 1726.

13. *Spectator* 10, 1:44–46.

14. McKendrick, Brewer, and Plumb, *Birth of Consumer Society,* 269.

15. Parker, "Addison's Modesty," 178.

16. Cicero, *Tuscalan Disputations,* trans. J. E. King, Loeb Classical Library, 5.4.10, 434–35 (New York: G. P. Putnam's Sons, 1927); quoted in Klein, *Shaftesbury,* 42.

17. Mackie, *Market á la Mode,* 2.

18. Power, "Coins and Circulation," 80, 89, 94.

19. Addison, *Works,* 1:22–27. See Terry, *Poetry,* 50–51, 289–90.

20. Addison, *Discourse on Ancient and Modern Learning,* 13.

21. Addison, 23.

22. Ridout, *Scenes from Bourgeois Life,* 58–61.

23. McKendrick, Brewer, and Plumb, *Birth of a Consumer Society,* 13–16; Mackie, *Market á la Mode,* 2.

24. For Addison's affinity to Horace, see Haan, "Twin Augustans," 338–39. On Addison's "double principle" linking literary pleasure, learning, and the act of comparison, see Walsh, "Addison as Critic," 109–10. For a standard historical overview of the shifting relation between theatricality and the expanding market in the period, see Agnew, *Worlds Apart.*

25. Ridout, *Scenes from Bourgeois Life,* 74–75, 92–93. See also Powell, 209–10. On the general importance of modest irony (and self-irony) in Addison's work and its professed ambitions, see Parker, "Addison's Modesty," 179–80.

26. *Spectator* 555, 4:492.

27. *Spectator* 1, 1:1.

28. Montaigne, *Essays,* 12. For a discussion of race and Addison's ambiguous use of the description "black" here and elsewhere, see chapter 3 and Ridout, *Scenes from Bourgeois Life,* 111–13.

29. *Spectator* 1, 1:5.

30. Sherman, *Telling Time*, 113–15. Sherman reads the uncanny silence of the Spectator in terms of the daily paper as a turned inside-out publicly performed diary: "Mr. Spectator is the first figure, real or feigned, to appear in print day by day, and is also the first print *eidolon* to define his whole character in terms of an obsessively cultivated privacy about his own experience."

31. Black, "Social and Literary Form."

32. For an admirable analysis of Addison's translation of the Actaeon passage, see Hopkins, "Addison as Translator," 36–39.

33. Davis, "Was Addison a Poet?," 63.

34. "The Round Table No. 2" (8 January 1815), 27; quoted in Dart, "Addison and the Romantics," 291.

35. Dart, 293.

36. Miller, "Whig Interpretation," 61, 63, 75–76.

37. Young, "Addison and the Victorians"; DeMaria "Addison, Samuel Johnson, and the Test of Time," 270–71. Young provides an important reevaluation of Aikin's biography (322–27).

38. Miller, "Strange Career of Joseph Addison," 660.

39. Davis, "Introduction," 17.

40. McCrea, *Addison and Steele*; Miller, "Strange Career," 651.

41. Eliot, *Use of Poetry*, 59.

42. Eliot, 62; Pope, "Epistle to Dr Arbuthnot," ll. 192–214, in Pope, *Major Works*, 343.

43. Eliot, "Metaphysical Poets," 288–89.

44. The ambivalence of the literary Modernist *Vatermord* lies in its reluctance to name the father as father (e.g., Addison as progenitor) and thus to take up the father's enemies and challenges as likely overlapping with the descendant's own. Through the childish fantasy of rejecting the literary predecessor as one's actual progenitor (acted out as vehemently dismissive critique), the Modernist writer acts out what is likely more derived from a childish fear of the literary father's weaknesses in the face of a common enemy than it is from an adult fear of the literary father himself as an enemy rather than a potential distant ally.

45. Joyce, *Portrait of the Artist*, 130–31.

46. *Spectator* 225, 2:375–76.

47. Davis, "Was Addison a Poet?," 61–79.

48. *Spectator* 225, 2:376.

49. *Spectator* 225, 2:375.

50. Aikin, for instance, treated Addison's religious sensibility seriously; see Young, "Addison and the Victorians," 326–27. For the importance of Addison's sincere faith to his reception in the French Enlightenment, see Boulard-Jouslin, "Addison and France," 248–49.

51. *Spectator* 39, 3:495.

52. *Spectator* 39, 1:164–65.

53. *Spectator* 39, 1:165.

54. Ellison, *Cato's Tears*, 4–9.

55. *Spectator* 40, 1:169.
56. Axelsson, *Political Aesthetics*, 4.
57. McCrea, *Addison and Steele*, 30.
58. McCrea, 27–28.
59. Womersley, "Introduction," *Cultures of Whiggism*, 12.
60. Lewis, "Addison," 164–65.
61. Lewis, 165–66.
62. Lewis, 154–55.
63. *Round Table*, no. 32 (3 March 1816), 143; quoted in Dart, "Addison and the Romantics," 301.
64. Dart, 304.
65. Orr, *British Enlightenment Theatre*, 31–32; Broadus, "Addison's Influence," 123–34.
66. Addison, *Discourse on Ancient and Modern Learning*, 24.
67. Miller, "Strange Career," 657.
68. Macaulay, "Life and Writings," 613.
69. Lewis, "Addison," 166–67.
70. *Spectator* 464, 4:139; emphasis in original.
71. *Spectator* 464, 4:139.
72. Lewis, "Addison," 161.
73. Parker, "Addison's Modesty," 165–66.
74. Courthope, *Addison*, 156.
75. Lewis, "Addison," 168.
76. Miller, "Strange Career," 652.
77. Klein, "Joseph Addison's Whiggism," 113.
78. Womersley, "Introduction," *Cultures of Whiggism*, 19.
79. Henry Butterfield's *The Whig Interpretation of History* (1931) is discussed in Miller, "Whig Interpretation," 66.
80. Womersley, "Introduction," *Cultures of Whiggism*, 11.
81. Addison, *Discourse on Ancient and Modern Learning*, 13–14.
82. Womersley, "Introduction," *Augustan Critical Writing*, xi–xiv. See also Womersley, "Introduction," *Cultures of Whiggism*, 11.
83. Womersley, "Introduction," *Augustan Critical Writing*, xviii.
84. Womersley, "Introduction," *Cultures of Whiggism*, 11.
85. Addison, *Discourse on Ancient and Modern Learning*, 8.
86. Womersley, "Introduction," *Cultures of Whiggism*, 11.
87. Axelsson, *Political Aesthetics*, 35–142.
88. Rounce, "Akenside's Clamors," 228.
89. Womersley, "Introduction," *Cultures of Whiggism*, 20.
90. Miller, "Strange Career," 657.
91. Axelsson, *Political Aesthetics*, 15.
92. Womersley, "Introduction," 20.
93. Wollstonecraft, *Vindication of the Rights of Woman*, 24.
94. See Steele's 1720 pamphlet *A Nation A Family*, discussed in chapter 7.
95. Lewis, "Addison," 167.

96. For the two versions of "What the Bird Said Early in the Year," see Lindskoog, "Carved in Stone."

97. The Whig John Dunton's twice-weekly *Athenian Mercury* printed questions from readers with anonymous answers, offering women the first "open platform for voicing their views and experiences": Clery, *Feminization Debate*, 29, 26–50 passim, particularly 43–44 in reference to *The Spectator;* Shevelow, *Women and Print Culture*, 58–92. On the *Female Tatler*, see Ellis, "Sociability and Polite Improvement," 156–57.

98. Clery, *Feminization Debate*, 44.

99. Wilson, *Race of Female Patriots*, 3–4, 1–9 passim.

100. Prescott, *Women, Authorship, and Literary Culture*, 142, 141–86 passim; Prager, "Elizabeth Singer Rowe"; Clery, *Feminization Debate*, 32–41, 46–49.

101. Mackie, *Market à la Mode*, 3.

102. Shevelow, *Women and Print Culture*, 140–41, 3, 52.

103. Shevelow, 135.

104. Shevelow, 1.

105. Shevelow, 141. In *Spectator* 15, Addison presents the contrast starkly in the virtuously ideal Aurelia and the satirically frivolous Fulvia; see Shevelow, 137–40.

106. Clery, *Feminization Debate*, 45–46.

107. McKeon, *Secret History of Domesticity*, 169–70. For *The Spectator*'s role in constructing a "polarized separation of spheres: public/social masculine versus private/familiar/feminine" and women as "angels in the house," see Mackie, *Commerce of Everyday Life*, 19.

108. *Spectator* 10, 1:46. Such sexist depictions have encouraged the perpetuation of the historical fallacy of real "separate spheres" for women and men in line with the ideological "domesticization" project discussed above. For recent work debunking this fallacy and analyzing the rhetoric that goes on producing it, see Chico, *Designing Women*, 36–38; and Backscheider and Dykstal, *Intersections of the Public and Private Spheres*.

109. Shevelow, *Women and Print Culture*, 56.

110. Smithers, *Life*, 365.

111. *Spectator* 10, 1:46.

112. Mackie, *Market à la Mode*, 76–79, 189–93.

113. Mackie, 192. For queer identities in the period, see O'Driscoll, "Molly and the Fop." Addison's naturalization of binary, sexual difference included his critique of a "narcissistic" fondness between women and "fancy men," as well as blaming aberrations in gender expressions on "feminine lapse." Mackie, 187–89, 201–2.

114. *Spectator* 34, 1:142. Mackie, *Market à la Mode*, 193.

115. Young, "Addison and the Victorians," 325.

116. *Spectator* 81, 1:349.

117. Wilson, *Race of Female Patriots*, 7–9; Marsden, *Fatal Desire*, 169–71.

118. Janet Todd, *Sensibility: An Introduction* (London: Methuen, 1986, 20); quoted in Shevelow, *Women and Print Culture*, 145; Knights, *Representation and Misrepresentation*, 140–42. See *Freeholder* 32, 181–85.

119. For Addison's construction of a graceful feminine ideal combining "women's physical and intellectual beauty," see Chico, *Designing Women*, 198.

120. King, *Gendering of Men*, 223.

121. Nussbaum, "Unaccountable Pleasure of Eighteenth-Century Tragedy."
122. Young, "Addison and the Victorians," 308–16.
123. Woolf, *Orlando*.
124. Woolf, *Common Reader*, 139–40.
125. Woolf, 11; Janes, "Femicons," 124.
126. Woolf, 140.
127. Woolf, 141.
128. For fashion in *The Spectator* as a crucial site of anxious, critical negotiation between individuals living through a rapid process of intensified commercialization and the "naturalization of the market and the rationalization of capitalism," see Mackie, *Market à la Mode*, 30, 76–79.
129. *Spectator* 435, 4:27.
130. Chico, *Designing Women*, 106, 113.
131. Spence, *Observations*, 1:80; discussed in Winn, "More Sensual Delights," 138–41. For one example demonstrating the threatening environment for "queer" sexuality at the time, see Defoe (1707) arguing that sodomy trials should remain secret in order to avoid inadvertently encouraging the crime (Norton, "Daniel Defoe").
132. Addison, *Drummer*, 4.1, 29–30.
133. The young hero's name is, of course, already a merger of his two parents' names: Hermes (Zeus's divine messenger) and Aphrodite (the goddess of beauty). *Spectator*, 1:27n1; Addison, *Works*, 1:139.
134. *Spectator* 435, 4:28–29.
135. The "Cavalier" style was associated strongly with royalists and the Stuart courts of Charles II, the exiled James II, and (at the time of Addison's writing) his son, James III, known as "the Pretender."
136. *Spectator* 435, 4:28–29.
137. Woolf, *Common Reader*, 145.
138. Woolf, 150.
139. Woolf, 145–46.
140. Addison and Steele, *Tatler* 153, 2:359. (Subsequent references to *The Tatler* are to this edition.)
141. Woolf, *Common Reader*, 147–48.
142. Woolf, 142.
143. Addison, *Discourse on Ancient and Modern Learning*, 1–2.
144. Woolf, *Common Reader*, 141.
145. Woolf, 151.
146. Cibber, *Apology*, 272.
147. *Tatler* 249, 3:269–73. For an analysis of Addison's identification with the shilling in this prototypical "it-narrative," see Smith, *Empiricist Devotions*, 129–35; and Power, "Coins and Circulation," 92.

2. Everyday Prose after Newton

1. Elkanah Settle's spectacular heroic play *The Empress of Morocco* (1673) was based on this work. Orr, *Empire on the English Stage*, 99–103.

2. Kohler, "Addison, Lancelot," 189. Kohler wrote that, in spite of Lancelot's bias toward his own creed, and even though seventeenth-century England had a very small Jewish population, "it must be conceded that his work exhibited a liberality of view and a keenness of perception not often encountered at that time." For Joseph's positive portrayal of Jews and Jewish life, see Miller, "Strange Career," 655–56.

3. Champion, *Pillars of Priestcraft*, 115–16.

4. Rob Iliffe and Scott Mandelbrote, editors, "Books in Newton's Library," The Newton Project (Oxford University, 2017), http://www.newtonproject.ox.ac.uk/his-library/books-in-newtons-library, compiled chiefly from John Harrison, *The Library of Isaac Newton* (Cambridge: Cambridge University Press, 1978.)

5. Haan, *Vergilius Redivivus*, 3.

6. Davis, "Misguided by the Tuneful Throng," 88–89; Smithers, *Life*, 42, 54–55, 79–81, 89–90, 104–7. In a letter to his father's direct superior at Lichfield, Addison reported on his private meetings with two towering intellects in Paris: Malebranche spoke about his theory of colors (in contrast to those of Descartes and Newton), and Boileau praised Corneille (for his invention of admiration as a passion appropriate to tragedy) and Homer (for his depiction of Ulysses's character through showing rather than telling.) "21. To Dr. John Hough, Bishop of Lichfield (29 November 1700)," in Addison, *Letters*, 25–26. He met Newton's rival, Leibniz, during the time when the latter was writing his *New Essays on Human Understanding*, a rebuttal of John Locke's *Essay*.

7. Ayres, *Classical Culture*, 1. For the networks of Whig patronage, linking aristocrats to poets and Tonson, the printer, see Williams, "Patronage and Whig Literary Culture," 149–72. Alexander Pope, Addison's contemporary and sometime friend, was one of the first "professional" writers to successfully make a living almost exclusively from his writing. His ambition in this regard had much to do with his exclusion from traditional university education and patronage as a Roman Catholic; see "Alexander Pope," in Greenblatt and Abrams, *Norton Anthology of English Literature*, 1:2493.

8. For a study of Addison's highly esteemed Latin poetry, see Haan, *Vergilius Redivivus*.

9. Ayres, *Classical Culture*, xv, xiii–iv, 3.

10. Foucault, *Security, Territory, Population*.

11. Addison, *Discourse on Ancient and Modern Learning*, 3.

12. Hall and Tilling, *Correspondence*, 4:195n1; Smithers, *Life*, 37–38.

13. Loftis, *Politics of Drama*, 41.

14. Johnson, "Addison," 343–44.

15. *Spectator* 34, 1:144–45.

16. Smithers, *Life*, 226.

17. Steele, "To Mr. Congreve," xii–iii.

18. Williams, *Poetry and the Creation of a Whig Literary Culture*, 219.

19. Tickell, "Preface," Addison, *Works*, x.

20. Plato, *Phaedo*, 78a, 114d–8a.

21. Their official governmental work on medals and longitude indirectly suggests the intriguing possibility of collaboration, but the evidence is lacking. Sherman, *Telling Time*, 163–65.

22. Hall and Tilling, *Correspondence,* 4:350n1; 5:xliii–lvi; Harrison, *Library of Isaac Newton.*

23. See, for instance, Newton, *Certain Philosophical Questions.* Newton developed the groundwork of his mathematical, physical, and optical theories while sequestering from the Great Plague of 1665–66 at his childhood home in Woolsthorpe-by-Colsterworth, before returning as a fellow in 1667 to Cambridge and his reopened alma mater.

24. For both Newton and Addison, the work of empiricism, of decoding nature's laws, was not understood as secularizing or primarily disenchanting but as uncovering and deciphering a divine, providential order, a work of devotion and religious meditation. Smith, *Empiricist Devotions.*

25. An idea of his extensive reading can be gleaned from the books he left to his daughter, see Leigh and Sotheby, *Catalogue.*

26. Lovejoy, *Great Chain of Being,* 99.

27. Lovejoy, 103, 109.

28. Lovejoy, 115, 110.

29. Addison, "Oration," 184, capitalization in original; Lovejoy, 125; Hunter, *Science and the Shape of Orthodoxy,* 165.

30. *Spectator* 543, 4:442; Hunter, *Science and the Shape of Orthodoxy,* 165n44.

31. Addison, "Oration," 184–85.

32. Addison, 186.

33. For related contemporary philosophical debates over scientific realism, see Hacking, "Do We See through a Microscope?"; and Cordero, "Scientific Realism."

34. Smithers, *Life,* 134–35, 154. For blindness in the eighteenth century, see Mounsey, *Sight Correction.* For Addison's emphasis on sight, see Winn, "More Sensual Delights."

35. *Spectator* 111, 1:457–58.

36. Lovejoy, *Great Chain of Being,* 247. For the gospel of gradual perfection, see Jost, *Prose Immortality,* 53–60. For an intellectual history of ambition, see Goebel, *Ambition.*

37. Lovejoy, 242–43, 247–48.

38. Lovejoy, 52–64, 245–46. The revised, progressive Chain solved the period's theological quandary about newly excavated ancient fossils by positing that they could be extinct creatures from an earlier stage of the universe and/or latent, half-formed beings awaiting an emergence in a later stage. (The more reactionary theological view claimed fossils were not extinct creatures but simply lower kinds of creations—divine thoughts—between mineral and living.)

39. Jost, *Prose Immortality,* 195.

40. *Spectator* 111, 1:459.

41. Brewer, *Pleasures of the Imagination,* 92.

42. *Spectator* 162, 2:136–37.

43. Lovejoy, *Great Chain of Being,* 250.

44. Marlowe's tragedy portrays an individual life distant from the divine incarnation and seemingly distant again from the second coming: some more ahistorical theological contract is in place.

45. *Spectator* 159, 2:125–26.

46. Agnew, *Worlds Apart*.

47. Weber, *Theatricality as Medium;* Egginton, *How the World Became a Stage.* Modern archeology was proving the radical extent to which time transformed every place on the Earth.

48. For a related meditation on the ambivalence of "classical" ground, see Addison's poetic epistle to Charles Montagu, "Letter from Italy." I argue elsewhere that the fundamentally new world-picture of Montagu's friend Newton subtly drives that poem's optical dialectic: Poston, "Still on Classic Ground," 67–77. For another interpretation of "The Vision of Mirzah," stressing Addison's "consistent attempt to invoke Islamic parallels" to Christian and Western philosophical ideas, see Orr, *British Enlightenment Theatre*, 32.

49. Westfall, *Never at Rest*, 63.

50. Russell, "Copernican System," 227.

51. Newton, *Certain Philosophical Questions*, 336.

52. Blumenberg, "Die Kopernikanische Konsequenz," 74.

53. For scientific progress as characterized by large, unsettling paradigm shifts with periods of more procedural scientific work in between, see Kuhn, *Structure of Scientific Revolutions.*

54. Shaftesbury, "Moralists," in *Characteristics*, 279

55. Pope, *Essay on Man*, 34 (epistle 2, ll. 31–34); emphasis in original.

56. Pope, 7; emphases in original.

57. *Tatler* 216, 3:132–33.

58. For an overview of Addison's critiques of scientists of "minutiae," see Smithers, *Life*, 258–59. On Newton and Newtonian's links to empire, see Jacob and Stewart, *Practical Matter.*

59. Pope, *Essay on Man*, 14 (epistle 1, l. 154.)

60. Pope, 12–13 (ll. 123–28).

61. Pope, 18 (ll.189–94).

62. Pope, 23 (ll. 264–65).

63. Pope, 20–21 (ll. 226–28).

64. *Spectator* 519, 4:345.

65. *Spectator* 519, 4:346–47.

66. *Spectator* 519, 4:347–48.

67. *Spectator* 519, 4:348.

68. Smith, *Empiricist Devotions*, 138.

69. *Tatler* 119, 2:206–7, 209.

70. *Spectator* 565, 4:529–30.

71. Jost, *Prose Immortality*, 303, 49–53. Robert Burns reported that two of his earliest literary pleasures were Addison's "Vision of Mirzah" and his hymn "How Are Thy Servants Blest, O Lord!" printed in *Spectator* 489, both of which thematized the vulnerability of human life to being swallowed by the sea, with only divine salvation possible. (The hymn was based on a violent storm Addison experienced on a ship in the Gulf of Genoa.) Davis, "Was Addison a Poet?," 66.

72. *Spectator* 121, 1:496.

73. *Spectator* 121, 1:496.
74. *Spectator* 565, 4:532.
75. Sherman, *Telling Time*, 113–15.
76. *Spectator* 465, 4:142.
77. Smithers, *Life*, 257.
78. *Spectator* 465, 4:144.
79. "Essay on Virgil's Georgics," in Addison, *Works*, 1:160.
80. Smith, *Empiricist Devotions*, 138. For Addison as both a "pioneer of literary criticism and theory" and a forerunner of Romantic poetics, see Walsh, "Addison as Critic and Critical Theorist," 95–96.
81. *Spectator* 465, 4:144; emphasis in original.
82. *Spectator* 465, 4:145.
83. *Spectator* 465, 4:145.
84. Jager, *Book of God*, 22–23. See also Shrock, *Choral Monuments*, 178.
85. Book 7 of Virgil, *Aeneid*; quoted in Freud, *Interpretation of Dreams*, 608n1.
86. For Addison's modern reconsideration of Virgil in his turn-of-the-century poem, "A Letter from Italy," written to Charles Montagu, see Poston, "Still on Classic Ground." For Addison's identification with Virgil and the georgic project of husbandry, see the introduction of this book.
87. Saintsbury, *Peace of the Augustans*, 12.
88. Smithers, *Life*, 259.
89. Addison anglicized the term tulipomania, so colorful in the history of finance.
90. *Tatler* 218, 3:142–43.
91. Ridout, *Scenes from Bourgeois Life*, 94.
92. Pollock, "Neutering Addison and Steele," 729
93. Ridout, *Scenes from Bourgeois Life*, 64–66.
94. Sherman, *Telling Time*, 109–13; Anderson, *Imagined Communities*, 33–35.
95. George Eliot, "Prelude," *Middlemarch*, in *The Clarendon Edition of the Novels of George Eliot*, ed. David Carroll (Oxford: Oxford University Press, 1992), 1.
96. *Spectator* 69, 1:294. For the gaze of the statue-sovereign and the mixed religious and theatrical aspects of the scene Addison therein describes, see Roach, *Cities of the Dead*, 87–88.
97. Norton, "Aesthetics," 640–41; Axelsson, *Political Aesthetics*, 14; Jost, *Prose Immortality*, 42.
98. *Spectator* 441, 4:49.
99. For the "Newtonian sublime" and its links to the celebration of British imperial mastery, see O'Brien, "These Nations Newton Made," 289–97.
100. Addison, "VIII," *Latin Prose and Poetry*.

3. Slavery in Addison's Discourse

1. *Spectator* 287, 3:19.
2. *Freeholder* 5, 56–57, 59.
3. Addison, *Discourse on Ancient and Modern Learning*, 20.

4. See, for instance, *Spectator* 287, 3:22, discussed below.

5. *Spectator* 287, 3:19.

6. Hobbes wrote his paradigmatic treatise under Louis XIV's protection among exiled Stuart royalists. His radically materialist arguments earned the *Leviathan* immediate condemnation from both the church and royalists, even though his overriding call for a unitary head of state with blanket religious and political authority might have been to their liking. The "monstrosity" of Hobbes's new logical formulation of the ultimate sovereign uncomfortably exposed the essential ambiguity latent in the testy alliance between Louis and the pope: Which of them, after all, was to be the legitimate terrestrial law-giver? Ironically, Hobbes's forceful apology for absolutism forced him into the second exile of homecoming—to the expediently tolerant Protestant Commonwealth.

7. Political office in Addison's England was tied to territorial seats and obtained through a mixture of elite negotiations, purchasing the right to office, and local elections; in this sense, the kind of diverse, liberal representation that Addison advocated was much more republican than democratic. With the exception of the Queen, women were excluded from almost all land ownership and political offices, so their social and educational emancipation in Addisonian terms would not amount to their full, equal participation in governance.

8. *Spectator* 287, 3:21–22, emphasis in the original.

9. *Spectator* 287, 3:21.

10. "There is increasing consensus among historians that changes in the economy and class structure of England in the eighteenth century were underwritten by returns on investments in an Atlantic economy fueled by slave labor." Dillon, *New World Drama*, 36. See also Roach, *Cities of the Dead*, 75–76.

11. Dillon, *New World Drama*, 31–32.

12. *Spectator* 215, 2:339–40.

13. Orr, *British Enlightenment Theatre*, 37–39.

14. *Spectator* 215, 339–40.

15. Carey, "Accounts of Savage Nations," 142, 138–43.

16. Patterson, *Slavery and Social Death*, vii–ix.

17. Prager, "Problem of Slavery," 314. For the omission of Atlantic slavery in progressive Whig writing and the alternative focus on religious tolerance and opposition to absolutism, see also Orr, *British Enlightenment Theatre*, 24–25.

18. After Gulston's sudden death, Addison struggled for years to recover his brother's estate and close his accounts in Madras: Smithers, *Life*, 149–50.

19. Orr, *British Enlightenment Theatre*, 42.

20. Addison, "The Late Tryal and Conviction of Count Tariff," in *Miscellaneous Works*, 2:271.

21. Addison, 2:267–72. The Blooms found Addison's pamphlet morally distressing, since they believed he was objecting to the treaty's restrictions on the number of human beings that the British could yearly sell. This would have been an extremely disturbing (and out of character) argument for Addison to have made. It seems clear from the pamphlet text, however, that the Blooms likely misread Addison's argument: he does

employ patriotic, economic grounds to object to the treaty, but his argument is *against* overall British involvement in the slave trade, *not* for the loosening of restrictions on it. Bloom and Bloom, *Joseph Addison's Sociable Animal*, xii, 51–52.

22. Roach, *Cities of the Dead*, 6; Morrison, *Playing in the Dark*, 38.

23. Roach, 75.

24. R. D. Hume, *Reconstructing Contexts*, 172.

25. *Tatler*, 3:256 fn. 26. The ad likely referred to a boy from India or Asia, or a West Indian of African descent: Fryer, *Staying Power*, 78; 110. The term "Black" in the period could refer to "people from the Indies, the Americas, Africa, or the South Pacific, or the Irish, and in general to laboring classes, especially coalminers and chimney sweeps." Nussbaum, *Limits of the Human*, 151.

26. Ashton, *Social Life in the Reign of Queen Anne*, 63.

27. *Tatler* 245, 3:252–56.

28. Ashton, *Social Life*, 62.

29. Hayes, "Black Atlantic," 44–146.

30. Zacharias Conrad von Uffenbach, *London in 1710: From the Travels of Zacharias Conrad von Uffenbach*, ed. and trans. W. H. Quarrell and Margaret Mare (London: Faber & Faber, 1934), 88; quoted in Ridout, *Scenes of Bourgeois Life*, 76.

31. For the visibility and legal/social status of free and enslaved Black people and people of color in London (since the Roman conquest) and the general awareness of colonial matters in Addison and Steele's milieu, see Ridout, 76–77, 116–22.

32. Ashton, *Social Life*, 61–62.

33. *Tatler* 132, 2:268.

34. *Spectator* 287, 3:21.

35. Pincus, "Addison's Empire," 108–11, 116.

36. *Spectator* 287, 3:21. The specter of a formerly supreme Roman church lingered threateningly in Addison's time, so his railing against "Popery" carried his sense of Protestantism as still a "protest" and wedge between church and absolute monarchy.

37. The oft-repeated idea that the asiento year 1713 was a "watershed" year for Britain's dominance of the slave trade is somewhat misleading. During the later seventeenth century, Spain had virtually ceased shipping large numbers of enslaved people to the Americas. By the first years of the eighteenth century, Britain was already shipping tens of thousands each year. Portugal had been the dominant slave trader in the Atlantic and remained active in the "industry" until the end of the eighteenth century. It was not until 1719, the year of Addison's death, that Britain significantly overtook Portugal's yearly shipping totals; from then on, Britain remained the largest slave-trading nation until the end of the eighteenth century. The Dutch were the third most active slave-trading nation in the Atlantic from the mid-seventeenth century until the French supplanted them at the beginning of the eighteenth century (after which the Dutch remained a stable, very active, fourth slaving power.) As British slave-trading numbers declined rapidly in the nineteenth century, Portugal began to ship more, and Spain entered the trade again, remaining active until 1866. "Estimates Database."

38. The famous scandal of the South Sea Bubble, for instance, revolved around the slave-trading South Sea Company's takeover of veteran pensions and many middle-class people's investments.

39. Patterson, "Freedom, Slavery, and the Modern Construction of Rights," 118–19; Patterson, *Slavery and Social Death*, 30–32, 157.
40. Gillingham, "French Chivalry in Twelfth-Century Britain," 8.
41. *Spectator* 1, 1:1.
42. Gillingham, "French Chivalry," 8; Donoghue, "Out of the Land of Bondage," 954.
43. Hudson, *Oxford History of the Laws of England*, 871–1216:424–28.
44. Gillingham, "French Chivalry," 8.
45. *The Digest of Justinian*, ed. Theodor Mommsen and Paul Krueger, trans. Alan Watson (Philadelphia: University of Pennsylvania, 1985), 1.5.3.35, vol. 1, 15; quoted in Skinner, "John Milton and the Politics of Slavery," 3–7; and Lovett, "Freedom, History Of," 388.
46. Zwierlein, "Grace in Deformity," 63–67; Ross, *Making of the English Literary Canon*, 213–20.
47. Skinner, "John Milton and the Politics of Slavery," 2, 12–14.
48. Skinner, 15.
49. Skinner, 18–20.
50. Donoghue, "Out of the Land of Bondage," 952.
51. Donoghue, 947–53. Donoghue argues for calling coerced European laborers "bond slaves" to avoid perpetuating the propaganda of "indentured servitude" used by enslaving marketers in the period to lure destitute people across the ocean under dramatically false pretenses about legal protections and the grueling, dangerous labor they would find there (including its temporary status). Eventually resultant colonial legal disputes deciding whom could and could not be enslaved for life catalyzed modern race constructions.
52. Pestana, *English Atlantic*, 185.
53. Donoghue, "Out of the Land of Bondage," 951.
54. Donoghue, 954.
55. Pestana, *English Atlantic*, 191–92. Dividing different classes of servants and slaves with racial, national, and status lines facilitated a stable, large, exploitative labor structure. An earlier experiment with colonial slavery, the Providence Island Company, had shown how the solidarity of less firmly differentiated English bond slaves, servants, and African slaves could manifest itself in mixed groups organizing resistance and escape attempts against their colonial masters. See Kupperman, *Providence Island*, 179–80.
56. Pestana, *English Atlantic*, 220.
57. An additional estimated 300,000 enslaved African people were shipped to the Americas by American ships. In the same time period approximately 5.9 million were shipped by the Portuguese, 1.3 million by France, 1 million by Spain, and 0.6 million by the Dutch. All numerical estimates were taken from "Estimates Database."
58. Donoghue, "Out of the Land of Bondage," 958–59; Dillon, *New World Drama*, 99; Pestana, *English Atlantic*, 6–7, 192.
59. Dillon, 71.
60. From *Declaration . . . against Spain*, quoted in Dillon, *New World Drama*, 72.
61. Dillon, 72, 75.
62. Donoghue, "Out of the Land of Bondage," 945–47, 961, 965–70. A strong net-

work of ex-colonial leaders, whose utopian puritan community on Providence Island had fallen apart after the first large slave revolt in the English colonies, had also played a pivotal role in Charles I's fall. Kupperman, *Providence Island*, 1; Bossert, "Slavery and Anti-Republicanism," 96–99.

63. Pestana, *English Atlantic*, 220–22; Dillon, *New World Drama*, 103.
64. Dillon, 100–101.
65. Locke, *Second Treatise on Government*, 24.1–3, 284; emphasis in original.
66. Locke, 23.13–15, 284.
67. Locke, 22.1–6, 283.
68. Greenblatt and Abrams, *Norton Anthology of English Literature*, 2829–30.
69. Patterson, "Freedom, Slavery, and the Modern Construction of Rights," 126.
70. Donoghue, "Out of the Land of Bondage," 967.
71. Springborg, "Republicanism," 867–68.
72. *Spectator* 11, 1:47–51.
73. Mallipeddi, *Spectacular Suffering*, 51–73, 84.
74. Mallipeddi, 18.
75. Morrison, *Playing in the Dark*, 37–38.
76. Orr, *British Enlightenment Theatre*, 35–36.
77. Bloom and Bloom, *Joseph Addison's Sociable Animal*, 50–52. Put into a sequence with *Spectator* 50, these three 1711 essays are an anniversary reflection on the 1710 visit of the Four Iroquois "kings" to London.
78. *Spectator* 55, 1:236.
79. *Spectator* 56, 1:240.
80. Pincus, "Addison's Empire," 116.
81. Orr, *British Enlightenment Theatre*, 34–35.
82. Pincus, "Addison's Empire," 109, 102–6.
83. Smith, *Empiricist Devotions*, 129; Pincus, 110. Smith argues that a twenty-first-century, critically disenchanted view on "emergent capitalist society" can cloud our understanding of Addison's encomium on the market, which situated trade inside more humanistic and religious commitments.
84. *Spectator* 69, 1:294.
85. Saintsbury, *Peace of the Augustans*, 13.
86. Ogée, "Nature and Imagination," 277–79.
87. Addison, *Discourse on Ancient and Modern Learning*, 17.
88. Dillon, *New World Drama*, 58.
89. Dillon links these processes more generally to the "primitive accrual" of capital in Britain and its colonies, which jump-started and fed the modern capitalist economy (35, 121).
90. Dillon, 16, 56.
91. For an insightful meditation on *Spectator* 235 (2:413–16), see Ridout, *Scenes of Bourgeois Life*, particularly 61–62, 103–4 (for the Trunk-Maker as theater critic), 111–13 (on the meaning of "Black" at the time), 125–26 (for the Trunk-Maker as "the black double of the white Mr. Spectator"). Ridout (122) cites the origin of his particular use of the term "political unconscious" as Simon Gikandi, *Slavery and the Culture of Taste* (Princeton, NJ: Princeton University Press, 2011).

4. Addison's Theory of the Imagination

1. Engell, *Creative Imagination*, 4, vii–ix; Guyer, *Values of Beauty*, 5.
2. McKeon, *Secret History of Domesticity*, 359–60.
3. Many of those ideas had to do with the psychologizing of criticism: Abrams, *Mirror and the Lamp*, 274–75. See also Youngren, "Addison and the Birth of Eighteenth-Century Aesthetics," 268. Basker cites Addison's essay as the best example of an eighteenth-century transition from "the classical emphasis on the ideals of form and their codification by critics, to a focus on the power of art to affect their critics" ("Criticism and the Rise of Periodical Literature," 322). See also Hipple, *Beautiful, Sublime, and Picturesque*, 13–24.
4. Mackie, *Commerce of Everyday Life*, 30–32.
5. Habermas, *Structural Transformation*, 40.
6. Szécsényi, "Jesuit Thread," 50–51, 56–58. Coming full circle, nineteenth-century reception of Addison's imagination essay inspired the "aesthetic revolution" in Spanish thought that challenged the accepted Aristotelian concept of art as mimesis at the time; see Rodríguez Sánchez de León, "Varying Life," 111–27.
7. Engell, *Creative Imagination*, 33.
8. Smithers, *Life*, 132, 159, 175, 178, 191, 202, 235.
9. *Spectator* 409, 3:530–51.
10. Sonnet 19, in Milton, *Selected Poetry*, 87.
11. Engell, *Creative Imagination*, 7.
12. Engell, 6.
13. McKeon, *Secret History of Domesticity*, 360.
14. Engell, *Creative Imagination*, 7.
15. Plato, *Phaedo*, 109a–b, 114d.
16. Norton, "Spectator, Aesthetic Experience," 87–104.
17. Hansen, "Addison on Ornament"; Addison, *Some Portions of Essays*.
18. *Spectator* 221, 2:359.
19. *Spectator* 221, 3:535; emphasis in original.
20. Lucretius, *De rerum natura*, 1:926–28.
21. Lucretius, 1:930–50, 4:11–25.
22. Newton's 1686 copy of Lucretius shows heavy signs of study, several of his unpublished drafts reference Lucretius, and the last query of the second edition of *Opticks* (1718) contains a declaration of his belief in atomism that elaborately paraphrases *The Nature of Things*. Johnson and Wilson, "Lucretius and the History of Science," 141–42.
23. McKeon, *Secret History of Domesticity*, 361.
24. *Spectator* 411, 3:536.
25. *Spectator* 411, 3:537. The primary and secondary division echoes and modifies Locke's similar division of the characteristics of objects; Baudot, "Joseph Addison's Lucretian Imagination," 910. On the relation between Addison's, Hobbes's, and Lucretius's theories of a material basis for the imagination, see Baudot, 902; and Walsh, "Addison as Critic," 101. See chapter 2 of Hobbes's *Leviathan* for his concept of imagination consisting of "decaying sense."
26. *Spectator* 411, 3:537.

27. See Steele's notes from a 1711 planning meeting for *The Spectator*, quoted in Ellis, "Sociability and Polite Improvement," 147. Ellis cites add. MS61688f.65, British Library, London, quoted in Alexander Lindsay, "Some Drafts by Richard Steele for *The Tatler, The Spectator,* and *The Guardian,*" *British Library Journal* 20 (1994): 163–73, 172.

28. *Spectator* 93, 1:396. The historical specificity of the allegory lies in the "everyman" being an aspirational, middling owner of stock.

29. *Spectator* 411, 3:539. Walsh notes that Addison's emphasis on a healthful reason for the use of imagination shows his theories proximity to Hobbes rather than Locke ("Addison as Critic," 102–3).

30. *Spectator* 411, 3:537–38.

31. See also: Zeitz, "Addison's Imagination Papers."

32. *Spectator* 411, 3:537.

33. McKendrick, Brewer, and Plumb, *Birth of Consumer Society*, 1–2, 9–12.

34. *Spectator* 411, 3:538.

35. McKeon, *Secret History of Domesticity*, 364.

36. See chapter 3 for how this structure of argumentation (in the explicit realm of foreign policy) justified Whiggish/English "moral" colonial efforts in contrast to Tory/Spanish exploitative efforts.

37. *Spectator* 412, 3:544, 542.

38. Combined with Addison's other writings in *The Spectator* on the Great Chain of Being (echoed later in the imagination essay), his thought seems to anticipate the Darwinian theory of sexual evolution and speciation.

39. *Spectator* 413, 3:545.

40. For the importance of novelty in Addison's aesthetic theorization of human pleasure and its separation from an eternal divine sphere, see Black, "Addison's Aesthetics of Novelty," 269–88. For Addison's belief that "the aesthetic pushes the agent onwards in his religious and moral engagements," see Axelsson, *Political Aesthetics*, 35.

41. *Spectator* 413, 3:545–46.

42. *Spectator* 413, 3:546–47.

43. Norton, "Aesthetics, Science," 652. The quote is from Aphra Behn's 1688 translation of Fontenelle's *Conversations on the Plurality of Worlds,* which was reprinted after Addison's death in revised form with his own defense of "Newtonian Philosophy"; see chapter 2.

44. *Spectator* 413, 3:547.

45. *Spectator* 414, 3:550–51.

46. *Spectator* 414, 3:548n1.

47. *Spectator* 415, 3:557.

48. *Spectator* 416, 3:558.

49. *Spectator* 416, 3:558. The Latin translation here is my own. The Latin of Lucretius reads: "Quatinus hoc simile est illi, quod mente videmus / atque oculis, simili fieri ratione necessest." Lucretius, *De rerum natura*, 4:750–51.

50. *Spectator* 416, 3:558–61.

51. Abrams, *Doing Things with Texts,* 28; Norton, "Aesthetics, Science," 641, 652.

52. *Spectator* 417, 3:563.

53. *Spectator* 417, 3:563.

54. *Spectator* 417, 3:564–66. A poet Addison never names, Dante, seems to particularly haunt this paper. On Dantean echoes in *Cato,* see chapter 6.

55. *Spectator* 418, 3:566–68. The passage's connection to Freud's late theory (*Beyond the Pleasure Principle*)—along with the Aristotelian theory of tragic pleasure—could be further explored, especially in Addison's suggestion that the comparative pleasure attendant on description/understanding actually increases the pleasure the mind takes in the original sources of pleasure.

56. *Spectator* 418, 3:568.

57. *Spectator* 418, 3:569.

58. *Spectator* 419, 3:573.

59. *Spectator* 420, 3:574.

60. Horace, *The Art of Poetry,* ed. Christopher Smart, trans. Theodore Alois Buckley (New York: Harper & Brothers, 1863), Perseus Digital Library, http://data.perseus.org/citations/urn:cts:latinLit:phi0893.phi006.perseus-eng1:99-124.

61. I have not been able to find a similar alteration in an edition of Horace, indicating that the alteration—with the surrounding matching declensions—is likely Addison's, not the result of a differing Latin edition.

62. *Spectator* 420, 3:574.

63. *Spectator* 420, 3:574.

64. *Spectator* 420, 3:575.

65. *Spectator* 420, 3:576.

66. O'Brien, *Literature Incorporated,* 71.

67. *Spectator* 420, 3:576–77.

68. *Spectator* 420, 3:577.

69. Addison, *Works,* 1:136.

70. Bloom, "Addison as Translator," 32.

71. Addison omitted all but Ovid's first colorfully sexually suggestive simile from his translation, perhaps out of prudishness, perhaps following a then standard critique of Ovid's untranslatable ludic prolixity; see Hopkins, "Addison as Translator," 23–24. See also Gippert, *Joseph Addison's Ovid.*

72. Without comment, Addison changes the protagonist's name in this passage from the masculine "Hermaphroditus" to "Hermaphrodite." In Ovid's Latin and in other translations, the name is not mentioned or changed here. Addison, *Works,* 1:139.

73. The rumor was pernicious enough in Rome that Vitruvius attempted to debunk it in print; Vitruvius, *On Architecture,* 2.8.12.

74. Addison, *Works,* 1:136.

75. Palmer, *Reading Lucretius,* 106, 109. Palmer notes that this Ovid quote (from *Amores,* book 2, poem 15, lines 23–24) was widely known by Renaissance and medieval scholars who "must have read [it] with some bitterness in the years when the *De rerum natura* seemed lost forever." The rediscovery of the poem thus signified a kind of rebirth of the world.

76. *Spectator* 421, 3:577.

77. McKeon, *Secret History of Domesticity,* 362.

78. *Spectator* 421, 3:578.
79. *Spectator* 421, 3:578. Addison's arguments here (and in other parts of the essay) echo Philip Sidney's *Defence of Poesie*.
80. *Spectator* 421, 3:579.
81. *Spectator* 421, 3:579.
82. The mention of ruined Babylon conjures up the fantasy of ancient Orientalized spaces and the concluding melancholic earth-bound gaze of Addison's "Vision of Mirzah" in *Spectator* 159, discussed in chapter 2.
83. *Spectator* 420, 3:579.
84. See *Spectator* 201's caution against too much inward devotion—the imagination exciting itself—discussed in Klein, "Sociability, Solitude, and Enthusiasm," 164–66.
85. *Spectator* 420, 3:580.
86. Staton, "Ovidian Elements in *A Midsummer Night's Dream*," 165–78.
87. Baudot, "Joseph Addison's Lucretian Imagination."
88. See Locke's account of property: *Second Treatise on Government*, 288 (chapter 5, §27).
89. McKeon, *Secret History of Domesticity*, 381–82; Paul Guyer, *Values of Beauty*, 5; Baudot, "Joseph Addison's Lucretian Imagination," 893; Cahill, *Liberty of the Imagination*, 4.
90. Szécsényi, "Jesuit Thread," 63.
91. Abrams, *Mirror and the Lamp*, 274–75.
92. Grindle, "Virgil's Prospects," 192.
93. Walker, "Ideology and Addison's Essays," 77.
94. Saccamano, "Sublime Force of Words," 87–91.
95. *Spectator* 412, 3:542–43.
96. The image might also be ghosted (for the poet Addison in particular) by the figure of Milton. For the reasons for that resonance, see chapter 1 and Davis, "Was Addison a Poet?"
97. Saccamano, "Sublime Force of Words," 104.
98. Stout, "How Vergil Established for Aeneas a Legal Claim," 152–60; Giusti, *Carthage in Virgil's Aeneid*.
99. Erskine-Hill, *Augustan Idea in English Literature*, especially chapters 5–7.
100. Ovid, *Heroides*. 83, ll. 13–14.
101. Ovid, 95, ll. 146–7.
102. Jung, *Tavistock Lectures*, 105.
103. For Freud's meditation on the connection between the human being's hermaphroditic constitution, the glorification of sight, and evolving human progress, see *Civilization and its Discontents*, 105–7n3.
104. Montaigne, *Essays*, 91–98.
105. For an overview of the modern theory of sublimation, including its crucial literary-historical contexts, see Goebel, *Beyond Discontent*.
106. Montaigne, *Essays*, 100–102.
107. Robinson, "Salmacis and Hermaphroditus," 212–23; Romano, "Invention of Marriage," 543–61.
108. See chapter 1 and Winn, "More Sensual Delights."

109. Lacan, "Mirror Stage."
110. *Spectator* 237, 422.
111. *Spectator* 237, 2:421.
112. *Spectator* 237, 2:422.
113. Letter from Addison to Bishop Hough, Marseilles, 29 November 1700; printed in Aikin, *Life of Joseph Addison*, 1:92–93. Voltaire later favorably compared Addison's *Cato* to Corneille's *Pompey* (*Letters Concerning the English Nation*, 178). For a further discussion of admiration and Addison's revision of the tragic, see Poston, "Passionsspiel Der Geschichte."

5. Staging a Shadow King

1. Macaulay, "Life and Writings of Addison," 606.
2. Thomson, *Cambridge Introduction to English Theatre*, 91.
3. Hone, "Isaac Newton and the Medals," 135.
4. Williams, *Poetry and the Creation of a Whig Literary Culture*, 159.
5. Pincus, "Addison's Empire," 101.
6. Hone, *Literature and Party Politics*, 11.
7. Greenblatt and Abrams, *Norton Anthology of English Literature*, 1:1816.
8. *Freeholder* 54, 268. For an overview of Addison's anti-"Popery" and anti-French Whig politics, see Axelsson, *Political Aesthetics*, 45–48.
9. Borsay, *English Urban Renaissance*, 282; quoted in Knights, *Representation and Misrepresentation*, 54. See also Axelsson, *Political Aesthetics*, 115–16.
10. *Freeholder* 54, 270. On Addison's "non-partisan" partisanship, see Wilson, *Race of Female Patriots*, 7. On the friendship between Addison and Sacheverell, see Cowan, "Mr. Spectator and the Doctor," 40–60.
11. *Spectator* 125, 510.
12. Hone, *Literature and Party Politics*, 105.
13. Womersley, *Augustan Critical Writing*, xix. See chapter 1 in this volume.
14. Addison, *Works*, 1:4–5.
15. Addison, 1:5.
16. Addison, 1:7–8.
17. Addison, 1:9.
18. Habermas, *Structural Transformation*, 63.
19. David Walker, "Addison's *Cato*," 103.
20. Hone, *Literature and Party Politics*, 4–5.
21. Smithers, *Life*, 92.
22. Smithers, 103.
23. Smithers, 101.
24. In addition to his ministerial roles, Addison was MP for Lostwithiel (1708–9) and Malmesbury (1710–19) in Westminster; he also represented Cavan Borough (1709–13) in Dublin. D. W. Hayton, "Addison, Joseph," in *The House of Commons, 1690–1715*, ed. Eveline Cruickshanks, Stuart Handley, and D. W. Hayton, 6 vols. (Cambridge: Cambridge University Press, 2002), iii:11–14; cited in Cowan, "Mr. Spectator and the Doctor," 40.

25. Loftis, *Politics of Drama*, 35.

26. R. D. Hume, "Theatres and Repertory," 59.

27. Carlson, *Haunted Stage*; Roach, *Cities of the Dead*.

28. For the history outlined above, see Williams, *Poetry and the Creation of a Whig Literary Culture*; Hone, *Literature and Party Politics*; Walker, "Addison's *Cato*"; and Gregg, "Was Queen Anne a Jacobite?"

29. Smithers, *Life*, 263–64.

30. "Pope to Caryll 30 April 1713," in Pope, *Correspondence*, 174–75.

31. Lord Castlecomer reported, for instance, on Tory rumors "that Cato must mean either the Lord Treasurer [Harley] or Bolingbroke." Smithers, *Life*, 265

32. Two weeks after the rebellion, on the evening before Essex's execution, the triumphant Queen had the pardoned Chamberlain's Men reperform the play at Whitehall Palace. Six months afterward, she is reported to have said to her archivist, in reference to Shakespeare's play, "I am Richard II, know ye not that?" The lines portraying Richard's deposition were suppressed in all printings of the play until after Elizabeth's death. Kantorowicz, *King's Two Bodies*, 40–41.

33. In 1956, Carl Schmitt made the well-known argument that the undeniable force of foundational theatrical masterpieces like *Hamlet* derived from the eruption of then-present events and conflicts into the fiction of the drama. Schmitt, *Hamlet or Hecuba*.

34. Smith, "Last of All the Heavenly Birth," 138, 148.

35. For a relevant (if highly culturally and temporally divergent) take on the performance of sameness as a tool of influential persona development, see Phelan, "Same."

36. Sharpe, *Rebranding Rule*, 615.

37. Smith, "Last of All the Heavenly Birth," 148–49. It is arguable, of course, that the ritual continues—and not in a less religious form—in the grace of celebrities and contemporary monarchs in descending to greet, give autographs for, and sometimes also touch their followers.

38. Smith, 146.

39. Smith, 147.

40. William Congreve, *A Pindarique Ode Humbly Offer'd to the Queen on the Victorious Progress of Her Majesty's Arms under the Conduct of the Duke of Marlborough* (1706), 6; quoted in Smith, "Last of All the Heavenly Birth," 147. See also Yates, "Queen Elizabeth as Astraea," 51–68.

41. Williams, *Poetry and the Creation of a Whig Literary Culture*, 231.

42. Hall and Tilling, *Correspondence*, 4:195n1, 282, 283n1. During the Exclusion Crisis, members of what would become the Whig Party wore a 1681 medal that celebrated the 1st Earl of Shaftesbury's vindication from charges of high treason, which had stemmed from his attempts to pass legislation excluding the future James II from the throne on the grounds of his Catholicism. The medal's obverse featured Shaftesbury, founding father of the Whigs, and the reverse featured London Bridge and the Tower with the inscription "Laetamur" (we rejoice). Williams, 63–74. At the behest of Charles II, Dryden satirized the movement in *The Medall*. Hone, "Isaac Newton and the Medals," 134.

43. Addison, *Works*, 1:267–68; Smithers, *Life*, 53. Although Addison circulated and published a few writings on medals before he died—Newton's library contained an

essay on medals by him printed in 1715—his *Dialogues on Medals* were only published posthumously. An agreement with Tonson seems to show a plan to publish the work before August 1713, possibly in conjunction with the premiere or publication of *Cato*, but this did not come to fruition for unknown reasons. Gámez, "And Art Reflected Images," 259; Harrison, *Library of Isaac Newton*. For an analysis of the *Dialogues*, see Power, "Coins and Circulation," 81–91.

44. Hone, *Literature and Party Politics*, 58–59. Newton's private notes show that he was heavily involved in medal design, seemingly immersing his mind in the task alongside other long-running intellectual projects: "Ideas for designs are interleaved with—and often jotted in the margins of—pages of complex sums or biblical chronology. Possible subjects for George I's coronation medal mingle with both calculations relating to the *Principia* and notes on Persian history." Hone, "Isaac Newton and the Medals," 126. John (Johann) Croker, a German jeweler who had been employed since 1697 at the Mint, was the principal medalist in Queen Anne's reign. John Craig, *Newton at the Mint*, 54. For Addison's discussion of medal design as an "art of peace," see *Guardian* 96, 344–45 in Addison and Steele, *Guardian*.

45. Hone, "Isaac Newton and the Medals," 128–29.

46. Kantorowicz, *King's Two Bodies*; Axton, *Queen's Two Bodies*.

47. Hone, "Isaac Newton," 129. Newton planned—a never realized—"sustained campaign of medallic propaganda disseminating" the image of Anne as Pallas (132).

48. Smithers, *Life*, 94–99.

49. Davis, "Was Addison a Poet?," 71–73.

50. Addison, *Works*, 1:42.

51. Addison, 1:43.

52. Addison, 1:46.

53. Addison, 1:48.

54. Addison, 1:51.

55. Addison, 1:53.

56. Addison, 1:52–53.

57. Addison, 1:44.

58. A further, more metaphorical meaning might refer to the English Civil Wars and their long aftermath, which shook "pale Britannia" to the core in the previous century.

59. Addison, *Works*, 1:49–50.

60. Williams, *Poetry and the Creation of a Whig Literary Culture*, 141.

61. Hone, *Literature and Party Politics*, 116.

62. Williams, *Poetry*, 142.

63. Smith, "Last of All the Heavenly Birth," 147.

64. Hawkins, Franks, and Grueber, *Medallic Illustrations*, 246.

65. Craig, *Newton at the Mint*, 52–54; Hone, *Literature and Party Politics*, 147. Before 1703, the tradition had been that engravers at the Mint could cut medals for private trade as a way of practicing their skill and supplementing their income. Newton later reobtained royal permission for this privilege of the engravers but only with a promise that he would approve all designs personally and that the medals would feature only "plain historical designs and inscriptions" (54).

66. Loftis, *Politics of Drama*, 37.

67. Hammond, "Joseph Addison's Opera," 608–9, 621–22.

68. Winn, *Queen Anne*, 441.

69. Williams, *Poetry and the Creation of a Whig Literary Culture*, 144.

70. Hammond, "Joseph Addison's Opera," 616, 619–20, 623. "The verdict of history" was that, "while Addison's lyrics were exceptionally successful, the opera was sabotaged by its execrable music." Hammond, 601. On *Rosamond* and Addison's poor musical taste, see Winn, "More Sensual Delights," 115, 130–31, 134.

71. Addison, *Works*, 1.4, 1:63. To praise Marlborough and the war itself was increasingly a politicized gesture at the time since Tory dissatisfaction with the war had grown. Allegory was necessary, not only to preserve a surface escapist entertainment value for a general audience but also because Charles Killigrew, Master of the Revels, exercised a heavy censorial hand over political and religious subjects. Loftis, *Politics of Drama*, 44–45.

72. Addison, *Works*, 1:73.

73. Smith, "Last of All the Heavenly Birth," 147.

74. Smithers, *Life*, 215.

75. Anne's dismissal of her Whig ministers, preceding the Whigs' electoral defeat a few months later, was a reaction to the Sacheverell trial, in which a High Church Anglican clergyman was charged for sedition because of a popular and inflammatory sermon he gave and had printed against the Whig separation of church and state. Sacheverell inspired a fervent following of Tories, Catholics, and Jacobites. When he was convicted but given a light sentence, riots against the government broke out in London, and he became a folk hero in much of England. The Whigs admitted in the trial that their long-standing objections to the legitimacy of James III's birth were unfounded, meaning, therefore, that Anne was monarch "by virtue of parliamentary rather than hereditary right." None of this, it might be guessed, was met by Anne with much pleasure. Gregg, "Was Queen Anne a Jacobite?," 370.

76. Gregg, *Queen Anne*, 123. One sign of the intensity of Anne's rivalry with Sophia might be the Queen's managing to survive, in spite of her famously failing health, until a month after Sophia's death.

77. Gregg, "Was Queen Anne a Jacobite?," 368.

78. Erskine-Hill, "Twofold Vision," 910.

79. Walker, "Addison's *Cato*," 93.

80. Johnson, "Addison," 10.

81. Erskine-Hill, "Twofold Vision," 910. The Jacobite threat remained a substantial undercurrent of British politics up until the failed rebellion of 1745.

82. Gregg, "Was Queen Anne a Jacobite?," 358.

83. Gregg, 367.

84. Erskine-Hill, "Twofold Vision," 911.

85. *Spectator* 10, 1:44.

86. One of the more interesting outputs of this cultivated diplomacy was a 1703 letter in which Addison (on behalf of Jacob Tonson) requested that Leibniz describe and obtain a drawing of the buffalo kept by the king of Prussia, a request with which Leibniz apparently complied. "39. To Gottfried Wilhelm Leibnitz (10 July 1703)," in Addison, *Letters*, 43–44; Junqua, "Moment in Amsterdam," 44–46.

87. Smithers, *Life*, 243–44.
88. John Byrom, "An Admonition against Swearing. Address'd to an Officer in the Army," *Chetham Society Publications* n.s. 30 (1894), 572; quoted in Erskine-Hill, "Twofold Vision," 913.
89. Smithers, *Life*, 128, 131, 145.
90. Snyder, "Duke of Marlborough's Request"; Gregg, "Was Queen Anne a Jacobite?," 369.
91. Gregg, 369–70.
92. "Berkeley to Percival April 16th, 1713," in Rand, *Berkeley and Percival*, 113.
93. Bolingbroke recounted the tale of his shrewd efforts on behalf of the Pretender in a published apologia, the 1717 *Letter to Sir William Wyndham*. Erskine-Hill, "Twofold Vision," 912.
94. Cannon, *Samuel Johnson*, 36–67. For the reasonableness of Addison's fears of civil war in England, see Miller, "Strange Career," 654.
95. The original minutes are held in Miscellaneous Literary MSS and Papers, MSS Dep c 293, Special Collections, Bodleian Library, Oxford University.
96. Gregg, "Was Queen Anne a Jacobite?," 359–60.
97. Boyer, *Political State of Great Britain*, 140–42.
98. Axelsson, *Political Aesthetics*, 18.

6. Addison's Cato

1. Carlson, *Haunted Stage*, 51.
2. *Tatler* 167, 2:423.
3. *Tatler* 167, 2:423.
4. Roach, *Cities of the Dead*, 74.
5. Roach, 92, 94.
6. Roach, 75, 82.
7. Roach, 77–78.
8. Roach, 105.
9. Goodall, *Stage Presence*, 12.
10. Roach, *Cities of the Dead*, 116–17.
11. Loftis, *Politics of Drama*, 42.
12. Roach, *Cities of the Dead*, 93.
13. Roach, 115.
14. *Tatler* 167, 2:424.
15. *Spectator* 26, 1:108–11.
16. See also Roach, *Cities of the Dead*, 85, 91–92.
17. Smithers, *Life*, 426.
18. *Tatler* 161, 2:397–401.
19. Smithers, *Life*, 56.
20. Smithers, 79.
21. Later, fuller formulations of this idea from thinkers influenced by Addison's theory of the imagination are now more famous, such as those published by Fontenelle (in the 1720s), Batteux, and Hume. See D. Hume, "Of Tragedy," in *Selected Essays*, 126–33.

22. "Von Homer bis Goethe ist eine Stunde, von Goethe bis heute 24 Stunden." See Benn, "Doppelleben," 160.

23. Brockett and Hildy, *History of the Theatre*, 50–51.

24. Terry, "Revolt in Utica," 123.

25. O'Brien, *Literature Incorporated*, 69.

26. For *Spectator* readership as distance learning, see Justice, "*Spectator* and Distance Education," 265–99.

27. Smithers, *Life*, 468.

28. Sherman, *Telling Time*, 109–13; Anderson, *Imagined Communities*, 33–35.

29. Mazurkewycz, "Chronic Time, Telling Texts," 23–24. For Sherman's standard work, see previous note.

30. Mazurkewycz, 22, 27.

31. Mazurkewycz, 14.

32. The "reality media" Trump presidency created a similar effect—in a historically overdetermined manner—given the true gigantic combined institutional sizes of the executive branch and the Trump media empire when matched against the staged singular, transgressive colloquial voice of the imaginary Twitter POTUS character.

33. Quoted in James William Johnson, *Formation of English Neo-Classical Thought*, 276–77n5.

34. Ayres, *Classical Culture*, 47.

35. Jensen, "Creating Cato," 235–36.

36. Jensen, 233.

37. Taylor, "Medieval Proverb Collections," 25.

38. Taylor, 32.

39. James William Johnson, *Formation of English Neo-Classical Thought*, 98.

40. Johnson, 96.

41. Addison, *Cato*, 2.1.1–10 (30). Reference: act.scene.lines (page). Subsequent references to *Cato* are to the same edition.

42. *Cato*, 1.3.42 (16). For a similar recent take on Sempronius's efficacy, see Taylor, "Cato and the Crisis of Rhetoric," 216. In an analysis of *Cato* as a play in search of "a means of reclaiming the civic utility of rhetoric," Taylor shows that Addison modelled the debate in the Senate on the debate in Pandaemonium in book 2 of *Paradise Lost*. Taylor, 213–15.

43. *Cato*, 1.1.4–6 (7–8).

44. *Cato*, 5.4.103–6 (96).

45. Edwards, "Modelling Roman Suicide?," 216.

46. Axton, *Queen's Two Bodies*, 11.

47. For a discussion of *Cato* as "a religious play" from a slightly different perspective (i.e., that Addison's intent was "to set up an ideal of heroic virtue"), see Kelsall, "Meaning of Addison's Cato," 161.

48. Book 5.12 in Augustine, *City of God*, 201–3.

49. We have no record of Addison discussing Dante's work, but some familiarity is likely, considering his travels through Italy as well as his steeping in Milton and Protestant theology. For Dante's seventeenth-century reception among English Protestants,

see Havely, "Dante's Reception." An earlier champion of European Protestantism, the modern imagination, and tragic admiration, Philip Sidney mentions Dante and Cato in close proximity in a passage of his *Defence of Poesy* mundane to Addison's interest in poetic justice and history writing; Sidney, "Defence of Poesy," 225 ll. 530–73. I analyze the Dantean aspect of Addison's *Cato* elsewhere: Poston, "Passionsspiel Der Geschichte."

50. Smithers, *Life*, 27.

51. Walker, "Addison's *Cato*," 92, 96.

52. *Cato*, 4.4.151–60 (87).

53. Malek, "Fifth Act." Halsband had earlier also emphasized Addison's late composition of act 5 and revisions of the entire play, showing evidence for several important late changes—including an increased emphasis on "liberty"—at the behest of Lady Mary Wortley Montagu, the wife of Addison's close associate Edward Wortley Montagu. Halsband, "Addison's *Cato* and Lady Mary Wortley Montagu."

54. In his autobiography, Colley Cibber indicates such reasons for Addison's delay in presenting the drama to the public after showing the first four acts to Cibber in 1703. Cibber, *Apology*, 267; Reed, "Some Unpublished Notes," 181.

55. Some rumors held that Addison wrote the fifth act under pressure from colleagues—John Hughes in particular—who believed it would be useful as a needed bulwark against Jacobitism. See Wilson, *Race of Female Patriots*, 23.

56. For such readings, see Armistead, "Drama of Renewal," 271; Radford, "Alas!," 32; Freeman, "What's Love Got to Do with Addison's *Cato*?"; and Terry, "Revolt in Utica."

57. Wolloch, "Cato the Younger," 71.

58. Plutarch, *Cato the Younger*, 70.5–6. Plutarch may have exaggerated the irrational and gruesome aspects of Cato's death, perhaps to critique Cato or perhaps more passively echoing propagandistic distortions in sources like Caesar's lost *Anti-Cato*. Zadorojnyi, "Cato's Suicide in Plutarch," 219–20.

59. *Cato*, 5.4.93–5 (96).

60. Plutarch, *Cato the Younger*, 59.5.

61. Faller, *Popularity of Addison's Cato*, 72; Radford, "Alas!," 35; Terry, "Revolt in Utica," 136–37; Wolloch, "Cato the Younger," 68

62. Stadter, *Plutarch*, 307–12.

63. *Spectator* 243, 2:444.

64. Montaigne, *Essays*, 247–49.

65. See *Spectator* 265, discussed in the context of Addison's relation to Marlborough in Smithers, *Life*, 215.

66. *Spectator* 548, 4:463–64.

67. Kantorowicz, *King's Two Bodies*, 3.

68. As a sleeping "Lucifer," his name more imaginatively suggests a playful reversal of Marlowe's *Dr. Faustus*. Here, the devil works by simply falling asleep in the midst of one of history's biggest tumults, thus keeping the would-be scholar Brutus from the balm of literature and pleasing entertainment, condemning him and Rome to the real hell of politics and worry unallayed by art.

69. Shakespeare, *Julius Caesar*, 2.1.10–19 (197–98).

70. Daniell, "Introduction," 17–21.

71. In *How the World Became a Stage*, William Egginton argues that theatricality as a constantly realizable breakage in time was constitutive of modernity.

72. "Perpetual Easter Calculator: Julian/Gregorian Easter Sunday and Jewish Passover," https://webspace.science.uu.nl/~gent0113/easter/easter_text4c.htm. The printed Wyvill sermon, for instance, prints both dates for Easter: "April 5/16 1713." Wyvill, *Sermon Preach'd*.

73. See: "Appendix: Plutarch's Lives," in Shakespeare, *Julius Caesar*, 323–71.

74. Plutarch, *Cato the Younger*, 66.1–3.

75. *Cato* belongs to the genre of military siege dramas.

76. *Cato*, 4.4.4–6 (80).

77. Radford, "Alas!," 35.

78. Middleton, *History of the Life of Cicero*, 419–20; Shakespeare, *Julius Caesar*, 152.

79. Bruyn, "Reference Guide," 390.

80. Hogan, *Shakespeare in the Theatre*, 9–11; Avery, *London Stage 1660–1800*, 137, 206, 299, 301.

81. For an overview of different critical responses, see Terry, "Revolt in Utica," 121–22, 133–35.

82. *Cato*, 4.4.66 (83).

83. Saintsbury, *Peace of the Augustans*, 39.

84. A contemporary critic indicated that Cato's wrathful grief came through in performance later during the same scene when the he saw Marcus's body. *Examiner* 45 (April 27–May 1, 1713); quoted in Bloom and Bloom, *Addison and Steele*, 267–68. On Booth, see Reed, "Some Unpublished Notes," 181.

85. Walker, "Addison's *Cato*," 91; Loftis, *Politics of Drama*, 58; Freeman, "What's Love Got to Do with Addison's *Cato*?," 464. The pamphlet war over *Cato* was something of a reperformance of an original Roman pamphlet war over Cato and his character after his death, in which Caesar wrote his lost *Anti-Cato*. Kelsall, "Meaning of Addison's Cato," 151.

86. Johnson, "Addison," 338.

87. R. D. Hume, "Theatres and Repertory," 57.

88. "Gay to Maurice Johnson, Jr. 23 April 1713," in Burgess, *Letters of John Gay*, 2–3.

89. "Berkeley to Percival April 16th, 1713," in Rand, *Berkeley and Percival*, 113.

90. Cibber, *Apology*, 268.

91. Faller, *Popularity of Addison's Cato*, 6.

92. Faller, 84–88.

93. Plutarch, *Cato the Younger*, 66.4–70.1. Addison's bedroom soliloquy is likely based on the extended reading soliloquy of Cato written by Thomas May (the secretary of the Long Parliament) in his 1630 continuation of Lucan's unfinished *Pharsalia*: May, *A Continuation*, book 4, 60–65. See *Notes and Queries*, series 1, vol. 3: March 1, 1851, 70:167 and April 12, 1851, 76:279–80.

94. *Cato*, 5.1 (88–9).

95. *Cato*, 5.4.31–4 (93).

96. Shakespeare, *Julius Caesar*, 196.

97. *Cato*, 4.4.98–9 (85)

98. *Cato*, 4.2 (73–4); Ellison, *Cato's Tears*, 60.

99. Rosenthal observes the scene's specific reversal of racist stereotypes of African/Roman masculinity in regard to rape ("Juba's Roman Soul," 73).

100. *Cato*, 1.5 (24–6), 1.6.11–17 (26), 4.1.20–21 (72).

101. *Cato*, 4.3.41 (70).

102. The navel of the tragedy, the scene uncannily expresses the play's unconscious murder and replacement of the historical, tightly related Roman Brutus by a free, exogamous foreign prince.

103. *Cato*, 4.3.97 (79).

104. *Cato*, 2.4.79–80 (44).

105. Radford, "Alas!," 36.

106. *Cato*, 5.4.96–112 (96–97).

107. Armistead, "Drama of Renewal." For Addison on the tragicomedy, see *Spectator* 40, 1:168–72. My argument is not that Addison intended *Cato*, a highly regular neoclassical Aristotelian tragedy, as a tragicomedy; rather, it is that the metatheatrical, providential plotline transforms *Cato* into a historical passion play, granting its concluding family tableaux a comic weight as redeeming, serious "gospel."

108. Faller, *Popularity of Addison's Cato*, 75; Edwards, "Modelling Roman Suicide?"

109. Joseph Roach influentially defined the theatrical effigy as "a set of actions that hold open a place in memory into which many different people may step according to circumstances and occasions." Roach, *Cities of the Dead*, 36.

110. "Pope to Caryll, 30 April 1713," in Pope, *Correspondence*, 175. After Addison's death, Steele touted his audience-packing at *Cato*'s premiere as proof of his service to his friend and as ensuring the popular success of the tragedy. Steele, "To Mr. Congreve," xv–vi.

111. Pope, *Correspondence*, 175. Pope's precise meaning in his phrase "more [from] the Hand than the Head" is unclear: the missing "from" adds ambiguity, and earlier printings of this letter use "and" instead of "than." Pope, *Letters*, 195–96.

112. Rosenthal, "Juba's Roman Soul"; Freeman, "What's Love Got to Do with Addison's *Cato*?"; Armistead, "Drama of Renewal"; Radford, "Alas!" For Pope's claim, see Smithers, *Life*, 271; and Halsband, "Addison's *Cato* and Lady Mary Wortley Montagu," 1125n21.

113. Robert Shiels, *The Lives of the Poets of Great Britain and Ireland*, vol. 3 (London, 1753), 315–6; quoted in Battersby, "Johnson and Shiels," 532.

114. Freeman, "What's Love Got to Do with Addison's *Cato*?," 461, 470.

115. Ellison, "Cato's Tears," 592–93.

116. Hale likely quoted *Cato* in his famous death speech: "I only regret that I have but one life to lose for my country." Shaffer, *Performing Patriotism*, 30–32. See also Ellison, *Cato's Tears*, 67–69.

117. The occasional verses surrounding the play's immediate reception demonstrated "a preoccupation with gender," both with manliness and women's responses to the play. Pope and Rowe even satirized the gender-laden hyperbolic praise of Addison's tragedy—for example, in Pope's sharp, parodic poem "On a Woman Who Pist at the Tragedy of *Cato*." See Wilson, *Race of Female Patriots*, 22, 26–30.

118. *Cato*, 4.4.152–53 (87).

119. Pope, *Correspondence*, 175.

120. For a reading that, to the contrary, stresses the misogyny and racism in Addison's depiction of Marcia and Juba disciplining themselves to "shine" like the white patriarch, see Canfield, *Heroes and States,* 161–62.

121. The historical Cato's marriage was less than conventional: according to Plutarch, he "loaned" his wife to a friend for several years for the purpose of child-rearing. Pope poked fun at this fact in an epilogue to Rowe's *Jane Shore* the year after *Cato*'s premiere: "Plu-Plutarch, what's his name, that writes his life? / Tells us, that Cato dearly lov'd his wife: / Yet if a friend, a night or so, should need her, / He'd recommend her as a special breeder." Quoted in Clery, *Feminization Debate,* 110.

122. Book 2:100 in Appian, *Civil Wars,* 433. Addison's Juba may imaginatively merge King Juba and the prince Juba II, who was still an infant when Caesar took him from Utica to Rome and who later achieved greatness as a writer and theater historian.

123. *Cato* 1.4 (17–24) and 2.5 (44–51).

124. Rosenthal, "Juba's Roman Soul," 66–67. Taylor reads Juba's mixed rhetoric as providing the solution to the "crisis of rhetoric," in keeping with Whig integrationist national-imperial ideology: Taylor, "Cato and the Crisis," 227–30.

125. *Cato,* 4.4.17–51/127–28 (80–82, 86).

126. Ellison, *Cato's Tears,* 52.

127. *Cato,* 4.4.94 (84).

128. Rosenthal, "Juba's Roman Soul," 74.

129. Armistead, "Drama of Renewal," 279.

130. Freeman, "What's Love Got to Do with Addison's *Cato?*," 466.

131. Rosenthal, "Juba's Roman Soul," 67–68.

132. *Cato,* 5.4.88–90 (96).

133. Reed, "Some Unpublished Notes," 182.

134. Rosenthal, "Juba's Roman Soul," 68–69. See Gildon's 1694 open letter to Dryden; discussed in Orr, *Empire on the British Stage,* 22–25.

135. The "second" couple (Lucia and Portius) in the play's closing tableaux would have politely evoked Princess Anne and Prince George, biding their time in the royal suburbs.

136. Rosenthal, "Juba's Roman Soul," 75.

137. Addison, *Freeholder* 34, 192.

138. Walker, "Addison's *Cato,*" 104.

139. Milton, *Samson Agonistes,* 115–19 (ll. 1577–end).

140. Milton, 65.

141. Seneca, *De Providentia,* 2.12; quoted in Edwards, "Modelling Roman Suicide?," 206–8.

142. Milton, *Samson Agonistes,* 115 (ll. 1595–1600). For a differing brief comparison of the two plays, see Kelsall, "Meaning of Addison's Cato," 162.

143. Hoole, *Catonis Disticha,* 10.

144. Agamben, *Homo Sacer,* 8.

145. Seneca, *De Providentia,* 2.9; quoted in Edwards, "Modelling Roman Suicide?," 207–8.

146. *Cato,* 5.1.27–31 (89).

147. Ayres, *Classical Culture,* xiv.

148. Augustine, *City of God*, 1:23–24 (34–35).
149. Plutarch, *Cato the Younger*, 71.1.
150. Wolloch, "Cato the Younger," 78–80.
151. Plutarch, *Cato the Younger*, 71.2.
152. Smithers, *Life*, 264.
153. Wolloch, "Cato the Younger," 66.
154. Voltaire, *Letters Concerning the English Nation*, 178–79. Voltaire lamented the play's "dull love plot," which he believed Addison added on to fit his age and milieu's "effeminate" theatrical taste, inherited from the French. But his argument was colored by his own long-running frustration with demands from actors and others that he himself insert love plots into his own dramas. See Carlson, *Voltaire*, 27, 42, 46, 56, 75.
155. Smithers, *Life*, 276–77.
156. Smithers, 293, 299, 301–3.
157. Smithers, 293.
158. "Pope to Caryll, 30 April 1713," in Pope, *Correspondence*, 175; Steele, "To the Author of the Tragedy of Cato," in Addison, *Works*, 1:162.
159. Johnson, "Addison," 19.
160. "39. From Jonathan Swift (09 July 1717)," in the appendix of Addison, *Letters*, 504.
161. Swift, "Sentiments of a Church of England Man," 348.
162. *Cato*, 1.2.42–45 (14). The mostly lost irony of the speech is that Portius and Sempronius turn out to be the least deserving, though arguably most darkly successful, of *Cato*'s cast of characters. Voltaire, though, found Addison and his circle deserving of their rewards and the English meritocratic culture in this regard admirable in comparison to France. Voltaire, *Letters Concerning the English Nation*, 224–26.

7. *Cato*'s Coda

1. Young, *Conjectures on Original Composition*, 48; emphasis in original.
2. See chapter 1.
3. The five chapters of the book recall the five acts of a neoclassical tragedy.
4. Joyce, *Portrait of the Artist as a Young Man*, 171. Joyce's novel was originally published in 1914–15 as a series within Dora Marsden's journal, the *Egoist*.
5. Axelsson, *Political Aesthetics*, 20.
6. On Young's *Night Thoughts* as the shadow of *The Spectator*'s diurnality, see Jost, *Prose Immortality*, 69–102.
7. Young, *Conjectures on Original Composition*, 3.
8. Young, 47; emphasis in original.
9. Young, 43–44.
10. Jost, *Prose Immortality*, 92–99.
11. Young, *Conjectures on Original Composition*, 45–48.
12. Young, 48.
13. Young, 48–49.
14. I take this "Roachian" term from Shaffer, *Performing Patriotism*, 8, 34–35.
15. Klein, "Addisonian Afterlives," 114.

16. Klein, "Joseph Addison's Whiggism," 112.

17. Smithers, *Life*, 312.

18. Steele, "Prologue at the Opening of the Theatre-Royal."

19. Williams, *Poetry and the Creation of a Whig Literary Culture*, 232; Thomson, *Cambridge Introduction to English Theatre*, 77; Milhous and Hume, *London Stage*, 481–91.

20. Smithers, *Life*, 63, 78; Cibber, *Apology*, 267.

21. *Remarks on Several Parts of Italy*, in Addison, *Works*, 1:392; Hammond, "Joseph Addison's Opera," 602–3. Hammond notes that Addison continued to regularly attend operas throughout his European tour.

22. Addison's reaction to the competitive theatrical form—mocking its scenery, machines, and foreign language—can be found in *Spectators* 5, 13, 14, 18, 29, and 31. Milhous and Hume, *London Stage*, 597, 620–21. His criticism of Italian opera was linked to his project of stabilizing British national identity; see Axelsson, *Political Aesthetics*, 131–42, 241.

23. Johnson later passed on malicious hearsay that Addison's lack of promotion was due to his unsuitability for administrative work, but Smithers found no archival evidence for that claim and a fair amount of evidence strongly to the contrary. Smithers, *Life*, 302–4n6. Addison's staging of Queen Anne's funeral on the night of August 23–24, 1714, was praised in Edward Young's epistle "To Joseph Addison." In Young, *Poems* 2:242.

24. Budgell, *Letter to Cleomenes King of Sparta*, 208–11.

25. Smithers, *Life*, 324.

26. Smithers, *Life*, 304–5.

27. Addison's engagement in the classical poetic convention of praising the object of primary admiration through praise of its artistic representation is discussed in Davis, "Misguided by the Tuneful Throng," 86–87.

28. Monod, *Jacobitism and the English People*, 173–78.

29. Addison, *To Her Royal Highness*, 7.

30. Addison, 8–9.

31. Dryden, "To Sir Godfrey Kneller," in *Works*, 4:461–66. Dryden's well-known poem, more blatantly ambiguous in its slight treatment of William III, was published in 1694, when the young Addison was in close working contact with him about Latin translations.

32. Addison, *To Her Royal Highness*, 1–4.

33. Smithers, *Life*, 312, 323, 341, 364. At the time of their marriage, Addison was forty-four and Myddelton thirty-six. Her previous husband had died in 1701, three years after their marriage—a fate that Addison was to share. For a brief biographical study on Charlotte Myddelton, see Cooke, "Addison's Aristocratic Wife."

34. Smithers, *Life*, 314. The point speaks to the growing gulf between professional writers and professional politicians since the British Augustan age, even if one counts in significant later exceptions (e.g. Sheridan, Goethe, Disraeli, Neruda).

35. Smithers, 318, 341.

36. Pliny, in a letter to Severus, says the speech (Addison's classical model) was part of his duty as a newly appointed consul to offer thanks to the emperor on behalf of the state. Letter 18 in Pliny the Younger, *Epistulae*, 3:76–77.

37. *Freeholder* 2, 43–47.
38. Smithers, *Life,* 384, 375–81.
39. Smithers, 388–93.
40. Smithers, 390, 397–8. That James Francis Edward Stuart still enjoyed support from many high places—not just in England—is confirmed by a report from Francis Manning, ambassador at Bern, to Addison about a meeting between the Pretender and the Pope in 1717: "the interview is said to have been very mournful, and plenty of tears was shed between them." Smithers, 402.
41. Sheehan, *Balance of Power,* 108–9.
42. Smithers, *Life,* 400, 403.
43. Armistead, "Drama of Renewal," 281–82; Walker, "Addison's *Cato,*" 99–100; Smithers, *Life,* 324, 341, 370, 414.
44. Addison, *Drummer;* Baker, "Witchcraft, Addison, and the Drummer," 174–81.
45. Smithers, *Life,* 356.
46. McKendrick, Brewer, and Plumb, *Birth of a Consumer Society,* 96.
47. Smithers, *Life,* 370, 414, 419, 437.
48. Theobald, "Life and Character of M. Cato," 267.
49. Kelsall, "Meaning of Addison's *Cato,*" 151–52; Wolloch, "Cato the Younger," 70–71.
50. Smithers, *Life,* 126–27; Miller, "Strange Career," 660.
51. *Spectator* 370, 3:393.
52. *Spectator* 576, 4:569.
53. Smithers, *Life,* 448–52.
54. Steele, *Conscious Lovers.*
55. O'Brien, *Literature Incorporated,* 97; Knight, *Political Biography of Richard Steele,* 231, 236.
56. Knight, 189–90.
57. O'Brien, 99–102.
58. O'Brien, 101. In 1693, Edmond Halley had published the first life expectancies based on empirical data in response to a failed tonine: "Estimate of the Degrees of the Mortality of Mankind."
59. O'Brien, 81–82, 98. The monopoly functioned as a Tory answer to the long-existing, Whig-controlled East India Company and Bank of England.
60. O'Brien, 90–93. The medals on *Cato's* title page had originally served as a kind of copyright protection or guarantee of authenticity; perhaps they also indicated Addison's belief that the tragedy would be his "enduring" work.
61. O'Brien, 91; Bailyn, *Ideological Origins of the American Revolution,* 51.
62. Bailyn, 43.
63. O'Brien, *Literature Incorporated,* 24. For some examples of how Cato was used as a political spokesperson after Addison's death, see Higgins, "Remarks on Cato's Letters," 127–46.
64. To John Grigsby (8 June 1719), in Addison, *Letters,* 407.
65. Ault, "Pope and Addison."
66. Weinbrot, *Augustus Caesar in Augustan England,* 5–7.
67. Smithers, *Life,* viii.

68. The designation could, ambiguously, be to Bolingbroke or any number of exiled Jacobites, or even to James Frances Edward Stuart, himself.

69. Deschamps, *Cato*.

70. Smithers, *Life*, 356–57; Boulard-Jouslin, "Addison and France," 244.

71. Klein, "Addisonian Afterlives," 101–3. For a survey of the first hundred years of *Spectator* volumes printed in the British Isles that describes many of the contrasting, similar, and novel features in different editions, see Wilkinson, "Complete *Spectator*"; and Wilkinson, "Appendix."

72. DeMaria, "Addison, Samuel Johnson, and the Test of Time," 253–55, 259–60, 267–68. Shakespeare, Dryden, and Pope are more heavily quoted in Johnson's dictionary, but their oeuvres were much larger (259).

73. John H. Middendorf, ed., *The Yale Edition of the Works of Samuel Johnson*, vols. xxi–xxiii (New Haven, CT: Yale University Press, 2010), xx, 546; quoted in DeMaria, "Addison, Samuel Johnson," 266–67.

74. Boulard-Jouslin, "Addison and France," 249–50.

75. Boulard-Jouslin, 241, 246. Some of Addison's more critical passages on France and Louis XIV were omitted or remitted in French editions. Boulard-Jouslin, 248. On Addison's "othering" of France, see also Axelsson, *Political Aesthetics*, 126–28.

76. *Encyclopédie*, xvi (1765), 517 (Tragedy), translated and discussed in Boulard-Jouslin, 244.

77. Tocqueville, *Democracy in America*, 2:846.

78. *Universal Spectator and Weekly Journal*, 10 April 1731; quoted in Loftis, *Politics of Drama*, 82. The contained Dryden quote is from the anti-Whig satirical poem, *Absalom and Achitophel*.

79. Tocqueville, 2:847.

80. *Spectator* 463, 4:136–37.

81. Walker, "Addison's *Cato*," 104.

82. Smithers, *Life*, 267–8.

83. Voltaire, *Letters Concerning the English Nation*, 178.

84. Voltaire, "Preface to *Socrates*," 283–85. Writing as "Mr. Fatima," Voltaire's assertion that his play is a translation of an English version written by James Thomson from Addison's sketch is generally taken to be an utter fabrication. It remains, nonetheless, a telling piece of "Addisonia." See R.M. Davis, "Thomson and Voltaire's *Socrates*."

Bibliography

Abrams, M. H. *The Mirror and the Lamp: Romantic Theory and the Critical Tradition.* Oxford: Oxford University Press, 1953.
———. *Doing Things with Texts: Essays in Criticism and Critical Theory.* New York: W. W. Norton, 1989.
Adams, Henry. *The Education of Henry Adams.* Boston: Houghton Mifflin, 1918.
Addison, Joseph. *A Discourse on Ancient and Modern Learning.* London: T. Osborne, 1739.
———. "An Oration in Defence of the New Philosophy." In *A Week's Conversation on the Plurality of Worlds,* by Bernard Le Bovier Fontenelle. 6th ed. London: A. Bettesworth, 1737.
———. *Cato: A Tragedy, and Selected Essays.* Edited by Christine Dunn Henderson and Mark E. Yellin. Indianapolis: Liberty Fund, 2004.
———. *Some Portions of Essays Contributed to "The Spectator" by Mr. Joseph Addison.* Edited by J. Dykes Campbell. Glasgow: Bell & Bain, 1864.
———. *The Drummer; or, The Haunted House.* 2nd ed. London: John Darby, 1722.
———. *The Freeholder.* Edited by James Leheny. Oxford: Oxford University Press, 1979.
———. *The Latin Prose and Poetry of Joseph Addison.* Translated by Dana F. Sutton. Birmingham: University of Birmingham, 2005.
———. *The Letters of Joseph Addison.* Edited by Walter Graham. Oxford: Oxford University Press, 1941.
———. *The Miscellaneous Works of Joseph Addison.* Edited by A. C. Guthkelch. 2 vols. London: G. Bell & Sons, 1914.
———. *The Present State of the War.* London: J. Morphew, 1708.
———. *The Works of Joseph Addison.* 6 vols. London: George Bell & Sons, 1903.
Addison, Joseph, and Richard Steele. *The Guardian.* Edited by John Calhoun Stephens. Lexington: University of Kentucky Press, 1982.
———. *The Spectator.* Edited by Donald F. Bond. 5 vols. Oxford: Oxford University Press, 1987.
———. *The Tatler.* Edited by Donald F. Bond. 3 vols. Oxford: Oxford University Press, 1987.
Addisoniana. Vol. 1. London: Printed for Richard Phillips by T. Davison, 1803.
Agamben, Giorgio. *Homo Sacer: Sovereign Power and Bare Life.* Translated by Daniel Heller-Roazen. Palo Alto, CA: Stanford University Press, 1998.

Agnew, Jean-Christophe. *Worlds Apart: The Market and the Theater in Anglo-American Thought, 1550–1750.* Cambridge: Cambridge University Press, 1988.

Aikin, Lucy. *The Life of Joseph Addison.* 2 vols. London: Longman, Brown, Green & Longmans, 1843.

Alsop, J. D. "New Light on Joseph Addison." *Modern Philology* 80, no. 1 (1982): 13–34.

Anderson, Benedict. *Imagined Communities: Reflections on the Origin and Spread of Nationalism.* New York: Verso, 2006.

Arendt, Hannah. *The Origins of Totalitarianism.* New York: Houghton Mifflin Harcourt, 1968.

Armistead, J. M. "Drama of Renewal: Cato and Moral Empiricism." *Papers on Language & Literature* 17, no. 3 (Summer 1981): 271.

Appian. *Civil Wars.* Vol. 4 of *Roman History.* Translated by Brian McGing. Cambridge, MA: Harvard University Press, 2020.

Ashton, John. *Social Life in the Reign of Queen Anne.* London: Chatto & Windus, 1904.

Augustine, Aurelius. *The City of God.* Vol. 1. Translated by Marcus Dods. Edinburgh: T. & T. Clark, 1871.

Ault, Norman. "Pope and Addison." *Review of English Studies* 17, no. 68 (1941): 428–51.

Austin, J. L. *How to Do Things with Words.* 2nd ed. Cambridge, MA: Harvard University Press, 1975.

Avery, Emmett L., ed. *The London Stage 1660–1800.* Vol. 2, *1700–1729.* Carbondale: Southern Illinois University Press, 1960.

Axelsson, Karl. *Political Aesthetics: Addison and Shaftesbury on Taste, Morals, and Society.* London: Bloomsbury Academic, 2019.

Axton, Marie. *The Queen's Two Bodies: Drama and the Elizabethan Succession.* London: Royal Historical Society, 1977.

Ayres, Philip. *Classical Culture and the Idea of Rome in Eighteenth-Century England.* Cambridge: Cambridge University Press, 1997.

Backscheider, Paula R., and Timothy Dykstal, eds. *The Intersections of the Public and Private Spheres in Early Modern England.* London: Routledge, 1996.

Baker, Donald C. "Witchcraft, Addison, and the Drummer." *Studia Neophilologica* 31, no. 2 (1 January 1959): 174–81.

Barbauld, Anna Laetitia. *Selections from the "Spectator," "Tatler," "Guardian," and "Freeholder."* Vol. 1. London: J. Johnson, 1804.

Barry, Jonathan. "Introduction." In *The Middling Sort of People: Culture, Society, and Politics in England, 1550–1800,* edited by Jonathan Barry and Christopher Brooks, 1–27. New York: Palgrave Macmillan, 1994.

Battersby, James L. "Johnson and Shiels: Biographers of Addison." *Studies in English Literature, 1500–1900* 9, no. 3 (1969): 521–37.

Basker, James. "Criticism and the Rise of Periodical Literature." In *The Cambridge History of Literary Criticism.* Vol. 4, *The Eighteenth Century,* edited by H. B. Nisbet and Claude Julien Rawson, 316–34. Cambridge: Cambridge University Press, 2005.

Bailyn, Bernard. *The Ideological Origins of the American Revolution.* Cambridge, MA: Harvard University Press, 1992.

Baudot, Laura. "Joseph Addison's Lucretian Imagination." *ELH* 84, no. 4 (2017): 891–918.

Benn, Gottfried. "Doppelleben." In *Autobiographische und vermischte Schriften, Ges. Werke IV.* Wiesbaden: Limes VLG, 1961.
Bentham, Jeremy. *The Works of Jeremy Bentham.* Vol. 4. Edited by John Bowring. Edinburgh: William Tait, 1843.
Black, Scott. "Addison's Aesthetics of Novelty." *Studies in Eighteenth-Century Culture* 30, no. 1 (2001): 269–88.
———. "Social and Literary Form in *The Spectator.*" *Eighteenth-Century Studies* 33, no. 1 (1999): 21–42.
Bloom, Edward Alan, and Lillian D. Bloom. *Joseph Addison's Sociable Animal: In the Market Place, on the Hustings, in the Pulpit.* Providence, RI: Brown University Press, 1971.
Bloom, Edward Alan, and Lillian D. Bloom, eds. *Addison and Steele, the Critical Heritage.* London: Routledge, 1980.
Bloom, Lillian D. "Addison as Translator: A Problem in Neo-Classical Scholarship." *Studies in Philology* 46, no. 1 (1949): 31–53.
Blumenberg, Hans. "Die Kopernikanische Konsequenz für den Zeitbegriff." In *The Reception of Copernicus' Heliocentric Theory,* 57–77. New York: Springer, 1973.
Bond, Donald F. "The First Printing of *The Spectator.*" *Modern Philology* 47, no. 3 (1950): 164–77.
Bossert, A. R. "Slavery and Anti-Republicanism in Sir Ralph Freeman's *Imperiale, a Tragedy* (1639)." *Early Theatre* 13, no. 1 (2010): 83–108.
Boulard-Jouslin, Claire. "Addison and France." In Davis, *Joseph Addison,* 232–50.
———. "Introduction." In Boulard-Jouslin and Ertler, *Addison and Europe,* 11–21.
Boulard Jouslin, Claire and Klaus-Dieter Ertler, eds. *Addison and Europe / Addison et l'Europe.* Berlin: Peter Lang, 2020.
Bowers, Terence. "Universalizing Sociability: *The Spectator,* Civic Enfranchisement, and the Rule(s) of the Public Sphere." In *The Spectator: Emerging Discourses,* edited by Donald J. Newman, 150–74. Newark: University of Delaware Press, 2005.
Boyer, Abel. *The Political State of Great Britain.* Vol. 8. London: John Baker, 1714.
Brewer, John. *The Pleasures of the Imagination: English Culture in the Eighteenth Century.* London: Routledge, 2013.
Broadus, Edmund K. "Addison's Discourse on Ancient and Modern Learning." *Modern Language Notes* 22, no. 1 (1907): 1–2.
———. "Addison's Influence on the Development of Interest in Folk-Poetry in the Eighteenth Century." *Modern Philology* 8, no. 1 (1910): 123–34.
Brockett, Oscar G., and Franklin J. Hildy. *History of the Theatre.* 10th ed. New York: Pearson, 2010.
Bruyn, Frans de. "Reference Guide." In *Shakespeare in the Eighteenth Century,* edited by Fiona Ritchie and Peter Sabor, 349–436. Cambridge: Cambridge University Press, 2012.
Budgell, Eustace. *A Letter to Cleomenes King of Sparta.* London: Printed for A. Moore, 1731.
Burgess, C. F., ed. *The Letters of John Gay.* Oxford: Oxford University Press, 1966.
Cahill, Edward. *Liberty of the Imagination: Aesthetic Theory, Literary Form, and Politics in the Early United States.* Philadelphia: University of Pennsylvania Press, 2012.

Canfield, J. Douglas. *Heroes and States: On the Ideology of Restoration Tragedy*. Lexington: University Press of Kentucky, 2000.

Cannon, John. *Samuel Johnson and the Politics of Hanoverian Britain*. Oxford: Oxford University Press, 1994.

Carey, Brycchan. "'Accounts of Savage Nations': *The Spectator* and the Americas." In Newman, *Spectator*, 129–49.

Carlson, Marvin. *The Haunted Stage: The Theatre as Memory Machine*. Ann Arbor: University of Michigan Press, 2001.

——— . "The Iconic Stage." *Journal of Dramatic Theory and Criticism* 3, no. 2 (1989): 3–18.

——— . *Performance: A Critical Introduction*. 2nd ed. New York: Routledge, 2003.

——— . "Theorizing the Performative Event." In *The Oxford Handbook of the Georgian Theatre, 1737–1832*, edited by Julia Swindells and David Francis Taylor, 53–69. Oxford: Oxford University Press, 2014.

——— . *Voltaire and the Theatre of the Eighteenth Century*. Westport, CT: Greenwood, 1998.

Champion, J. A. I. *The Pillars of Priestcraft Shaken: The Church of England and Its Enemies, 1660–1730*. Cambridge: Cambridge University Press, 1992.

Chico, Tita. *Designing Women: The Dressing Room in Eighteenth-Century English Literature and Culture*. Lewisburg, PA: Bucknell University Press, 2005.

Cibber, Colley. *An Apology for the Life of Colley Cibber, Comedian, and Late Patentee of the Theatre-Royal*. London: John Watts, 1740.

Clery, E. J. *The Feminization Debate in Eighteenth-Century England: Literature, Commerce, and Luxury*. New York: Palgrave Macmillan, 2004.

Cooke, Arthur L. "Addison's Aristocratic Wife." *PMLA* 72, no. 3 (June 1957): 373–89.

Cordero, Alberto. "Scientific Realism and the Divide et Impera Strategy: The Ether Saga Revisited." *Philosophy of Science* 78, no. 5 (1 December 2011): 1120–30.

Council, Norman. "'O Dea Certe': The Allegory of 'The Fortress of Perfect Beauty.'" *Huntington Library Quarterly* 39, no. 4 (1976): 329–42.

Courthope, W. J. *Addison*. London: Macmillan, 1884.

Cowan, Brian William. "Mr. Spectator and the Doctor." In Davis, *Joseph Addison*, 40–60.

——— . *The Social Life of Coffee: The Emergence of the British Coffeehouse*. New Haven, CT: Yale University Press, 2005.

Craig, John Herbert McCutcheon. *Newton at the Mint*. Cambridge: Cambridge University Press, 1946.

Daniell, David. "Introduction." In Shakespeare, *Julius Caesar*, 1–147. London: Bloomsbury, 1998.

Dart, Gregory. "Addison and the Romantics." In Davis, *Joseph Addison*, 290–307.

Davis, Paul. "Addison's Forgotten Poetic Response to *Paradise Lost*." *Milton Quarterly* 49, no. 4 (2015): 243–74.

——— . "Introduction." In Davis, *Joseph Addison*, 1–17.

——— . "'Misguided by the Tuneful Throng': Addison at the Rubicon." In Boulard-Jouslin and Ertler, *Addison and Europe*, 79–91.

——— . "Was Addison a Poet?" In Davis, *Joseph Addison*, 61–79.

Davis, Paul, ed. *Joseph Addison: Tercentenary Essays.* Oxford: Oxford University Press, 2021.

Davis, Rose Marie. "Thomson and Voltaire's *Socrate.*" *PMLA* 49, no. 2 (June 1934): 560–65.

Defoe, Daniel. *Robinson Crusoe.* Oxford: Oxford University Press, 1988.

DeMaria Jr., Robert. "Addison, Samuel Johnson, and the Test of Time." In Davis, *Joseph Addison,* 251–71.

Dennis, John. *Remarks upon Cato, a Tragedy.* London: B. Lintott, 1713.

Deschamps, François-Michel-Chrétien. *Cato: A Tragedy: As It Is Acted at the Theatre in Lincolns-Inn-Fields.* London: E. Curll, 1716.

Diamond, Elin. "Brechtian Theory/Feminist Theory." *TDR* 32, no. 1 (1998): 82–94.

Dillon, Elizabeth Maddock. *New World Drama: The Performative Commons in the Atlantic World, 1649–1849.* Durham, NC: Duke University Press, 2014.

Doms, Misia Sophia. *"Spectator"-Type Periodicals in International Perspective: Enlightened Moral Journalism in Europe and North America.* Berlin: Peter Lang, 2019.

Donoghue, John. "'Out of the Land of Bondage': The English Revolution and the Atlantic Origins of Abolition." *American Historical Review* 115, no. 4 (2010): 943–74.

Dryden, John. *The Works of John Dryden.* Vol. 4, *Poems, 1693–1696.* Edited by A. B. Chambers, William Frost, and Vinton A. Dearing. Oxford: Oxford University Press, 1974.

Edwards, Catharine. "Modelling Roman Suicide? The Afterlife of Cato." *Economy and Society* 34, no. 2 (2005): 200–222.

Egginton, William. *How the World Became a Stage: Presence, Theatricality, and the Question of Modernity.* Albany: State University of New York Press, 2012.

Eliot, T. S. "The Metaphysical Poets." In *Selected Essays,* 2nd ed., 281–91. London: Faber & Faber, 1934.

———. *The Use of Poetry and the Use of Criticism.* London: Faber & Faber, 1933.

Ellis, Markman. "Coffee-Women, *The Spectator,* and the Public Sphere in the Early Eighteenth Century." In *Women, Writing, and the Public Sphere, 1700–1830,* edited by Elizabeth Eger, Charlotte Grant, Clíona Ó Gallchoir, and Penny Warburton, 27–52. Cambridge: Cambridge University Press, 2001.

———. *Eighteenth-Century Coffee-House Culture.* Vol 1. London: Routledge, 2017.

———. "Sociability and Polite Improvement in Addison's Periodicals." In Davis, *Joseph Addison,* 142–63.

———. "Time and the Essay: *The Spectator* and Diurnal Form." In *On Essays: Montaigne to the Present,* edited by Thomas Karshan and Kathryn Murphy, 97–113. Oxford: Oxford University Press, 2020.

Ellison, Julie. "Cato's Tears." *ELH* 63, no. 3 (1996): 571–601.

———. *Cato's Tears and the Making of Anglo-American Emotion.* Chicago: University of Chicago Press, 1999.

Engell, James. *The Creative Imagination: Enlightenment to Romanticism.* Cambridge, MA: Harvard University Press, 1981.

Erskine-Hill, Howard. *The Augustan Idea in English Literature.* London: E. Arnold, 1983.

———. "Twofold Vision in Eighteenth-Century Writing." *ELH* 64, no. 4 (Winter 1997): 903–24.

Ertler, Klaus-Dieter, Yvonne Völkl, Elisabeth Hobisch, Alexandra Fuchs, and Hans Fernández, eds. *Storytelling in the Spectators / Storytelling Dans Les Spectateurs*. Bern: Peter Lang, 2020.

Ertler, Klaus-Dieter. "Addison, Lecteur de Bayle." In Boulard-Jouslin and Ertler, *Addison and Europe*, 93–107.

"Estimates Database. 2013. Voyages: The Trans-Atlantic Slave Trade Database." http://www.slavevoyages.org/assessment/estimates.

Faller, Lincoln B. *The Popularity of Addison's "Cato" and Lillo's "The London Merchant," 1700–1776*. New York: Garland, 1988.

Fenollosa, Ernest, and Ezra Pound. *"Noh", or, Accomplishment: A Study of the Classical Stage of Japan*. London: Macmillan, 1916.

Fitzmaurice, Susan. "Coalitions, Networks, and Discourse Communities in Augustan England: *The Spectator* and the Early Eighteenth-Century Essay." In *Eighteenth-Century English: Ideology and Change*, edited by Raymond Hickey, 106–32. Cambridge: Cambridge University Press, 2010.

Foucault, Michel. *Security, Territory, Population: Lectures at the Collège de France, 1977–1978*. Translated by Graham Burchell. New York: Palgrave Macmillan, 2009.

Franklin, Benjamin. *The Autobiography and Other Writings on Politics, Economics, and Virtue*. Edited by Alan Houston. Cambridge: Cambridge University Press, 2004.

Fraser, Nancy. "Rethinking the Public Sphere: A Contribution to the Critique of Actually Existing Democracy." *Social Text*, no. 25/26 (1990): 56–80.

———. "What's Critical about Critical Theory? The Case of Habermas and Gender." *New German Critique*, no. 35 (1985): 97–131.

Freeman, Lisa A. *Character's Theater: Genre and Identity on the Eighteenth-Century English Stage*. Philadelphia: University of Pennsylvania Press, 2013.

———. "What's Love Got to Do with Addison's *Cato*?" *Studies in English Literature, 1500–1900* 39, no. 3 (1999): 463–82.

French, H. R. *The Middle Sort of People in Provincial England, 1600–1750*. Oxford: Oxford University Press, 2007.

Freud, Sigmund. *The Interpretation of Dreams*. Vol. 4 of *The Standard Edition of the Complete Psychological Works of Sigmund Freud*, edited by James Strachey. London: Hogarth, [1900] 1953.

———. *Civilization and its Discontents*. Vol. 21 of *The Standard Edition of the Complete Psychological Works of Sigmund Freud*, edited by James Strachey, 57–146. London: Hogarth, [1930] 1953.

Fryer, Peter. *Staying Power: The History of Black People in Britain*. London: Pluto, 1984.

Gámez, Luis Rene. "'And Art Reflected Images to Art': Addison's Use of Numismatics in *Cato*." *Modern Philology* 85, no. 3 (1988): 256–64.

Genovese, Michael. *The Problem of Profit: Finance and Feeling in Eighteenth-Century British Literature*. Charlottesville: University of Virginia Press, 2019.

Gillingham, John. "French Chivalry in Twelfth-Century Britain." *Historian*, no. 122 (Summer 2014): 6–10.

Gippert, Susanne. *Joseph Addison's "Ovid": An Adaptation of the "Metamorphoses" in the Augustan Age of English Literature.* Remscheid: Gardez!, 2003.

Giusti, Elena. *Carthage in Virgil's "Aeneid": Staging the Enemy under Augustus.* Cambridge: Cambridge University Press, 2018.

Goebel, Eckart. *Ambition: An Essay on the Burning Desire to Rise.* Translated by James C. Wagner. New York: Bloomsbury, 2022.

———. *Beyond Discontent: "Sublimation" from Goethe to Lacan.* Translated by James C. Wagner. New York: Bloomsbury, 2012.

Goodall, Jane. *Stage Presence.* New York: Routledge, 2008.

Graham-Jones, Jean. *Evita, Inevitably: Performing Argentina's Female Icons before and after Eva Perón.* Ann Arbor: University of Michigan Press, 2014.

Greenblatt, Stephen, and M. H. Abrams, eds. *The Norton Anthology of English Literature.* 2 vols. 8th ed. New York: W. W. Norton, 2006.

Gregg, Edward. "Was Queen Anne a Jacobite?" *History* 57, no. 191 (1972): 358–75.

Grindle, Nick. "Virgil's Prospects: The Gentry and the Representation of Landscape in Addison's Theory of the Imagination." *Oxford Art Journal* 29, no. 2 (1 June 2006): 185–95.

Guyer, Paul. *Values of Beauty: Historical Essays in Aesthetics.* Cambridge: Cambridge University Press, 2005.

Haan, Estelle. "Twin Augustans: Addison, Hannes, and Horatian Intertexts." *Notes and Queries* 52, no. 3 (September 2005): 338–46.

———. *Vergilius Redivivus: Studies in Joseph Addison's Latin Poetry.* Philadelphia: American Philosophical Society, 2005.

Habermas, Jürgen. *The Structural Transformation of the Public Sphere: An Inquiry into a Category of Bourgeois Society.* Translated by Thomas Burger. Cambridge, MA: MIT Press, 1989.

Hacking, Ian. "Do We See through a Microscope?" In *Images of Science: Essays on Realism and Empiricism,* edited by Paul M. Churchland and Clifford A. Hooker, 133–52. Chicago: University Of Chicago Press, 1985.

Hall, A. Rupert, and Laura Tilling, eds. *The Correspondence of Isaac Newton.* Vols. 4–5. Cambridge: Cambridge University Press, 1976.

Halsband, Robert. "Addison's *Cato* and Lady Mary Wortley Montagu." *PMLA* 65, no. 6 (December 1950): 1122–29.

Hammond, Brean S. "Joseph Addison's Opera *Rosamond:* Britishness in the Early Eighteenth Century." *ELH* 73, no. 3 (30 August 2006): 601–29.

Hansen, David A. "Addison on Ornament and Poetic Style." In *Studies in Criticism and Aesthetics, 1660–1800: Essays in Honor of Samuel Holt Monk,* edited by Howard Anderson and John S. Shea. 94–127. Minneapolis: University of Minnesota, 1967.

Harrison, John. *The Library of Isaac Newton.* Cambridge: Cambridge University Press, 1978.

Havely, Nick. "Dante's Reception in the English-Speaking World." In *English Writing and Culture: High and Late Medieval, 1066–1485,* edited by Kate Ash-Irisarri, Rory Critten, David Fuller, Natalie Hanna, Hugh Magennis, Jamie McKinstry, Sarah Peverley, and Sebastian Sobecki. Vol. 1.2.1.02 of *The Literary Encyclopedia,* edited by Jo

Ann Cavallo, 2009. https://www.litencyc.com/php/stopics.php?rec=true&UID=5773.

Hawkins, Edward, Augustus Wollaston Franks, and Herbert A. Grueber. *Medallic Illustrations of the History of Great Britain and Ireland to the Death of George II*. London: British Museum, 1885.

Hayes, Richard W. "The Black Atlantic and Georgian London." In *Colonial Frames, Nationalist Histories: Imperial Legacies, Architecture, and Modernity*, edited by Mrinalini Rajagopalan and Madhuri Desai, 137–60. Surrey: Ashgate, 2012.

Heavilin, Barbara A. "'A Love for Joseph Addison': Wit, Style, and Truth in Steinbeck's *America and Americans*." *Steinbeck Review* 6, no. 2 (1 September 2009): 39–54.

Henderson, Christine Dunn. "On Bourgeois Dignity: Making the Self-Made Man." In *Dignity: A History*, edited by Remy Debes, 269–90. Oxford University Press, 2017.

Herrick, Marvin T. "Aristotle's Pity and Fear." *Philological Quarterly*, no. 9 (1 January 1930): 141.

Higgins, Ian. "Remarks on *Cato's Letters*." In Womersley, *Cultures of Whiggism*, 127–46.

Hill, H. "Dionysius of Halicarnassus and the Origins of Rome." *Journal of Roman Studies* 51, pts. 1–2 (1961): 88–93.

Hipple, Walter John. *The Beautiful, the Sublime, and the Picturesque in Eighteenth-Century British Aesthetic Theory*. Carbondale: Southern Illinois University Press, 1957.

Hogan, Charles Beecher. *Shakespeare in the Theatre, 1701–1800*. Vol. 1. Oxford: Clarendon, 1952.

Hone, Joseph. "Isaac Newton and the Medals for Queen Anne." *Huntington Library Quarterly* 79, no. 1 (Spring 2016): 119–48.

———. *Literature and Party Politics at the Accession of Queen Anne*. Oxford: Oxford University Press, 2017.

Hoole, Charles, trans. *Catonis Disticha de Moribus with One Row English and Another Latin*. London: n.p., 1659.

Hopkins, David. "Addison as Translator." In Davis, *Joseph Addison*, 18–39.

Hudson, John. *The Oxford History of the Laws of England*. Vol. 2, *871–1216*. Edited by Sir John Baker. Oxford: Oxford University Press, 2012.

Hughes, Derek. "Restoration and Settlement: 1660 and 1688." In *The Cambridge Companion to English Restoration Theatre*, edited by Deborah Payne Fisk, 127–41. Cambridge: Cambridge University Press, 2000.

Hume, David. *Selected Essays*. Edited by Stephen Copley and Andrew Edgar. Oxford: Oxford University Press, 1996.

Hume, Robert D. *Reconstructing Contexts: The Aims and Principles of Archaeo-Historicism*. Oxford: Oxford University Press, 1999.

———. "Theatres and Repertory." In *The Cambridge History of British Theatre*, vol. 2, *1660–1895*, edited by Joseph Donohue, 53–70. Cambridge: Cambridge University Press, 2004.

Hunter, Michael Cyril William. *Science and the Shape of Orthodoxy: Intellectual Change in Late Seventeenth-Century Britain*. Woodbridge: Boydell & Brewer, 1995.

Jacob, Margaret C., and Larry Stewart. *Practical Matter: Newton's Science in the Service of Industry and Empire, 1687–1851. Cambridge, MA: Harvard University Press, 2004.

Jager, Colin. *The Book of God: Secularization and Design in the Romantic Era*. Philadelphia: University of Pennsylvania Press, 2007.

Jameson, Fredric. "Periodizing the 60s." *Social Text*, nos. 9–10 (1984): 178–209.

Janes, Regina. "Femicons." *Salmagundi*, nos. 135–36 (2002): 103–26.

Jensen, Freyja Cox. "'Creating' Cato in Early Modern England." In *Concepts of Creativity in Seventeenth-Century England*, edited by Rebecca Herissone and Alan Howard, 233–52. Woodbridge: Boydell & Brewer, 2013.

Johnson, James William. *The Formation of English Neo-Classical Thought*. Princeton, NJ: Princeton University Press, 1967.

Johnson, Monte, and Catherine Wilson. "Lucretius and the History of Science." In *The Cambridge Companion to Lucretius*, edited by Stuart Gillespie and Philip Hardie, 131–48. Cambridge: Cambridge University Press, 2007.

Johnson, Samuel. "Addison." In *The Lives of the Poets*, vol. 3, edited by Roger Lonsdale, 1–38. Oxford: Oxford University Press, 2006.

Jost, Jacob Sider. *Prose Immortality, 1711–1819*. Charlottesville: University of Virginia Press, 2015.

Joyce, James. *A Portrait of the Artist as a Young Man*. New York: Random House, 1916.

Jung, C. G. *The Tavistock Lectures: On the Theory and Practice of Analytical Psychology*. In *The Symbolic Life: Miscellaneous Writings*, translated by R. F. C. Hull, 1–182. Vol. 18 of *The Collected Works of C. G. Jung*, edited by Sir Herbert Read, Michael Fordham, Gerhard Adler, and William McGuire. Princeton, NJ: Princeton University Press, 1955.

Junqua, Amélie. "A Moment in Amsterdam—Joseph Addison and Jacob Tonson in 1703." In Boulard-Jouslin and Ertler, *Addison and Europe*, 37–48.

Justice, George. "*The Spectator* and Distance Education." In Newman, *Spectator*, 265–99.

Kantorowicz, Ernst H. *The King's Two Bodies: A Study in Mediaeval Political Theology*. Princeton, NJ: Princeton University Press, 1997.

Kelsall, Malcolm Miles. "The Meaning of Addison's *Cato*." *Review of English Studies* 17, no. 66 (1966): 149–62.

King, Thomas Alan. *The Gendering of Men, 1600–1750*. Madison: University of Wisconsin Press, 2004.

Klein, Lawrence E. "Addisonian Afterlives: Joseph Addison in Eighteenth-Century Culture." *Journal for Eighteenth-Century Studies* 35, no. 1 (1 March 2012): 101–18.

———. "Coffeehouse Civility, 1660–1714: An Aspect of Post-Courtly Culture in England." *Huntington Library Quarterly* 59, no. 1 (1996): 31–51.

———. "Joseph Addison's Whiggism." In Womersley, *Cultures of Whiggism*, 108–26.

———. *Shaftesbury and the Culture of Politeness: Moral Discourse and Cultural Politics in Early Eighteenth-Century England*. Cambridge: Cambridge University Press, 1994.

———. "Sociability, Solitude, and Enthusiasm." *Huntington Library Quarterly* 60, nos. 1–2 (1997): 153–77.

Knight, Charles A. *A Political Biography of Richard Steele*. London: Routledge, 2015.

Knights, Mark. *The Devil in Disguise: Deception, Delusion, and Fanaticism in the Early English Enlightenment.* Oxford: Oxford University Press, 2011.

———. *Representation and Misrepresentation in Later Stuart Britain: Partisanship and Political Culture.* Oxford: Oxford University Press, 2006.

Kohler, Max J. "Addison, Lancelot." In *The Jewish Encyclopedia,* edited by Isidore Singer, 189. New York: Funk & Wagnalls, 1901.

Kuhn, Thomas S. *The Structure of Scientific Revolutions.* Chicago: University of Chicago Press, 2012.

Kupperman, Karen Ordahl. *Providence Island, 1630–1641: The Other Puritan Colony.* Cambridge: Cambridge University Press, 1995.

Lacan, Jacques. "The Mirror Stage as Formative of the I Function as Revealed in Psychoanalytic Experience." In *Écrits,* translated by Bruce Fink, 75–81. New York: W. W. Norton, 2006.

Leigh and Sotheby. *A Catalogue of the Valuable Library, of the Late Celebrated Right Hon. Joseph Addison....* London: n.p., 1799.

Lewis, C. S. "Addison." In *Selected Literary Essays,* edited by Walter Hooper, 154–68. Cambridge: Cambridge University Press, 1979.

Lindskoog, Kathryn. "Carved in Stone: What the Bird Did Not Say Early in the Year." *Lewis Legacy,* no. 75 (1998). https://www.discovery.org/a/715/.

Locke, John. *The Second Treatise on Government.* In *Two Treatises of Government,* edited by Peter Laslett, 265–428. Cambridge: Cambridge University Press, 1988.

Loftis, John. *The Politics of Drama in Augustan England.* Oxford: Clarendon, 1963.

Lovejoy, Arthur O. *The Great Chain of Being: A Study of the History of an Idea.* Cambridge, MA: Harvard University Press, 1936.

Lovett, Frank. "Freedom, History Of." In *International Encyclopedia of the Social and Behavioral Sciences,* vol. 9, 2nd ed., edited by James D. Wright, 387–91. New York: Elsevier, 2015.

Lucretius Carus, Titus. *De rerum natura: On the Nature of Things.* Translated by William Ellery Leonard. New York: E. P. Dutton, 1916.

Macaulay, Thomas Babington Baron. "Life and Writings of Addison." In *Essays, Critical and Miscellaneous,* 594–623. Philadelphia, PA: Carey & Hart, 1846.

Mackie, Erin. *Market à la Mode: Fashion, Commodity, and Gender in "The Tatler" and "The Spectator."* Baltimore, MD: Johns Hopkins University Press, 1997.

———. *Rakes, Highwaymen, and Pirates: The Making of the Modern Gentleman in the Eighteenth Century.* Baltimore, MD: Johns Hopkins University Press, 2009.

Mackie, Erin, ed. *The Commerce of Everyday Life: Selections from "The Tatler" and "The Spectator."* New York: Bedford/St. Martin's, 1998.

Malek, James S. "The Fifth Act of Addison's *Cato.*" *Neuphilologische Mitteilungen* 74, no. 3 (1973): 515–19.

Mallipeddi, Ramesh. *Spectacular Suffering: Witnessing Slavery in the Eighteenth-Century British Atlantic.* Charlottesville: University of Virginia Press, 2016.

Marsden, Jean I. *Fatal Desire: Women, Sexuality, and the English Stage, 1660–1720.* Ithaca, NY: Cornell University Press, 2006.

May, Thomas. *A Continuation of the Subject of Lucan's Historical Poem, Till the Death of Julius Cæsar.* London: Peter Parker, 1679.

Mazurkewycz, Christine. "Chronic Time, Telling Texts: Forms of Temporality in the Eighteenth Century." PhD diss., University of Iowa, 2013.
McCrea, Brian. *Addison and Steele Are Dead: The English Department, Its Canon, and the Professionalization of Literary Criticism.* Newark: University of Delaware Press, 1990.
McKendrick, Neil, John Brewer, and J. H. Plumb. *The Birth of a Consumer Society: The Commercialization of Eighteenth-Century England.* Bloomington: Indiana University Press, 1982.
McKenzie, Jon. *Perform or Else: From Discipline to Performance.* London: Routledge, 2001.
McKeon, Michael. *The Secret History of Domesticity: Public, Private, and the Division of Knowledge.* Baltimore, MD: Johns Hopkins University Press, 2005.
Middleton, Conyers. *The History of the Life of Marcus Tullius Cicero.* Vol. 2. London: W. Innys, 1741.
Milhous, Judith, and Robert D. Hume. *The London Stage, 1660–1800.* Unpublished draft, 2017. http://personal.psu.edu/hb1/London%20Stage%202001/.
Mill, John Stuart. *On Liberty.* Edited by Stefan Collini. Cambridge: Cambridge University Press, 1989.
Miller, Henry Knight. "The 'Whig Interpretation' of Literary History." *Eighteenth-Century Studies* 6, no. 1 (1972): 60–84.
Miller, Stephen. "The Strange Career of Joseph Addison." *Sewanee Review* 122, no. 4 (2014): 650–60.
Milton, John. *Milton's Selected Poetry and Prose.* Edited by Jason Philip Rosenblatt. New York: W. W. Norton, 2011.
———. *Samson Agonistes.* In *The Complete Works of John Milton,* vol. 2, *The 1671 Poems,* edited by Laura Lunger Knoppers, 65–120. Oxford: Oxford University Press, 2008.
Monod, Paul Kleber. *Jacobitism and the English People, 1688–1788.* Cambridge: Cambridge University Press, 1993.
Montaigne, Michel de. *The Essays of Montaigne.* Translated by John Florio. London: David Nutt, [1603] 1892.
Morrison, Toni. *Playing in the Dark: Whiteness and the Literary Imagination.* New York: Vintage, 1992.
Mounsey, Chris. *Sight Correction: Vision and Blindness in Eighteenth-Century Britain.* Charlottesville: University of Virginia Press, 2019.
Newman, Donald J., ed. *The Spectator: Emerging Discourses.* Newark: University of Delaware Press, 2005.
Newton, Isaac. *Certain Philosophical Questions: Newton's Trinity Notebook.* Edited by J. E. McGuire and Martin Tamny. Cambridge: Cambridge University Press, 1983.
Nevalainen, Terttu, and Heli Tissari. "Contextualising Eighteenth-Century Politeness: Social Distinction and Metaphorical Levelling." In *Eighteenth-Century English: Ideology and Change,* edited by Raymond Hickey, 133–58. Cambridge: Cambridge University Press, 2010.
Norton, Brian Michael. "Aesthetics, Science, and the Theater of the World." *New Literary History* 51, no. 3 (2020): 639–59.

———. "*The Spectator,* Aesthetic Experience, and the Modern Idea of Happiness." *English Literature* 2 (2015): 87–104.
Norton, Rictor, ed. "Daniel Defoe, on the Public Prosecution and Punishment of Sodomites, 1707." In *Homosexuality in Eighteenth-Century England: A Sourcebook,* 2002. http://www.rictornorton.co.uk/eighteen/defoe.htm.
Nussbaum, Felicity A. *The Limits of the Human: Fictions of Anomaly, Race, and Gender in the Long Eighteenth Century.* Cambridge: Cambridge University Press, 2003.
———. "The Unaccountable Pleasure of Eighteenth-Century Tragedy." *PMLA* 129, no. 4 (October 2014): 688–707.
O'Brien, John. *Literature Incorporated: The Cultural Unconscious of the Business Corporation, 1650–1850.* Chicago: University of Chicago Press, 2015.
O'Brien, Karen. "'These Nations Newton Made His Own': Poetry, Knowledge, and British Imperial Globalization." In *Postcolonial Enlightenment: Eighteenth-Century Colonialism and Postcolonial Theory,* edited by Daniel Carey and Lynn Festa, 281–303. Oxford: Oxford University Press, 2009.
O'Byrne, Alison. "The Spectator and the Rise of the Modern Metropole." In *The Cambridge Companion to the City in Literature,* edited by Kevin McNamara, 57–68. Cambridge: Cambridge University Press, 2014.
O'Driscoll, Sally. "The Molly and the Fop: Untangling Effeminacy in the Eighteenth Century." In *Developments in the Histories of Sexualities: In Search of the Normal, 1600–1800,* edited by Chris Mounsey, 145–72. Lewisburg, PA: Bucknell University Press, 2013.
Ogée, Frédéric. "Nature and Imagination: The Posterity of Addison's 'Pleasures' in British Enlightenment Culture." In Davis, *Joseph Addison,* 272–89.
Orr, Bridget. *British Enlightenment Theatre: Dramatizing Difference.* Cambridge: Cambridge University Press, 2020.
———. *Empire on the English Stage, 1660–1714.* Cambridge: Cambridge University Press, 2001.
Ovid. *Heroides. Amores.* Translated by G. P. Goold and Grant Showerman. Cambridge, MA: Harvard University Press, 1914.
Palmer, Ada. *Reading Lucretius in the Renaissance.* Cambridge, MA: Harvard University Press, 2014.
Parker, Fred. "Addison's Modesty, or the Essayist as Spectator." In Davis, *Joseph Addison,* 164–81.
Patterson, Orlando. "Freedom, Slavery, and the Modern Construction of Rights." In *The Cultural Values of Europe,* edited by Hans Joas and Klaus Wiegandt, 115–51. Liverpool: Liverpool University Press, 2008.
———. *Slavery and Social Death: A Comparative Study.* Cambridge, MA: Harvard University Press, 1982.
Pestana, Carla Gardina. *The English Atlantic in an Age of Revolution, 1640–1661.* Cambridge, MA: Harvard University Press, 2004.
Pfizenmaier, Thomas C. "Was Isaac Newton an Arian?" *Journal of the History of Ideas* 58, no. 1 (1997): 57–80.
Phelan, Peggy. "The Same: Reflections on Andy Warhol and Ronald Reagan." *Umbr(a)* 1 (2002): 65–70.

———. *Unmarked: The Politics of Performance*. New York: Routledge, 1993.
Pincus, Steve. "Addison's Empire: Whig Conceptions of Empire in the Early Eighteenth Century." *Parliamentary History* 31, no. 1 (2012): 99–117.
Plato. *Phaedo*. Translated by Harold North Fowler. In *Plato in Twelve Volumes,* vol. 1. Cambridge, MA: Harvard University Press, 1966.
Pliny the Younger. *Epistulae*. Vol. 3. Edited by Peter G. Walsh. Oxford: Oxford University Press, 2006.
Plutarch. *Cato the Younger*. In *Plutarch's Lives*, vol. 8, translated by Bernadotte Perrin, 235–411. Cambridge, MA: Harvard University Press, 1919.
Pollock, Anthony. "Neutering Addison and Steele: Aesthetic Failure and the Spectatorial Public Sphere." *ELH* 74, no. 3 (2007): 707–34.
Pope, Alexander. *An Essay on Man*. London: J. & P. Knapton, 1753.
———. *Letters of Mr. Pope, and Several Eminent Persons, from the Year 1705 to 1735*. London: T. Cooper, 1735.
———. *The Correspondence of Alexander Pope*. Vol. 1, *1704–1718*. Edited by George Sherburn. Oxford: Oxford University Press, 1956.
———. *The Major Works*. Edited by Pat Rogers. Oxford: Oxford University Press, 2006.
Poston, Dan. "Passionsspiel der Geschichte. Joseph Addisons *Cato* und die Poetik der Bewunderung." In *ZwischenSpielZeit. Das Theater Der Frühaufklärung*, edited by Jörn Steigerwald and Leonie Süwolto, 81–107. Paderborn: Fink, 2021.
———. "Still on Classic Ground: Joseph Addison's Italy." In Boulard-Jouslin and Ertler, *Addison and Europe*, 67–77.
Powell, Manushag N. *Performing Authorship in Eighteenth-Century English Periodicals*. Lewisburg, PA: Bucknell University Press, 2012.
Power, Henry. "Coins and Circulation in Addison's Prose." In Davis, *Joseph Addison*, 80–94.
Prager, Carolyn. "Elizabeth Singer Rowe: Gender, Dissent, and Whig Poetics." In Womersley, *Cultures of Whiggism*, 173–99.
———. "The Problem of Slavery in *The Custom of the Country*." *Studies in English Literature, 1500–1900* 28, no. 2 (1988): 301–17.
Prescott, S. *Women, Authorship and Literary Culture, 1690–1740*. New York: Palgrave Macmillan, 2003.
Puchner, Martin. *The Drama of Ideas: Platonic Provocations in Theater and Philosophy*. Oxford: Oxford University Press, 2010.
Radford, Leslie. "'Alas! I Fear I've Been Too Hasty!' And Other Reconsiderations of Addison's *Cato*." *Restoration and Eighteenth Century Theatre Research* 10, no. 2 (1995): 32.
Rancière, Jacques. *The Politics of Aesthetics*. Translated by Gabriel Rockhill. London: Bloomsbury, 2013.
Rand, Benjamin, ed. *Berkeley and Percival*. Cambridge: Cambridge University Press, 1914.
Raphael, Timothy. *The President Electric: Ronald Reagan and the Politics of Performance*. Ann Arbor: University of Michigan Press, 2009.
Reed, Edward B. "Some Unpublished Notes of Lord Macaulay." *Modern Language Notes* 23, no. 6 (1908): 181–83.

Ridout, Nicholas. *Scenes from Bourgeois Life*. Ann Arbor: University of Michigan Press, 2020.
Roach, Joseph. *Cities of the Dead: Circum-Atlantic Performance*. New York: Columbia University Press, 1996.
———. *It*. Ann Arbor: University of Michigan Press, 2007.
———. "Territorial Passages: Time, Place, and Action." In *Of Borders and Thresholds: Theatre History, Practice, and Theory*, edited by Michal Kobialka, 110–24. Minneapolis: University of Minnesota Press, 1999.
Robinson, M. "Salmacis and Hermaphroditus: When Two Become One (Ovid, *Met.* 4.285–388)." *Classical Quarterly* 49, no. 1 (1999): 212–23.
Rodríguez Sánchez de León, María José. "'Varying Life': The Idea of Fiction in the Spanish Version of Joseph Addison's 'The Pleasures of the Imagination.'" In Boulard-Jouslin and Ertler, *Addison and Europe*, 111–27.
Romano, Allen J. "The Invention of Marriage: Hermaphroditus and Salmacis at Halicarnassus and in Ovid." *Classical Quarterly* 59, no. 2 (2009): 543–61.
Rosenthal, Laura J. "Juba's Roman Soul: Addison's *Cato* and Enlightenment Cosmopolitanism." *Studies in the Literary Imagination* 32, no. 2 (Fall 1999): 63–76.
Ross, Trevor. *The Making of the English Literary Canon: From the Middle Ages to the Late Eighteenth Century*. Montreal: McGill-Queen's University Press, 1998.
Rounce, Adam. "Akenside's Clamors for Liberty." In Womersley, *Cultures of Whiggism*, 216–34.
Russell, John L. "The Copernican System in Great Britain." In *The Reception of Copernicus' Heliocentric Theory*, 189–239. New York: Springer, 1973.
Saccamano, Neil. "The Consolations of Ambivalence: Habermas and the Public Sphere." *MLN* 106, no. 3 (1991): 685–98.
———. "The Sublime Force of Words in Addison's 'Pleasures.'" *ELH* 58, no. 1 (Spring 1991): 83–106.
Saintsbury, George. *The Peace of the Augustans: A Survey of Eighteenth-Century Literature as a Place of Rest and Refreshment*. London: G. Bell & Sons, 1916.
Santner, Eric L. *The Royal Remains: The People's Two Bodies and the Endgames of Sovereignty*. Chicago: University of Chicago Press, 2012.
Scarry, Elaine. *Dreaming by the Book*. Princeton, NJ: Princeton University Press, 2001.
Schechner, Richard. *Between Theater and Anthropology*. Philadelphia: University of Pennsylvania Press, 1985.
Schmitt, Carl. *Hamlet or Hecuba: The Intrusion of the Time into the Play*. Translated by David Pan and Jennifer R. Rust. New York: Telos, 2009.
Seneca, Lucius Annaeus. "On Providence." In *Dialogues and Essays*, edited by John Davie and Tobias Reinhardt, 3–17. Oxford: Oxford University Press, 2008.
Sennett, Richard. *Authority*. New York: W. W. Norton, 1993.
Shaffer, Jason. *Performing Patriotism: National Identity in the Colonial and Revolutionary American Theater*. Philadelphia: University of Pennsylvania Press, 2007.
Shaftesbury, Anthony Ashley Cooper, Earl of. *Characteristics of Men, Manners, Opinions, Times*. Edited by Lawrence E. Klein. Cambridge: Cambridge University Press, 2000.

Shakespeare, William. *Julius Caesar.* Edited by David Daniell. London: Bloomsbury, 1998.

Sharpe, Kevin. *Rebranding Rule: Images of Restoration and Revolution Monarchy, 1660–1714.* New Haven, CT: Yale University Press, 2013.

Sheehan, Michael. *The Balance of Power: History and Theory.* London: Routledge, 1996.

Shelley, Percy Bysshe. *The Complete Poetry.* Vol. 3. Edited by Donald H. Reiman, Neil Fraistat, and Nora Crook. Baltimore, MD: Johns Hopkins University Press, 2012.

Sherman, Stuart. *Telling Time: Clocks, Diaries, and English Diurnal Form, 1660–1785.* Chicago: University of Chicago Press, 1996.

Shevelow, Kathryn. *Women and Print Culture: The Construction of Femininity in the Early Periodical.* London: Routledge, 1989.

Shrock, Dennis. *Choral Monuments: Studies of Eleven Choral Masterworks.* Oxford: Oxford University Press, 2017.

Siebert, Fred S. "The Authoritarian Theory of the Press." In *Four Theories of the Press,* by Fred S. Siebert, Theodore Peterson, and Wilbur Schramm, 9–38. Urbana: University of Illinois Press, 1956.

Skinner, Quentin. "John Milton and the Politics of Slavery." In *Milton and the Terms of Liberty,* edited by Graham Parry and Joad Raymond, 1–22. Cambridge: Boydell & Brewer, 2002.

Sidney, Sir Philip. *The Defence of Poesy.* In *The Major Works,* edited by Katherine Duncan-Jones. Oxford: Oxford University Press, 2009.

Smith, Anthony D. *The Nation Made Real: Art and National Identity in Western Europe, 1600–1850.* Oxford: Oxford University Press, 2013.

Smith, Courtney Weiss. *Empiricist Devotions: Science, Religion, and Poetry in Early Eighteenth-Century England.* Charlottesville: University of Virginia Press, 2016.

Smith, Hannah. "'Last of All the Heavenly Birth': Queen Anne and Sacral Queenship." *Parliamentary History* 28, no. 1 (2009): 137–49.

Smithers, Peter. *The Life of Joseph Addison.* 2nd ed. Oxford: Clarendon, 1968.

Snyder, Henry L. "The Duke of Marlborough's Request of His Captain-Generalcy for Life: A Re-Examination." *Journal of the Society for Army Historical Research* 45, no. 182 (1967): 67–83.

Spence, Joseph. *Observations, Anecdotes, and Characters of Books and Men.* Edited by J. M. Osborn. 2 vols. Oxford: Clarendon, 1966.

Springborg, Patricia. "Republicanism, Freedom from Domination, and the Cambridge Contextual Historians." *Political Studies* 49, no. 5 (2001): 851–76.

Stadter, Philip A. *Plutarch and His Roman Readers.* Oxford: Oxford University Press, 2014.

Staton, Walter F. "Ovidian Elements in *A Midsummer Night's Dream.*" *Huntington Library Quarterly* 26, no. 2 (1963): 165–78.

Steele, Richard. *The Conscious Lovers.* In *The Plays of Richard Steele,* edited by Shirley Strum Kenny. Oxford: Oxford University Press, 1971.

———. "The Prologue at the Opening of the Theatre-Royal, the Day after His Majesty's Publick Entry." London: n.p., 1714.

———. "To Mr. Congreve." In Addison, *Drummer,* iii–xviii.

Stout, S. E. "How Vergil Established for Aeneas a Legal Claim to a Home and a Throne in Italy." *Classical Journal* 20, no. 3 (1924): 152–60.
Swift, Jonathan. "The Sentiments of a Church of England Man [1708]." In *The Works of the Rev. Jonathan Swift*, vol. 2, edited by Thomas Sheridan and John Nichols, 347–80. London: Nichols & Son, 1801.
Szécsényi, Endre. "The Jesuit Thread in Joseph Addison's Aesthetics." In Boulard-Jouslin and Ertler, *Addison and Europe*, 49–66.
Taylor, Barry. "Medieval Proverb Collections: The West European Tradition." *Journal of the Warburg and Courtauld Institutes* 55 (1992): 19–35.
Taylor, David Francis. "*Cato* and the Crisis of Rhetoric." In Davis, *Joseph Addison*, 212–31.
Terry, Richard. *Poetry and the Making of the English Literary Past, 1660–1781*. Oxford: Oxford University Press, 2001.
———. "Revolt in Utica: Reading *Cato* against Cato." *Philological Quarterly* 85, nos. 1–2 (Winter 2006): 121.
Theobald, Lewis. "The Life and Character of M. Cato of Uticca." In Addison, *Cato*, 253–71.
Thomson, Peter. *The Cambridge Introduction to English Theatre, 1660–1900*. Cambridge: Cambridge University Press, 2006.
Tickell, Thomas. "To The Right Honourable The Earl of Warwick, &c." In Addison, *Works*, vol. 1, xiii–vi.
Tocqueville, Alexis de. *Democracy in America*. Vol. 2. Edited by Eduardo Nolla. Translated by James T. Schleifer. Indianapolis: Liberty Fund, 2012.
Voltaire. *Letters Concerning the English Nation*. London: C. Davis, 1733.
———. "Preface to *Socrates*." In *The Works of Voltaire*, vol. 10, translated by William F. Fleming, 283–86. New York: E. R. DuMont, 1901.
Walker, David. "Addison's *Cato* and the Transformation of Republican Discourse in the Early Eighteenth Century." *Journal for Eighteenth-Century Studies* 26, no. 1 (2003): 91–108.
Walker, William. "Ideology and Addison's Essays on the Pleasures of the Imagination." *Eighteenth-Century Life* 24, no. 2 (1 April 2000): 65–84.
Walsh, Marcus. "Addison as Critic and Critical Theorist." In Davis, *Joseph Addison*, 95–114.
Weber, Samuel. *Theatricality as Medium*. New York: Fordham University Press, 2004.
Weinbrot, Howard D. *Augustus Caesar in Augustan England: The Decline of a Classical Norm*. Princeton, NJ: Princeton University Press, 2015.
Westfall, Richard S. *Never at Rest: A Biography of Isaac Newton*. Cambridge: Cambridge University Press, 1983.
Westminster Abbey, Dean and Chapter of. "Joseph Addison," 2019. https://www.westminster-abbey.org/abbey-commemorations/commemorations/joseph-addison.
Wilkinson, Hazel. "Appendix: The Complete *Spectator*, 1712–1812—A Bibliographical Catalogue." In Davis, *Joseph Addison*, 329–90.
———. "The Complete *Spectator*: A Bibliographical History." In Davis, *Joseph Addison*, 182–211.

Williams, Abigail. "Patronage and Whig Literary Culture in the Early Eighteenth Century." In Womersley, *Cultures of Whiggism*, 149–72.
——. *Poetry and the Creation of a Whig Literary Culture, 1681–1714*. Oxford: Oxford University Press, 2005.
Williams, Raymond. *Drama in a Dramatised Society: An Inaugural Lecture*. Cambridge: Cambridge University Press, 1975.
——. *The Long Revolution*. New York: Columbia University Press, 1961.
Wilson, Brett D. *A Race of Female Patriots: Women and Public Spirit on the British Stage, 1688–1745*. Lewisburg, PA: Bucknell University Press, 2012.
Winn, James A. "'More Sensual Delights': Visual Pleasure and Musical Anxiety in Addison's Aesthetics." In Davis, *Joseph Addison*, 115–41.
——. *Queen Anne: Patroness of Arts*. Oxford: Oxford University Press, 2014.
Wolloch, Nathaniel. "Cato the Younger in the Enlightenment." *Modern Philology* 106, no. 1 (1 August 2008): 60–82.
Wollstonecraft, Mary. *A Vindication of the Rights of Woman*. 3rd ed. Edited by Deidre Shauna Lynch. New York: W. W. Norton, 2009.
Womersley, David. "Introduction." In Womersley, *Augustan Critical Writing*, xi–liv.
——. "Introduction." In Womersley, *Cultures of Whiggism*, 9–26.
Womersley, David, ed. *Augustan Critical Writing*. London: Penguin, 1997.
——. *"Cultures of Whiggism": New Essays on English Literature and Culture in the Long Eighteenth Century*. Newark: University of Delaware Press, 2005.
Woolf, Virginia. *The Common Reader*. New York: Harcourt, Brace, 1925.
——. *Orlando: A Biography*. London: Hogarth, 1928.
Wyvill, John. *A Sermon Preach'd . . . upon Easter Sunday . . . 1713, Etc*. London: T. Childe, 1713.
Yates, Frances A. "Queen Elizabeth as Astraea." *Journal of the Warburg and Courtauld Institutes* 10 (1947): 27–82.
Young, Brian. "Addison and the Victorians." In Davis, *Joseph Addison*, 308–27.
Young, Edward. *Conjectures on Original Composition*. Edited by Edith J. Morley. Manchester: University of Manchester Press, [1759] 1918.
——. *The Poems of Edward Young*. Vol. 2. Edited by Sir Herbert Croft. Chiswick: C. Whittingham, 1822.
Youngren, William H. "Addison and the Birth of Eighteenth-Century Aesthetics." *Modern Philology* 79, no. 3 (1982): 267–83.
Zadorojnyi, Alexei V. "Cato's Suicide in Plutarch." *Classical Quarterly* 57, no. 1 (2007): 216–30.
Zeitz, Lisa M. "Addison's 'Imagination' Papers and the Design Argument." *English Studies* 73, no. 6 (1992): 493–502.
Zwierlein, Anne-Julia. "'Grace in Deformity'. Praxeologien des Klassischen und Literarische Geschmacksbildung am Beispiel des Englischen 'Nationaldichters' John Milton im Frühen 18. Jahrhundert." In *Europäische Regelsysteme des Klassischen*, edited by Heribert Tommek, 57–71. Regensburg: Schnell + Steiner, 2020.

Index

abolition movement: early stirrings of, 135; motivations for, 140, 146; nonexistence in Britain (1711), 122; progressivism and, 21; relative invisibility of slavery in Europe, effect on, 133; tale of Inkle and Yarico in, 139

Abrams, M. H., 150; *The Mirror and the Lamp,* 31

Actaeon and Diana myth, 48

Act of Settlement (1701), 193, 207, 208, 216, 229

Act of Union (1707), 205

Addison, Charlotte (daughter), 278, 279, 294n25

Addison, Gulston (brother), 123

Addison, John (paternal uncle), 80–81

Addison, Joseph: achievements, list of, 7–9; aristocrat status upon marriage, 269, 273, 276; Bilton estate purchased by, 111, 269; birth (1672), 2; as celebrity of his times, 257–58, 283n1; as champion of the individual, 6, 19, 30, 34, 55; colonial affairs under direction of, 7, 194, 269, 270–71; compared to Hobbes, 302n29; compared to Pope, 19, 38; compared to Swift, 19; cultural esteem for, 257–58; death (1719), 4; deathbed scene of, 51–52, 262; education of, 81; as envoy to Hanoverian court, 208, 218, 267; family background of, 7, 26, 80–82; father figures of, 80–86; as "First Victorian," 30, 49; as founder of modern aesthetics, 8, 9, 11, 13, 150, 301n6; goals of his writings, 22, 39–41, 59–61, 85, 140, 159, 169, 212, 261, 263; gravestone and inscription, 2, 86; health problems of, 273; as humanist, 24, 54; Indian colonial business and brother, 123; international influence of, 29, 280, 287n105, 288n12; legacy of, 4, 6, 9, 19, 35, 48, 60, 261, 264, 279; in literary history, 3, 9, 25, 30, 37, 46, 48–49, 57, 259; London life of, 27, 47; marriage to Countess of Warwick, 269, 273, 276; modern rejection/disappearance and misreading of, 5, 23, 30, 35, 38, 59, 237, 261; as national Censor, 29, 65; as neoclassical poet at start of literary career, 48, 81, 90; out-of-office time during Tory supremacy, 85, 152, 210; as paradigm of literary taste, 263; as philosopher, 34, 151, 153, 172–73, 179, 262, 301n3; philosophical and political differences with Steele, 217–18, 274–75; as poet-statesman, 4–5, 35, 189–90, 257, 265; political/administrative career of, 8, 34–35, 82, 114, 189, 194, 201, 265, 305n24; political moderation and nonpartisanship of, 191, 250; as political propagandist, 269, 270; private papers, disappearance of, 279; Prussian court of Frederick William I, visit to, 218, 308n86; religious motto of, 39; same-sex love life, speculation on, 75, 185, 284n22, 291n113; as secretary of state, 7–8, 85, 210, 212, 257, 258, 265, 269; self-

Addison, Joseph (*continued*)
deprecation and modesty, 39–40, 48, 75, 160, 288n25; social position of, 26, 265; statue in Westminster, 4, 283n6; Steele's friendship and partnership with, 7, 217, 222; Steele's split from, 35, 274–76; unconventional life of, 8, 265; vision problems of, 91, 151; world of, 6, 47, 61, 114; writing styles of, 5, 30, 33, 37, 46, 65, 144, 262, 264, 272

Addison, Joseph, works by: *An Account of the Greatest English Poets*, 44; *The Campaign*, 7, 34, 201–5, 211, 257; *Dialogues upon the Usefulness of Ancient Medals*, 7, 85, 200, 307n43; *Discourse on Ancient and Modern Learning*, 20–21, 38, 144; *The Drummer*, 75, 272, 280; *Evidences of the Christian Religion*, 228, 273; "A Letter from Italy," 82, 200, 295n48, 296n86; letter to father's direct ecclesiastical superior, 187, 293n6; on mole's life, 105–6; "Mr. Addison's Defence of the Newtonian Philosophy," 89–90, 102; *Old Whig* pamphlets, 275; *Pax Gulielmi Auspiciis Europae Reddita*, 81; *A Poem to His Majesty*, 46, 81, 192; *The Present State of the War*, 209, 218; prologue to Steele's *The Tender Husband*, 42; Psalm 19 rewritten by, 108–9; *Remarks on Several Parts of Italy, &c.*, 7, 82, 266; *Rosamond*, 7, 34, 204–6, 211, 266, 279, 308n70; *To Sir Godfrey Kneller*, 267; translation of Ovid's tale of Salmacis and Hermaphroditus, 170–76, 179–80, 184–85, 303n72; translations of Ovid and Virgil, 48, 81; *The Trial of Count Tariff*, 123, 297–98n21; on Virgil's *Georgics*, 80, 107; "The Vision of Marraton" (*Spectator* 56), 142; "Vision of Mirzah" (*Spectator* 159), 95–96, 295n71, 304n82. See also *Cato; Freeholder; On the Pleasures of the Imagination; Spectator, The; Tatler, The*

Addison, Lancelot (father), 80–82, 186; *The First State of Mahumedism*, 81; *The Present State of the Jews*, 81, 293n2; *West Barbary, or a Short Narrative of the Revolutions of the Kingdoms of Fez and Morocco*, 81

Aeneid (Virgil): allusions in Addison's *On the Pleasures of the Imagination*, 175, 181–85; Cacus in, 181, 182; Dido in, 181–82, 186–87; Marlborough compared to Aeneas, 202; Mercury in, 181, 183

aesthetics: Addison as founder of modern aesthetics, 8, 9, 11, 13, 150, 301n6; in Addison's world, 54–55, 64; aesthetic disinterestedness, 150, 179; bourgeois/middling, 12, 33–34, 179–80; Newton's impact on, 16, 18, 31. See also *On the Pleasures of the Imagination*

afterlife, depiction of, 217
Agnew, Jean-Christophe, 97
Aikin, Lucy, *Life of Addison*, 49, 71, 289n50
Albemarle, Duke of (George Monck), 283n2
ambition, 17, 26, 39, 91–93, 101–2, 190, 201, 293n7, 294n36; Addison as figure for others', 3, 19, 23, 61, 73, 259; Addison's, 21, 24, 34, 42–43, 47–48, 111, 221, 229, 264, 282
American Revolution, 246, 278
Anglicanism, 57, 85, 245. See also Protestantism
Anne (English queen): in Addison's poem *To Sir Godfrey Kneller*, 268; Addison's support for, 218; in Addison's *The Campaign*, 202, 203–4; attempt to perform warrior and martial monarch, 199, 206; coronation medal for, 200–201; echoing Elizabeth I's

reign, 34, 196–201, 207, 209, 210; funeral under Addison's direction, 35, 257, 265, 316n23; Marlborough and, 204–6, 257; middle-class character of, 190; secret packet burned after death, 210–11; shadow sovereigns during reign of, 198, 206, 214–16, 256; succeeding William and Mary, 199; succession as major issue of reign of, 194–96, 206–11, 218, 226, 249; surrogate images of heroic kingship during reign of, 214, 216; Tories and, 142, 152, 194, 207; Tudor reign's end mirrored by Stuart reign's end, 198, 207; Whigs and, 194–95, 200, 202, 204, 206–7, 209, 308n75
Aphrodite, 170
Apollonian systems, 75, 175, 185, 238
archeology, 4, 294n38, 295n47
Arendt, Hannah, 34
aristocracy: Addison gaining status of via marriage, 269, 273, 276; Addison living in time of dominance of, 13, 82–83, 86, 185; Addison's satire of, 67, 70; fashion and, 14, 70–71; social change and, 3, 11, 14–15, 27, 61, 67, 83, 98, 147, 153, 190; South Sea Company and, 127. *See also* feudalism and serfdom; Tories
Aristotle, 29, 55, 89–90, 91, 98, 160, 187, 219, 251
Armistead, J. M., 249
Ashton, John, 125–26
Astell, Mary, 67; *Reflections upon Marriage*, 138
atheism, 227
Athenian Mercury, 67–68
Augustan Age, 50, 72, 124–25; echoing Elizabethan Age, 34; partisan rifts, 56–58; poet-statesman role in, 111, 189–90; theater in, 195. *See also* Anne (English queen)
Augustine (saint), 228, 230, 255
Augustus (Roman emperor), 119

avarice: Addison's condemnation of, 35, 123, 140–43, 145, 179; age of Walpole's imperial greed, 274
Axelsson, Karl, 212, 261
Ayres, Philip, 224

Babel's Tower, 175
Babylon, 175, 181, 304n82
Bacon, Francis, "Of Regiment of Health," 156
Baldwin, Abigail (Ann/Anne), 28
bans on theater, 213, 219–20, 227, 253
Barbados: Slave Code (1661), 136; sugar plantations of, 123, 132
Barbauld, Anna Laetitia, 17, 21
Barton, Catherine, 86
Basker, James, 301n3
Battle of Glen Shiel (1719), 278
Battle of Hastings (1066), 129
Battle of Philippi (42 BC), 234, 244
Baudot, Laura, 34
beauty, 8, 33, 77, 111–12, 150–51, 160
Behn, Aphra, 67, 72, 302n43
Benn, Gottfried, 220
Berkeley, George, 29, 210, 240
Betterton, Thomas, 41, 214–17, 218, 238, 256
Bickerstaff, Isaac, Esq (fictional *Tatler* author), 111–14, 126
Bilton estate of Addison, 111, 269
Black people living in London, early eighteenth century, 125, 298n31
Blenheim, Marlborough's victory at, 201, 205
Blenheim Palace gifted to Marlborough, 204, 205
Bloom, Edward and Lillian, 21–22, 141, 297n21
Boileau-Despréaux, Nicolas, 82, 187, 260, 284n47, 293n6
Bolingbroke, Lord (Henry St John), 100–101, 127, 142, 196–97, 210–11, 257–58, 309n93
bond slavery, 134, 299n51, 299n55

Booth, Barton, 197, 238–39
Bothmer, Hans Casper von, 210
Boulard-Jouslin, Claire, 280
bourgeoisie: Addison's ambivalent legacy in regard to, 21; empowerment of bourgeois public sphere, 19, 31, 82, 126, 253, 256–57, 278; materialism and, 113; paradigm of bourgeois aesthetics, 179–80
Bowers, Terence, 15
Brewer, John, 94
Britain: ancient Roman paradigm, 221, 233; attaining modern, imperial status, 5, 221; Cato adopted as father to early quasi-Republic, 246; as foremost diplomatic power in Europe, 271; Julian calendar of, 235
British Leeward Islands, 121
Bruno, Giordano, 88, 89
Brunswick House, 265, 267
Brutus (in Addison's *Cato*). See *Cato*
Brutus (in Shakespeare's *Julius Caesar*), 233–35, 238, 242
Buckingham, Second Duke of (George Villiers), *The Rehearsal*, 181
Buckley, Samuel, 28
Burnet, Thomas, *A Sacred Theory of the Earth*, 114
Burns, Robert, 295n71
Byrom, John, 209

Cacus (monstrous giant in the *Aeneid*), 181, 182
Caesar. *See* Julius Caesar
capitalism, 3, 5, 89, 112, 127, 300n83, 300n89
Carey, Brycchan, 122
Caribbean, slavery in, 132–34, 138. *See also* Barbados
Carlos II (Spanish king), death of, 193
Carlson, Marvin, 306n27, 309n1, 315n154
Caroline (princess of Wales, daughter-in-law of George I), 267, 269
Cartesianism. *See* Descartes, René

Cassius (in Shakespeare's *Julius Caesar*), 238, 244
catharsis, 45, 55, 78, 219, 220, 251
Catholicism: absolute monarchs and, 8, 119; Addison's opposition to restoration of, 250; British fear of "Popery" and return to civil war, 89, 126, 127, 159, 193, 228, 298n36, 306n42; English Bill of Rights barring Catholic from taking throne, 192; French slavery ended by, 129; Gregorian calendar of, 235; politico-religious authority replaced by Westphalian sovereignty, 135. *See also* religious unrest and change
Cato (Addison), 34–35, 219–58; actor from Shakespeare's *Julius Caesar* appearing in, 238; advertising in *The Spectator*, 9, 245; anticolonialism in, 144–45; Brutus (husband of Cato's daughter), 218, 224, 237; Cato compared to Othello, 227; Cato reading Plato in, 241, 254–55; Cato recognized as figure of cultural authority, 225, 254; Cato's heirs, 246–48, 251; Cato's monologue in final act, 242, 254; Cato's suicide in, 227, 229, 237, 241, 254; change in Addison's view of Cato and tragedy, 230; as "crowning" achievement of Addison's career, 7, 212; domestic peace and cosmopolitanism reflected in marriage at conclusion, 249; epigraph in printed edition, 252, 254; fatal error of Cato, 218, 237; final act written later than the other acts, 218, 229–30, 311nn53–55; form of the play, 225–29; international readership of, 7, 29–30, 256, 280–81; interracial couple in closing tableaux, 12, 144, 248, 250; Johnson's evaluation of, 78; Juba (Black Numidian prince), 145, 147, 239, 242–43, 247–50, 257, 314n122, 314n124; Julius Caesar's approach in, 197, 219, 225, 242, 249, 254–56; legacy

of, 7, 35, 280–81; liberty as ideal in, 116; love as victorious in, 253, 256; love plots, 243, 246–47, 255–56, 314n135, 315n154; Lucia (love interest of Portius and Marcus), 239, 243, 248, 257, 314n135; Lucius (loyal friend to Cato), 225–27, 233–39, 241–44; Marcia (daughter of Cato and love interest of Juba), 242–43, 247–48, 250, 257; Marcus (son of Cato), 224, 226–27, 229, 239, 241–43, 245–47, 249, 312n84; metatheatrical, tragicomedy nature of, 35, 242, 244–45, 249, 313n107; as middle-class/bourgeois tragedy, 35; modern rejection and misreading of, 5, 38, 237; national unity's emergence in, 35, 221–22, 230, 250–51; as nonpartisan and transcending political milieu, 240, 250–51; North Africa as setting of, 187, 219, 225; old order yielding to new age of bourgeois selves and national empire, 244; operas competing for audience share against, 265–66; out-of-office time of Addison deployed in writing, 210; pamphlet war over interpretations of, 240, 312n85; in political context of Addison's world, 34, 189–97, 221, 230; Pope's prologue, 37; popularity of and positive reception of, 34, 38, 79, 212, 228, 240, 245, 256–57, 280–82; Portius (brother to Marcus), 227, 239, 242, 243, 247–49, 255, 257, 258, 314n135, 315n162; premiere of (1713), 188, 196–97, 210, 220, 225, 245, 265, 281; as preparation for Addison's own death, 262; as prequel to Shakespeare's *Julius Caesar,* 233–45; as Protestant passion play, 227–28, 252, 313n107; re-visionary history, 35, 229–31, 256; revival at Drury Lane theater (1716), 279; rewriting of Plutarch, 231, 241; Roman medals on title page of original publication, 24, 277, 317n60; Roman Republic in, 220–21, 225–26, 231, 233–34, 246–49, 255; Roman virtue, 232, 240, 242–43, 247–49, 252; in scientific context of Addison's world, 255; Sempronius (villain), 225–27, 237–38, 242–43, 247–49, 258, 315n162; sentimental tone at end of play, 239, 243, 253; sophistication of viewing audience, 240–41; staged in 1730s as attacks on Walpole, 282; staged in 1764 as *Cato without the Love Scenes,* 246; Steele's prologue, 265, 281; Stoicism in, 227, 231–32, 237–39, 243, 247–49, 252; symbolism of hero Cato, 188–89, 196–97, 256–58, 306n31; Syphax (Northern African rebel), 144, 227, 239, 242, 248; timed to rebirth of republicanism and rise of imperialism, 220–21, 230; tragic praxis of audience, 56, 252; Utica citizens gathering to mourn Cato's death, 255; women in love plots, 246–47; women's response to, 313n117; Woolf's evaluation of, 78–79; in Woolf's *Orlando,* 73; writing/rewriting of, 85, 218, 228–30, 246, 311nn53–55

Cato the Elder (Cato the Censor): Addison taking modern role of Censor from, 29, 65; as model for bourgeois revolutionaries, 278; *Origenes,* 182

Cato the Younger (Marcus Porcius Cato Uticensis): American appropriation of, 246; Augustine's praise for, 228; familiarity of Addison's audience with, 223–24; influence on Addison, 264; as link between Socrates and Jesus, 233; perilous political situation of, 19, 187; Plutarch on, 231, 236, 241, 254–55, 311n58, 314n121; representing defiant but defeated Republic, 220, 224; as self-martyr, 186–87, 234, 244, 247–48, 254; Seneca and, 252; Socrates as model for, 86; Steele on death of, 274; suicide of, 220, 230, 231–32; William and Mary's association with, 82. See also *Cato*

Censor, Addison taking national role of, 29, 65
Centlivre, Susanna, 72
Chain of Being. *See* Great Chain of Being
Chalmers, Alexander, 25
Champion, Justin, 81
Charles I (English king), 130, 132, 172, 181, 182, 300n62
Charles II (English king), 60, 84, 135, 199, 268, 283n2, 292n135, 306n42. *See also* Restoration
Chaucer, Geoffrey, 44, 205
Chico, Tita, 75
Christianity, 53, 66, 92, 238, 252–53, 264. *See also* Protestantism
Churchill, John. *See* Marlborough, Duke of
Churchill, Sarah (wife of Duke of Marlborough), 204, 206–7, 211, 279
Cibber, Colley, 38, 79, 240, 311n54
Cicero, 43, 82, 130, 214, 224, 231, 264–65
Cincinnatus, 278
civil politics constructed by Addison. *See* public opinion and discourse
Civil Wars, English: avoiding through moderation of political discourse, 190–91; cause of and consequences of, 25; colonists returning to England to fight in, 131–32, 135; Hobbes's *Leviathan* and, 119; literacy rates during, 28; resolution enabled by moving slavery offshore, 133, 191; Roman civil wars compared to, 181; threat of returning, 11, 89, 159, 228
classical models: Addison on Ancient tragedies, 54; Addison's identification with Actaeon, 48; Addison's *On the Pleasures of the Imagination* as Latin poem, 33, 180–87; British school children learning, 223–24; *Distichs of Cato* used in Latin education, 224; English literature and law based on, 15, 221; golden age of Latin poetry, 171, 180; Horace's influence on Addison, 59, 166, 167, 180–81; Lucretius's influence on Addison, 155–56, 159, 163, 166, 170, 172, 176, 180, 260; Ovid's tale of Salmacis and Hermaphroditus as translated by Addison, 170–76, 179–80, 184–85, 303n72; Plato's influence on Addison, 34, 141, 156, 157, 172–74, 263; popularity of Roman stories from late Republic, 224; Socrates's influence on Addison, 40, 42, 85–86, 107, 112, 264; Virgil's influence on Addison, 20–21, 59, 111, 180, 184, 285n57; as warning of dangers that destroyed Roman liberty, 224

class structure, 126, 217, 297n10; broad cross-section of society represented in Addison's writing, 59, 79. *See also* aristocracy; middle (middling) class; working class
Clayton, Thomas, 205
Clery, E. J., 69
Clifford, Rosamond, 205
Clio (muse of history), 35, 181; C-L-I-O, Addison's essays signed with letters of, 45
Codex of Justinian, 130
coffeehouse culture: Black workers in, 125; ideally suited to reformist Whig project, 7, 27–29, 270; inheriting theater's role as site of social debate, 216–17; middle-class revolution linked to, 40, 85, 126; names of coffeehouses reflecting knowledge of slave trade, 125; reading aloud and circulating journals in, 46, 283n16; similarity to Socrates's and Plato's schools, 28, 42; as training ground for going to the theater, 124, 215
coins and medals: Addison's enthusiasm for, 34, 200, 306–7n43; coronation medals, 200–201, 307n44; Great Recoinage, 200; Harley's control over images, 204; literature and, 44, 214; Marlborough's image on

medal, 204; Newton's roles at Mint, 200–201, 204, 307n44, 307n65; Pretender's medal in circulation, 209; Roman medal associated with Addison's print edition of *Cato*, 277, 317n60; *Tatler* 249 essay on life of antique silver shilling's passage through multiple hands, 79, 292n147; Whigs' issuance with Anne's image, 200, 204

Coleridge, Samuel Taylor, 158; *Friend*, 59; "Frost at Midnight," 158

colonialism: Addison's responsibilities in Ireland and Americas, 194, 269, 270–71; anti-Walpole sentiment in colonies, 278; British exploitation of, 5, 123, 142–43; British supply of indentured servants, 131; Great Migration (and return of colonists to England), 131–32, 135; plantation system, 123, 135; theatrical performances depicting effect of, 145; Western Design of Cromwell, 32, 134, 138. *See also* slavery and slave trade, African chattel

commercial revolution, 14–15, 44–47, 157–58, 179

Congreve, William, 44, 200

consensus. *See* national unity and consensus

consumerism. *See* commercial revolution

contingency of human knowledge and decision, 16–17, 31–32, 54, 60, 62, 97, 99, 104–9, 113, 153, 158, 176–77, 186–87, 252, 255, 260–61

Cooper, Anthony Ashley. *See* Shaftesbury, 3rd Earl of

Copernican system, 88, 99

Corneille's tragedy on Pompey, 187, 293n6, 305n113

cosmography, 31, 88–99, 102–6, 115, 155

cosmopolitanism, 8, 17, 25, 28–29, 35, 94–96, 110, 117–18, 140, 146, 192–93, 202, 230

Courthope, William John, 8, 22, 25, 49, 60

Coverley, Sir Roger de (*Spectator* character), 43, 68, 76

Craggs, James, the Younger (Addison's successor and heir to his works), 277

Craig, John, 204

Croker, John (Johann), 200, 307n44

Cromwell, Oliver, 32, 132, 134–35, 138, 142, 202, 229, 278

cross-dressing, 76

currency reform, silver vs. gold standard, 79, 275. *See also* coins and medals

cynicism, 81, 113, 137

Daily Courant, 28

Daniell, David, 235

Dante Alighieri, 181, 228, 303n54, 310–11n49

Dart, Gregory, 48

Davenant, Charles, 142

Davenant, William, 215, 216, 238; *Salmacis Spolia* (with Jones), 172

David (biblical king), 105

Davis, Paul, 48, 49, 52

death and immortality, 63–64, 91, 261–62; literary immortality, 39, 40, 49

Deborah (biblical figure), 198–99

Defoe, Daniel, 123, 143, 292n131; *Robinson Crusoe*, 5, 126, 279; *The Storm*, 203

DeMaria, Robert, Jr., 280

democracy: consumerism and, 14; England transformed into first modern nation of, 29; progressivity in move toward, 11, 13, 273

Dennis, John, 78, 84, 238, 246

Descartes, René, 16, 88–90, 98, 158, 187; his haunting "evil genius" from *Meditationes de Prima Philosophia*, 173–74, 175; pleasure theory of, 164–65

Deschamps, François, *Cato*, 279

Diana and Actaeon myth, 48

Diderot, Denis, 280

Dido: in Ovid's *Heroides*, 183; in Virgil's *Aeneid*, 181–82, 186–87

Dillon, Elizabeth Maddock, 120, 145, 300n89

Dionysian frenzy, 75, 185
Diotima of Mantinea, 1, 173
discretion, 52–53
Distichs of Cato, 224
diversity, celebration of, 94, 103
Dobrée, Bonamy, 30
Domesday Book, 128
domestic peace, 8, 9, 32, 98, 100, 141, 191, 193, 209, 279
Donoghue, John, 299n51
Drake, Judith, *Essay in Defence of the Female Sex*, 138
Drury Lane theater: *Cato*'s premiere at (1713), 188, 197, 210, 220, 225, 245, 265; *Cato*'s revival at (1716), 279; *Rosamond* opera staged at, 205; Steele as manager, 276
Dryden, John, 44, 73, 81, 193; *Absalom and Achitophel*, 318n78; Addison as literary successor of, 257, 281; Addison's *Cato* drafts and, 228; "Fairie Way of Writing" and, 166, 167; *The Hind and the Panther*, 84; *Julius Caesar* altered by, 238; *The Medall*, 306n42; poem to Kneller, 268–69, 316n31; *The Rehearsal* (as satire of), 181; satirizing Whigs, 228; translation of Virgil's *Georgics*, 107
Dubois, Abbé, 271
Dunton, John, 291n97
Dutch Republic as colonial competitor, 143
Dutch slavers, 132, 135, 298n37
Dyson, Hugo, 66

education, universal, Addison as advocate for, 121, 127
Edward, Catherine, 227
Edward the Confessor, 1–2, 4, 5
egalitarianism, 9, 17, 21, 35, 104, 272, 275
Egerton, Francis. *See* Ellesmere, Earl of
egotism, Addison's coinage, 18, 19, 89, 285n55
eighteenth century, difficulty of analysis of, 18–19

Eliot, George, 113
Eliot, T. S.: evaluation of Addison, 30, 49–57, 60, 65–66, 78, 106, 115; *The Metaphysical Poets*, 50; on poetry's function, 50–51, 61; Tory perspective of, 57; *The Use of Poetry and the Use of Criticism*, 50; *The Waste Land*, 52
Elizabeth I (English queen): ban on religious plays, 227; burial vault of, 1, 2; imprisoned by Mary I, 205; Queen Anne's reign echoing, 34, 196–201, 207, 209, 210; reign in Addison's *On the Pleasures of the Imagination*, 182; theater mimicking politics during reign of, 197, 216, 306n32
Ellesmere, Earl of (Francis Egerton), 3, 49
Ellison, Julie, 32, 249
emancipation. *See* liberty
empathy, 55, 139, 140, 144, 145
Engell, James, 150
English Bill of Rights (1689), 192, 193
Enlightenment, 6; Addison's role in, 13, 20, 64, 87, 107, 253, 260, 261, 280–81; contemporary condemnation of, 19; gender roles and, 72; imagination as essential idea of, 34; inseparability of literature from politics in, 19; legacy of, 10–11; liberty as concept in, 117; potential of not attaining, 152; Young's guidance on, 261–63
Epicurean Platonism, 171
Epicurus, 155
epigraphs in Addison's works, 154. *See also Cato*; *On the Pleasures of the Imagination*
Erskine-Hill, Howard, 208
Essex's Rebellion (1601), 197, 306n32
Europe: governance in, 119, 126–27; near-invisibility of African enslaved persons in, 133. *See also* slavery of Europeans
Europeans (non-British), emancipation of, 118

"Fairie Way of Writing," 166, 167
Faller, Lincoln, 240

fashion, 14, 70–71, 74–75, 292n128
Faust / Faustian ideal, 94–95, 97, 163
Female Tatler, 67
femininity, 68, 70–71
feudalism and serfdom, 32, 125, 127, 128–31, 133, 136, 139–40, 145, 148, 260
Fielding, Henry, *The Tragedy of Tragedies*, 245
Fontenelle, Bernard Le Bovier de, *Entretiens sur la pluralité des mondes*, 89–90, 161, 302n43, 309n21
Foucault, Michel, 83
France: Addison's influence in, 280, 318n75; Addison's travels in, 81–82, 187, 260; as British adversary, 218, 228; influences on the English, 16; peace negotiated through Quadruple Alliance, 271. *See also* Louis XIV
Franklin, Benjamin, 5, 23, 278
Franklin, James, *New England Courant*, 278
Frederick William I (king of Prussia), 218
Freeholder, 117, 191, 250, 269–71
Freeman, Lisa A., 249–50
Freeport, Sir Andrew (*The Spectator*'s prototypical self-made merchant), 143
French Revolution, 278
Freud, Sigmund, 50, 110, 111, 303n55; pleasure principle and reality principle, 165
"Fundamental Constitution of Carolina," 138

Galileo Galilei, 88
gardening, 18, 111, 162; garden-laboratory of Newton, 113–14; landscape, 83, 145, 167; unkempt, 153
Gay, John, 240; *The What D'ye Call It*, 281
gender equality/inequality: Addison's presentation of, 118, 173, 183–85, 314n120; domestic role of women and, 71; early feminist writers on women's feudal reality, 138; exclusion of women from land ownership and political office, 297n7; progressivism and, 21; Restoration's progress and, 69
gender stereotypes: Addison's *Cato*'s audience and, 313n117; Addison's condescension and, 6, 31; domestic role of women and, 291n108; middle-class wife and mother, 67–70; Platonic trope of "bad" feminization, 173; social ideal of, 68; women's plight as natural slaves, 138; Woolf on Addison's treatment of "the fair sex," 75–77
George I (English king): Addison in charge of arrival in England of, 35, 257, 265; Addison promoted to secretary of state by, 266, 269; Addison's diplomacy under, 272; arrival in England, 266–68; in feud with son (future George II), 273; Jacobite riots upon coronation of, 267–68; portrayal in Addison's poem *To Sir Godfrey Kneller*, 267–69. *See also* Hanoverian Succession
George II (English king), 272–73, 279
George of Denmark (husband of Queen Anne), 211
georgic aesthetics, Addison's identification with as "British Virgil" or society's "husband," 21, 42, 61, 80, 107–15, 140, 180–81, 182–83, 285n57, 285n63, 296n86
German Romanticism, 259
Gildon, Charles, 250; *The Life of Mr. Thomas Betterton, the Late Eminent Tragedian*, 214
Gillingham, John, 129–30
Globe Theatre, 235
Glorious Revolution, 24, 63, 82, 118, 133, 200, 216, 224, 250. *See also* William and Mary
Godolphin, Sidney, 201
Goethe, Johann Wolfgang von, 94–95, 163, 259
Goodall, Jane, 216

Gordon, Thomas, *Cato's Letters* (with Trenchard), 277
governance: bureaucracy replacing royal court, 194–95; parliamentary authority over monarchy, 193; primary legal texts establishing, 189; representative legislature, 118–20; transition to mixed republican-monarchical empire, 35, 183. *See also* monarchy; Parliament; representative legislature
Gracián, Baltasar, 150
Great Chain of Being, 88, 91–93, 98, 100–104, 147, 153, 294n38, 302n38
Great Migration, and return of colonists to England, 131–32, 135
greed. *See* avarice
Gregg, Edward, 207, 208, 210
Gregorian calendar, 235
Guinea Company, 134
Gulston, Jane (mother of Addison), 81

Habermas, Jurgen, 6–7, 25–27, 71
Hale, Nathan, 246, 313n116
Halifax, Earl of. *See* Montagu, Charles
Halley, Edmond, 317n58
Hammond, Brean, 205, 316n21
Handel, George Frideric, 109, 265; *Rinaldo*, 265–66; *Teseo* (*Theseus*), 266
Hanover Club, formation of, 209
Hanoverian Succession, 5, 8, 195–96, 206–10, 218, 250, 257; succession as major issue of reign of Queen Anne, 194–96, 206–11, 218, 226, 249. *See also* George I
Harley, Robert, 127, 142, 204, 209–10
Haydn, Franz Joseph, *The Creation*, 109–10
Hazlitt, William, 58
health and imagination's effect on body and mind, 33, 156–59, 167, 177, 179, 302n29
Hedges, Charles, 194
Henderson, Christine Dunn, 12
Henry, Patrick, 246
Henry II (English king), 205

Hercules, 181
Hermaphrodite / Hermaphroditus: British nation as hermaphroditic construction of ancient Rome and gothic tradition, 221; hermaphrodite as eighteenth-century epithet for homosexual, used by Pope against Addison and Steele, 75; hermaphroditic aesthetic, 74–76, 244; hermaphroditic discourse, 18, 185, 247, 260, 262; Ovid's tale of Salmacis and Hermaphroditus as translated by Addison, 33, 76, 170–76, 179–80, 184–85, 303n72; Plutarch's Cato as classical hermaphroditic figuration, 255. *See also* Ovid
Hermes, 170
Hervey, Lady Elizabeth, 240
Hobbes, Thomas, 89, 96; Addison and, 156, 159, 177; *Leviathan*, 119, 130, 155, 251, 297n6, 301n25
Holland House (Kensington), 273, 276
Homer, 15, 83, 164, 180, 293n6
Hone, Joseph, 190, 192, 203
Horace, 45–46, 62, 65, 144, 288n24; *Ars Poetica*, 167; epigraphs from, 46, 162, 164, 166, 167; *Epistles*, 166, 181; influence on Addison, 59, 166, 167, 180–81; *Odes*, 59, 164
House of Commons, 131, 177, 275–76
House of Hanover, 208, 212. *See also* Hanoverian Succession
House of Lords, 275–76
House of Nassau, 192
human reason: in Addison's neoclassical thinking, 33, 54, 107; deception exposed by Newtonian science, 98, 104–5; in healthful balance of the body, 33, 156–59, 167, 177, 179, 302n29; reconstituting society according to, 87, 99
Hume, David, 8, 309n21
Hume, Robert D., 124
humility. *See* modesty
Hunt, Leigh, 48
hypocrisy, 4, 60, 125, 126, 138, 248

imagination, 8, 18, 149–87; historical context supplying meaning of, 67; Jung on, 184; as *Lex Continui* of European public discourse, 149; middle (middling) class and, 178; modern psychoanalytic analysis of, 184–85; Montaigne on, 184–85; progressivism and, 149–51, 177, 245; sentimentality and, 54; sovereignty of, 186; understanding vs., 33, 157–61, 166, 169, 172, 176. See also *On the Pleasures of the Imagination*
immortality. *See* death and immortality
imperialism, 11, 32; Addison's poetry on, 193; Addison's role in, 83; Newtonian sublime linked to, 296n99
indentured servitude, 126, 299n51
individualism (individual sovereignty), 6, 19, 30, 33, 55, 99, 147, 158, 177, 275
industrialization, 42, 64, 94, 113, 143, 244
Inkle and Yarico (tale), 139, 141
intellectual biography, 24, 30
Iphis, myth of, 184
Iroquois, 142, 300n77
Islam, 81, 295n48
Italianate opera, 266. *See also* Handel, George Frideric

Jacobites: Addison suppressing rebellions of, 257; Battle of Glen Shiel (1719), 279; failed rebellion (1715), 210, 270; failed rebellion (1745), 308n81; French assistance to, 192, 199; French version of *Cato* and, 279; network and plots by, 35, 208; probability of victory of, to Addison and Whigs, 152, 209, 250; Queen Anne and succession after her, 194, 196, 206–12; riots upon George I's coronation, 267–68; South Sea Company and, 127. *See also* Stuart, James Francis Edward
Jager, Colin, 110
James I (English king), 130, 182

James II (English king), 60, 193–94, 196, 199, 200, 229, 292n135, 306n42
James III. *See* Stuart, James Francis Edward
Jesus of Nazareth, 233; crucifixion of, 171
Job (biblical figure), 106–7
Johnson, James William, 224
Johnson, Samuel, 22–23, 316n23, 318n72; on Addison's *Cato*, 207, 210, 240; admiration of Addison, 40, 78, 280; *Life of Addison*, 23, 29; Woolf agreeing with evaluation of Addison, 73, 77
Jones, Inigo, 182; *Salmacis Spolia* (with Davenant), 172
journalism: one origin in fantasy of Mr. Spectator, 47
journals: daily, 31, 289n30; female readership of, 27–28; popularity and circulation of, 28, 283n16; public mind-shaping by reading, 222; replacing stage as setting for public discourse, 217
Joyce, James, *A Portrait of the Artist as a Young Man*, 51, 72–73, 259–60
Judaism, 81, 293n2
Judges (biblical book), 252
Julian calendar, 235
Julius Caesar: British public's knowledge of, 224; Cato's rivalry with, 19; imperial rise of, 276; refounding of Carthage, 182; triumph of (49 BC), 220; Virgil's reaction to death of, 181. *See also Cato*; Shakespeare, William
Jung, Carl, 184
Jupiter, 181–82, 186, 200–201
Justinian Codex/law on slavery, 130

Kant, Immanuel, 164
Kantorowicz, Ernst H., 233; *The King's Two Bodies*, 35, 306n32, 307n46, 311n67
Killigrew, Charles, 308n71
King, Thomas Alan, 72
king's two bodies, the (doctrine), 34–35, 201, 210–12, 272–73, 277, 279

Kit-Kat Club, 82, 194, 200, 270
Klein, Lawrence E., 4, 12, 62, 264
Kneller, Godfrey, 267–68
Kohler, Max J., 293n2

la Bonde, Charles François de, 211
Lacan, Jacques, 185
Las Casas, Bartolomé de, *Tears of the Indians: Being an Historical and True Account of the Cruel Massacres and Slaughters of above Twenty Millions of Innocent People*, 134
Leibniz, Gottfried Wilhelm, 82, 293n6, 308n86
Lewis, C. S.: evaluation of Addison and Augustan Age, 30, 57–62, 65–67, 70, 73, 75, 78
liberty, 9, 11, 113, 116–20; Addison compared to Locke, 178, 218; in Addison's *Cato*, 247; cosmopolitan approach to, 117–18; democracy and, 11; disconnect from racialized slavery, 32, 120; expansion of, 116–17, 193; from feudalism, 128–30, 138, 145, 148; free expression rights, 11, 31; Hobbes on, 119; in reaction to slavery, 124, 125; Roman/Norman origin of British identity tied to, 147–48; Whig discourse of, 136–44; worker's autonomy and, 18. *See also* gender equality/inequality
Lincoln's Inn Field theater, 279
literacy in England, 28, 222
literary history: Addison's place in, 3, 9, 25, 30, 37, 46, 48–49, 57, 259; construction and persistence of partisan rift in, 62–63, 65; transition from theater to novel, 5, 35, 41, 45–46, 237, 244–45, 279; Young's recognition of two currents in, 259. *See also* Modernism; Romanticism
literary immortality, 63, 262
Locke, John, 301n25; Addison's dissemination and imitation of, 16, 104, 147; Addison succeeding as commissioner of appeal in excise, 201; property views of, compared to Addison, 177–78; on rational system of government, 16; *Second Treatise on Government*, 137; Whiggish discourse following, 137–38, 140, 143, 218
London: Black people living in, early eighteenth century, 125, 298n31; growth of, 1600 to 1800, 14; servitude culture, 126; split into two worlds, 15; transition into imperial city, 220
Louis XIV (French king): Addison's critiques of, 280, 318n75; English triumph against, 221, 229; harboring and supporting Stuart Pretender, 192, 196–97, 200, 207, 209; Hobbes's protection by, 297n6; peace negotiations in War of Spanish Succession and, 141, 142; slave trade and, 127; Treaty of Utrecht and, 226
Lovejoy, Arthur O., 88–89, 91–92, 94, 98–99
Lucius (in Shakespeare's *Julius Caesar*), 233–36, 241
Lucius Junius Brutus (founder of Roman Republic), 234, 236
Lucretius: epigraphs from, 154, 170, 171; influence on Addison, 155–56, 159, 163, 166, 170, 172, 176, 180, 260; materialist theory of the simulacra in, 163; *On the Nature of Things*, 154–55, 159, 163, 166, 301n22, 303n75; Ovid admiring work of, 170–71; as popularizer of Epicurean Platonism, 171

Macaulay, Thomas, 21–22, 49, 59, 73, 78, 189, 250
Mackie, Erin, 43, 70
Magdalen College, Oxford, 66, 85
Malebranche, Nicolas, 82, 187, 293n6
Malek, James, 229–30
Mallet, Elizabeth, 28
Manning, Francis, 317n40
Marcia (second wife of Cato the Younger), 247

Marlborough, Duke of (John Churchill), 199–212; in Addison's *Rosamond,* 204–6; Addison's support for, 250, 263; Addison's *The Campaign* written for, 201–5, 257, 308n71; in Addison's *The Drummer,* 272; Blenheim Palace gifted to, 204, 205; Blenheim victory of, 201, 205; Bolingbroke and, 197; compared to Aeneas, 202; Hanoverian succession favored by, 196, 209; military role of, 196, 199, 204, 228; Queen Anne's dismissal of, 206–7, 209; Queen Anne's elevation of, 204; return from exile and parade through London upon George I's accession, 211, 272; as shadow warrior-king, 205–6, 256; Tories and, 196, 250; Whigs and, 197, 206, 208, 211, 226, 250

Marlowe, Christopher, 94–95, 97, 294n44, 311n68

Martial, epigraph from, 159–60, 180

Mary I (English queen), 1, 2, 199, 205

Mary II (English queen), 199, 250. *See also* William and Mary

masculinity, 19, 66, 68, 70–72, 75–76, 184–85, 246, 313n99

materialism, 33, 113, 155–56, 163

May, Thomas, 312n93

Mazurkeywycz, Christine, 223

McCrea, Brian, 56; *Addison and Steele Are Dead: The English Department, Its Canon, and the Professionalization of Literary Criticism,* 50

McKenzie, Jon, 285n67

McKeon, Michael, 69

medals. *See* coins and medals

mercantilism, expansion of, 14, 92

Mercury, 181, 183

metatheatrical staging, 35, 42, 79, 97, 215, 235, 244, 252, 272, 313n107

microscopic discoveries, 90, 98, 102–3

middle (middling) class, 3; Addison as progenitor of, 8–9, 31, 42–43, 60, 83, 140, 146, 183, 265; Addison's politics attached to, 12–13; coffeehouse culture linked to, 40, 85, 126; Eliot's disapproval of values of, 61–62; imagination and, 33, 153, 177–78; Queen Anne styled as, 190; rise of, 3, 11, 14–15, 27, 61, 67, 83, 98, 147, 153, 190; scientific and philosophical justification and impetus of, 17, 60, 87–88, 98–99, 105, 112–14, 152–53; terminology of "middling," 26; theatrical commons of, 145–46; time's organization and, 223; transition to novel as literary choice of, 5, 35, 41, 45–46, 237, 244–45, 279; tripartite division of English society and, 286n88

Middleton, Conyers, *Life of Cicero,* 223

Miller, Stephen, 26, 64

Mills, John, 238

Milton, John: Addison and, 16, 18, 20, 52, 91, 130, 144, 177, 228, 251, 278; in Addison's *On the Pleasures of the Imagination,* 164–65, 168; blindness of, 152; *Declaration . . . against Spain,* 134–35, 136; *Eikonoklastes,* 130; on freedom, 130–31; Gordon and Trenchard following in steps of, 278; on head of state, 16, 252; *Paradise Lost,* 16, 110, 310n42; *Pro populo Anglico defensio,* 130; psychological discourse and, 18; *Samson Agonistes,* 251–52; Sonnet 19, 152; *The Tenure of Kings and Magistrates,* 130; Whigs as heirs of, 142

Mirzah, 95–97, 105, 304n82

moderation, 100, 190–92, 206, 232, 261

Modernism: Addison and, 19, 30–33, 44, 49, 50–52, 56, 59, 61, 111, 223, 289n44; aesthetic taste and poetry of, 50–51; Freud and, 110, 111; on great art, 79; imaginative space of, 33, 51; Joyce and, 260; Mr. Spectator similar to a roving figure of, 47; Newton and, 98; politicized poetry criticized by, 64; sentimentality, dismissal of, 18–19, 30–32 modernity: Addison and, 22, 33; gender roles and, 72; genealogy from Descartes to Coleridge, 158; insights from past into our disenchantment in, 233; new sovereignty of trade and global exchange in, 101; Newtonian paradigm shift as dividing line for, 161; works of imagination refining the senses in, 174

modesty, 24, 40, 59–60, 75, 152, 160, 288n25

monarchy: absolute, 32, 119, 142, 193, 297n6; Addison on, 218, 250; Addison's *Cato* as rallying drama for anti-monarchical movements, 218; Cato of history merging with spiritual king in Addison's *Cato,* 225; split between monarchists and republicans in Queen Anne's reign, 198, 208; succession chosen by Parliament, 188, 194, 208; sugar planters' loyalty to, 132; theater's relationship with, 196. *See also* Anne (English queen); Hanoverian Succession; Restoration

Montagu, Charles (Earl of Halifax), 84–86; as Addison's patron and mentor, 2, 84, 86, 266; *The City Mouse and the Country Mouse,* 84; death of, 269; as envoy to Hanoverian court, 208; George I and, 266–67; memorial to, 2; Mint role of, 200; Newton and, 84–86; as poet, 44; as president of Royal Society, 85

Montaigne, Michel de, 13, 19–20, 46–47, 89, 184–85, 232

moralism, 4, 6, 53, 144, 199, 260. *See also* performance/performativity

Morrison, Toni, 124, 139

Mr. Spectator: Addison identified with, 4, 48, 114; afterlife of, 280; autobiographical details of, 129; on Black "Trunk-Maker" at theater, 146–47, 300n91; *Cato*'s theatrical commons formed by, 282; finding positive sentiment in noisy markets, 102; Job's despair and, 106; loss of British readership, 5; marvelings akin to scientific discoveries of the era, 97–98; mass appeal of, 222; meditation on human species' place in the universe, 106, 217; privileged bourgeois status of, 112; religious bent of, 84; as silent journalistic onlooker, 47; as Socrates for his time, 42–43; women readers and, 28; women's fashion critiqued by, 74

Myddelton, Charlotte (Countess of Warwick, wife of Addison), 269, 316n33

national unity and consensus: Addison's *Cato* constructing, 35, 221–22, 230, 250–51; Addison's role in constructing, 8, 22–23, 65, 140, 250–51; creation of cosmopolitanism vs., 117; Newton's role in forming, 11; in Restoration, 89

nation-state, emergence of, 118, 136, 264–65

Native Americans, 134, 139, 142

natural philosophy, 160, 162

nature: communing with and decoding of, 107–8, 111, 294n24; individual's connection to, 159; sights on landscape tour in the imagination, 155–56, 167

neoclassical culture: Addison as representative of, 62, 82–83, 108, 144–45; condemnation of slavery in, 130; Newton and, 108, 114; of William and Mary's reign, 82. *See also* classical models

newspapers. *See* journals; *Spectator, The; Tatler, The*

Newton, Isaac: Addison's dissemination and imitation of, 16–18, 23, 79, 90, 98–99, 101, 114, 157, 223; Addison's personal relationship with, 85–86; background of, 86–87, 294n23; on Burnet, 114; compared to Addison, 294n24; cosmography of Romans revalidated by, 155; effect of discoveries, 87–88, 177, 183; library containing works by Lancelot Addison and Joseph Addison, 81, 306–7n43; on line between understanding and delusion, 162; Lucretius and, 155, 301n22; as middle-class philosopher, 87; Mint role of, 200–201, 204, 307n44, 307n65; Montagu and, 84–86, 269; neoclassicism of, 108, 114; *Opticks,* 301n22; Platonism and, 86, 88–89, 98, 162; *Principia,* 99, 223; scientific role analogous to Addison's social role, 98, 183; on sight, 151–53, 160, 165

Newtonian science, 294n23; Addison's essay on, 89–90, 102; Addison's optimism on, 104–5; in Addison's poetic and theatrical work, 33, 89–99, 107, 168, 174, 187, 261; Cartesians vs., 16, 89, 98; Chain of Being and, 92–93; effect on Addison's view of humanity, 31, 33, 87, 106; gravitation, 99; light, discoveries about, 17, 86, 88; mathematical laws, 98; neoclassicism and, 108, 114; paradigm shifts associated with, 11, 13, 16–18, 87, 161, 177, 254; Pope's attack on, 101–2; progressivism and, 94, 104, 177. *See also* sight

nihilism, 33, 104, 138, 233, 251

Norman Conquest. *See* William the Conqueror

North, Thomas, translation of Plutarch's Lives, 236

North Africa, Europeans taken as slaves in, 131

Norton, Brian Michael, 154

numismatics. *See* coins and medals

Nussbaum, Felicity, 72, 139

O'Brien, John, 169, 277

Oedipus, 105, 161

Ogée, Frédéric, 33

oneness, cultivation of, 213–14

On the Pleasures of the Imagination (Addison), 32–33, 150–87; as Addison's principal contribution to philosophy, 34, 151, 153, 172–73, 179, 301n3; architecture's role, 33, 167, 176; art for art's sake vs. art appreciation, 33, 162, 178, 179; Babylon allusions, 175, 181, 304n82; Cartesian pleasure principle, 164–65, 173–74, 175; classical guides chosen for three imaginative pleasures, 164; classical poetry, 164–67, 176; concept of "pleasures" in, 156–57; delusive ability of secondary pleasures, 166, 179, 184; epigraphs, 33, 154–56, 180; final installment and tale of Salmacis and Hermaphroditus, 170; first draft without epigraphs, 154; focusing on greatness, novelty, and beauty, 33, 160, 164–65; healthy imagination, 33, 156–59, 167, 177, 179, 302n29; Hobbes and, 156, 177; Homer as guide to the great, 164; Horace's epigraphs, 162, 164, 166, 167; human actors in divine imaginative theater, 161; imagination vs. understanding, 33, 157–61, 166, 169, 172, 176; international influence of, 301n6; as Latin poem, 180–87; Locke and, 177, 178; Lucretius's epigraphs, 154–55, 163, 166; "A Man of a Polite Imagination," meaning of, 158, 178; Martial's epigraph, 159–60, 180; Milton as sublime example in, 164–65; mimetic arts, 163, 173, 301n6; modern psychoanalytic analysis of, 184; narcissism, 172–73, 176; nature providing pleasure through imagination, 159, 162, 167, 173, 180; "new Principle of Pleasure," 165; Newton's visionary work and, 33, 160–62, 165, 169; North African self-martyrs of Dido and Cato, 186–87; optics of, 170, 174, 176, 178, 187; Orestes, allusion in Virgil's *Aeneid,* 175; Ovid as guide to the strange or novel, 164; Ovid's epigraphs, 160, 170, 171; Ovid's *Heroides* compared to, 183; Ovid's tale of Sal-

On the Pleasures of the Imagination (*continued*)
macis and Hermaphroditus, 170–76, 179–80, 184–85, 303n72; perceiver's stance and radical subjectivization, 164; phantasm of two suns, two Apollonian systems, two civilizational eras, and two world pictures, 175, 183; poetry stimulating the brain and its traces of pleasant places, 164; primary pleasures, 162–63, 165–68, 171; property linked to pleasure rather than ownership, 158, 178, 179; Saturday sermons, published as, 156, 174, 176; scientific writing, 168–69; secondary pleasures, 163–68, 175; self-reflexive criticism in last installment, 174; sequential reading of, 180–81; sights on landscape tour in the imagination, 155–56, 163, 165, 176; spiritual experience of imagination, 179; symmetry between first and last epigraphs, 170; tragic gaze and reality principle, 165; transition from Lucretius to Ovid, 171–72; two concluding figures in, 175–76; veracity of writers not of concern compared to ability to move imagination, 168; Virgil as guide to the beautiful, 164; Virgil's epigraph, 166; writing as an art, 163–66, 167

opera: Addison attending, 316n21; as aristocratic spectacle, 35; in competition to Addison's *Cato*, 266, 316n22. *See also* Handel, George Frideric

optimism, 17, 92, 152, 155, 250, 266, 272; epistemological, 33, 104; religious, 143

Orestes, allusion in *Aeneid* (Virgil), 175, 181, 183–84

Orientalism, 95, 187

Orr, Bridget, 10, 140

Ovid: Acteon and Diana myth in, 48; Addison's translation of, 48, 81, 176, 303n71; epigraphs from, 160, 170, 171; Hermaphroditus in, 33, 76, 170–76, 179–80, 184–85, 303n72; *Heroides*, 183; influence on Addison, 172, 176, 177, 180; influence on Shakespeare, 176–77; Iphis myth in, 184; *Metamorphoses*, 48, 76, 170, 176

Ozell, John, 279

Palmer, Ada, 303n75
paradigm shifts, 11, 13, 16–18, 72, 161, 177, 179, 254, 257, 295n53
Parliament: balance of powers and, 126, 193–94, 198, 211; role in 1713 political arena, 226; royal succession chosen by, 188, 194, 208. *See also* House of Commons; House of Lords
Parliamentarians, 57, 131–33
paternalism, 18, 68, 218, 248, 261
pathos, 16, 51, 99, 161, 172, 254, 261
patriarchal traditionalism, 12, 139–40, 198, 243, 248, 261
patriotism, 19, 32, 117, 129, 203, 205, 225, 245–46, 247
Patterson, Orlando, 122
Peerage Bill (proposed 1719), 275–76
penal slavery, 132
penny papers, 24, 25, 44
Pentheus, allusion in Virgil's *Aeneid*, 175, 181, 183, 185
performance/performativity, 9–11, 17, 19–24, 28–30, 39, 41–49, 63–65, 79, 83, 114–15, 188–89, 198–200, 216–17, 237, 260–65, 274–75, 312n85. *See also* theatricality and theatrical culture; tragedy
Phelan, Peggy, 285n67, 306n35
Phidias (Greek sculptor), 268
Phillips, John (Milton's nephew), 134
philosophy: Addison's role as philosopher, 34, 151, 153, 172–73, 179, 262, 301n3; kingship of, 264. *See also specific types of philosophy and philosophers by name*
Pincus, Stephen, 142, 190
Plato: in Addison's *Cato*, 237, 241, 254–55, 262; ban on theater advocated by, 213, 219; dialogues' similarity to

British journals, 28–29; Great Chain of Being and, 91; influence on Addison, 34, 141, 156, 157, 172–74, 263; *Phaedo*, 85–86, 241, 254; *Phaedrus*, 91, 152; *The Republic*, 213, 219–20; Seneca compared to, 186, 232

Platonism: Epicurean, 171; familiar to Addison's audience, 223; imagination and, 33, 172, 177; mising of thought and feeling, 54; Newton and, 86, 88–89, 98, 162; resyncretism of Christianity with, 53, 85

pleasure. See *On the Pleasures of the Imagination*

Pliny, *Panegyricus*, 270, 316n36

Plotinus, 91

Plutarch, 191, 231, 241, 254–55, 311n58, 314n121; *Lives*, 236

politeness, 2, 11–13, 129, 274

politics: access to political office in Addison's England, 297n7; Addison's art link with, 53, 261; increase in political writing at end of seventeenth century, 190; middle class as Addison's focus in, 12; moderation, Addison as advocate of, 190–91; political representation, social benefits of, 118–20

Pollock, Anthony, 112

Polyphemus (mythical figure), 51

Pompey, 187, 224, 225

Pompey's theater (Rome), 220, 253

Pope, Alexander, 99–105; on Addison's *Cato*, 196, 245–47, 313n111, 313n117; on Addison's ideology, 22, 101–4; admiration of Addison, 257; Augustan Age of mixed sentimentality and, 56, 58; as Catholic Tory, 57, 100; *Cato* prologue, 37; compared to Addison, 19, 38, 98, 101–4; compared to Swift, 19; *Dunciad*, 63; Eliot's agreement with, 50; epilogue to Rowe's *Jane Shore*, 314n121; *Epistle to Augustus*, 279; *Epistle to Dr. Arbuthnot*, 50, 279; *Epistle to Mr. Addison*, 116; *An Essay on Man*, 100–101, 103, 116; eulogy for Addison, 39, 288n6; Great Chain of Being and, 101, 103–4; Lewis on, 60; Newton's work viewed as sociologically dangerous by, 101; on premiere of Addison's *Cato*, 196, 245; on same-sex relations of Addison and Steele, 75; as self-supporting author, 293n7; as specialized literary writer, 273; in Woolf's *Orlando*, 73

popular sovereignty, 61, 89, 120, 145; middling class and, 5, 98

Porcius (historical son of Cato), 247, 255, 257–58

Portia (daughter of Cato), 238, 247–48, 279. See also *Cato*

Portuguese slavers, 132, 298n37

Pound, Ezra, 52, 80

Powell, George, 238

Powell, Manushag, 31

Preliminary Articles of September 1711, 209

pride, 101–2

Prior, Matthew, *The City Mouse and the Country Mouse* (with Montagu), 84

progressivism: Addison's position in history of, 12, 21, 32, 61; imagination and, 149–51, 177, 245; Newtonian science and, 94, 104, 177; Whiggish, 27, 57; in women's liberty, 21, 69

Protestantism, 8, 57, 64, 68, 87, 119, 191, 228, 263, 298n36

Providence Island Company, 299n55

Providence Island puritan community, 300n62

Psalm 19, 108–10

public opinion and discourse: Addison setting new standard for, 8, 11–12, 64, 222; Addison's goal to create, 40–41, 212; England transformed into modern nation of, 29; journals as mirror to readers', 15; taste expressed as, 150; upward movement of common discourse, 150; Whigs democratizing, 192. See also national unity and consensus

Quadruple Alliance (1718), 271
Queen's Theatre in Haymarket, 200, 266
queer identities: Addison's sexuality, speculations about, 75–76, 185, 284n22; in Addison's time, 291n113, 292n131

race and racial steeotypes, 6; Addison's ambiguity on, 117–18; in Addison's *Cato,* 12, 144, 248, 250; Black "Trunk-Maker" at theater in *The Spectator* 235, 146–47, 300n91; construction of, 117, 122, 128, 137; hierarchy, creation of, 133; segregation, 67. *See also* Inkle and Yarico (tale); Iroquois; slavery and slave trade, African chattel
Radford, Leslie, 238, 243
Rancière, Jacques, 13
randomness of human knowledge and decision, 107. *See also* contingency of human knowledge and decision
realism: in Addison's *On the Pleasures of the Imagination,* 166; balanced realism of Addison, 31, 39, 141; scientific, 100; Victorian, 259
reason. *See* human reason
reconciliation. *See* national unity and consensus
religious convictions of Addison, 32, 53, 84, 113, 141, 228, 289n50. *See also* theology and God
religious unrest and change: Addison's role in stabilizing, 8, 57; Newton's effect on, 11, 17; threat of civil wars, 11, 25, 89, 119, 159, 228
representative legislature, 35, 118–20, 297n7. *See also* Parliament
Restoration: in Addison's *On the Pleasures of the Imagination,* 177, 181–82; conditions leading up to, 135; fashion and masculinity in, 70; literacy, drop in, 28; Milton and, 16; slavery during, 133; social change of, 89, 98; women in literature and theater of, 69–70, 72. *See also* Charles II

Rich, Edward (Addison's stepson). *See* Warwick, Earl of
Richardson, Samuel, 259, 262
Ridout, Nicholas, 45, 112, 146
Roach, Joseph, 10, 124, 214–16, 283n1, 313n109
Roman Empire: end of, 219, 233; governance of, 119; rise of, 182
Roman Republic, 35, 155. *See also Cato*
Romanticism: Addison considered in light of, 31, 48, 57–59, 64, 93, 107, 109–10, 259, 261; German, 259; origins of, 31, 38. *See also* Coleridge, Samuel; Goethe, Johann Wolfgang von
Roscius (classical Roman actor): Addison compared to, 10, 263; as exemplar of virtue and grace, 214
Rosenthal, Laura J., 249–50, 313n99
Rounce, Adam, 64
Rousseau, Jean-Jacques, 255, 280
Rowe, Elizabeth, 67, 69, 313n117, 314n121
Royal African Company, 135, 138
Royal Exchange, 113, 143
Royal Society, 85, 88

Saccamano, Neil, 180, 181
Sacheverell, Henry, 191, 308n75
Sackville-West, Vita, 73
Saintsbury, George, 144
Salmacis and Hermaphroditus, tale of, 170–76, 179–80, 181–82, 185
Samson, 152, 251–52
Schmitt, Carl, 306n33
Scholasticism, 89–90
scientific discoveries and writing, 168–69, 222. *See also* Newtonian science
Scotland invasion by French-backed Stuart Pretender, 209
secret packet of Queen Anne, 210–11
Seneca, 186, 232, 253–54; *De Providencia,* 252, 254
Sennett, Richard, 18
sensoriolum, 106, 108, 114, 274
sentimentalism/sentimentality: in Addison's *Cato,* 239, 243, 253; in Addison's

paraphrase of Psalm 19, 110; combining thought and feeling, 54, 55, 56; identification with distant others, 147; Modernist dismissal of, 18–19, 30–32; neoclassicism and, 114; Pope's condemnation of, 102; slavery and, 139–40; women's role and, 69
serfdom. *See* feudalism and serfdom
Settle, Elkanah, 292n1
Shaffer, Jason, 246
Shaftesbury, 1st Earl of (Lord Ashley), 138, 306n42
Shaftesbury, 3rd Earl of (Anthony Ashley Cooper), 11–12, 72, 83, 98, 99; *Characteristicks*, 153
Shakespeare, William: acting legacy passed through Davenant to Betterton, 214–16; Addison compared to, 13, 60, 176–77, 233; in Addison's *On the Pleasures of the Imagination*, 166; borrowing from North's translation of Plutarch's *Lives*, 236; Caliban, 161; *Hamlet*, 306n33; history plays, 61; *Julius Caesar*, 231, 233–36, 238, 244, 251; Lear, 161; magical transformations derived from Ovid in, 176–77; *A Midsummer Night's Dream*, 176; as national bard, 215–16; *Othello*, 227, 250; relationship with Elizabethan monarchy, 196, 198; *Richard II*, 197, 306n32; Roman plays, 182
Shelley, Percy Bysshe, 37
Sherman, Stuart, 223, 289n30
Shevelow, Kathryn, 68–69
Shiels, Robert, 246
Sidney, Philip, 304n79, 311n49
sight: Addison's interest in and personal troubles with, 91, 151; eye favoring color over all else, 160; Lucretius's epigraph and, 155; Newton's discoveries about, 16, 31, 88, 99, 105, 151, 160, 162
silver and silver age, 31, 77, 79, 198, 275
Skinner, Quentin, 130
slavery and slave trade, African chattel: Addison's *Cato* resonating with, 250; Addison's connections to American plantations and slave trade, 123; Addison's silence on or minimal treatment of, 6, 32, 118, 120–27, 140–43; asiento of Treaty of Utrecht (1713), 122–23, 127, 298n37; British discourse on and disconnect from, 32, 120, 128–31, 136–44; British exploitation of and participation in, 5, 32, 127, 131–32, 134, 136, 140–43, 274, 298n37; as driven by economic competition, 126–27, 145–46; Dutch slavers, 132, 135, 298n37; feudalism conflated with, 127, 128–31; labor structure and, 299n55; Locke on, 137–38; numbers of enslaved persons shipped, 133, 298n37, 299n57; offshoring, 131–35, 191; political-economic implications of, 127, 138, 142, 297n10; Portuguese slavers, 132, 298n37; racialized slavery, acceptability of, 32, 133, 136; slave revolt on Providence Island, 300n62; South Sea Company's monopoly on, 277, 317n59; *The Tatler* advertising slave sales, 124, 298n25
slavery of Europeans: under absolute monarchies, 119, 126–27; after fall of Roman Empire, 128; associated with feudalism, 125, 126; British slaves freed by Britain and forced into navy service, 126; defining who qualified to be a slave, 128–29; Locke on, 137; Norman Conquest as demarcation of change in Britain, 128–29, 189; by North Africans, 131. *See also* feudalism and serfdom
small-mindedness, 52–53
Smith, Courtney Weiss, 300n83
Smith, Edmund, 81
Smith, Hannah, 198, 204
Smithers, Peter, 21–22, 24–25, 40, 70, 84, 194, 257, 265, 269–71, 316n23
sociability vs. sociality, as salient difference in Addison and Steele's separate outlooks, 217–18, 274–75

social change: in Addison's era, 273; aristocracy and, 3, 11, 14–15, 27, 61, 67, 83, 98, 147, 153, 190; of Restoration, 89, 98–99; social contract and, 119; theatrical performances depicting, 145. *See also* middle (middling) class

social norms: Addison and Steele constructing, 11, 15–16; link of salutary society to Addison, 21; tripartite division of English society, 286n88

social purpose of literature and theater, 30, 45, 60–62

Socrates: Addison compared to, 29, 153, 288n12; in Addison's *Cato*, 241; Addison's popularizing, 15; Addison's unwritten tragedy, 282; ban on theater advocated by, 219–20; Cato the Elder as figuration of, 29; in chain with Addison and Plato, 262; choice of Athens's birth myth, 214; Cicero's appraisal of, 43; imagination and, 152–53; influence on Addison, 40, 42, 85–86, 107, 112, 264; link with Jesus, 233; Mr. Spectator taking role of, 42–43; on preparing for death, 262; *The Republic*, 219–20; sight as shared concern with Addison, 91

Sophia (electress of Hanover), 82, 193, 195, 207, 211, 308n76

soul, 16, 18, 91, 158, 169–70, 175, 241

South Sea Bubble, 276–77, 298n38

South Sea Company, 127, 277, 278, 298n38

sovereignty: Addison's formulation of, 33, 159, 177–78, 181, 186; Hobbes's formulation of, 159, 297n6; human sovereignty supported by divine theatricality, 166; individual, 6, 19, 30, 33–34, 55, 99, 147, 158, 177, 275; modernity's new sovereignty of trade and global exchange, 101; Westphalian, 135. *See also* popular sovereignty

Soyinka, Wole, 213

Spain: Cromwell's aggression against, 32, 134, 138; as negative model of greedy, bloody imperialism (the "Black Legend"), 134, 142; slave trade, 298n37; in Treaty of Utrecht, 122; Triple Alliance negotiations with, 271

Spectator, The: Addison's contributions to, 7, 49; Addison's goals in, 39, 59–61, 140, 169; coffeehouse culture and, 7, 27–29; commercial revolution and, 44–47; as daily, 95, 223; eleven issues devoted to *On the Pleasures of the Imagination*, 33; epigraph preceding each essay, 154; female readership of, 67; Habermas on role of, 26; influence of, 7, 9, 16; international readership of, 29–30; international reprints and imitations of, 7, 282; Johnson reprinting, 280; legacy of, 60; out-of-office time of Addison deployed in writing, 85, 152, 210; popularity of, 7, 15; public discourse as result of, 31; readership of, 42, 222, 257, 283n16; Saturday sermons in, 8, 53–54, 156, 174, 176; sentimentalization in, 140; theatricality of, 45; unique aspects of, 58; women readership of, 246; women's depiction in, 69, 291n105, 291n108. *See also* Mr. Spectator

Spectator, The, individual numbers: *1*, 46–47; *2*, 143; *10*, 69–70, 208; *11*, 139; *15*, 291n105; *26*, 217; *34*, 71; *39*, 54; *40*, 55; *49*, 216; *50*, 300n77; *55* and *56*, 141–42; *69*, 113, 143; *81*, 71; *93*, 156; *111*, 91, 93; *121*, 105; *125*, 191; *159*, 95–96, 295n71, 304n82; *166*, 24; *214*, 126; *215*, 120–23, 126, 139; *225*, 52; *235*, 146, 300n91; *237*, 186, 232; *243*, 231; *256*, 206; *287*, 116, 118–19, 127; *370*, 274; *409*, 150–51; *411*, 150, 154–56, 166–67; *412*, 150, 159–60, 167, 180; *413*, 150, 160, 167; *414*, 150, 162, 167; *415*, 150, 162, 167, 175; *416*, 150, 163, 167; *417*, 150, 164, 167, 181; *418*, 150, 165–66, 167, 181, 219; *419*, 150, 166–67, 181; *420*, 150, 167; *421*, 150, 173, 175, 181; *433* and *434*, 77; *435*, 74–76; *441*, 113;

463, 282; *464*, 59–60; *465*, 107–9; *477*, 111; *489*, 295n71; *519*, 102–3; *543*, 90; *548*, 232; *565*, 105–6; *576*, 275
Spencer, Charles (Earl of Sunderland), 194, 209
Spenser, Edmund, 199–200
Stadter, Philip A., 231
Stationer's Company, end of monopoly of (1695), 29, 190
Steele, Richard: Addison's friendship and partnership with, 7, 217; on Addison's political success, 265–66; Addison's split from, 35, 274–75; admiration of Addison and praise for *Cato*, 257, 313n110; aristocracy of old world challenged by, 11–12; classical figures brought to English public's attention, 223; on coffeehouse's role, 216–17; commercial revolution and, 14–15, 44–47; daily exposition by, 106; as Drury Lane theater manager, 276; eulogy to Betterton, 214, 217; on evolving social scene, 274; Hazlitt on role of, 58; literary style compared to Addison's, 65; inheritance of plantation with enslaved people, 123; marketing of Addison's *Cato*, 9, 245; on middling public sphere, 140–41; on Montague-Addison relationship, 85; Peerage Bill (proposed 1719) as subject of spat with Addison, 275–76; philosophical and political differences with Addison, 217–18, 274–75; on pleasure, 156, 214; radical Whiggism and, 218; same-sex love life, speculation on, 75; slavery views of, 123–25, 138–41; Stoicism, compared to Addison on, 274; theatergoing's benefits acknowledged by, 213–14; theater's doubling effect linked to Whig politics, 213; theatricality of times of, 10–11, 45; women's depiction by, 68–71
Steele, Richard, works by: *Cato* prologue, 265, 281; *The Christian Hero*, 230, 274; *The Conscious Lovers*, 276; *A Nation a Family*, 277; *Plebian* pamphlets, 275; tale of Inkle and Yarico (*Spectator* 11), 139, 141; *The Tender Husband*, 42; *Theatre*, 276. See also Bickerstaff, Isaac, Esq; Mr. Spectator; *Spectator, The; Tatler, The*
Stephen, Leslie, 40, 49, 73
Stoicism: Addison compared to Steele on, 274; in Addison's *Cato*, 227, 231–32, 237–39, 243, 247–49, 252; familiar to Addison's audience, 223; imagination and, 33, 153, 156; Job's despair and, 106; Plutarch's Cato and, 241; resyncretism of Christianity with, 53; Seneca and, 186. See also Seneca
Stuart, James Francis Edward (Stuart Pretender), 192, 195–97, 200, 206–11, 226, 317n40
Stuart court, 68, 172, 292n135, 297n6
Stuart Pretender. See Stuart, James Francis Edward
Stuart restoration. See Restoration
sublimation, 185
Sunderland, Lord Lieutenant, 269
Swift, Jonathan: on Addison, 29, 258; Augustan Age of mixed sentimentality and, 56, 58; Catholicism and, 57; compared to Pope and Addison, 19, 98; Lewis on, 60; in Woolf's *Orlando*, 73

Tarquin kings of Rome, 234
Tatler, The: Addison's contributions to, 7; Addison's goals in, 39; Habermas on role of, 26; legacy of, 60; popularity of, 15; public discourse as result of, 31; readership of, 283n16; sentimentalization in, 140; slave sales advertised in, 124, 126, 298n25; unique aspects of, 58; women's depiction in, 69
Tatler, The, individual numbers: *119*, 104; *132*, 124, 126; *161*, 218; *167*, 213; *216*, 100; *218*, 111; *245*, 124–25; *249*, 79, 292n147
Taylor, Barry, 224, 310n42, 314n124

telescopic discoveries, 90, 98, 102–3, 105, 168, 186
Terence, *Andria*, 276
Thackeray, William Makepeace, 73
theatricality and theatrical culture: Addison compared to Shakespeare, 176–77, 233; Addison's world and thinking, 9–11, 33, 41–42, 45, 60–61, 166, 189–90, 215, 237, 288n24; Betterton as shadow monarch, 214–16; central paradigm and expertise of the age, 9–11, 16, 41–44; colonial relation shown in, 145; of death, 263; double vision of, 213; female roles performed by females in Restoration theater, 72; Hanoverian introduction of sympathetic merchant as its hero, 216; impersonalness of Addison's writings due partially to, 65; literary transition from theater to novel, 5, 35, 41, 45–46, 237, 244–45, 279; metaeffigy in Augustan theater, 215–16; national unity's emergence from, 55, 216; in Queen Anne's reign, 195; recovering Enlightenment sense of peak of, as a golden age of acting, 10–11, 41, 56, 237–39; as social act, 45, 55, 60; Steele's views of, 10–11, 45, 213–15; unique aspects of theater, 213. See also *Cato*; performance/performativity
Theobald, Lewis, 273
theology and God, 91, 94, 103–10, 113; in Addison's *On the Pleasures of the Imagination*, 175; contemplating nature of Supreme Being, 160; imagination and theodicy, 157; in light of ancient excavations, 294n38
Thirty Years' War, 89, 159
Thomson, Peter, 190
Tickell, Thomas, 3, 262, 285n57
time: new daily/diurnal organization of time and social life, 94–95, 106, 222–23; progress and temporalization of the Great Chain of Being, 91–97; slip in timeliness enabling tragic outcome, 233, 242, 244; variety of timekeeping systems in Europe, 235
Tocqueville, Alexis de, 281
Tolkien, J. R. R., 66
Tonson, Jacob, 29, 81, 287n104, 288n6, 307n43, 308n86
Tonson, Jacob, Jr., 287n104
Tories: Addison's performative nonpartisanship and, 68, 191; alliance with Queen Anne, 142, 152, 194, 207; Astell as, 67; avarice of, Addison's critique of, 141–42; Behn as, 67; in conflict between Protestants and Catholics, 60; interpretation of Addison's *Cato*, 250; Marlborough's removal by, 196, 250; in Restoration era, 182; resurgence of power of, 85, 142, 152, 194, 207–11, 218, 226; South Sea Company and, 127. See also aristocracy; Treaty of Utrecht
tragedy, 7, 10, 33–35, 45–46, 54–56, 187, 219–20, 228–29, 232, 247, 249, 252. See also *Cato*
tragicomic synthesis, 35, 225, 242, 244–45, 249, 313n107
Treaty of Utrecht (1713), 122–23, 141, 226, 230, 246, 297–98n21
Trenchard, John, *Cato's Letters* (with Thomas Gordon), 277
Triennial Act (1694), 190
Triple Alliance, 271
tulip mania (tulipomania), 111–12

unity. See national unity and consensus
universal rights, 6; education, 121, 127; to own and use land, 159
universe, Copernican model of, 88–89, 99
utilitarianism, 159

Vanbrugh, John, 200, 205, 208, 279
Venus, 181, 253
Victorianism, 9, 23, 30, 48, 59, 66, 259
Virgil: epigraph from, 164; *Georgics*, 80, 107, 181, 285n63; influence on Addi-

son, 20–21, 59, 111, 180, 184, 285n57. See also *Aeneid*
vision. *See* sight
Voltaire, 16–17, 280, 282, 305n113, 315n154, 315n162, 318n84; *Letters Concerning the English Nation*, 256; *Socrates*, 282

Walker, William, 34, 179
Walpole, Robert, 35, 270, 272, 274–75, 276–77, 279, 282
Walsh, Marcus, 302n29
war: religion-based, 228; sensibility toward, 202. *See also* Civil Wars, English; domestic peace; *specific wars*
Ward, Ned, *London Spy*, 31
War of Spanish Succession (1701–14), 141, 191–92, 221, 226. *See also* Treaty of Utrecht
Warwick, Earl of (Addison's stepson), 51–52, 262
Washington, George, 246
wealth creation: spoils of empire and, 142; virtuous circle of, 120; Whigs and doctrine of, 93, 143
Western Design of Cromwell in American colonies, 32, 134, 138
Westmacott, Richard, 2
Westminster Abbey: Addison and Steele's visits inspiring afterlife description, 214–17; Poet's Corner, 1–2, 4, 86; site of new national monuments to "middling" people and actors, 98, 218
Westphalian sovereignty, 135
Whigs and Whiggism: Addison as reformer and champion of, 34, 40, 60, 62, 65, 82, 96, 119, 208, 250; Addison's *Cato* marking triumph of, 221; democratizing political discourse, 192; Dryden satirizing, 229; fall from power and resurgence of Tory power, 85, 142, 152, 194, 207–11, 218, 226; history and theory of literature of, 62–69; Jacobite portrayal by, 207;

liberty goals, 6, 32, 124, 128, 131, 133, 136–37; Locke and, 104; marginalization of female Whig writers, 67; Marlborough and, 197, 206, 208, 211, 226, 250; medals, issuance of, 200; middle class and, 12, 82, 182; modern British freedom and, 119–20, 126; Newtonian science and, 101; progressivism and liberalism's precursor, 27, 57; public ethic of polite discourse as focus of, 12; Queen Anne and, 194–95, 200, 202, 204, 206–7, 209, 308n75; representative legislature and, 118–20; Restoration role of, 182; slavery and liberty, discourse of, 32, 136–44; social utility of literature and, 30; South Sea Company and, 127, 277; Steele and, 218; Stuart Restoration seeming improbable to, 152, 209, 250; theater patronship of, 200; wealth creation, theory and doctrine of, 93, 143; "Whig Interpretation of History," teleology of, 62. *See also* Hanoverian Succession
William and Mary, 82, 190, 193, 200, 250
Williams, Abigail, 204
Williams, Raymond, 42
William the Conqueror, 129, 189
William III (English king), 81, 192, 194, 199, 201, 218, 229, 316n31. *See also* William and Mary
Winn, James A., 284n22, 285n73, 308n68
Wollstonecraft, Mary, 26, 64
women: in Addison's *Cato*'s love plots, 246–47, 255–56; Addison's presentation of, 28, 31, 67–79, 173, 291n119; analogy of women as natural slaves to Black slaves, 138; femininity, 68, 70–71; as journal contributors and publishers, 28, 291n97; as journal readers, 27–28, 67. *See also* gender equality/inequality; gender stereotypes
Womersley, David, 62–64, 192

Woolf, Virginia: *The Common Reader*, 73; evaluation of Addison, 30, 31, 64, 69, 72–79; *Orlando*, 73, 76
Wordsworth, William, *Tintern Abbey*, 149
working class, 3, 13, 14, 67, 123
Wyatt's Rebellion (1554), 205

Young, Edward, 19, 259, 261–63, 271, 316n23; *Conjectures on Original Composition*, 10, 37, 259, 261–62; *Night Thoughts*, 261–62

zero-sum games, 13, 93, 104, 111–12, 282

www.ingramcontent.com/pod-product-compliance
Lightning Source LLC
Chambersburg PA
CBHW030603230426
43661CB00053B/1822